On Kubrick

ON KUBRICK

James Naremore

For Darlene

First published in 2007 by the
BRITISH FILM INSTITUTE
21 Stephen Street, London W1T 1LN

There's more to discover about film and television through the BFI.
Our world-renowned archive, cinemas, festivals, films, publications
and learning resources are here to inspire you.

Cover design by Eureka!
Cover image: Keir Dullea as David Bowman in *2001: A Space Odyssey* (1968)

Set by D. R. Bungay Associates, Burghfield, Berkshire
Printed in the UK by St Edmundsbury Press, Bury St Edmunds, Suffolk

British Library Cataloguing-in-Publication Data
A catalogue record for this book is available from the British Library

ISBN 978–1–84457–142–0 (pbk)
ISBN 978–1–84457–143–7 (hbk)

Contents

Preface and Acknowledgments

On Kubrick is a critical survey of Stanley Kubrick's films, intended for readers who already know his work and for those who might be approaching it for the first time. As its title suggests, the book takes a somewhat discursive form, allowing me to explore a variety of personal interests while providing basic information about the production history of the films. The discussion is divided into six parts, the first of which ('Prologue') addresses foundational issues: Kubrick's biography and the cultural context of his early work; his paradoxical relationship with the Hollywood industry; and certain pervasive qualities of style and tone in his films. Here and elsewhere I've emphasised that Kubrick belongs both to Hollywood and to the twilight of international modernism. I'm also interested in the affective or emotional aspects of his work, which is usually inflected by the grotesque, the uncanny, the fantastic and the blackly humorous.

In the middle sections of the book I discuss the films in chronological order, omitting *Spartacus* (1959–60) on the grounds that it was a project over which Kubrick had little control. I've tried to synthesise my treatment of various formal concerns, giving as much attention to acting and literary matters as to camera and cutting. When the occasion demands, I've also tried to deal with philosophical, ideological and political issues, including representations of race, gender and sexuality. The discussion is organised according to phases of Kubrick's career: his early, artisanal films; his collaborations with James B. Harris and Kirk Douglas; his major productions; and his last two pictures, both of which have a spare quality and an unorthodox form. Where these last works are concerned, I haven't employed the term 'late style' – a concept Edward Said borrows from Theodor Adorno and applies to an analysis of several musical artists – but I've tried to suggest a late moment when Kubrick reflects back on his earliest pictures (an allegorical war movie and an especially dreamlike film noir), bringing his career full circle and indicating his greater willingness to disturb the unities or logics of realist narrative.

Finally, in the closing section ('Epilogue'), I offer some concluding observations along with a discussion of Steven Spielberg's *A. I. Artificial Intelligence* (2001), which is based on a project Kubrick had worked on for over a decade. An intriguing film on many levels, *A. I.* enables me to contrast the styles of two famous directors in relation to certain themes that recur in the book as a whole – among them Kubrick's emotional propensities, his interest in automata and his particular blending of Freudianism and post-humanism. This section also gives me an opportunity to speculate about the historical transition from photographic to digital cinema – a significant development for an artist like Kubrick, who began as a photographer.

Like any viewer, I value some of Kubrick's films over others (I vastly prefer *Barry Lyndon* to *A Clockwork Orange*), yet it seems to me that time has been good to him; his pictures improve with age and his body of work shows an unusually consistent intelligence, craft and artistry. I've found him to be a challenging subject, but as Charles Baudelaire once remarked, any critic who comes late on the scene enjoys certain advantages. Whatever my shortcomings, I at least have the ability to see Kubrick's career in retrospect, after his reputation is secure and at a point when we know a good deal about how his films were made. I've benefited from numerous critics and historians who came before me and whose work I've cited on many occasions in the pages that follow. Several individuals have also given me personal help, advice and assistance. I owe special thanks to Rob White, my original editor at the BFI, who encouraged me to embark on the project. Jonathan Rosenbaum talked with me at length about Kubrick and provided me with ideas, important historical information, and useful suggestions about the completed manuscript. Tom Gunning was an equally generous and insightful reader and a supporter from the beginning, who sharpened my thinking about several issues. Michael Morgan gave me good advice about the structure of the book. I was also aided in various ways by David Anfam, David Bordwell, Simon Callow, Laurence Goldstein, Don Gray, Miriam Hansen, Joan Hawkins, Barbara Klinger, Robert Kolker, Bill Krohn, Nancy Mellerski, Andrew Miller, Gene D. Phillips, Robert Ray, Jason Sperb and Gregory Waller. Portions of the book, in slightly different form, appeared originally in *Film Quarterly* and *Michigan Quarterly Review*, and I'm grateful to the editors of those journals for their support. Barbara Hall at the Margaret Herrick Library of the Motion Picture Academy in Los Angeles gave me help with my research, as did Rebecca Cape at the Lilly Library in Bloomington and Michelle Hilmes and Dorinda Hartmann at the Wisconsin Center for Film and Theater Research in Madison. At the BFI, Rebecca Barden was a patient editor and Sarah Watt, Tom Cabot and Sophia Contento were immensely helpful in the production of the book. I also owe thanks to Indiana University for a Humanities Initiative Fellowship that supported me in the early stages of my research and writing. Darlene Sadlier, to whom the book is dedicated, gave intellectual and emotional support, putting up with me through the usual highs and lows of writing.

Part One

PROLOGUE

I. The Last Modernist

> The Art House Transmission that Stanley received so deeply in the forties was still manifesting in the early sixties, when I spent my nights and a lot of afternoons rocketing between the Bleecker Street Cinema, the Thalia, the New Yorker, and the Museum of Modern Art.... And so if I got weepy when the end credits rolled on *Eyes Wide Shut* and the waltz played one more time, it wasn't just because the movie was over, or because it was the final work of a man I admired and loved, but because that tradition, with its innocence, or anyway its naivete, and a purity that only someone born before 1930 could continue, had come to a certain end, as most traditions do. It's gone and it won't be returning.
>
> Michael Herr, *Kubrick*, 2000

Stanley Kubrick (1928–1999) was, in several ways, a paradoxical and contradictory figure. Though he rarely appeared in public, he achieved stardom. A fierce autodidact who possessed intellectual sophistication and breadth of knowledge, he was also a showman and businessman who, for most of his career, maintained at least some rapport with the popular audience and the Hollywood studios. His pictures seemed both hand-made and technologically advanced and, despite his apparent eccentricity and iconoclasm (fear of flying, aversion to Los Angeles), he became a sort of brand name. His successes, moreover, entailed a certain estrangement from the centres of movie-industry power. A native New Yorker who never lost his Bronx accent, Kubrick lived in apparent exile from America from the 1960s onward, creating visions of space travel, the Vietnam War and New York City all within driving distance of his English country home.

During his lifetime Kubrick was often depicted by the press as living in Xanadu-like isolation or as having retreated into Axel's castle. He gave interviews to publicise his films and made himself available to a few scholars and critics, especially to Michel Ciment, Gene D. Phillips and the late Alexander Walker, but most of his published remarks have the feeling of carefully chosen, editorially polished statements. He was photographed many times and his picture appears on the covers of several of the books about him, but he rarely appeared on TV and never acted in his or anyone else's pictures. Most of his socialising was done at his own dinner table or over the telephone. In the best record we have of his working methods, his daughter Vivian's documentary, *The Making of 'The Shining'*, which aired on the BBC in 1980, he seems both authoritative and shy, standing at the margins during the social interludes, hidden by a scruffy beard and a baggy jacket. Despite his apparent reclusiveness, however, a powerful aura surrounded his name and bizarre legends began to accumulate about his activities. In the US, a conspiracy cult maintained that NASA never landed a man on the moon; the TV broadcast of the voyage, the cultists argued, was staged and directed for the government by Stanley Kubrick. (Ironically, Peter Hyams directed *Capricorn One* [1978], a movie about a fake TV broadcast of the moon landing, and later directed Arthur C. Clarke's *2010* [1984].) Kubrick also became the victim of identity theft. In the early 1990s a pathetic con-man named Alan Conway, who looked and sounded nothing like Kubrick and barely knew his movies, was easily able to impersonate him. Introducing himself to various Londoners as 'Stanley', Conway obtained dinners, theatre tickets, drinks, drugs and gay sex from people who thought they might profit from knowing the great director. After his con-game was exposed, Conway became a minor celebrity, whose impersonation was documented on the BBC and turned into a film, *Color Me Kubrick* (2005), written by Kubrick's long-time associate Anthony Frewin, directed by another associate, Brian Cook, and starring John Malkovich.[1]

Another paradox: even though Kubrick was one of the cinema's indisputable auteurs, a producer-director who supervised every aspect of his films from writing to exhibition, he never benefited from the support of the auteurists. This may have been due to the fact that his films seemed different from one another, or to the fact that most of them were literary adaptations – although only one was based on a book of such international fame and artistic excellence that most critics would say it reads better than what the director made from it. The *Cahiers du cinéma* critics, including Jean-Luc Godard, thought Kubrick was overrated; Andrew Sarris placed him in the 'Strained Seriousness' category; *Movie* never listed him in their pantheon; and David Thomson described him as 'sententious', 'nihilistic', 'meretricious' and 'devoid of artistic personality'.[2] Even the anti-auteurist Pauline Kael relentlessly attacked his films, and many others in the New York critical establishment, from Bosley Crowther in the 1950s and 1960s down to Anthony Lane in the present day, have been either slow to appreciate him or hostile towards his work. His chief journalistic supporters in the US have tended to come from the alternative press or from newspapers outside New York. In Britain his leading advocate was Alexander Walker, and in Paris his admirers have been associated with *Positif*, a film journal with historical links to surrealism and left-anarchism.

Whatever the critical reception of Kubrick's films, and whatever might be thought of his desire to retain his privacy, he has left a mark on the popular culture of the past fifty years that few directors can rival. The mad scientist Dr Strangelove and the Strauss music that opens *2001: A Space Odyssey* (1968) are known by everybody, and several Kubrick films have been endlessly parodied or quoted in all sorts of media. (To mention only a couple of recent examples from television: *The Simpsons* has made several episodes based on Kubrick, and Bartholomew Cousins has made an MTV video filled with references to *The Shining* [1980].) Passing time has also revealed Kubrick as the last major representative of an important artistic tradition that Michael Herr seems to be describing in the epigraph above. In making this statement, let me emphasise that I'm not saying good movies are no longer made; my point is simply that Kubrick can be viewed as one of the few – arguably the last and the most successful – of the modernist directors who worked for the Hollywood studios.

In using the term 'modernist', I refer not to what David Rodowick and other scholars have called the 'political modernism' of directors like Jean-Luc Godard, who broke radically from the conventions of illusionist cinema;[3] nor to the avant-garde provocations of Andy Warhol, who was born in the same year as Kubrick and became a more revolutionary figure; nor to Fredric Jameson's claim that the celebrated auteurs of classic Hollywood were all modernists. I have in mind a more ordinary notion of 'modern art' usually associated with the first half of the twentieth century, which had a demonstrable impact on Kubrick's work. Several writers, among them Jameson, have argued that Kubrick's late films are 'postmodern', but if that term designates retro and recycled styles, waning of affect, lack of psychological 'depth', loss of faith in the 'real' and hyper-commodification, then Kubrick was a modernist to the end. He was an avid reader of the Anglo-European and largely modernist literary and philosophical canon of dead white men that was established by mid-century (plus a great deal of pulp fiction and scientific literature), and he maintained a lifelong interest in Nietzsche, Freud and Jung. As Thomas Elsaesser has pointed out, most of his films are rather like 'late modernist' manifestations of the aesthetic detachment we find in Kafka and Joyce, or of the 'cold' authorial personality in Brecht and Pinter.[4] A similar point could be made in more specifically cinematic terms: a gifted cinematographer, Kubrick began his career as a photo-journalist in the heyday of New York street photography, which has been hailed as a form of modernist art; and as a director he made pictures that, however much they might resemble Hollywood genres, were very close in spirit to the Euro-intellectual cinema of the 1960s.

Like the high modernists, Kubrick forged a distinctive style, which evolved, as all styles do. He also showed a preoccupation with several of the leading ideological or aesthetic tendencies of high modernism: a concern for media-specific form, a resistance to censorship, a preference for satire and irony over sentiment, a dislike of conventional narrative realism, a reluctance to allow the audience to identify with leading characters and an interest in the relationship between instrumental rationality and its ever-present shadow, the irrational unconscious. His pictures often tell the story of how a carefully constructed plan fails because of what the surrealists called 'objective chance', or the conflict between reason and the masculine libido. (In Robert Kolker's words, the films are about 'a process that has become so rigid that it can neither be escaped nor mitigated – a stability that destroys'.)[5] Two of his favourite subjects were war and scientific technology, the privileged domains of rational planning and male authority; and partly for that reason Molly Haskell has placed him along with Orson Welles and John Huston in 'the mainstream of American misogyny'.[6] Nevertheless, he made three films about the American nuclear family, all of which are satires of patriarchy. Few directors have been more critical of military and scientific institutions, more sharply attuned to the fascistic tendencies in male sexuality and more aware of how machines function in male psychology as displacements for Eros and Thanatos.

Tom Gunning once suggested to me in conversation that Kubrick might be viewed not simply as the last modernist but also as the last of the Viennese auteurs. This observation strikes me as highly relevant. Even though in one sense Kubrick never left the Bronx, his ancestry can be traced to Austro-Hungary and he was intrigued by the proto-modernist, largely Jewish culture that originated in pre-World War I Vienna. In addition to Freud, he was interested in Stefan Zweig and Arthur Schnitzler, and he often stated his admiration for the films of Max Ophuls, which are sometimes associated with fin-de-siècle Viennese luxury. The Viennese cultural nexus may not seem evident in a film like *2001*, but that film is at least distantly related to Lang's *Metropolis* (1927), and the famous image of a shuttle docking in a revolving space station to the music of 'The Blue Danube' not only makes a sly Freudian joke but also evokes memories of Ophuls's *La Ronde* (1950) and *Lola Montez* (1955).

Notice, moreover, that as the director of *2001*, Kubrick might additionally be regarded as the last futurist. Certainly, his visionary future differs from the future-is-now of Godard's *Alphaville* (1965), the retro-future of George Lucas's *Star Wars* (1977) and the dystopian future of Ridley Scott's *Alien* (1979). If Fredric Jameson is correct that the death of futurism is precisely the moment when postmodernism becomes the cultural dominant, then we have another reason why Kubrick can be described as a modernist. One of the many oddities of *2001*, however, is that it seems to transcend or circumvent the utopian/dystopian distinction upon which futurism depends. Interestingly, its success led Kubrick to spend almost seventeen years developing *A. I. Artificial Intelligence* (2001), a project strikingly relevant to a hyper-modern period when the definition of the human is no longer clear and when the ostensibly opposite fields of machine intelligence and psychoanalysis have begun to illuminate one another. In both *A. I.* and its predecessor, Kubrick's generally Freudian and pessimistic view of human relations was ameliorated by his futuristic embrace of android technology, which, paradoxically, allowed him to express an otherwise repressed spirituality.

Kubrick often recommended three writers to fledgling movie directors: V. I. Pudovkin, Sigmund Freud and Konstantin Stanislavsky. His work was influenced by all three, but he also described the director as a 'taste machine' – a specialised computer devoted to keeping all the scenes in memory and making hundreds of decisions every day about script, acting, costuming, photography, editing and so forth.[7] This is a good description of his particular approach to his job, which involved obsessive attention to detail and gave him the reputation of a relentless and sometimes exasperating perfectionist. Aside from William Wyler, no other director was so prone to retakes, always in search of a mysterious I-don't-know-what that presumably he would recognise. Kubrick's particular taste, how-ever, has human sources in the cultural environment of New York City during his youth. The major events of his early life, which have been recounted many times (most thoroughly by Vincent LoBrutto), need only brief mention here, but are worth recalling. He was born into a secular Jewish family, the only male child of a Bronx medical doctor, and enjoyed what appears to have been a loving, even indulgent upbringing. Undoubtedly his Jewish ancestry influenced his later artistic development (this is the subject of an entire book: Geoffrey Cocks's *The Wolf at the Door*, which has a good deal to say about Kubrick as a post-Holocaust artist), but equally important was his freedom to explore the city and develop his own interests. A poor to indifferent high-school student, he played drums in the school's swing band and briefly dreamed of becoming a jazz musician (Eydie Gorme was a classmate). He was also a devoted moviegoer who visited every kind of theatre, from the Museum of Modern Art (MoMA) to grind houses. Much of his time was spent engaged in two hobbies his father had taught him – chess and photography, at which he was prodigiously talented. In 1945, at the age of seventeen, his photograph of a New York news vendor mourning the death of Franklin Roosevelt was purchased by *Look* magazine and he became a member of the magazine's photographic staff – a job that sent him travelling around the US and Europe and resulted in the publication of over 900 of his pictures.

By the end of the 1940s, Kubrick had acquired a pilot's licence, married his high-school sweetheart, moved to Greenwich Village, audited Mark Van Doren's literature class at Columbia and begun thinking of how he might become a film-maker. His immediate neighbourhood was filled with talent and ideas. Also living in Greenwich Village was America's leading film critic, James Agee, who wrote reviews for *The Nation* and *Time* and collaborated with photographer Walker Evans on *Let Us Now Praise Famous Men*. In 1952 Kubrick worked as a second-unit photographer on *Mr. Lincoln*, a television film written by Agee and directed by Norman Lloyd, which, if my memory of seeing it as a child can be trusted, might be the best film ever made on the subject; and, in 1953, after viewing Kubrick's first feature film, Agee gave the young director private encouragement. Agee's love of documentary realism and admiration for the films of John Huston may well have been an influence on Kubrick's early features, which were shot in natural light and thematically related to films that Huston had recently made. But there were plenty of other influences. New York during the late 1940s and 1950s had become the world's major centre for modern art, a place where, at one time or another, Jackson Pollock, Jack Kerouac, Marlon Brando and Miles Davis could all be found. The films of Jean Vigo, Carl Dreyer and the Italian neo-realists were playing in New York art houses, and by the mid-1950s the 'theatre of the absurd' was influencing New York playwrights. Kubrick was aware of these developments and during his years at *Look* he was at least indirectly involved with an important art movement: the 'New York school' of photographers, which included Lee Friedlander, Robert Frank, Diane Arbus and several others. Like Kubrick, many in this group were from Jewish-immigrant families, and their livelihood was made possible by the burgeoning market for photo-journalism in the picture magazines and tabloid newspapers. They tended to work on the borderland between mass and museum culture, and were responsible for the distinctive, black-and-white imagery of Manhattan that everyone now identifies with the city and the period.

The senior and most famous representative of the New York school of photographers was the tough, relatively uneducated and constantly self-promoting Arthur Felig, aka 'Weegee', who became famous for his photo-flood newspaper pictures of crime and accident scenes. A freelance photographer in the 1930s, Weegee had occasionally lectured at the New York Photo League, a Popular Front organisation that helped foster the careers of Berenice Abbott, Morris Engle, Lisette Model and many others. In 1940 he began publishing photographs in *PM Daily*, and in 1943, at about the time when young Stanley Kubrick was becoming seriously interested in cameras, his work was featured in an exhibit entitled 'Action Photography' at MoMA. His best-selling 1945 book of photographs, *Naked City*, inspired the street scenes in Jules Dassin's *The Naked City* (1948) and influenced the look of Hollywood film noir over the next decade. (Christiane Kubrick's *Stanley Kubrick, A Life in Pictures* [2002] contains two photos by the young Kubrick showing Weegee taking pictures with his Speed Graphic camera on the New York set of Dassin's movie.)

Weegee's chief importance to the younger generation of photographers lay in the fact that he immersed himself in the active life of the streets, eschewing the large-format cameras associated with the art-gallery pictures of Alfred Stieglitz. Like Walker Evans and the Farm Security Administration photographers of the 1930s, he could be distantly related to the 'Ash Can' painters of the early twentieth century, but his work was more urgent, sensational and 'existential'. Kubrick was, in some ways, influenced by this style; in general, however, he avoided flashbulbs and achieved altogether more artfully composed effects. *Look* was a slicker publication than *PM* and had a substantial readership in Middle America; hence Kubrick's pictures, many of which have recently been shown in European museum exhibits and collected in a coffee-table art book, are less shocking than Weegee's and deal with a wide range of 'human interest' subjects from the world outside New York.[8] Kubrick photographed fraternity boys at the University of Michigan, union organisers in Indiana and fishing villagers in Portugal. One of his major assignments was a study of contrasts between the poor and the prosperous in Chicago. Another was a pictorial on Dixieland musicians working in New York. (Among the Dixieland photographs is a portrait of the artist as a young man: Kubrick poses himself as a jazz drummer surrounded by black musicians, who seem to be ignoring him.) He often did stories on show business or sports celebrities, including Montgomery Clift, Frank Sinatra, Rocky Graziano and Errol Garner. Some of his assignments were merely cute: a baby seeing himself for the first time in a mirror, a couple necking in a theatre and people at the zoo viewed from the perspective of the animals. Some were faked and made to look spontaneous.

Kubrick took a series of supposedly candid shots of people riding the New York subway – a subject associated with Walker Evans – and he photographed showgirls, circus performers, street kids and people in paddy wagons, just as Weegee had done. Out of the welter of images he produced, however, something of a personal style or sensibility began to emerge. One of the distinctive qualities of his photographs, as Alexandra Von Stosch and Rainer Crone have written, is 'the conscious wish to stage his shots, to deliberately shape reality'.[9] This quality results in part from the fact that *Look* needed photographs that would instantly hook the viewer, delivering a message or telling a story. The magazine was 'cinematic', and many of Kubrick's images have the look of dynamic shots from movies: a seated Frank Sinatra viewed from a low angle, his face framed through the arm of a man who is leaning on a table in the foreground; an over-the-shoulder image of a travelling saleslady seen from the back seat of her car as she stops at a 'road closed' sign and consults a roadmap. Very often Kubrick arranges figures so that available light creates dramatic effects: a backlit scene of a college sweater girl lighting a cigarette for a fraternity boy; a black man and his daughter framed by an open door, looking into a dark hallway as they stand outside in the sun. Perhaps more significantly, given what we know of Kubrick's later work, the shots are sometimes composed to create surreal effects: a Chicago model wearing a girdle and a bra, blowing smoke from a cigarette while a fully clothed woman in glasses works at a desk behind her; a five-year-old female circus acrobat with scruffy knees, striking a pose in front of a line of elephants, who are also striking a pose.

Kubrick's celebrated films sometimes allude to other photographers, and sometimes borrow ideas from his own images for *Look*. In 1949 he photographed a nude woman modelling for the cartoonist Peter Arno; the woman stands with her back to the camera, her hips slightly cocked, in a pose almost exactly like Nicole Kidman at the beginning of *Eyes Wide Shut* (1999). At about the same time, Kubrick photographed a couple of men standing beside a row of artificial legs, all of which are 'dressed' in shoes and socks – an eerie shot that foreshadows Kubrick's lifelong preoccupation with mannequins, prosthetics and automata. The most direct connection between the still photographs and the films, however, is between a 1949 *Look* story on middleweight prize-fighter Walter Cartier and a sixteen-minute documentary about Cartier entitled *Day of the Fight* (1950–1), which was Kubrick's first motion picture. (Several shots from the documentary were almost exactly reproduced in Kubrick's second fiction film, *Killer's Kiss* [1955].) The magazine piece features full-length, remarkably still and statuesque images of Cartier and his opponents slugging it out in the ring, viewed from beneath the ropes at the level of the canvas.

In addition to the shots of athletic violence, the story also has a 'human interest' angle: it shows Cartier, who lived in Greenwich Village, attending a Catholic church, enjoying a day at the beach with a female friend and spending time at home with his family. One of its more curious aspects, which at times almost subverts the cosy scenes of private life, is that Cartier has an identical twin, Vincent, who accompanies him to the fights and helps him in training. The photographs of the twins have a surreal, uncanny feeling – something Kubrick exploits to an even greater extent in his documentary film about Cartier, which, for all its matter-of-fact narration and insistence that the fighter is an ordinary fellow, occasionally leaves a noir-like impression of something bizarre or oneiric.

George Toles has remarked that 'to a greater degree than the images of most directors', the individual shots in Kubrick's films 'aspire to self-sufficiency, to the lucid character of a firmly articulated thought'.[10] This may explain the unusually large number of iconic images Kubrick produced – shots that can be used to represent the film or even the cinema (Major Kong riding the hydrogen bomb, the Star Child floating in space, Alex leering at the audience and so forth). And Kubrick's 'thoughts', or more properly the feelings generated by his thoughts, have something in common. As many people have observed, photography is ideally suited for surrealistic effects, especially when it documents unusual juxtapositions, revealing something haunted, humorous or crazy that emerges from the social unconscious. Kubrick was very much attuned to this phenomenon; his films often create the impression of a creepy, unsettling force somewhere beneath a carefully composed, sharply focused cinematography. He was attracted to myths and fairy tales, and most of his work generates an emotional atmosphere that can be described with a family of related effects that belong to the fairy-tale genre – the uncanny, the darkly humorous, the strange, the absurd, the surreal, the fantastic and the grotesque – all of which are heightened by photographic realism. These effects have an important role to play in modern art (even if they don't originate in the twentieth century) and their various poetic functions have been theorised by modern authors. Freud's essay on the 'The Uncanny' was published in 1919, and his 1928 essay, 'Humour', influenced the surrealist André Breton's conception of *humour noir*, which was articulated in 1940; 'strange-making' or 'estrangement' was a vital concept for both the Russian formalists and Bertolt Brecht in the 1920s and 1930s; the 'absurd' was a term applied to experimental theatre in the 1950s; and the 'fantastic' was an important mode in Tzvetan Todorov's formalist theory of narrative poetics in the 1960s.

I don't mean to suggest that Kubrick's work was directly affected by these writings (though he was certainly aware of several of them), only that he partakes in a current of feeling often identified with modernity and given cultural significance by modernist aesthetics. The following book will occasionally comment on all the terms I've listed, indicating how they apply to specific films. I plan to give special attention to the 'grotesque' but, in advance of discussing that subject, it may be useful to address some more material concerns. What follows is a brief overview of Kubrick's career as a producer-director and his relationship to the American motion-picture industry.

II. Silence, Exile, and Cunning

> I will try to express myself in some mode of life or art as freely as I can and as wholly as I
> can, using for my defence the only arms I allow myself to use, silence, exile, and cunning.
>
> Stephen Dedalus in James Joyce's *A Portrait of the Artist as a Young Man*, 1916

Kubrick's films were nearly always made and received in the aura of art. This was chiefly due to his own aspirations, but he also wanted and needed commercial success. Prior to any critical examination of his films, we should at least briefly take into account the nature of the film industry during his lifetime and the financial circumstances under which his projects were produced (or in some cases not produced).

In the best account yet written of Kubrick's business relationship with Hollywood, to which a fair amount of the following information is indebted, Robert Sklar has pointed out that while Kubrick is often portrayed as a maverick and an exile, the truth is slightly more complicated:

> Stanley Kubrick's career as a filmmaker is deeply interconnected with the American
> motion picture industry. He has worked at one time or another with nearly all the so-
> called 'majors:' United Artists, Universal, Columbia, MGM, and Warner Bros. These
> companies have distributed his films and have participated in financing some of them.
> These connections have enmeshed Kubrick and his films in the structures of the American
> film business; despite his geographical self-exile from Hollywood, Kubrick continues to be
> regarded as an American filmmaker, while other expatriate directors, like Richard Lester
> and Joseph Losey, worked more closely with British and continental production and
> distribution companies and came to be seen as members of the Anglo-European film
> community.[11]

The terms 'exile' and 'expatriate' are often used synonymously, but an exile is a resident forced to live in another country rather than a voluntary expatriate or émigré. Kubrick, it should be emphasised, remained a US citizen and retained close contacts with Hollywood for virtually all his career. Sklar appropriately calls him a 'self-exile', as opposed to a figure like Joseph Losey, who was driven out of the US for political reasons and no longer functioned as a Hollywood director. It also seems to me that Kubrick isn't the same sort of American abroad as Orson Welles, despite the significant similarities between the two. Jonathan Rosenbaum has pointed out that Kubrick and Welles made exactly the same number of films and 'ended up making all the films they completed after the 1950s in exile, which surely says something about the creative possibilities of American commercial filmmaking over the past four decades'.[12] The basic point here is valid and important, but it's also important to note that Welles was often *persona non grata* in Hollywood and became a peripatetic citizen of the world, whereas Kubrick, who had a successful career as an American director, established a settled existence in England, remaining close to American production facilities but far enough away from Hollywood to protect his art. In Sklar's words, Kubrick 'hardly ever hesitated from playing the American film business game', much of the time 'by his own rules' (p. 114).

There was always a certain tension between Kubrick's artistic aims and Hollywood's conventional way of manufacturing entertainment, but Kubrick rarely had to yield authority over his films. His ability to maintain control was due in part to the fact that, when taking the first steps in his career, the film industry was undergoing major changes. A 1948 Supreme Court ruling had recently divested the major Hollywood studios of their theatre chains and the popular audience was increasingly obsessed with television. In the early 1950s a good many of television's dramatic programmes were being produced in New York, so that Kubrick might have entered the film industry by the same path as Daniel Mann or John Frankenheimer, who began as television directors. Alternatively, he might have moved to Hollywood and tried to become a professional cinematographer. Perhaps he was fortunate that his lack of film-making or theatrical experience forced him to invent ways of producing his own movies.

Kubrick's boyhood friend Alexander Singer worked with the *March of Time* documentaries, a newsreel unit of Time–Life in New York, and with Singer's help Kubrick made *Day of the Fight*, his sixteen-minute documentary about boxer Walter Cartier. Kubrick and Singer photographed the film with a rented Eymo camera and also played bit parts as fight fans. Another friend, Gerald Fried, a Julliard student, composed a music score and recorded it, eventually becoming the composer for Kubrick's first three feature films. Douglas Edwards, who would soon become a television anchor of CBS news, was the narrator. The film cost $3,900 of Kubrick's own savings, a considerably lower cost than the average documentary of the period, and was sold to RKO for $4,000. On the strength of its quality, RKO advanced Kubrick $1,500 to make a nine-minute short entitled *Flying Padre* (1952) about a New Mexico priest who flew to his far-flung parishioners in a Piper Cub. (At the time Kubrick was an amateur pilot who was pleased to have an opportunity to photograph aerial scenes.) The next year Kubrick took a job as director-photographer of *The Seafarers*, a thirty-minute promotional documentary funded by the Seafarers International Union, which was shot in colour and narrated by Don Hollenbeck, a CBS news reporter who would soon become a victim of the McCarthy-era witch hunts.

During all this time Kubrick had plans to produce a feature film – a remarkable ambition if we consider that between 1948 and 1954 movie-house attendance in the US declined by some 40 million. Hollywood responded to the box-office crisis with colour, CinemaScope and 3-D. Meanwhile, however, two developments in the world of exhibition created markets for low-budget, independent producers: the drive-in or 'passion pit', which favoured certain types of exploitation film, and the urban or college-town art theatre, which specialised in foreign pictures. In the period between 1952 and 1956, when many of the traditional showplaces were going out of business, the second of these newer forms of exhibition grew fairly steadily in urban locations. By the mid-1950s, at least 470 theatres located in various parts of the country were exclusively devoted to what was described as 'art' or 'adult entertainment', and at least 400 others made a policy of featuring 'art' on a part-time basis. Art houses had, of course, existed before World War II, especially in the biggest cities, but they relied chiefly on revivals of older products such as *The Cabinet of Dr. Caligari* (1920); after the war, enterprising distributors began to circulate new foreign films, obtaining more exhibition venues and a great deal of critical attention. Olivier's British-made *Henry V* (1945) and *Hamlet* (1948) were highly successful on the American market, as was the French-Italian production of Autant-Laura's *Devil in the Flesh* (1946), which was regarded in some quarters as scandalously sexual. Most important of all were Italian neo-realist pictures such as Rossellini's *Open City* (1945), De Sica's *The Bicycle Thief* (1947) and De Santis's *Bitter Rice* (1948), which helped to reveal a 'lost audience' and laid the groundwork for an art-cinema boom.[13]

In the trade, the art theatres came to be known as 'sure-seaters' because their audiences were loyal and their films tended to attract strong reviews from critics.[14] The films were sometimes labelled 'mature', presumably because they were enjoyed by sophisticated and discriminating viewers, but also because they were more openly sexual than Hollywood's typical products. In those innocent times, a publicity still from *Bitter Rice* showing a large-breasted Silvana Mangano as a proletarian labourer standing in a rice field with her skirts hiked up was enough to make Mangano an international star. As a result, art cinema rubbed shoulders with a softly pornographic sensationalism. Arthur Mayer, an ex-Paramount executive who worked as an independent distributor during the period, has given an amusing account of how promotion worked:

> 'Open City' was generally advertised with a misquotation from *Life* adjusted to read: 'Sexier than Hollywood ever dared to be,' together with a still of two young ladies deeply engrossed in a rapt embrace, and another of a man being flogged, designed to tap the sadist trade. The most publicized scene in 'Paisan' showed a young lady disrobing herself with an attentive male visitor reclining by her side in what was obviously not a nuptial couch. 'The Bicycle Thief' was completely devoid of any erotic embellishments, but the exhibitors sought to atone for this deficiency with a highly imaginative sketch of a young lady riding a bicycle.[15]

Inevitably, the foreign films encountered resistance from censors; but in 1952 the Supreme Court issued a landmark ruling against the state of New York, which had attempted to prohibit screenings of De Sica's *Miracle in Milan* on the grounds that the Catholic Legion of Decency deemed it 'sacrilegious'. The court ruled that motion pictures, like books or other forms of art, were entitled to First Amendment protection. From then until the 1970s, Hollywood's virtually complete dominance of the market was challenged by 'mature' productions from both outside and inside the country.

At first, few if any American film-makers seemed aware of the new circumstances. Stanley Kramer caused something of a stir with his independent productions of *Home of the Brave* (1949) and *Champion* (1949), but those pictures were conceived, exhibited and received as Hollywood products rather than as art films. David Bradley, a wealthy young Chicagoan, produced and directed his own low-budget adaptations of *Peer Gynt* (1940) and *Julius Caesar* (1950), featuring a Northwestern University student named Charlton Heston, but neither film had a national distribution. John Cassavetes's shoe-string production of *Shadows*, which owed something to the Italian neo-realists, did not appear until 1961. During the early 1950s, the only American who made inexpensive, English-language films that found a natural home in art houses was Orson Welles, whose *Othello* (1952) and *Mr. Arkadin* (1955) were European imports, produced in advance of an art-house distribution network.

Enter Stanley Kubrick, whose cinephilia had been nourished by regular attendance at New York art theatres and the Museum of Modern Art, and who can legitimately claim the distinction of being the first American director of an entirely independent American art film in the post-World War II era. In 1950 Kubrick approached Richard de Rochement, a New York newsreel producer and journalist, with the idea of making a feature-length, allegorical war picture based on a script by Kubrick's former high-school friend Howard O. Sackler. De Rochement's brother Louis was in charge of *The March of Time* and had recently become a Hollywood producer of ground-breaking docudramas such as *House on 92nd St.* (1945); in 1949, he also independently produced *Lost Boundaries*, a fiction film about racial segregation in America, which was developed at MGM but released through an independent distributor and exhibited mostly in art houses. Richard de Rochement may have been interested in following in his brother's footsteps; in any case he was impressed with Kubrick's youthful intensity and talent; when de Rochement came to produce *Mr. Lincoln*, the TV film by James Agee and Norman Lloyd, he recommended Kubrick as one of the photographers, and he eventually provided part of the financing for Kubrick's feature film.

The bulk of the money for the feature came from Kubrick's maternal uncle, Martin Perveler, who was credited as producer. Kubrick did practically everything but act in this picture, which he shot on location in the San Gabriel Mountains outside Los Angeles. Historians have differed in their reports of the budget, but the best estimate seems to be that the film was shot in five weeks without sound for about $9,000 and then went through several months of post-production sound recording during which the cost increased another $20–30,000. By the time all fees were calculated, the total pre-release budget had risen to $53,500. Hollywood distributors rejected the film, but ultimately Kubrick attracted the interest of a legendary distributor of foreign art films – Joseph Burstyn, the man who, together with Arthur Mayer, had brought *Open City*, *The Bicycle Thief* and Renoir's *A Day in the Country* to America, and who had fought and won against the state of New York in the '*Miracle*' case. 'He's a genius!' the excitable Burstyn purportedly said after meeting the twenty-four-year-old Kubrick and seeing his film, which at that point was entitled

The Shape of Fear. Burstyn immediately declared it an 'American art film', changed the title to the more provocative *Fear and Desire* (1953), and in March 1953 booked it into New York City's Guild Theatre, an art house located in Rockefeller Center, where Kubrick himself designed a photographic display to attract customers. *Fear and Desire* received a 'B' rating from the Legion of Decency because of a sex scene involving a woman strapped to a tree, but it also enjoyed a remarkable degree of mostly favourable critical attention, especially given the fact that it was a low-budget production from an unknown director. (No doubt Kubrick's connections in the world of glossy news magazines had something to do with the extent to which the film was noticed.) It subsequently played San Francisco, Chicago, Detroit and Philadelphia, and then reappeared in New York at the Rialto Theatre, where, according to Vincent LoBrutto, it was sold as a 'sexploitation picture' (p. 90).

Kubrick was eventually able to repay his investors, though not with the meagre returns from *Fear and Desire*. Nor did he receive profits from his next film, the slightly more orthodox *Killer's Kiss*, which was financed by Kubrick's relatives and Bronx pharmacist Morris Bousel for a cost of roughly $75,000. This film was shot in a little over three months on the streets of New York and in a few minimalist sets (the generous shooting schedule was made possible by the fact that the actors and crew worked for almost nothing). Once again Kubrick was director, photographer and editor, and once again the soundtrack was post-recorded. This time, however, Kubrick was able to find a Hollywood distributor – United Artists (UA), formerly the studio of Griffith, Pickford, Fairbanks and Chaplin, which had recently been rescued from bankruptcy by the management team of Arthur Krim and Robert Benjamin. UA was in the process of transforming itself into a new type of financing and distributing organisation; it sometimes offered production facilities, but mostly it shared expenses and profits with movie stars and other talent who were breaking free of their studio contracts and forming their own production companies.[16] Krim and Benjamin ultimately achieved great commercial success with this formula, which became a standard practice in the industry, and they became famous among film lovers for supporting Woody Allen's career in the late 1960s and 1970s. When Kubrick approached them, they were still trying to put the UA organisation back on its feet and were simply buying cheap product that they wouldn't have to produce. They gave *Killer's Kiss* national distribution, but it had almost no publicity and was booked in bargain-price theatres, usually at the bottom half of a double feature. I myself saw it in a fleapit called the Majestic in Lake Charles, Louisiana, which normally showed nothing but re-runs.

According to Vincent LoBrutto, at about this time Kubrick complained to one of his friends at the Marshall Chess Club in New York about the frustrations of getting started in the film business: "'I have talent,' he said. 'I know I'm good. I just can't get a backer or a producer'" (p. 106). Not long afterward, his luck changed. James B. Harris, born within a week of Kubrick, had served in the US Army Signal Corps alongside Kubrick's friend Alexander Singer and afterward, aided by his wealthy father, had co-founded a motion-picture and television distribution company in New York. He had met Kubrick on a few occasions and, when Kubrick approached him in 1955 about the possibility of distributing *Fear and Desire* on TV, Harris recognised a kindred spirit. He immediately suggested that they form a production company. Grounded in a friendship between two confident, sharply intelligent young men who had similar tastes in literature and film, Harris-Kubrick Pictures was to become one of the most artistically important collaborations of the 1950s.

Kubrick was the chief creative partner, but Harris was a skilful producer with an eye for talent and sufficient capital to acquire properties and writers. He immediately purchased the rights to Lionel White's thriller *Clean Break*, which provided the basis for Kubrick and Jim Thompson's script for *The Killing* (1955–6). UA agreed to finance and distribute the film if Harris and Kubrick could find a star. After Harris unsuccessfully approached Jack Palance, the script fell into the hands of Sterling Hayden, the star of *The Asphalt Jungle* (1950), who seems at first to have confused Stanley Kubrick with Stanley Kramer, but who nevertheless agreed to act in the picture. Because Hayden's career was on the wane, UA offered a miniscule budget of $200,000. James Harris added $130,000 of his own money, which demonstrated his great faith in Kubrick and bought extra days of shooting. The film was photographed on locations around Los Angeles and San Francisco and in the old Chaplin studios at UA. Kubrick took no pay, deferring his fee until UA recovered its investment, living entirely on loans from Harris. Unfortunately, the completed film was disliked by Sterling Hayden's agent and by executives at UA, who were dismayed by its confusing time scheme. (One can only wonder if they read the script when they agreed to the project.) At one point Kubrick tried to re-edit everything in chronological fashion, but he quickly abandoned the idea when he saw that it made the picture look conventional and lifeless. Released in the form Harris and Kubrick had originally intended, *The Killing* earned no profit, largely because UA treated it as a B movie and dumped it on the lower end of the market; nevertheless, the camera style and the modernistic, backward-and-forward shifts of the plot caught the eye of critics, prompting a *Time* magazine reviewer to compare Kubrick with the young Orson Welles. To cognoscenti, it was evident that the director had turned low-budget, formulaic material into a silk purse.

Even before *The Killing* went into development, Harris and Kubrick began to explore the possibility of making additional films, nearly all of which would have been based on controversial properties. In 1955, they contemplated an adaptation of another Lionel White novel, *The Snatchers*, but the Production Code Administration (PCA) frowned upon the project because it involved a detailed account of a kidnapping. Soon afterward, they wrote to Geoffrey Shurlock of the PCA about the possibility of adapting Felix Jackson's novel *So Help Me God*, which was an attack on the House Un-American Activities Committee. In convoluted language, Shurlock replied that the novel was totally unacceptable: 'This would hardly seem to be in conformity with the Code requirement that prominent institutions be not misrepresented.... [A]ny attempt to make a picture which would seem to have as its aim the discrediting of the Un-American Activities Committee would appear to be of such a highly controversial nature that it might get into the area of questionable industry policy.'[17]

Next, Harris-Kubrick floated the idea of adapting Calder Willingham's *Natural Child*, a novel about intellectuals in New York and their love affairs. Again Shurlock wrote that the proposed book was 'basically unacceptable', not only because it involved an abortion, but also because it adopted 'a light and casual approach' to illicit sex.

The situation looked as if it might change slightly when a pre-release print of *The Killing* caught the eye of MGM production chief Dore Schary, who tried to buy the film from UA and distribute it through his own studio. Schary had begun to transform the once conservative MGM into a home for social-problem pictures and film noir; he had already contracted director Anthony Mann and cinematographer John Alton to work on a series of excellent low-budget thrillers, including *Border Incident* (1949), *Side Street* (1949) and *The Tall Target* (1951), and he had strongly supported John Huston's production of *The Asphalt Jungle*. Harris-Kubrick seemed to fit perfectly with Schary's agenda, so he invited the two men to form their own unit at MGM, giving them office space, a secretary and money to develop their next project.

Soon after Harris-Kubrick set up shop in Culver City, Kubrick proposed they adapt Humphrey Cobb's 1935 novel about World War I, *Paths of Glory*. When he and Harris brought the idea to Schary, however, they were told it was unsuitable. Schary was probably still suffering from the troubles he had encountered with John Huston's stark, uncompromising adaptation of Stephen Crane's *The Red Badge of Courage* (1951), and didn't relish the prospect of another anti-war picture with actors dressed in historical costumes – especially since the picture in question had no chance of being exhibited in the French marketplace. (When *Paths of Glory* eventually became a film, it was banned in France for almost two decades.) He politely informed Harris and Kubrick that they should limit themselves to properties already owned by the studio.

After surveying the available material, Kubrick settled on *Burning Secret*, a novel by Stefan Zweig, who had provided the source for Max Ophuls's *Letter from an Unknown Woman* (1948). A Viennese contemporary of Freud and Schnitzler, Zweig usually wrote about bourgeois sexuality – in this case an Oedipal story about a boy who tries to protect his mother when his father discovers she has been having an affair. (Zweig's novel had been filmed in Germany in 1933 by Robert Siodmak and would be filmed again in a German-British co-production in 1988.) To develop a screenplay, Harris-Kubrick hired Calder Willingham, the author of *Natural Child*, one of the books Kubrick had recently considered adapting. (Willingham had previously adapted his own novel, *End as a Man*, under the title *The Strange One* [1957], a frank and memorable film about life in a military school, featuring a distinguished performance by the young Ben Gazzara.) Meanwhile, despite Kubrick's arrangement with MGM, he and Jim Thompson began to moonlight on a script for *Paths of Glory*.

Willingham's adaptation of *Burning Secret* was delayed by troubles with censors and became a victim of studio economics and politics. Less than a year after Harris and Kubrick arrived, Dore Schary was fired as production chief and the two New Yorkers were unceremoniously dumped from the studio. The entire movie business was changing; MGM would soon be distributing such oddities as *Hootenanny Hoot* (1963), and the industry would be driven mostly by producers and stars who controlled their own production units. The new conditions nevertheless created opportunities for a young talent like Kubrick, who soon made the acquaintance of a powerful and intelligent star. Kirk Douglas, the muscular, dimple-chinned, intensely emotional actor who was a vivid presence in such pictures as *Detective Story* (1951) and *Lust for Life* (1956), was at the height of his fame during the period, and had been much impressed with *The Killing*. When Douglas saw a script for *Paths of Glory* – which by that time had been revised by Calder Willingham – he offered to take the leading role and to pressure United Artists into financing and distributing the picture. The price Douglas exacted, however, was considerable: Harris–Kubrick had to agree to move their operation to Douglas's Bryna Production Company and Kubrick had to make five other pictures with Bryna, two of which would star Douglas. Harris and Kubrick were uneasy about these arrangements, but ultimately agreed to the deal. Soon afterward, *Paths of Glory* went before cameras, budgeted at approximately $1 million. Its star received over a third of that sum, and its large cast worked on locations near Munich, Germany – as far from Hollywood as Kubrick had ever been. Harris and Kubrick again waived their fees and agreed to work for a percentage of the picture's profits, if profits ever came.

Even though the working relationship between Douglas and Kubrick was sometimes tense, *Paths of Glory* (1957) was one of the most critically admired films in the director's career. Kubrick gained no monetary profit, but he acquired a good deal of cultural capital and the reputation of having collaborated with a major star. Moreover, his new contract led to his being hired to direct Douglas's next film, the widescreen epic *Spartacus*, produced by Bryna and Universal Pictures, which was budgeted at $12 million. At the time, this was the most expensive movie ever shot inside the US. (Some of the crowd scenes were photographed in Spain, but nearly everything else was done on the Universal back lot.) MGM's remake of *Ben-Hur* (1959) in the previous year had been slightly more expensive, but was done completely in Europe, where Hollywood companies were able to obtain tax advantages and cheaper labour. In fact, during the 1960s the so-called 'flight' from domestic production, coupled with the turn towards expensive spectacles, had become so commonplace that several industry insiders questioned the wisdom of making *Spartacus* in Hollywood. When the film opened, the recently elected President John F. Kennedy made a special point of attending a showing at a regular theatre in Washington, DC, thereby calling attention to Douglas and Universal's attempt to keep US money at home.

Like most other commentators on Kubrick, I've chosen to omit critical discussion of *Spartacus*. Let me note, however, that it's one of the best of Hollywood's toga movies, in part because it deals with Romans vs slaves rather than Romans vs Christians (although it does make Spartacus a kind of Christ figure). It has literate dialogue and effective action sequences, and, somewhat like *The Robe* (1953), it runs slightly against the grain of its genre by offering a liberal political message. Nevertheless, it was the only alienated labour of

Kubrick's film career and has very few moments when one can sense his directorial personality. The climactic battle scene between the slave army and the Romans is sometimes
attributed to Kubrick, but was designed by Saul Bass. Anthony Mann was in charge of the
opening sequences, which are as good as any others in the picture. Kubrick's hand seems
most evident in the sexually kinky moments – the visit of Roman aristocrats and their wives
to the gladiator school, and the not-so-veiled homosexual conversations between Crassus
(Laurence Olivier) and his slave, Antoninus (Tony Curtis). Elsewhere Kubrick functioned as
a sort of choreographer or traffic cop who could manage tensions between Olivier and
Charles Laughton, two theatrical icons with large egos. He had no voice in the casting or the
development of the screenplay, nor did he supervise the editing. He disliked the script,
which he described to Michel Ciment as 'dumb' and 'rarely faithful to what is known about
Spartacus', who had twice led his victorious army to the borders of Italy and could have easily escaped: 'What the reasons were for this would have been the most interesting question
the film could have pondered. Did the intentions of the rebellion change? Did Spartacus lose
control of his leaders who by now may have been more interested in the spoils of war than
freedom?'[18] (Kirk Douglas has said that, in spite of such complaints, Kubrick offered to take
credit for the work of blacklisted screenwriter Dalton Trumbo; Douglas rejected the idea
and broke the blacklist, defying an attempted boycott of the film from the American
Legion.) To make matters worse, Kubrick had trouble with director of photography Russell
Metty, a Universal Pictures veteran who had photographed Welles's *Touch of Evil* (1958) and
several of the Douglas Sirk melodramas. Probably as a result of Metty's intransigence, very
few scenes in *Spartacus* employ the source illumination we identify with Kubrick. Notice in
particular the bright, three-point lighting inside the Roman forum – a far cry from *Barry
Lyndon*. The entire experience provided a lesson Kubrick would never forget. As he told
Ciment, 'If I ever needed any convincing of the limits of persuasion a director can have on
a film where someone else is the producer and [the director] is merely the highest-paid member of the crew, *Spartacus* provided proof to last a lifetime' (p. 151).

Ironically, *Spartacus* gave Kubrick his first big payday. (Kirk Douglas never profited
from the film, which did less business than expected through domestic rentals.) He then
went on to earn still more money by helping to develop a picture he never directed: Marlon
Brando's production of *One-Eyed Jacks* (1961). Once again Kubrick was frustrated by having to work for a producer-star, and he left the project during pre-production. Even though
his involvement was brief, his shadow hovers over parts of the completed film, perhaps
because two of his former collaborators remained on the job: Calder Willingham wrote
the script and Timothy Carey has an effective scene as a raunchy, sadistic cowboy. Brando
directed the film, which is an exceptionally good Western, marred only by a tacked-on
happy ending.

During these years Kubrick and Harris were planning to make more films together.
One of their projects was a script by Kubrick and Jim Thompson for a Kirk Douglas vehicle,
I Stole $16,000,000, based on the autobiography of safe-cracker Herbert E. Wilson. Another

was *The 7th Virginia Cavalry Raider*, an unfinished script by Kubrick for a film about Confederate guerrillas in the US Civil War. Still another was *The German Lieutenant*, intended to star Alan Ladd, which centred on a German paratroop unit in the final days of World War II. (The script of this film, written by Kubrick and Richard Adams, is discussed in some detail by Geoffrey Cocks.)[19] Harris and Kubrick also contemplated making a satiric TV series starring the surreal comic Ernie Kovacs, based on the character Kovacs had played in Richard Quine's *Operation Mad Ball* (1957). This, like the other projects, did not get far. Meanwhile, Kubrick asked to be released from his contract with Douglas, and Douglas generously consented. There was bad blood between the two, but Douglas had done more than anyone to advance Kubrick's career. As far as Hollywood was concerned, the most impressive thing on Kubrick's résumé was *Spartacus*, which showed that he could manage a super-colossal picture brimming with big stars.

Another opportunity soon arose. Kubrick and Harris had read Vladimir Nabokov's *Lolita* just prior to its publication and, at the urging of Richard de Rochement and several others, they immediately acquired the film rights. (As a hedge against the book's controversial subject matter, they also bought the rights to *Laughter in the Dark* [1938], an earlier Nabokov novel involving a roughly similar erotic situation, told against the background of the movie industry in Weimar Germany.) When *Lolita* became a sensational best-seller, Warner Bros. promised a million-dollar budget if Harris-Kubrick Productions could obtain Code approval. According to Jack Vizzard's account of the workings of the Production Code Administration, Harris, Kubrick and others involved in the film hired Martin Quigley, the editor of *Motion Picture Daily* and one of the authors of the 1930 Production Code, to give them advice and help smooth *Lolita*'s passage through the PCA and past the Catholic Legion of Decency.[20] Harris-Kubrick soon gave up on the deal with Warner because the studio wanted too much control over creative aspects of the film. They talked briefly with Columbia Pictures but signed no agreement. Ultimately, through Harris's connections in an old-boy network dating back to his school days, they obtained financial backing from Eliot Hyman, the head of a new company called Associated Artists, and from Ray Stark, Kirk Douglas's former agent. Kubrick and Harris decided to shoot the film in England, where, under the recently enacted 'Eady Plan', they could enjoy substantial tax advantages if at least 80 per cent of the people they employed were British citizens. This arrangement provided Kubrick with distance from Hollywood's usual ways of doing business and probably emboldened him in his treatment of the sexual themes of the novel. He enjoyed working with a British crew (even though they called him 'Governor' and insisted on tea breaks) and was pleased by the production facilities. The film, with a final budget of approximately $2 million, was made without a distributor but was ultimately released by MGM. It was the least critically successful but the most profitable of the Harris-Kubrick pictures, earning almost twice its cost in the US alone.

Lolita's relative box-office success, following closely on the heels of *Spartacus*, gave Kubrick cachet in Hollywood and marked a turning point in his career. He would make all his remaining films in England, where his dark humour and gifts for caricature flourished, and he would end his collaboration with James B. Harris, who had long wanted to become a director. Soon after Harris and Kubrick began planning their next project, a suspense film about nuclear war based on British novelist Peter George's *Red Alert*, the two men amicably dissolved their partnership. Harris went on to direct several pictures, among them *The Bedford Incident* (1965), a suspense melodrama about a right-wing US naval commander's confrontation with a Soviet nuclear submarine, and *Some Call It Loving* (1973), an off-beat retelling of the Sleeping Beauty fairy tale. Kubrick, meanwhile, became his own producer and entered the major phase of his creative life.

The suspense film Kubrick and Harris had been working on was transformed into *Dr. Strangelove or: How I Learned to Stop Worrying and Love the Bomb* (1963–4), produced by Columbia Pictures and Kubrick's new company, Hawk Films, for a cost of $1.8 million. The star, Peter Sellers, who would soon appear on US screens as Inspector Clouseau in *The Pink Panther* (1963), was about to become a major celebrity. Columbia thought he was the only bankable element in the off-beat film and proposed that he play several characters on the model of his work in *The Mouse That Roared*, a British comedy that Columbia had distributed in 1959. At Sellers' insistence, *Strangelove* was shot in England, where he was undergoing a complicated divorce. Kubrick, who was loath to work in Hollywood and who regarded British studios as superior to anything he could find in New York, was pleased to accept this condition. When the risky, highly unorthodox film was completed, some of Columbia's executives hated it, and after the initial preview Kubrick revised the ending, dropping a manic pie-throwing sequence. But *Strangelove* was embraced by younger audiences and went on to become the studio's biggest hit of 1964, earning $5 million from the domestic box office alone. Both Robert Sklar and Charles Maland have pointed out, that *Strangelove* scored its greatest success in big cities and college towns, where it prefigured the youth rebellions of the later 1960s.[21] This audience would support Kubrick for the next fifteen years, but his inability or disinclination to attract crowds in the provinces would eventually cause problems.

Kubrick moved back to Manhattan and began work on an even more risky project. He and Arthur C. Clarke collaborated on a 'novelisation' of a proposed science-fiction movie entitled *Journey beyond the Stars*, which ultimately became *2001: A Space Odyssey*. MGM agreed to finance and distribute the picture along with the Cinerama Corporation for a 6 per cent interest charge, half ownership and permanent distribution rights. Kubrick again chose to do his shooting and editing in England, this time at MGM's studios at Boreham Wood. The initial cost estimate for the production was $6 million, but Kubrick's innovative special effects drove the price of the final negative up to $10,964,080. His financing arrangement stipulated that his production company wouldn't begin to receive a share of profits (25 per cent of gross rentals) until MGM earned 2.2 times its negative and advertising costs (Sklar, p. 118). After a disappointing screening for Hollywood executives and bad reviews from some of the New York critics, he shaved nineteen minutes from the running time of the deliberately enigmatic film and added new titles. *2001* went on to become one of the biggest money-makers in MGM history, but for a long time Kubrick realised none of the profits. By 1973 the film had earned approximately $28 million in domestic and foreign rentals and MGM was still collecting its 6 per cent interest on the financing. Robert Sklar concludes that, at least until 1978, the relationship between the independent producer and the distributor of *2001* 'was hardly different from the norms Kubrick had experienced with his low-budget productions of the 1950s' (p. 119).

Close on the heels of *2001*, Kubrick planned an equally ambitious film in a dialectically opposite genre: an epic historical picture about Napoleon Bonaparte, the military genius and self-created emperor who, as much as anyone in the scientific or artistic world, could be credited with the birth of modernity. A Promethean and in some ways tragic figure, Napoleon was one of the most politically and sexually fascinating figures in modern history; Freud and Nietzsche have written about him in interesting ways, and many biographers and film-makers have told of his heroic, foolish and sometimes harrowing adventures. Kubrick probably identified with him on some level; in any case, Kubrick's proposed three-hour film, which would have been shot in Yugoslavia, Italy and other European locations, required a tactical brilliance, administrative skill and encyclopedic knowledge worthy of the great general himself. Kubrick amassed a vast library of books about Napoleon, hired graduate students from Oxford to compile a day-to-day record of Napoleon's life and created a semi-computerised picture file consisting of over 15,000 items from the Napoleonic era. He commissioned historian Felix Markham to act as an advisor to the film and used Markham's biography of Napoleon as his chief source for the script, which he completed and submitted to MGM in November 1968. In a memo appended to the script, he told MGM executives that he planned to keep production costs down by casting lesser-known actors (the actor he had in mind for Napoleon was Jack Nicholson, who was about to win a sup-porting-player Oscar for *Easy Rider* [1969]), hiring cheap extras in Yugoslavia, and making use of the front-projection system he had devised for *2001*. With the aid of super-fast lenses and specially engineered film stock, he also planned to avoid building large sets; he would shoot in real interiors, sometimes using nothing but candlelight.

Kubrick's *Napoleon* screenplay, which was at one time available on the web and may soon be published, might have eventuated in a great screen biography, and by general agreement is the most tantalising unfulfilled project in the director's career. Even by Kubrick's standards, it has an unusually large amount of off-screen narration, blending a god-like historical narrator with the subjective voice of the eponymous hero. (At one point we hear long excerpts from Napoleon's letters to Josephine, while his military campaign is cross-cut with scenes of her love affair with a young officer in Paris.) The battle sequences would doubtless have been executed with Kubrick's customary skill, but the script is equally interesting for its dramatisation of Napoleon's sex life. In somewhat Freudian fashion, it depicts the emperor as a mother's boy and gives Josephine, the older woman who is the major love of his life, a mirrored bedroom that becomes the setting for several highly charged erotic encounters. In the political scenes, Napoleon is treated in complex ways: we see him as a gifted leader who advances the ideals of the Enlightenment, as an autocratic ruler who overreaches and lives by war, and as a superstitious dreamer who neglects his campaign in Russia and condemns the Grand Army to a 'thousand mile march into oblivion'.[22] As in many of Kubrick's other films, the implied view of society is pessimistic: humanity is fatally flawed and even its progressive institutions are founded on a sublimated violence and will to power.

Despite all his work on the project, Kubrick and his associate producer Jan Harlan (who was also Kubrick's brother-in-law) were unable to secure financing for the Napoleon film. Both MGM and United Artists turned it down, in part because the industry was in a financial slump, but also because Sergei Bondarchuck's *Waterloo* (1970) appeared on US screens at about the same time as Kubrick submitted his script and turned out to be an epic flop. Kubrick's disappointment must have been ameliorated, however, when Warner Bros. offered him one of the most attractive contracts any director has ever received.

In 1970, John Calley, the executive vice-president for production at Warner, signed Kubrick for a three-picture deal in which he would have a unique relationship with the studio. He could remain in England, where Warner's London office would fund the purchase, development and production of properties for him to direct; he was guaranteed final cut of his films; and his company, Hawk Films, would receive 40 per cent of the profits.[23] The first picture made under this arrangement, *A Clockwork Orange* (1971), was budgeted at $2 million; by 1982 it had earned total box-office revenues of $40 million, making it the most profitable production of the director's career and one of the studio's biggest hits of the decade (Sklar, p. 121). The profits, moreover, were achieved despite the fact that *A Clockwork Orange* had a limited distribution. Soon after the film opened in England, the British press charged it with having prompted a series of copy-cat crimes; in response, Kubrick withdrew it from circulation in British theatres for the rest of his lifetime – an extraordinary action that no other director of the period had the power to take.

Part of the success of *A Clockwork Orange* was due to Kubrick's marketing campaign. For some time he had been involving himself in the promotion and exhibition of his films, even to the point of sending out assistants to control their screenings. In August 1962, for example, he wrote a letter to his film editor, Anthony Harvey, asking Harvey to supervise the early showings of *Lolita* in London theatres: 'check the screening print in the theater a day or so before it opens. It would be a good idea to set the sound level in the empty theater a bit too loud. When the theater is full, it is usually just right.'[24] He also paid a good deal of attention to the hiring of people who designed posters, advertisements and trailers for his films. The impressively edited and very funny trailer for *Dr. Strangelove*, for instance, was done by Pablo Ferro, who also designed the titles for the picture and became a sought-after figure within the industry.[25] The trailer for *A Clockwork Orange* is equally good – a sort of 'Lodovico treatment' for moviegoers, edited in hyper-accelerated tempo. Of greater importance to the success of this particular film, however, was Kubrick's ability to circumvent the controversy in the mainstream press by targeting the promotional campaign to a specific audience. In a 22 October 1971 letter to Warner Bros., Mike Kaplan, an associate of Kubrick at Hawk Films, announced that Kubrick was 'particularly concerned now with the college-underground outlets . . . . This is the prime audience for the film, being the strongest Kubrick followers, and most familiar with the book, etc.' Kaplan outlined a strategy for advertising not only in metropolitan areas such as New York, Los Angeles, San Francisco and Toronto, but also in every college newspaper in California. Particularly important to the campaign were such venues as the *LA Free Press*, *Village Voice*, *East Village Other*, *Berkeley Barb*, *Earth*, *Ramparts* and *Screw*. Kaplan emphasised that the film should also be advertised on FM radio, on 'progressive' rock stations and on classical music stations where the *2001* soundtrack had often been played. Finally, he proposed that 'small, discreet ads' be placed in the *New York Review of Books*, which was 'rarely used for films'.[26] Meanwhile, *Variety* reported that Kubrick had compiled a data bank on US and foreign markets and developed a worldwide booking strategy. This plan was so successful that, according to the journal, Kubrick was partly responsible for driving Norman Katz, the chief executive officer of Warner's international offices, out of his job. Ted Ashley, the head of the company, announced that Kubrick was a genius who combined 'aesthetics' with 'fiscal responsibility' (Sklar, p. 121).

Kubrick remained at Warner for the rest of his career. According to Thomas Elsaesser, he formed a 'personal bond' with CEO Steve Ross (also a friend of Steven Spielberg), deputy CEO Terry Semel and Julian Senior, who was head of the company offices in London (p. 138). His ascendancy in the early 1970s had something to do with the 'New Hollywood', a phenomenon he slightly predates, which is determined by the relative independence of US exhibition, the liberalisation of classic-era censorship codes and the rise of 'youth culture'. Auteurs such as Spielberg, Robert Altman, Martin Scorsese, Francis Coppola and George Lucas came to prominence in this decade and, by the late 1970s, Spielberg and Lucas were producing Hollywood blockbusters in the same British facilities Kubrick had used. But Kubrick's ability to attract sufficiently large audiences was about to end. After the success of *A Clockwork Orange*, he was determined to make the historical film he had long envisaged; the result was *Barry Lyndon* (1975), which employs many of the same themes and techniques that were planned for the unfilmed Napoleon project. Three years in production, the slightly over three-hour film cost $11 million. Its initial run earned only $9,200,000 in domestic rentals, barely placing in the top twenty-five grosses of the year; it performed better in Europe and eventually earned a profit, but *Variety* called it a 'flop' (Sklar, p. 121).

Writers in the trade press accused Kubrick of arrogance, in part because he hadn't allowed them on the set during the making of *Barry Lyndon* and had kept the nature of the production largely a secret. Since the late 1960s, perhaps in response to the poor critical reception of his films in some quarters of the US, he had refused to allow publicity photos of his work in progress. The bigger problem with his historical film, however, was that the industry was changing, especially at the level of distribution. The top money-maker in the year was *Jaws*, which earned $133 million, almost doubling the earnings record of any previous film. From this experience the studios learned new marketing practices: saturation booking of 'tent-pole' films across the entire country, massive TV advertising and huge promotional campaigns, pre-release payments from exhibitors and guaranteed playing time in theatres (Sklar, p. 121). The nation was becoming more geared towards corporate thinking and Big Money. In the 1980s Ronald Reagan would be elected, the movie studios would once again be vertically (and horizontally) integrated and the 'New Hollywood' would become a memory.

Kubrick's initial response to changing times was a highly commercial project: *The Shining*, a horror picture based on a Stephen King novel and starring Jack Nicholson. (He had declined Warner's offer to have him direct *The Exorcist* [1973], which went on to become one of the studio's most profitable investments.) The film was budgeted at $18 million and earned nearly $40 million in domestic rentals – a substantial sum, but not so terribly impressive in a year when Lucas's *The Empire Strikes Back* brought in $140 million. As Robert Sklar observes, the gap between 'aesthetics' and 'fiscal responsibility' was growing wider and Kubrick's inability to appeal to audiences beyond the sophisticated urban centres was becoming more noticeable (p. 123). Warner nevertheless remained faithful to him; Terry Semel believed that Kubrick strengthened the studio's image on Wall Street, and appreciated the fact that his late films were shot with relatively small, efficient crews. Even so, the periods of silence between his films grew longer. *Full Metal Jacket* (1987), which appeared late in a cycle of gritty pictures about Vietnam, was produced for $17 million and returned almost $23 million in domestic rentals (Cook, p. 525). At least two other projects – *Aryan Papers*, based on Louis Begley's *Wartime Lies*, a novel about a Jew who passes as a Gentile during World War II; and *A. I. Artificial Intelligence*, derived from a short story by Brian Aldiss about a robot child of the future – were abandoned. Kubrick's last film, *Eyes Wide Shut*, which starred Tom Cruise and Nicole Kidman and took a great deal of time in shooting, cost $65 million – a sum that reflects the massive inflation in the industry. US audiences expected to see a psychological thriller or a sex show, but what they got was one of the most unusual films of the decade; its initial earnings in the US were a disappointing $56 million, at a time when the price of movie tickets had become very expensive indeed.[27]

Despite fluctuations of profit at the box office, Kubrick's career was by no means commercially insignificant. As the century drew to a close, he may have seemed an aging maverick, but he had maintained a prominent image in Hollywood for over forty years and had been a clever showman who usually made money for himself and the studios. If he never became as successful as Spielberg, Lucas and James Cameron, he produced a more consistent body of artistically impressive films. Near the end of his life, when he was presented with the D. W. Griffith Award from the Directors' Guild of America, he used his acceptance speech to confirm his faith in big artistic ambition. Griffith's career, he recalled, had often been compared to the Icarus myth; 'but at the same time I've never been certain

whether the moral of the Icarus story should only be, as is generally accepted, "Don't try
to fly too high," or whether it might also be thought of as "Forget the wax and feathers and
do a better job on the wings."'

III. Grotesque Aesthetics

I don't think that writers or painters or film makers function because they have something
they particularly want to say. They have something that they feel.

Stanley Kubrick in *The Observer* (London), 4 December 1960

With the foregoing facts about Kubrick's career as background, let me now turn to questions of directorial style, and particularly to the affective qualities of Kubrick's films. I've
given this issue special emphasis because I want to counter the tendency of most critics
to treat Kubrick as if he were chiefly a man of ideas who makes philosophical statements.
The intellectual dimensions of his work can't be ignored, but we need to understand at the
outset that he was primarily an artist who was dealing in emotions.

The discussion of such matters isn't easy. In the stylistic analysis of films, how can we
account for such things as tone, mood and complex emotional affect, all of which are sub-
jectively perceived and describable only with impoverished adjectives? The question has
special relevance for the study of a director like Kubrick, whose films are often said to have
a 'cool' or 'cold' emotional tone, presumably expressive of his own personality. Kubrick's
public image may have contributed something to this reaction. To the world at large he was
an intellectual Mr Cool, a tough guy with a scholarly beard. Some of those who worked with
him believed he was misanthropic; for example, one of his early collaborators, the gifted
novelist Calder Willingham, wrote that Kubrick's major deficiency in directing *Paths of Glory*
was his 'near psychopathic indifference to and coldness toward the human beings in the
story . . . . [H]e doesn't like people much; they interest him mainly when they do unspeak-
ably hideous things or when their idiocy is so malignant as to be horrifyingly amusing.'[28]

Remarks such as these, plus the many critical references to what Pauline Kael called
the 'arctic spirit' of Kubrick's films, eventually prompted his friends to come to his defence,
assuring us of his love for his family and his deep affection for stray animals and household pets. 'I know from dozens of articles and a few too many books that Stanley was
considered to be cold,' Michael Herr writes in his touching memoir of working with Kubrick
on *Full Metal Jacket*, 'although this would have to be among people who never knew him.'[29]
Herr paints a picture of a 'gregarious' and convivial man, although he also notes that
Kubrick's personality resembled Lenny Bruce, and that he often leavened conversation
with sick humour. Where Kubrick's films are concerned, Herr goes to some length to refute
charges that the director's reputed coldness eventuated in sterility or lack of feeling – and,
in fact, it does seem odd that anyone who has seen *Lolita* or *Barry Lyndon* could accuse
Kubrick of being emotionless.

Herr's arguments aside, several features of Kubrick's style, most of them discussed in
the ever-increasing library of books about him, could be said to create an impression of
coolness, or at least an air of perfectionism and aesthetic detachment. First among these is
what *Time* magazine once called the 'lapidary' quality of his photographic imagery,[30]
which relies upon visibly motivated and rather hard light sources, and which usually
favours a deep-focus, crystal-clear resolution, like the world seen through the ground glass
of a fine optical instrument such as a Mitchell viewfinder.[31] Kubrick also had a fondness for
the wide-angle lens, which he employed in the manner of Orson Welles, to create an
eerie, distorted, sometimes caricatured sense of space. Like Welles and Max Ophuls, he was
a virtuoso of the moving camera, except that he usually created a more rigidly geometrical
feeling; his tracking movements follow the characters in a lateral direction, travelling
past objects in the foreground, or they advance remorselessly down a fearsome
corridor towards impending doom, rather like the inexorable march of a military manoeuvre. Set over against this technique is his repeated use of hand-held shots, often
positioned at bizarre angles, which usually depict violent combat. The radical shifts
between geometrical tracking and skittish, hand-held movements are in some ways
echoed in the performances of his actors, who depart from cinematic naturalism in two
ways: through a slow, sometimes absurdist playing of dialogue, in which equal weight is
given to every line, no matter how banal (see the exchanges between astronauts in *2001* and
almost all the conversations in *Eyes Wide Shut*); and through an over-the-top display of
mugging (see George C. Scott in *Dr. Strangelove* and Malcolm McDowell in *A Clockwork
Orange*). Both techniques have the effect of slightly alienating the audience, and this
alienation is consistent with Kubrick's tendency to avoid melodrama or sentiment. Most of
his films are obviously satiric, and are focused on flawed, criminal or even monstrous
protagonists.

And yet these important formal and thematic traits strike me as insufficient to explain
the effects of certain typical scenes in Kubrick. For instance, exactly what kind of response
is appropriate to Dr. Strangelove when he rises from his wheelchair, takes a twisted step
and shouts '*Mein Führer*, I can walk' with such resonating theatrical ecstasy? Or to Alex in
Clockwork Orange when he smashes the Cat Lady's head with a huge ceramic penis? Or to
the paralytic Sir Charles Lyndon in *Barry Lyndon* when his gleeful laughter turns into a
diseased cough and then into a heart attack? Or to Jack in *The Shining* when he loudly complains about 'the old sperm bank' he has married? To be sure, these moments are blackly
humorous, but they also provoke other kinds of emotion – shock, disgust, horror, obscene
amusement and perhaps even sadistic pleasure. To understand their effects and their bearing on Kubrick's so-called coolness, I would argue that we need to examine them in light
of what might be called the aesthetics of the grotesque, a term that appears often in literary and art criticism but seldom in film studies. First, however, since in ordinary parlance
'grotesque' means simply 'hideously ugly', it may be useful if we briefly consider the term's
cultural history and implications for poetics.

Unlike many important categories in the history of art, the 'grotesque' has a fairly specific birth date. It originates sometime around 1500, when excavations beneath the city of Rome unearthed a series of ornamental wall paintings in which animal, vegetable and mineral imagery mingled in bizarre fashion, deliberately confusing the animate with the inanimate: human heads grew from trees, the faces of animals were appended to human bodies, garlands of flowers sprang from candelabra and so forth. The paintings, which had been denounced as 'monstrous' and 'bastard' by the classical author Vitruvius in the age of Augustus, were discovered in *grotte* or caves, and from this 'underground' source derived the adjective *grottesco* and the noun *la grottesca*. Initially the two words referred solely to the ancient style of ornamentation, but not long afterward, the French author Rabelais used 'grotesque' to describe deformed or 'lower' aspects of the human body. By the eighteenth century in England and Germany, the term had become associated with artistic caricature, and it took on purely pejorative or critical connotations. Finally, during the Victorian period, British art historian John Ruskin gave it an important definition that has influenced virtually all subsequent uses. In *The Stones of Venice* (1851–3), Ruskin describes a series of 'monstrous' heads, 'leering in bestial degradation', which are carved on the Bridge of Sighs and other Venetian landmarks; and from these sculptures, all of them conceived in a 'spirit of idiotic mockery', he develops the following theory:

> [I]t seems to me that the grotesque is, in almost all cases, composed of two elements, one ludicrous, the other fearful; that, as one or the other of these elements prevails, the grotesque falls into two branches, sportive grotesque and terrible grotesque; but that we cannot legitimately consider it under these two aspects, because there are hardly any examples which do not in some degree combine both elements: there are few grotesques so utterly playful as to be overcast with no shade of fearfulness, and few so fearful as absolutely to exclude all ideas of jest.[32]

In typical Victorian fashion, Ruskin moralises the grotesque, admiring the types that belong to the festive, 'wayside' culture of medieval peasants and criticising those produced by the decadent Venetian aristocrats of the Renaissance, who created masked carnivals and played 'unnecessarily', engaging in 'restless and dissatisfied indulgence' (p. 208). He nevertheless finds examples of 'noble' grotesque in Dante's *Inferno* and in Shakespeare's *Othello* and *King Lear*. Ultimately, he argues that,

> there is no test of greatness in periods, nations, or men, more sure than the development, among them or in them, of a noble grotesque; and no test of comparative smallness or limitation ... more sure than the absence of grotesque invention. (p. 214)

The most elaborate scholarly attempt to explore the full implication of the grotesque can be found in Wolfgang Keyser's *The Grotesque in Art and Literature*, translated into English in 1963, which arrives at the notion (first articulated by G. K. Chesterton) that the form constitutes a psychological strategy aimed at defamiliarising the everyday world and thereby controlling or exorcising the absurdities and terrors of life.[33] Another influential theory is developed by Mikhail Bakhtin in *Rabelais and His World*, translated from Russian into English in 1968. Bakhtin confines himself almost entirely to the 'exuberant' or 'carnivalesque' features of medieval Billingsgate and lower-body comedy, which he explains as a popular social ritual devoted to various bodily excesses and directed against 'superior powers of the sun, the earth, the king, the military leader'.[34] For virtually all later writers, the grotesque is a somewhat broader category associated with both the carnivalesque and the terrifying – at one extreme with gross-out comedy and at the other with the monstrous, the uncanny or the supernatural. In all its visual and verbal manifestations, however, the grotesque is structured by a dual implication, and therefore has something in common with such rhetorical figures as ambiguity, irony and paradox. Its defining feature is what Philip Thompson describes as an '*unresolved*' tension between laughter and some unpleasant emotion such as disgust or fear.[35] In effect, it fuses laughing and screaming impulses, leaving the viewer or reader balanced between conflicting feelings, slightly unsure how to react.

The problem with such definitions is, of course, that individual viewers can react differently. In the last analysis, the grotesque is always to some extent in the eye of the beholder and, because it involves discordant effects, people sometimes disagree about what things it should include. Exactly what mixture of laughter, fear and disgust is needed to make something grotesque? To what degree is the grotesque a style or a subject matter? (To Victor Hugo, the grotesque was something that occurred in nature and not simply in art.) Is it an artistic mode, and if so, how does it contribute to such related modes as satire, caricature and black comedy? Nobody has given completely satisfactory answers to these questions, although reasonably convincing arguments have been made that the grotesque depends upon a more extreme style of exaggeration than simple caricature and that, unlike some types of black comedy, it's exclusively preoccupied with monstrous or repulsive images of the human body. Even so, satire and caricature frequently employ grotesque imagery, and at least one theorist has argued that the grotesque should be understood as a subcategory of black humour.[36]

For nearly all writers on the subject, it would seem that the grotesque is exclusively visual, rendered through pictures or descriptive language. By this account there is no such thing as grotesque music, although when Alex in *A Clockwork Orange* accompanies an evening of rape and 'ultraviolence' with his rendition of 'Singin' in the Rain', one could argue that the conjunction is grotesque. Some writers, chief among them Thomas Mann, have claimed that modernist literature's tendency to mix genres and tones is essentially a grotesque practice. The most common understanding of the term, however, involves deformed and disgusting representations of the body – especially when they place exaggerated emphasis on the anus, the vagina, or other orifices, or when they depict bodily secretions or fluids. The same could be said of images that mix the human anatomy with something alien – the head of an animal, the legs of a puppet and so forth. In the cinema, the grotesque can be created with masks, make-up, wide-angle close-ups, or simply with the casting of actors who seem grossly fat, emaciated, or ugly in ways that make their faces potentially both comic and frightening.

No matter how the grotesque is achieved, it isn't quite identical with the 'absurd', at least if we take that term to mean 'opposed to reason'. Nor is it quite identical with the 'bizarre', the 'macabre', or the 'uncanny', which are usually taken to mean 'very strange', 'associated with death' and 'apparently supernatural'. It nevertheless belongs to what I've already described as a family of these and other emotionally laden words with which it can sometimes blend and become confused. Grotesque figures often appear in the theatre of the absurd, in fairy tales and in ghost stories, and all artistic uses of the grotesque might be said to imply a deep-seated anxiety. One thing is certain: although the grotesque has a long history, artistic modernism is strongly marked by it. Consider, as only a few examples from the literary sphere, Franz Kafka's 'Metamorphosis', the 'Circe' episode of James Joyce's *Ulysses*, Nathaniel West's *Miss Lonelyhearts*, Djuna Barnes's *Nightwood*, Flannery O'Connor's 'A Good Man is Hard to Find', Gunter Grass's *The Tin Drum*, T. S. Eliot's *The Waste Land* and Sylvia Plath's *Ariel*. Where modern painting is concerned, grotesque effects can be seen in the 'Exquisite Corpse' drawings of the surrealists (which are in some ways analogous to the 'bastard' forms of the ancient Italian cave paintings), and in numerous images by Picasso and Francis Bacon. The list could be expanded considerably, to the point where the grotesque functions almost as a guarantee of artistic seriousness and authenticity during the first half of the twentieth century. As in previous eras, it has its 'sportive' and 'terrible' branches, but the terrible dominates. Even so, in the world of high-modernist grotesque we seldom encounter the pure supernatural. Modernism remains at bottom a secular aesthetic, in overt rebellion against genteel beauty, bourgeois realism and classical decorum; its uses of the grotesque are usually aimed at showing that this is, in fact, the way the world actually is or ought to be understood. Its hideous ghosts and monsters therefore tend to be given psychoanalytic explanations, or they occupy what Todorov calls the 'fantastic' mode, in which events are poised ambiguously between fantasy and reality.[37]

The twentieth century's most influential art form, the cinema, is filled with instances of the grotesque – in slapstick comedies ranging from *The Fatal Glass of Beer* (1933) to *Stuck on You* (2003), and in monster movies ranging from *The Bride of Frankenstein* (1935) to *Hellboy* (2004). At a more overtly 'artistic' level, similar effects can be seen in many celebrated films from Weimar Germany, among them Lang's *M* (1931), which is influenced by the grotesque caricatures of George Grosz. In fact, the grotesque is important to the entire history of international art cinema; we need only think of films by Eisenstein, Buñuel, Kurosawa, Polanski and, above all, Fellini. (More recent examples in the 'postmodern' sphere are Lynch, Cronenberg and the Coen brothers.) For roughly similar reasons, the modernist-inflected film noir of the 1940s and 1950s made use of the grotesque, as did several of the American directors who worked slightly against the grain of classic Hollywood – consider Von Stroheim's *Greed* (1925), Sternberg's *Blonde Venus* (1932) and *The Scarlet Empress* (1934) and especially Welles's *The Lady from Shanghai* (1948), *Mr. Arkadin, Touch of Evil* and *The Trial* (1962); where Hollywood directors of a more populist bent are concerned, consider also Aldrich, Fuller and Tashlin.

All of which brings us back to Kubrick, whose work is shaped by the artistic modernism he absorbed in New York during the late 1940s and 1950s, at the very moment when black humour and the theatre of the absurd were profoundly influencing American culture.[38] As a photographer for *Look*, Kubrick not only took pictures of George Grosz but also, as we've seen, worked alongside the cutting-edge, New York School photographic artists of the period, including two specialists in the grotesque: Weegee, the first American street photographer to have his work displayed at the Museum of Modern Art, and Diane Arbus, whose career transition from *Harper's Bazaar* to art photography followed close on the heels of Kubrick's move from *Look* to the cinema. Weegee is often described as a populist and a documentary realist, but the unsettling force of much of his imagery derives from the way he makes New Yorkers, whether operagoers or Bowery bums, look like participants in a carnival freak show. Arbus's more sharply disturbing pictures are devoted to people she herself described as 'freaks'. Susan Sontag, who intensely disliked the 'cool dejection' and apparent lack of 'compassionate purpose' in Arbus's work, accurately described the bewildered emotions it can produce. '[The] mystery of Arbus's photographs,' Sontag wrote, 'lies in what they suggest about how her subjects felt . . . . Do they see themselves, the viewer wonders, like *that*? Do they know how grotesque they are?'[39] Similar questions are raised by Kubrick's 1949 magazine story and 1951 documentary about Greenwich Village boxer Walter Cartier and his twin brother Vincent. Significantly, Kubrick later hired the aging Weegee as a still photographer for *Dr. Strangelove*, and he quoted Arbus's famously creepy photograph of twin girls in *The Shining*.

As we've also seen, Kubrick was arguably the first independent producer of a true American art film. *Fear and Desire*, his initial effort at directing a full-length feature, is a heavily allegorical drama containing a great many signs of 'modern art-ness', including Soviet-style montage, wide-angle photography, internal monologues and a sex scene involving bondage and attempted rape. As in most of his subsequent work, Kubrick also employs many of the formal strategies that David Bordwell has shown to be characteristic of the art cinema as a 'mode of film practice' – especially the use of actual locations and the sort of expressive 'realism' that depends on ambiguity, alienation, angst and absurdity.[40] What makes the film 'artistic' in a specifically Kubrickian sense, however, is its fascination with the grotesque. Its most effective sequence involves a nocturnal military raid in which a group of enemy soldiers are taken by surprise as they eat dinner. Kubrick shows a dying hand convulsively flexing in a bowl of greasy stew and squeezing a wet clump of bread through its fingers. The bodies of the dead, framed from the waist down, are dragged across the floor, their legs splayed at an angle that makes them look like stick figures or puppets.

At the end of the sequence, in an image designed to evoke both disgust and sardonic amusement, we see a large close-up of one of the victors as he gulps down a bowl of cold gruel from the dinner table, wipes off his slimy chin and grins with satisfaction.

Kubrick's next film, the low-budget thriller *Killer's Kiss*, illustrates this tendency even more clearly, particularly when it climaxes with a clumsy duel between a hero named Davy and a villain named Vince in a loft filled with naked department store mannequins. The two men, rivals for a dance-hall girl named Gloria, are armed respectively with a spear and a fire axe, but in the midst of their quasi-gladiatorial combat they pick up female mannequins and begin throwing body parts at one another. At one point, Davy tosses the entire body of a woman at Vince, who chops it in half with his axe. Later, Davy pushes Vince down on a pile of female bodies and tries to spear him, in the process getting the weapon caught in the lower half of a woman; as Davy waves the truncated torso around to shake it loose, Vince swings wildly with his axe and shatters the mannequin to pieces. Throughout, the suspense is charged with humour, partly because Kubrick's editing makes it difficult for us to distinguish the real figures from the mannequins, and partly because several of the wide or master shots run for a fairly long time, allowing us to see the sweaty, dusty combatants stumbling, floundering, falling and growing weary. Whenever I've shown the sequence to students, a few of them break into laughter. Their response seems to me

perfectly in keeping with at least part of the effect Kubrick is trying to achieve, in which the horrific, the uncanny and the sadistically amusing are suspended in an awkward, uncertain equilibrium.

In the history of art photography, there are many instances where similar effects are achieved by confounding the animate with the inanimate – a type of confusion that Wolfgang Kayser specifically connects with the grotesque. Kubrick's idea for the climax of *Killer's Kiss* probably derives from one of his *Look* photographs described above, but more generally from a tradition of surrealist-inspired photos involving department-store mannequins, much of which has recently been documented in a museum catalogue, *Puppen, Körper, Automaten: Phantasmen der Moderne*, edited by Pia Müller-Tamm and Katharina Sykora.[41] (Famous practitioners of such photography in the period between 1920 and 1945 include Eugene Atget, Umbo, Hans Bellmer and Werner Rohde.) There are also, as Kayser observes, even older scenes of the type in literature – for example, E. T. A. Hoffmann's *The Sandman*, in which the protagonist, Nathaniel, has fallen in love with an automaton named Olympia, who is constructed by a Professor Spalanzani. Entering the Professor's house one day, he finds the Professor and an Italian named Coppola battling with one another for possession of the body of a woman:

> Nathaniel recoiled in horror on recognizing that the figure was Olympia. Boiling with rage, he was about to tear his beloved from the grip of the madmen, when Coppola by an extraordinary exertion of strength twisted the figure out of the Professor's hands and gave him such a terrible blow with her, that Spalanzani reeled backwards and fell over the table among the phials and retorts . . . Coppola threw the figure across his shoulder and, laughing shrilly and horribly, ran hastily down the stair, the figure's ugly feet hanging down and banging like wood against the steps.

In his useful monograph on the theory of the grotesque, Philip Thompson quotes these lines to illustrate the way in which something 'disconcerting, perhaps even frightening' can also seem 'irresistibly comic, not least because of the slapstick nature of the brawl' (p. 52). The comic feeling depends as well on the way the human body is reduced to a clattering stick figure or mechanical object – imagery that preoccupied Kubrick throughout his career, most notably in *Dr. Strangelove*, in which the mad scientist is part man and part puppet; in *A Clockwork Orange*, whose very title indicates a grotesque combination of the organic and the mechanical; in *2001*, in which black comedy arises from a computer with an uncannily 'human' voice and personality; and in *A. I. Artificial Intelligence*, which concerns a humanoid robot.

Kubrick's third film and first true Hollywood production, *The Killing*, differs from its most important influence, John Huston's *The Asphalt Jungle*, chiefly by virtue of the fact that Kubrick gives us a veritable festival of grotesque imagery, much of it prompted by screenwriter Jim Thompson's sadistic humour and by the large cast, most of whom are pug-ugly veterans of the film noir. Among the players are a couple of newer, even more eccentric personalities. Maurice, the philosophical strong man hired to distract police during a race-track robbery, is Kola Kwariani, a real-life chess player and ex-wrestler Kubrick had known in New York; and Nikki, the sniper who shoots a horse, is Tim Carey, a method-trained actor who had previously worked with Elia Kazan. Kwariani has a cauliflower ear, a shaved head, a fat belly, a hairy torso and an almost impenetrable accent. The ruckus he starts in the race-track bar is truly carnivalistic – a cross between a Three Stooges slapstick routine, a monster movie and a wrestling match on 1950s' TV. For his part, Carey has a rep-tilian grin, a habit of talking through his teeth and the dreamy attitude of the sort of hipster we might encounter in a Jim Jarmusch movie. He seems especially strange in an early sequence involving a conversation with Sterling Hayden at a shooting range some-where outside the city. The first image in this sequence, accompanied by three rapid explosions of gunfire, is of three identical targets in the shape of comic-book gangsters who frown and point their pistols directly at us. The camera tilts over the targets and we see Carey and Hayden walking forward. As their conversation develops, we become aware of bizarre visual juxtapositions: parked in front of a ramshackle house in the background is an MG sports car, and cradled in Carey's arms is a lovable puppy. The three menacing tar-gets in the foreground seem both uncanny and vaguely comical, like the mannequins in

Killer's Kiss. Hayden launches into a rapid-fire monologue that explains his plans for the heist and, at one point during his long exposition, Kubrick cuts to a dramatic, low-angle close-up of Carey, viewed from across one of the targets in the extreme foreground, so that the cute little dog he is holding is framed by two monstrous heads. Carey softly strokes the puppy and reacts to Hayden's speech by leaning thoughtfully over the target and spitting on the ground.

The Killing has often been interpreted as a sort of existentialist parable, or as a philosophical commentary on what Thomas Allen Nelson calls the conflict between rational order and contingency.[42] But the film's immediate effect on audiences is emotional rather than philosophical or intellectual. The stolid (and sometimes inaccurate) voice-over narration supplying a time scheme is in ironic contrast to the bizarre imagery, functioning rather like what T. S. Eliot once described as 'meaning' in poetry: in the guise of offering rational information, it helps to keep the viewer's mind 'diverted and quiet . . . much as the imaginary burglar is always provided with a bit of nice meat for the house-dog'.[43] Meanwhile, the complex temporal disposition of the plot transforms a hyper-rational plan for a robbery into a splintered montage of lurid details or local situations. Consider Sterling Hayden's rubber clown mask – the first of several grotesque disguises in Kubrick, foreshadowing the adolescent thugs who wear phallic noses in *A Clockwork Orange*, the ghostly

figure who performs fellatio while wearing a pig mask in *The Shining* and the orgiastic revellers who wear Venetian carnival masks in *Eyes Wide Shut*. Consider also the more general
features of staging and performance in the scenes between Elisha Cook and Marie Windsor,
in the first of which a little man is posed at the feet of a hugely voluptuous, heavily made-
up woman whose size is exaggerated by the wide-angle lens and the placement of her body
in the frame. Everything here is caricatured but at the same time played in a measured
style and photographed in a smooth series of mesmerising long takes that somehow
heighten the feeling of a cruel burlesque.

   One could go on in this vein, proceeding film by film and noting elements of the
grotesque that recur in Kubrick's work: the leering hotel keeper named 'Swine' in *Lolita*,
the metallically wigged and mini-skirted 'Mum' in *A Clockwork Orange*, the grossly made-up
'Chevalier de Balibari' in *Barry Lyndon*, the pudgy Japanese men in bikini underwear in
Eyes Wide Shut and so forth. The list would reveal that, like Rabelais, Kubrick is interested in
scatology; hence his fondness for staging key scenes in bathrooms, as in *Lolita*, *A Clockwork
Orange*, *The Shining*, *Full Metal Jacket*, *Eyes Wide Shut* and even *2001*. By the same logic he's
drawn to coarse bodily images, such as the female statuary or 'furnishings' of the Korova
Milk Bar in *A Clockwork Orange* and the Rabelaisian architectural designs of giant open
mouths and other orifices that he commissioned from Chris Baker for *A. I. Artificial*

Intelligence. The point to be emphasised is that, although Kubrick is normally treated as an artist who deals in big, important ideas, the key to his style lies in his anxious fascination with the human body and his ability, which he shares with all black humorists and artists of the grotesque, to yoke together conflicting emotions, so that he confuses both our cognitive and emotional responses. This aspect of his work becomes increasingly marked during the course of his career, as Hollywood censorship is liberalised and as he gains greater control over his productions. Again and again he uses grotesque effects to unsettle social norms, whether liberal or conservative, thereby inducing a sort of moral and emotional disequilibrium. The loss of guideposts is probably least evident in *2001*, if only because the human beings in that film are dwarfed by the immensity of space; but even at the opposite extreme, when his satire is at its most overt and might be taken as a kind of humanism, he creates a troubling emotional ambiguity. The montage of exploding nuclear bombs at the end of *Dr. Strangelove* may not be a grotesque moment but it works according to a similar principle, so that horror mingles with a sort of detached appreciation of the sublime beauty of sun, sky and bursting clouds.

In my own view, Kubrick's films can be distinguished from those of other directors who make similar uses of the grotesque. For example, he and Orson Welles share not only certain technical mannerisms – especially the wide-angle lens and dynamic uses of the long take – but also a love of exaggerated performances and caricatured faces and bodies. The difference between the two is largely a matter of tone or emotional effect. In Welles, the grotesque is Shakespearian, inflected with affectionate, sentimental and even tragic emotions. When the fat, rumpled Captain Quinlan chews a candy bar in Tana's parlour in *Touch of Evil*, he seems childlike, pathetic and oddly noble. In *Mr. Arkadin*, when the title character looks down on the grubby, dying Jacob Zouk and chuckles to himself, Zouk asks what he is laughing at; 'Old age,' Arkadin says, in a tone reminiscent of *King Lear*. Especially in *Chimes at Midnight*, Welles delights in the same sort of earthy, festive pleasures that interested Ruskin and Bakhtin. Kubrick almost never ventures into that territory. In his films, it's as if the body is the source of a horror that can be held in check only with a kind of radical, derisive humour (which may explain why his work has always had a strong appeal for adolescent and college-age males who have artistic interests).

Perhaps I can best illustrate and summarise my argument by looking more closely at a single, representative scene. For my purposes, the best choice is the opening sequence of *Full Metal Jacket* – not because it is the most powerful moment I could select, but because to my knowledge it is the only place in Kubrick's entire *oeuvre* in which the word 'grotesque' appears in the dialogue. Viewers will recall that this sequence begins with a wide-angle travelling shot that retreats in front of Gunnery Sergeant Hartman (Lee Ermey) as he walks 360 degrees around the Marine barracks at Parris Island and inspects the new recruits, all of whom are shaved bald and standing at rigid attention in front of their bunks. Many things about the shot are typical of Kubrick: the long take; the deep-focus; the realist lighting that seems to spill from the barracks windows; and above all the dynamically forced perspective and tunnel-like effect created by the wide-angle lens as Hartman moves down the column of men. We are also in a familiar Kubrick world – masculine, militarised, filled with warriors. The photography emphasises the spit-and-polish cleanliness of the room, in which reflected light shimmers off the bare floor; the clarity, symmetry and aura of discipline, however, are in uneasy conflict with the slightly weird exaggeration of space, and with Hartman's loud, hyperbolic performance.

Holding himself ramrod straight, Hartman paces forward and glares at the troops, his eyes bulging as he yells out an angry speech filled with curses, obscenity, racist epithets and vivid scatological imagery. As the sequence develops, things become even stranger. Just when it looks as if Hartman couldn't get more abusive, we cut to closer views in which he confronts individual soldiers, giving them cartoonish nicknames ('Snowball', 'Joker', 'Cowboy' and 'Gomer Pyle') and terrorising them with threats, insults and physical violence. Most of us know from previous Hollywood movies about Marine training that drill instructors are supposed to be intimidating disciplinarians, but this one is so shocking that it's not clear how we are supposed to take him. (For instructive comparison, see the first ten minutes of *Take the High Ground* [1953], a Cold War movie about the Marines directed by Richard Brooks and photographed by John Alton, which shows the same physical and emotional harassment, the same clichéd character types and even the same jokes about the difference between a rifle and a gun, but which seems utterly benign; see also Jack Webb's *The D.I.* [1957], which is an important intertext for *Full Metal Jacket*.) Is Hartman completely serious? Is he nuts? Is this the way Marine sergeants really behave, or are we in the realm of satiric stylisation, à la *Dr. Strangelove*? Everything the drill instructor says is outrageously offensive but delivered with such theatrical flair and poetic talent for disgusting metaphors that it invites laughter. The movie seems to be hovering somewhere between realism and caricature, and throughout the sequence Hartman throws us off balance because he is revolting, scary and funny at the same time.

A good deal might be said about the sexual implications of Hartman's harangue: his tendency to call his troops 'ladies', 'queers', or 'peter puffers', his reference to the typical soldier's girlfriend as 'Mary Jane Rottencrotch', and his promise that Marines under his control will have their sexuality channelled into a love for their rifles. Granting the importance of such matters (which *Dr. Strangelove* treats in similar fashion), we should also notice that Hartman subordinates sexuality to an intense preoccupation with bodily secretions, especially shit, which is the prime source of his grotesque verbal humour. His discourse could easily be analysed in the same fashion as Klaus Theweleit has analysed the writings of the proto-fascist German *Freikorps* in the first volume of his disturbing study, *Male Fantasies* (1987), where we repeatedly encounter frightening images of mud, faeces and menstrual blood set against the hard bodies of patriotic soldiers.[44] The whole of *Full Metal Jacket* is constructed by such imagery, culminating in Vietnam's 'world of shit', which might seem the binary opposite of the immaculate cleanliness, obsessive order and tightened buttocks in the opening scene; significantly, however, the first half of the movie comes to a bloody climax in a toilet that Hartman, in inimitable fashion, orders two of his men to clean. ('I want you two turds to clean the head. I want that head so sanitary and squared away that the Virgin Mary herself would be proud to go in there and take a dump!')

From the opening moments, shit is never far from Hartman's mind. As he strides around the barrack room, his veins distending and his face turning red, he tells the recruits that they are 'nothing but amphibious, grabasstic pieces of shit' and threatens to punish them until their 'assholes are sucking buttermilk'. An equally important feature of his raging disquisition has to do with the psychology he uses to transform his men into cold killers. One of his tricks is to elicit an amused and frightened response – which is to say, the response elicited by the grotesque – and then to punish anyone who reacts. When Private Joker (Matthew Modine) mutters a derisive comment in imitation of John Wayne, Hartman races across the room to find the 'slimy little twinkle-toed shit communist cocksucker' who made the remark. 'I like you,' he sneers when he discovers Joker. 'You can come over to my house and fuck my sister!' Almost as soon as this sick joke registers, he punches Joker hard in the solar plexus and drops him to the floor. Kubrick cuts to a distorting, wide-angle close-up from Joker's subjective point of view, showing Hartman bending down, pointing his finger and shouting, 'You will not laugh! You will not cry!' When Joker stands up and

resumes his rigid position, Hartman warns, 'You had best unfuck yourself or I will unscrew your head and shit down your neck!' He then demands, 'Lemme see your war face!' Joker wildly contorts his features and tries to give a fearsome yell, but behind his round, scholarly glasses he looks somewhat comical and afraid. As far as Hartman is concerned the effect is insufficiently grotesque. 'You don't scare me,' he says as he turns away. 'Work on it.'

Moving down the row, Hartman stops in front of Cowboy (Arliss Howard) and asks, 'Are you shook up? Are you nervous?' Cowboy stares straight ahead and shouts, 'Sir, no sir!' Scowling contemptuously because 'Cowboy' is shorter than the other men, Hartman yells, 'I didn't know they stacked shit that high . . . . It looks to me like the best part of you ran down the crack of your mama's ass and ended up as a brown stain on the mattress!' The *pièce de résistance* of Hartman's performance, however, is his sadistic confrontation with the next figure – the tall, fat soldier he dubs 'Private Gomer Pyle' (Vincent D'Onofrio). An innocent hick who tries to maintain the rigid posture and blank, straight-ahead stare demanded of the troops, Pyle can't help smiling at Hartman's colourful rhetoric. Hartman looks him up and down, asking 'Did your parents have any children that lived? I bet they were grotesque. You're so ugly you look like a modern-art masterpiece!'

The more insulting Hartman becomes, the more difficult it is for Pyle to stop grinning. 'Do you think I'm cute, Private Pyle?' Hartman asks in hysterical rage. 'Do you think I'm funny?' Pyle says no, and Hartman yells, 'Then wipe that disgusting grin off your face!' Pyle struggles to keep his composure. 'I'm going to give you three seconds, exactly three seconds, to wipe that stupid looking grin off your face,' Hartman screams, 'or I will gouge out your eyeballs and skull fuck you!' The image of Hartman having intercourse with a skull is so horrible yet so ridiculous that Pyle can't control himself, and he begins to exhibit a kind of panicked amusement. Hartman orders, 'Get on your knees, scumbag!' Holding his hand at waist level, he commands Pyle to lean forward, place his neck in Hartman's palm and be choked. 'Are you through grinning?' he asks as he squeezes the recruit's windpipe. Pyle's grin disappears and his face changes colour. 'Yes, sir,' he gasps. 'Bullshit!' Hartman replies, 'I can't hear you. Sound off like you got a pair!' When Pyle manages to say yes a second time, Hartman releases him. As Pyle returns to his feet, his eyes wild with terror, Hartman warns, 'You had best square your ass away and start shitting me Tiffany cufflinks!'

Whether or not the opening sequence of *Full Metal Jacket* is what Hartman would call a 'modern-art masterpiece', it probably aspires to that condition. All its visual and verbal techniques are aimed at maintaining an exact style and a convincing picture of military life while at the same time making us cringe and laugh uncomfortably. In the last analysis, it can be understood both as a meta-commentary on Kubrick's art and as a systematic demonstration of how the grotesque, whether in life or in film, messes with our minds.

The chief irony of the sequence is that, even though Pyle's reaction to Hartman seems slow-witted, it's much like the reaction most viewers are likely to have – a bewildered mingling of amusement, fear and disgust that turns suddenly into outright shock. In contrast with the stony looks on the faces of the other recruits, Pyle's reaction is sensible and sane; only when forced to deny his feelings does he later turn into a murderer and a suicide. His confusion and bewilderment, moreover, are built into the very structure and texture of the film, which is designed to create a world that is both absurd and verisimilar.

This is the world Kubrick repeatedly tried to represent. If some people regard him as cold, it may be because he seldom allows us the comfort of secure responses. The emotions he elicits are primal but mixed; the fear is charged with humour and the laughter is both liberating and defensive. His control of photography, découpage and performance creates a sense of authorial understanding without immersion, as if volcanic, almost infantile feelings were being observed in a lucid, rational manner. Much like Franz Kafka, his most bizarre effects emerge from the very clarity with which his imagery is rendered. The result is a clash of emotions – a charged atmosphere that may not be the only virtue an artist can produce, but that gives Kubrick's work a good deal of its motivating energy and consistency of purpose. Kubrick's style is therefore more than the sum of his technical propensities, and more than his choices of subject matter; it grows out of a unified attitude towards such different issues as war, science, sexuality, European history and family life. At his best, like many other practitioners of the grotesque, he aims to show a paradoxical and potentially disturbing truth: at the farthest reaches of our experience, extremes meet and transform themselves. The coldest temperatures burn no less than fire. Especially where the human body is concerned, there is always something potentially comic about horror and horrible about comedy.

Notes

1. For a full account of the Conway affair, see Anthony Frewin, 'Color Him Kubrick!', *Stopsmiling*, no. 23, 2005, pp. 60–3, 91–3.
2. David Thomson, *A Biographical Dictionary of Film*, 3rd edn (New York: Alfred A. Knopf, 1994), p. 408.
3. D. N. Rodowick, *The Crisis of Political Modernism: Criticism and Ideology in Contemporary Film Theory* (Champaign: University of Illinois Press, 1988).
4. Thomas Elsaesser, 'Evolutionary Imagineer', in Hans-Peter Reichmann and Ingeborg Flagge (eds), *Stanley Kubrick*, Kinematograph no. 20 (Frankfurt am Main: Deutsches Filmmuseum 2004), pp. 136–47.
5. Robert Kolker, *A Cinema of Loneliness* (New York: Oxford University Press, 2000), p.110. All subsequent references are to this edition, and page numbers are indicated in the text.
6. Molly Haskell, *From Reverence to Rape: The Treatment of Women in the Movies* (Harmondsworth: Penguin, 1974), p. 204.
7. Joseph Gelmis, 'The Film Director as Superstar: Stanley Kubrick', in Gene D. Phillips (ed.), *Stanley Kubrick Interviews* (Jackson: University Press of Mississippi, 2001), p. 102.
8. See Rainer Crone (ed.), *Stanley Kubrick: Drama and Shadows: Photographs 1945–1950* (London: Phaidon, 2005).
9. Alexandra Von Stosch and Rainer Crone, 'Kubrick's Kaleidoscope: Early Photographs 1945–1950', in Crone, *Stanley Kubrick*, p. 22.
10. George Toles, 'Double Minds and Double Binds in Stanley Kubrick's Fairy Tale', in Robert Kolker (ed.), *Stanley Kubrick's 2001: A Space Odyssey* (New York: Oxford, 2006), pp. 157–57. All subsequent references are to this edition, and page numbers are indicated in the text.
11. Robert Sklar, 'Stanley Kubrick and the American Film Industry', *Current Research in Film Audience, Economics, and Law* vol. 4 (1988), p. 114. All other references are to this source, and page numbers are indicated in the text.
12. Jonathan Rosenbaum, 'In Dreams Begin Responsibilities: Kubrick's *Eyes Wide Shut*', in *Essential Cinema: On the Necessity of Film Canons* (Baltimore, MD: Johns Hopkins University Press, 2004), pp. 267–8. All other references are to this edition, and page numbers are indicated in the text.
13. See John E. Twomey, 'Some Considerations on the Rise of the Art-Film Theatre (1956)', in Gregory A. Waller (ed.), *Moviegoing in America* (Malden, MA: Blackwell, 2002), pp. 259–62. See also Stanley Frank, 'Sure-Seaters Discover an Audience (1952)', in Waller, *Moviegoing in America*, pp. 255–8.

14. See Barbara Wilinsky, *Sure Seaters: The Emergence of Art House Cinema* (Minneapolis: University of Minnesota Press, 2001).

15. Quoted in Twomey, 'Some Considerations on the Rise of the Art-Film Theater (1956)', p. 261.

16. For information on the history of United Artists, see Tino Balio, *United Artists: The Company Built by the Stars* (Madison: University of Wisconsin Press, 1976). See also Steven Bach, *Final Cut* (New York: New American Library, 1987).

17. Geoffrey Shurlock is quoted from the Production Code files, Margaret Herrick Library of the Motion Picture Academy, Los Angeles.

18. Michel Ciment, *Kubrick: The Definitive Edition* (New York: Faber and Faber, 2001), p. 151. All other references are to this edition, and page numbers are indicated in the text.

19. Geoffrey Cocks, *The Wolf at the Door: Stanley Kubrick, History, and the Holocaust* (New York: Peter Lang, 2004), pp. 151–4.

20. Jack Vizzard, *See No Evil* (New York: Simon & Schuster, 1970), pp. 266–71.

21. See Charles Maland, '*Dr. Strangelove* (1964): Nightmare Comedy and the Ideology of Liberal Consensus', in Peter C. Rollins (ed.), *Hollywood as Historian: American Films in a Cultural Context* (Lexington: University of Kentucky Press, 1983), pp. 209–10.

22. Stanley Kubrick, 'Napoleon: A Screenplay' (29 September 1969), ‹www.hundland.com›, p. 93.

23. David A. Cook, *Lost Illusions: American Cinema in the Shadow of Watergate and Vietnam, 1970–1979* (Berkeley: University of California Press, 2000), p. 308.

24. Correspondence file, Anthony Harvey collection, Lilly Library, Indiana University.

25. See Joel G. Cohn, 'Ferro-Gross: Titles, Trailers, and Spots, with Feeling', *T-Print* vol. 26 no.6 (November–December 1972), p. 49. I'm grateful to Keith Hamel for providing me with information about Ferro.

26. A 22 October 1971 letter from Mike Kaplan of Hawk Films to Warner Bros., Margaret Herrick Library of the Motion Picture Academy, Los Angeles.

27. Figures for *Eyes Wide Shut* come from The Internet Movie Data Base on the world wide web.

28. Calder Willingham quoted in Robert Polito, *Savage Art: A Biography of Jim Thompson* (New York: Vintage Books, 1996), p. 406.

29. Michael Herr, *Kubrick* (New York: Grove Press, 2000), p. 36. All further references are to this edition, and page numbers are indicated in the text.

30. 'The New Pictures', *Time*, vol. 67 (4 June 1956), p. 106.

31. See Alexander Singer's comments on Kubrick's love of the Mitchell viewfinder, quoted in Vincent LoBrutto, *Stanley Kubrick, A Biography* (New York: Da Capo Press, 1999), p. 127. All further references are to this edition, and page numbers are indicated in the text.

32. John Ruskin, 'Grotesque Renaissance', in *The Genius of John Ruskin*, ed. John D. Rosenberg (New York: George Braziller, 1963), p. 207. All subsequent references are to this volume, with page numbers indicated parenthetically in the text.

33. Wolfgang Keyser, *The Grotesque in Art and Literature*, trans. Ulrich Weisstein (Bloomington: Indiana University Press, 1963).

34. Mikhail Bakhtin, *Rabelais and His World*, trans. Helene Iswolsky (Bloomington: Indiana University Press, 1968), p. 352. All subsequent references are to this edition, and page numbers are indicated in the text.

35. Philip Thompson, *The Grotesque* (London: Methuen, 1972), p. 21. All subsequent references are to this edition, and page numbers are indicated in the text.

36. See Mathew Winston, '*Humour noir* and Black Humor', in Harry Levin (ed.), *Veins of Humor* (Cambridge, MA: Harvard University Press, 1972), pp. 269–84.

37. Tzvetan Todorov, *The Fantastic: A Structural Approach to a Literary Genre*, trans. Richard Howard (Ithaca, NY: Cornell University Press, 1973).

38. For a discussion of the history of black humour and its importance to another film-maker, see James Naremore, 'Hitchcock and Humour', in Richard Allen and Sam Ishii-Gonzales (eds), *Hitchcock Past and Future* (London: Routledge, 2004), pp. 22–36.

39. Susan Sontag, *On Photography* (New York: Farrar, Straus and Giroux, 1978), p. 36.

40. David Bordwell, 'The Art Cinema as a Mode of Film Practice', in Leo Braudy and Marshall Cohen (eds), *Film Theory and Criticism*, 5th edn (New York: Oxford University Press, 1999), pp. 716–24.

41. Pia Müller-Tamm and Katharina Sykora (eds), *Puppen, Körper, Automaten: Phantasmen der Moderne* (Dusseldorf, Kunstsammlung Nordrhein-Westfalen: Oktagon, 2004).

42. Thomas Allen Nelson, *Kubrick: Inside a Film Artist's Maze* (Bloomington: Indiana University Press, 2000), pp. 32–9. All further references are to this edition, and page numbers are indicated in the text.

43. T. S. Eliot, '"Difficult" Poetry', in *Selected Prose*, ed. John Hayward (Harmondsworth: Peregrine, 1963), p. 88.

44. Klaus Theweleit, *Male Fantasies: Volume I: Women, Floods, Bodies, History*, trans. Stephen Conway (Minneapolis: University of Minnesota Press, 1987).

Part Two

EARLY KUBRICK

I. No Other Country but the Mind

Fear and Desire, Kubrick's first feature, is seldom exhibited and therefore merits a brief plot summary for those who haven't seen it. As the film opens, four soldiers have crashed their plane behind enemy lines in an unnamed, abstract war. The downed men scout their immediate terrain and then construct a raft in order to float down a river and rejoin their unit. Their plan is delayed when an enemy reconnaissance plane flies overhead and nearly spots them. Through binoculars, they see a landing strip, plus an enemy command post housing a general and his military guard. They move to the cover of a forest and as night falls they come across another house where a couple of enemy soldiers are eating a meal. Storming the house, they kill the inhabitants, devour the leftover food and seize whatever weapons they can find. The next morning they return to the river, where three lovely young women are fishing with nets; when one of the women approaches, they take her prisoner, bind her to a tree and leave the youngest of their group to stand guard while the others camouflage the raft. But the young soldier is almost cracking under the strain of the mission and when left alone he goes berserk. Babbling incoherently, he embraces the girl and unties her. When she tries to escape, he shoots her and runs off into the forest.

At this point, the most aggressive of the remaining soldiers convinces the other two that their only meaningful action would be to attack the enemy outpost and kill its commanding general. He sets up a diversion: under cover of night, he floats down the river on the raft, firing at the general's guards. His two cohorts move quietly to the unguarded building and shoot the general and his aide; but in doing so, they seem to be killing older versions of themselves. (The general and his aide are played by the same actors who attack

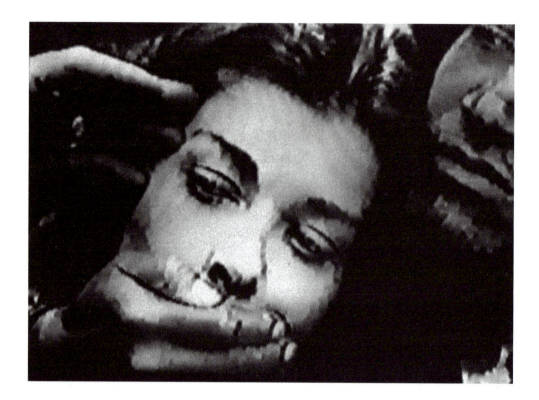

them.) Running to the nearby field, they board the enemy aircraft and fly back to their
unit. Meanwhile, the soldier on the raft, mortally wounded, floats further down river and
comes upon the insane young soldier who had run away. Back at home base, the two soldiers who escaped confer with their commanding officer and then go down to the river
and wait, hoping that their comrade on the raft will make it through. Out of a mist the raft
emerges, carrying the dead comrade and the young soldier, who is raving mad.

Baldly summarised, *Fear and Desire* might sound like a reasonably typical, if unusually
grim, war movie. Despite its familiar generic elements, however, the film is explicitly
designed as an allegory and bears the marks of 'artistic-ness' at every turn. On the literary
level, it employs stream-of-consciousness passages, philosophical soliloquies and allusions
to Mark Twain, John Donne, William Shakespeare and T. S. Eliot. (The closing shot of the
two men on the raft alludes to Gericault's nineteenth-century painting, *The Raft of the
Medusa*.) The photography, which involves striking *plein air* effects of mist, fog and dap-
pled light, reminded contemporary critics of Kurosawa's recent art-house hit, *Rashomon*
(1950). The editing, especially in scenes of grotesque violence, is strongly reminiscent of
Eisenstein and the Soviet school. The story is filled with symbols (including a dog named
'Proteus'), and everything comes to an end in a mood of despair and absurdity. Along the way,
the film also features the perversely sexy scene of the young woman being strapped to

a tree and lustfully embraced by the crazed soldier, thus offering titillating material for art-theatre advertisements. (Predictably, ads for the film emphasised this scene.)

This is not to say that *Fear and Desire* is a cynical pastiche. On the contrary, it's a personal work of high, if failed, artistic ambition. Financed with money Kubrick had borrowed from his father and a rich uncle, it involved only a small 'family' of collaborators. The script, originally weighing about three pounds and entitled *The Trap*, was written under Kubrick's supervision by Howard O. Sackler, who would later win the Pulitzer Prize for *The Great White Hope* on Broadway. The modernistic music was composed by Gerald Fried, who had first worked with Kubrick on *Day of the Fight*. Kubrick's then wife, Toba Metz, functioned as 'dialogue director' and production assistant, and Bob Dierks, one of Kubrick's studio assistants at *Look* magazine, was credited as 'production manager'. Most of the other work fell to Kubrick himself, who not only produced, directed, photographed and edited the film, but also chauffeured the cast and crew to locations in California's San Gabriel Mountains.

Fear and Desire was shot in 35mm black and white with a rented Mitchell camera (an instrument Kubrick had never used) equipped with a standard series of prime lenses: 25mm, 50mm, 75mm and 100mm. There are no complicated camera movements in the film, probably because Kubrick had no tracks or other equipment to facilitate movement. There is also no direct sound, in part because Kubrick was unfamiliar with sound-recording technology and in part because his earlier work as a director of documentaries had involved photographing everything silently and then adding narration, music and sound effects. He seems to have believed that the production would move more swiftly and economically and that he could be freer to compose dynamic compositions in available light if the soundtrack were completely post-synchronised. This proved a major error, affecting the artistic quality of the film, much of which sounds tinny, and greatly increasing its total cost.

Sometime in the 1960s, Kubrick removed the film from circulation. The only print known to have survived, located at George Eastman House in Rochester, New York, was shown without Kubrick's co-operation in 1991 at the Telluride Film Festival in Colorado and then again in 1994 at the Film Forum in New York, on both occasions to mixed responses. At the time of the latter showing, Kubrick issued a statement to the New York newspapers saying that *Fear and Desire* was nothing more than a 'bumbling, amateur film exercise ... a completely inept oddity, boring and pretentious'.[1] A quite different opinion has recently been offered by Paolo Cherchi Usai, the chief curator at Eastman House, who, in the course of a detailed critical analysis, argues that Kubrick tried to suppress his first picture because it 'proclaims with unadulterated immediacy the major creative strategies of the director's oeuvre that would follow in coming years'.[2] Undoubtedly, *Fear and Desire* has several things in common with other Kubrick films, but Usai's argument is unconvincing. Had the picture been an artistic success, there would have been no reason for Kubrick to want it forgotten, however much it revealed his future methods or interests. Few people who have been able to see the film would praise it as anything more than the work of an interesting director who suffered from insufficient resources and perhaps a certain artistic hubris. If it had no credits, we might never connect it with Kubrick. Because we know who directed it, however, we tend to search out the themes, images and 'expressive' elements that signal the auteur and portend his later work.

The most obvious connection between *Fear and Desire* and Kubrick's later pictures is that he often made war movies, guiding his actors through grisly battle scenes like a field general. He is usually described as an 'anti-war' director, but in certain respects that description is inadequate. Few if any directors – even John Wayne – are pro-war in the sense that they believe military combat is a virtue in itself; on the other hand, a great many directors are patriotic or propagandistic, justifying war in the name of democracy, socialism, humanitarianism, nationalism, religion or some other non-military value. What makes Kubrick distinctive is his refusal to provide a rationale for war or any explanation for military conflict beyond self-destructive human drives. In every film he made about the subject, the 'enemy' is either unseen or virtually indistinguishable from the protagonists and the violence is convulsive and arbitrary. (*Spartacus* is an exception to the rule and a film Kubrick disliked precisely because of its idealism and sentimentality.) At the same time, probably for much the same reason that he was fascinated with prize-fighting, Kubrick seems attracted to the stark dramatic conflicts and the *imagery* of war. A skilled director of scenes of violence, he often makes us see the physical grace and potentially beautiful geometry of military tactics alongside their chaos, brutality and absurdity.

Fear and Desire treats these interests in a more overtly allegorical and generalising fashion than Kubrick's later work, although it might be noted that several of his other pictures – especially *Spartacus*, *2001* and *A Clockwork Orange* – can be read as allegories. Notice as well that many generic war movies have something allegorical about them: put two men in a fox-hole or pose them against a barren, bombed-out landscape and, simply by virtue of emptying out the *mise en scène*, you have the makings of *Waiting for Godot* or some kind of symbolic commentary on the human condition. Likewise, almost any war movie that focuses on small groups in combat – John Ford's *The Lost Patrol* (1934), Denis Sanders's *War Hunt* (1962) and Kubrick's own *Full Metal Jacket* – tends to become a kind of allegory or parable. In certain Hollywood films about World War II, the symbolism is quite conscious; Howard Hawks's *Air Force* (1943), for example, gives us a bomber crew representing a cross-section of America and transforms a single aircraft into an emblem of the nation (a technique Kubrick would later satirise in *Dr. Strangelove*).

And yet *Air Force* and the other movies I've mentioned also elicit what Erich Auerbach calls a 'realist' mode of interpretation – that is, they deal with recognisable historical situations, even though most of their characters are fictional and have symbolic functions.[3] By contrast, *Fear and Desire* is manifestly ahistorical and anti-realist. The four soldiers are costumed somewhat oddly, not quite like the American military, and the aircraft that flies over their heads in an early scene is a commercial Piper Cub of the sort that young Kubrick himself piloted. At the very beginning, as the camera pans slowly across an empty landscape, an off-screen narrator tells us that we are supposed to read the story as pure allegory:

There is war in this forest – not a war that has been fought, nor one that will be, but any war. And the enemies that struggle here do not exist unless we call them into being. For all of them, and all that happens now, is outside history. Only the unchanging shapes of fear and doubt and death are from our world. These soldiers that you see keep our language and our time, but have no other country but the mind.

The lost patrol in *Fear and Desire*, like those in other war movies, is composed of men with sharply different personalities and social backgrounds; but unlike the quasi-allegorical figures in the typical combat picture, none of Kubrick's soldiers is especially like-able and the group never bonds into a single fighting unit. One of the most insistent motifs in the film is that, contra John Donne, each man is an island. At best, their various social classes, mental dispositions and ethnic or regional backgrounds tend to merge into a pes-simistic and sometimes pretentiously philosophical chorus. Lieutenant Corby (Kenneth Harp) is a WASP intellectual who tries to philosophise about war and ultimately finds it meaningless: 'it's all a trick we perform because we'd rather not die immediately'. Sergeant 'Mac' (Frank Silvera) is a dark-skinned proletarian who feels bitter resentment towards offi-cers and raging frustration about his empty life: 'I'm thirty-four years old and I've never done anything important – when this is over I'll fix radios and washing machines.' Private Fletcher (Steve Coit) is an easygoing, rather feckless southerner who becomes morbid and confused: 'I don't want what I used to want. But somehow there's nothing else to want . . . I'm all mixed up.' Private Sidney (Paul Mazursky) is a sensitive young New Yorker who lives in constant fear: 'Nobody's safe here! Are they watching me? . . . Don't die here!'

Norman Kagan has remarked that 'In a way, the four soldiers are like the exploded frag-ments of a personality.'[4] *Fear and Desire* could, in fact, be viewed as an allegory of the psyche – a form that dates at least as far back as the *Psychomachia* of Prudentius in the Middle Ages. But Kubrick has no cosmology and no coherent map of the mind (beyond a generalised notion of the intellect and the instincts) to support either a metaphysical or a psychological allegory. Instead, he offers a secularised, existential view of society, which he depicts in a per-petual state of combat – 'a blazing island with gunfire around it', as one of the characters says. The result is a country of the mind resembling the bleak, cruel world of Thomas Hobbes's *Leviathan*, minus Hobbes's conservative belief in the civilising authority of religion and roy-alty. Gilles Deleuze has made the intriguing observation that, in Kubrick's major films, 'the world itself is a brain, there is an identity of brain and world'.[5] That idea finds literal expres-sion in *Fear and Desire* but here, as in many of the later films, the 'brain' is in conflict with itself; Reason is unable to prevent Eros, Thanatos, or whatever uncontrolled, instinctive urges one might postulate from producing havoc or dissolution. The sense of crisis is even more acute at the level of phenomenology. In a particularly interesting discussion of the ontological status of the brain-as-world, Jason Sperb reminds us that later Kubrick pictures such as *The Shining* 'increasingly reveal the country of the mind as an arbitrary and often illu-sory . . . façade that masks the ambiguity of the story world beyond'.[6]

Kubrick himself, in a letter to Joseph Burstyn, described the film as both 'allegorical' and 'poetic', a drama of '"man" lost in a hostile world – deprived of material and spiritual foundations . . . . imperiled by an unseen but deadly enemy who, upon scrutiny, seems to be almost shaped from the same mould'.[7] Thus, when the four soldiers attack the house in the woods, the men they kill are shown chiefly as silhouettes, isolated body parts or corpses, and are barely distinguishable from their attackers. Inside the enemy command post, the aging general and his aide wear Germanic uniforms and drink heavily, but otherwise they are doubles for Lieutenant Corby and Private Fletcher. (Like Corby, the general broods pessimistically about the war: 'I'm trapped. What is a prison for me? I make a grave for others.' Like Fletcher, the aide is smiling, compliant and untalkative.) When Corby administers a *coup de grâce* to the dying general, who is pleading for mercy, Corby realises that he is looking into his own face. The only true 'other' in the film is the female captive (nicely played by Virginia Leith, a Kubrick 'discovery' who went on to have a brief Hollywood career), a mute objectification of the men's fear and desire, who dies a senseless death. The quotation marks that Kubrick placed around '"man"' in his letter to Burstyn seem to have been knowingly ironic, emphasising his intention to allegorise a specifically masculine psychology rather than a general human condition.

All this might have been powerfully disturbing, but parts of the film are weakly executed. Despite the dramatic ironies of the plot and Lieutenant Corby's occasional attempts at sardonic wit, *Fear and Desire* is Kubrick's most humourless picture. The pacing of the climactic episodes is lugubrious and the staging of the attack on the enemy command post is amateurish, lacking the dynamism Kubrick usually brought to such material. The acting doesn't help. Kenneth Harp's performance as Corby is stilted and pompous, rather like a bad television announcer, and Paul Mazursky (later to become an important writer and director) portrays Sidney with an unmodulated, annoying hysteria. The best actor of the group is Frank Silvera, a Jamaican who had attended Northwestern University Law School and then turned to theatre. The only true professional in the cast, Silvera played the rebel slave Nat Turner on the New York stage and went on to act in various ethnic roles in Hollywood – a Mexican in Elia Kazan's *Viva Zapata!* (1952) and an Italian in Roger Corman's *The St. Valentine's Day Massacre* (1967). He brings an authentic feeling of anger and self-loathing to the character of Mac, perhaps aided by the fact that this movie was a step down in his career.

But *Fear and Desire* also exhibits a good deal of cinematic talent. The daylight photography creates subtle variations of tone and mood in difficult outdoor locations, and Kubrick shows flair in his use of optical wipes, radical distortions of space and quick shifts between overt speech and inner monologue. Although he is associated with long takes and a moving camera, his style in this film is heavily dependent upon quick cutting between bold graphic compositions and is a forceful reminder that he had made a careful study of Pudovkin. He regularly suspends the rules of continuity, ignoring the 180-degree rule and using establishing shots sparingly; and, because he likes to jump from telephoto to wide-angle views, his cutting in the dialogue scenes has an almost cubist effect. His most powerful display of montage is the first assault on the two enemy soldiers in an isolated house, which is depicted in twenty-one brief shots with clever Foley effects and no background music. As in Soviet films, the sequence is composed of a kind of visual metaphor and metonymy: two dying men's heads lolling back at different angles; a table knife lying in a pool of dripping stew; a hand flailing at a bowl of food and squeezing it between the fingers; a hand relaxing and dropping a piece of soggy bread; a pair of bizarrely twisted legs seized by their pants and dragged off screen. At the end of the sequence, we see a dead hand in a bowl of stew and hear a voice saying, 'Sidney, better get something to eat.'

Another of the film's effective montages is the sex scene between Sidney and the female captive, which has a kinky, sadomasochistic quality typical of Kubrick. In this case, a young woman is wearing a light summer dress and is bound to a tree with a military belt. She never speaks, but her eyes show panic as she watches Sidney lose control. We see a close-up of his knee pressing between her legs. Her face registers fear, but then, as she realises that he might be persuaded to untie the belt, she smiles. When Sidney cups water in his hands and brings it to her, she smiles again, and in an extreme close-up she laps at the water and licks his palms. He runs his hands over her face and she throws her head back so that he can kiss her throat and shoulder. As he crouches to embrace her, she seems to dominate. Reaching around her body and groping at the belt, he mutters eagerly, 'You'll put your arms around me!' When she breaks free and runs, Sidney pleads for her to stop and then shoots her. She falls without a sound, and Kubrick cuts to two deliberately mismatched close-ups of her motionless face, showing it first as if she were lying on her stomach and then as if she were lying on her back.

Considered apart from the legacy of Kubrick's other films, *Fear and Desire* may seem insignificant – especially when we consider that it was released in the same year as Fritz Lang's *The Big Heat*, Alfred Hitchcock's *I Confess*, Howard Hawks's *Gentlemen Prefer Blondes*, Vincente Minnelli's *The Bad and the Beautiful*, Samuel Fuller's *Pickup on South Street*, Anthony Mann's *The Naked Spur* and George Sidney's *Kiss Me Kate*. (Among the non-Hollywood productions of 1953 were Herbert Biberman's *Salt of the Earth*, Federico Fellini's *I Vitelloni*, Kenji Mizoguchi's *Ugetsu*, Carol Reed's *The Man Between* and Roberto Rossellini's *Voyage in Italy*.) The biggest award-winning and box-office success of the year was another war movie: Fred Zinneman's *From Here to Eternity*. In this environment, Kubrick's film was anomalous and even a bit strange – not a Hollywood production, not a work of political agitation and not a foreign art film. Despite its unusual aspects and its claim of being 'outside history', however, *Fear and Desire* belongs to its own time in more ways than one. It can be viewed as what Thomas Allen Nelson calls 'a youthful grab-bag of 1950s bohemian negativism and existential self-congratulation' (p. 22), and, as we've seen, it received commercial exhibition by virtue of its suitability to the art cinema of the period. Notice also that it was made during the last months of the Korean War, a conflict that marked the end of the qualified optimism of the Roosevelt era. A blacklist was on its way, a conservative government had been elected and there were few idealistic causes in which intellectuals wanted to believe. *Fear and Desire*'s apparent retreat from history marks it as an historical artefact – a 'realist' allegory after all. The battle-weary faces of Kubrick's four soldiers were much closer in appearance to newsreel images of GIs in Korea than to the characters in almost any war movies Hollywood had produced during the 1950s. (Exceptions to the rule are Samuel Fuller's *The Steel Helmet* [1951] and *Fixed Bayonets* [1951] and Anthony Mann's *Men in War* [1957].) Moreover, unlike *From Here to Eternity* and every other Hollywood attempt to criticise the military, *Fear and Desire* offered no comforting suggestion that the basic institution was sound and healthy; it depicted warfare as inherently brutal and meaningless. In the future Kubrick would deal more directly with actual wars but in this instance he was responding, in at least some measure, to real conditions with a serious and not merely sophomoric pessimism.

II. Dream City

Soon after *Fear and Desire* opened in New York, Kubrick set out to make another low-budget feature under the auspices of his own company, which he dubbed 'Minotaur Productions'. In July 1953, via legal representatives, he submitted a script entitled *Along Came a Spider* to Joseph Breen of the Production Code Administration, who rejected the project on the grounds that it contained 'scenes of nudity and suggested nudity, excessive brutality, attempted rape, illicit sex ... treated with no voice of morality or compensating moral values'.[8] Kubrick then transformed the idea into a somewhat less sensational film, initially entitled *Kiss Me, Kill Me*. Once again, the script was written by Howard O. Sackler (without credit, using Kubrick's story-line), the music was composed by Gerald Fried and the cast was made up of Frank Silvera and a small group of inexperienced players. Kubrick was director, photographer and editor. At first he planned to shoot the picture with direct sound, but when the microphone boom interfered with his careful lighting of interiors, he abandoned the idea and once again constructed a completely post-synchronised soundtrack.

This time the project was a film noir – the sort of picture that was suited to mainstream entertainment but at the same time amenable to Kubrick's artistic touches. Eventually entitled *Killer's Kiss*, it concerns an erotic triangle between a failed New York prize-fighter named Davy Gordon (Jamie Smith), a self-destructive taxi-dancer named Gloria Price (Irene Kane) and a neurotic gangster named Vince Rapallo (Silvera). Shortly after being knocked out in the ring and deciding to give up his career in boxing, Davy sees Vince manhandling Gloria; he comes to her rescue, falls in love and persuades her to go with him to Seattle, where he plans to work on a horse ranch owned by his uncle. The jealous Vince, who is Gloria's employer in the Pleasure Land dance hall, intervenes and tries unsuccessfully to have Davy killed. In an eerie sequence staged in a loft filled with department-store mannequins, Davy has a fight with Vince and kills him. All this is narrated in flashback by Davy, who is waiting in Pennsylvania Station for the train to Seattle, hoping that Gloria will join him. At the last moment, she appears and they embrace passionately.

During the production, Kubrick was able to procure a photo spread about the making of the film in *Life* magazine, shot by his friend Alexander Singer. Censors required the deletion of two scenes, one showing Davy pushing Gloria down on her bed after he kisses her and the other showing an obviously homosexual man searching for an apartment in Davy's building; the PCA report also insisted that the climactic battle between the hero and the villain not go too far in 'exploitation of the nudity of the mannequins'.[9] Kubrick himself deleted a brief sequence halfway through the picture, showing Davy and Gloria walking together in the city and deciding to get married.

Much of the film's charm derives from the way it combines pulp fiction and a documentary feel for the streets of New York with a certain hand-crafted asperity. One of its most fascinating sequences reveals a vivid contrast between Kubrick's gritty realism and the emerging society of the spectacle: Davy and Gloria visit Gloria's workplace at 49th and Broadway during a peak hour of the evening as crowds are bustling past and bright lights are blinking everywhere. The sequence was shot on location with a hidden Eymo camera using high-speed, black-and-white film stock, and the actors, who were unknown to the public, mingled with pedestrians on the street. The soundtrack consists mostly of traffic noise. In the background are bizarrely animated advertisements, lit shop windows and the bubbling marquees of movie theatres featuring the latest CinemaScope and Technicolor productions; but the dense array of attractions looks like a crazy fairground, and life on the pavement, captured with grainy immediacy, is harsh and oppressive.

Sequences like this one prompted Gavin Lambert, writing a review of *Killer's Kiss* in *Sight and Sound*, to praise Kubrick for taking 'a kind of neo-realist approach to human behavior, a feeling for the place and moment'.[10] A documentary atmosphere had, in fact, become fairly typical of Hollywood in the period, especially in the film noir. Henry Hathaway's *Kiss of Death* (1947) and Jules Dassin's *The Naked City* use extensive footage of life on the New York streets; Rudolph Mate's *D.O.A.* (1950) contains scenes of Edmund O'Brien running down the crowded sidewalks of San Francisco; and Robert Aldrich's *Kiss Me Deadly*, released in the same year as Kubrick's film, provides a virtual roadmap of Los Angeles. A somewhat later film of the type, Alexander Mackendrick's *The Sweet Smell of Success* (1957), was photographed by James Wong Howe in locations very near to the ones in *Killer's Kiss*, although here, as in most of the other pictures I've named, police cordoned off the streets and extras were employed. What makes *Killer's Kiss* relatively special is that it documents the city with such immediate urgency and unglamorous authenticity. In his fine book on urban space in the American film noir, Edward Dimendberg compares Kubrick's film to photographer William Klein's 1956 book, *Life Is Good and Good for You in New York*, which depicts Manhattan as a world of 'anomie and seediness'.[11] Dimendberg argues that *Killer's Kiss* represents the metropolis 'to a degree unparalleled by most of the films noir of the 1940s' (p. 136), and that it constitutes a kind of allegory about a moment in history when the easily negotiable, pedestrian spaces of the city are beginning to give way to postmodern fragmentation, commodification and suburban dispersal: as he points out, the film opens with ground-level shots inside Pennsylvania Station (a landmark that would be destroyed in the 1960s), emphasising the open, almost contemplative waiting room and the peaceful light from the barrel-vaulted ceilings; then it takes us to the violent and tawdry spaces of a boxing arena, a dance hall, a bustling street and a mannequin factory – settings where Davy and Gloria become alienated and objectified.

If *Killer's Kiss* looks slightly different from other films noir, that is undoubtedly due to its raw, guerilla style of shooting and its indebtedness to a photographic tradition I've already described: the black-and-white street photography of the New York school. The film carries several allusions to the New York photographers – in its subway scenes, for example, and in an episode that makes an indirect reference to Weegee, who had worked as an advisor on Robert Wise's *The Set Up* (1949), a film noir about boxing photographed chiefly in a studio. Wise's film ends with an aging boxer being cornered in a blind alley and beaten to death by thugs. In Kubrick's film, two hoods beat a boxer's manager to death. The scene is staged in an actual alley rather than a studio set, and it feels truer to the blood and squalor of Weegee's crime photos. (As the terrified fight manager scurries from one corner of the alley to another, he moves past a sheet of plywood bearing a crudely painted sign: 'No Toilet.')

But Kubrick's style is also in many ways different from Weegee's. For one thing, Weegee's nocturnal photos have less to with the architecture of the city than with the grotesquerie of people caught in the glare of a flashbulb against a black limbo. Some of Kubrick's still-camera work for *Look* magazine, especially the photos of Walter Cartier that influenced the boxing sequences in *Killer's Kiss*, was unquestionably in this tradition; for the movies, however, Kubrick frequently employed wide-angle lenses, radically low- or high-level camera positions, silhouetted figures against dramatically lit backgrounds and a whole arsenal of techniques we associate with a director like Orson Welles. Some of the most arresting images in *Killer's Kiss* also draw on conventions of cityscape photography that date back to figures like Alfred Stieglitz (the stunning shot of the bright disk of the sun disappearing slowly behind the Manhattan skyline), or on a kind of poetic-naturalistic school of still-camera portraiture (the close-up of Gloria looking out of her apartment window, her face softly reflected in a pane of glass), or on a more ironic technique that shows people in relation to architecture and signage (the extreme wide-angle shot of Gloria mounting the stairs of Pleasure Land, where the floor is covered with a chessboard pattern and a sign above her head says 'Watch Your Step').

In this film and all his later work, Kubrick never forsook his predilection for the natural or 'practical' lighting he had used as a photo-journalist, but his images are more textural, more sensitive to gradations and qualities of light, than Weegee's ever were. Then, too, Weegee's pictures of ghetto life and the New York *demi-mondaine* are chiefly about human faces and tight groupings of highly individuated figures; his is a city of vivid characters, whereas Kubrick's is a city of anonymous crowds and empty spaces. Probably because Kubrick was shooting without official permission and with no money to hire extras, he photographed several key sequences in the grey light of dawn, when there were relatively few people around – for instance, the scenes in Pennsylvania Station, or the shots of Davy and Gloria exiting their apartment building on 8th Avenue. The dynamically shot and edited chase sequence near the end of the film, when Davy jumps out the window of a loft on 24th Street, runs down a blind alley, climbs a fire escape and sprints across a rooftop, has an eerie effect precisely because the city seems uninhabited. Even indoors, Kubrick couldn't afford to show crowds, so he gives us a prize-fight and a ballet in which the 'audience' is completely hidden in darkness. Through these and other techniques, he makes New York a surreal place, just as most of the tabloid photographers had done. In a photographer like Weegee, however, the surrealism is vernacular, unself-conscious and teeming with life. In *Killer's Kiss* it feels deliberate, uninhabited and untouched by a populist impulse.

Killer's Kiss is equally interesting at the level of the soundtrack. Kubrick's decision to avoid direct sound recording is less problematic here than in *Fear and Desire* because the dialogue is sparse, exposition being provided by off-screen narration. The narrative is so complex that we have two flashbacks within Davy's flashback – first, when Gloria talks about her confrontation with Vince and, second, when she talks at greater length about her childhood and the death of her family. The second of these retrospective stories is represented less like a conventional flashback than like a mental image or an avant-garde movie; on the visual level, it consists entirely of a ballet solo performed by Kubrick's second wife, Ruth Sobotka, a dancer and designer with the New York City Ballet, who performs against a black limbo. (Perhaps significantly, Sobotka had previously appeared in the Man Ray episode of Hans Richer's surrealist anthology film, *Dreams that Money Can Buy* [1947].) Even though Davy is presumably in charge of everything we see, the off-screen narration shifts easily from his voice to Gloria's, just as the visual point of view shifts between the three leading characters. Sometimes narration drops out altogether for long stretches during which the actors work mainly in pantomime. Several conversations occur on a telephone, which makes the job of dubbing somewhat easier, and the actors now and then deliver lines outside the frame or with their backs to the camera. On the few occasions when speech is photographed directly, there is a slight mismatch between the image and the ambient quality of the sound, but this only enhances the air of strangeness and oneiricism.

Gerald Fried's musical score is comprised chiefly of three interwoven elements: a martial theme associated with Davy's life in the ring, a romantic theme associated with Gloria and a Latin jazz theme associated with Vince and his gang (the Latin music anticipates Henry Mancini's score for Orson Welles's *Touch of Evil*). A great deal of what we see relies upon nothing more than non-diegetic music and dubbed sound effects in support of three fundamental editing techniques from the silent era – parallel editing, which historians tend to associate with Griffith, point-of-view editing, which is usually associated with Kuleshov or Hitchcock, and montage, which derives from Eisenstein and the Soviets. By virtue of its almost total reliance on editing rather than dialogue, *Killer's Kiss* could be described as what Hitchcock liked to call 'pure cinema'. It even contains several echoes of Hitchcock, among them a protagonist who gazes through his rear window, a painting that seems to mock one of the characters and a scream that dissolves into the sound of a train whistle.

Not unlike Hitchcock, Kubrick often told interviewers that he considered the average talking picture uncinematic. Speaking to Maurice Rapf in 1969, he remarked, 'In most films you have a bunch of guys talking to each other and you make use of about three or four sets and that's about it. There really isn't a lot to look at, and everybody is waiting for the big action sequence'.[12] *Killer's Kiss* offers plentiful evidence of his interest in the plastic qualities of the medium. He offers us a compendium of stock characters and situations from the universe of noir and he ends with a 'big action sequence', but through his dynamic, slightly unorthodox manipulation of image, sound and *mise en scène*, he makes the familiar seem strange.

Everything begins in primal movie fashion, with a dark screen and the chugging sound of a train starting on a journey. We see a low-level, deep-focus image of a young man wearing a knitted tie and a sports coat, smoking and pacing the nearly empty floor of Penn Station in soft grey light. As the credits appear, the sound of the train fades into the distance, followed by a public-address announcement of the next train and the ring of a bell. 'It's crazy how you can get yourself in a mess sometime,' the young man's off-screen voice says. He explains that his troubles originated a couple of days ago at the time of his big fight with a boxer named Rodriguez. A wavy dissolve accompanied by percussive martial music takes us into the past, where we see a brief montage copied almost directly from Kubrick's documentary about Walter Cartier: a fight poster hanging from a lamp post and another in a barbershop window show the face of the narrator and tell us that his name is Davy Gordon.

Cut to Davy's darkened one-room apartment. Wearing a polo shirt and slacks and viewed from a slightly high angle, he studies his face in a dressing-table mirror (another image borrowed from *Day of the Fight*). A quick series of inserts shows family photos pasted around the mirror: a farmhouse; a blurred image of a woman in rural dress standing near a front porch (next to it a couple of ticket stubs from 'Washland' on 9th Avenue); a cow; and an older man in the woods. No dialogue has been spoken, but we already know a good deal about the leading character. Davy continues studying his face, flattening his nose with a finger to see how it would look if it were broken; then he steps away from the mirror, crosses to a sink and pours a glass of water. As he paces, the camera pans and shows all four walls of the cramped room. Among the strange items hanging on the wall are a machete and a mandolin; we also see a window, outside of which, across a short, dark space, another window reveals an attractive blonde dressed in a sweater and skirt moving about her own room. Davy pays no attention and crosses towards the next wall, where he bends down to look at a goldfish bowl beneath a lamp. At this point Kubrick cuts to one of the film's most flamboyant images – an 'impossible' reverse-angle close-up, positioned in the space that

the wall occupied in the previous shot, looking through the bowl at Davy. His features, which were previously distorted by his own hand, are now grotesquely twisted. Kubrick uses a telephoto lens to flatten the perspective and at the same time uses the bowl to create a fisheye effect; as a result Davy looks at once mashed in and weirdly elongated, as if he had been beaten into putty.

Davy glances out of the window towards Gloria and then walks over to his bed, where he lays down fully dressed. An insert shows that his clock reads 6.50. Cut to another 'impossible' angle, the camera positioned in the wall space behind the clock and the bedside telephone, looking towards the window and the neighbouring apartment. Kubrick adds fascination to the minimal decor by arranging framed pictures within the picture; we've seen Davy framed by a mirror that holds several tiny snapshots and in this shot we see Gloria framed by two identical window frames. (To the right of her image is yet another frame – a picture tacked to the wall of Davy's room.) The tightly enclosed apartment becomes a sort of camera obscura, with a single opening that shows a brightly lit figure across the way.

The voyeuristic moment is interrupted by the ringing of a telephone. Davy's manager is calling from a payphone in a gym; strangely lit, as if he were standing in front of a process screen, he begins the film's first exchange of dialogue, making arrangements with Davy to meet for that evening's fight. Now Gloria's subjectivity is briefly introduced. We cut to her room – a space nearly identical to Davy's but decorated with curtains, a checquered tablecloth and nylons drying on a line. Sipping coffee, she paces around, goes to her window and looks out. A close-up shows her gazing at the adjacent apartment. Cut to a wide shot from her point of view through the two window frames, showing Davy as he packs a bag. In close-up, Gloria sips coffee and gazes for a long time. She might be interested in Davy, or she might be daydreaming. She finishes her coffee, takes a trenchcoat from her wardrobe and exits her apartment.

Kubrick continues to draw parallels by cross-cutting between the two characters as they individually walk down three flights of stairs to the street below. Davy arrives first and takes a letter from his mailbox. He and Gloria exit the building side by side, walking towards a bright new convertible parked at the curb. Davy turns and walks off down the street. Cut to a close view of Vince, who steps out of the convertible dressed in flashy gangster's attire. He stares at Davy, who looks back over his shoulder as he enters the 8th Avenue subway. After Vince puts Gloria into the car, he remarks, 'You're doing alright for yourself.' 'What do you mean?' she replies, and then realises what Vince is talking about. 'Oh,' she says, 'he just lives in the building.' But Vince recognises Davy and smiles. 'We can watch him tonight on TV,' he says as he starts the car and drives off.

On the almost empty New York subway, Davy reads the letter he just received, and we hear the unintentionally laughable, country-hick voice of Uncle George, the letter-writer: 'Deer Dayvee. We still haven't heard from yuh yet this month.' Davy smiles affectionately. A direct cut takes us to a wide shot of a boxing arena, where two fighters can be seen in a pool of light, surrounded by blackness from which an unseen crowd cheers wildly. Cut to a dressing room, where Davy's hands are being taped by his manager as the crowd outside continues to cheer. Here and in the subsequent shots of the fight, Kubrick restages scenes from his documentary on Walter Cartier, using the same hand-held Eymo camera, the same low-level camera positions and the same jagged cutting style. First, however, he gives us a shot of Times Square at night, followed by a brief descriptive montage of the busy city. The choice of documentary shots is odd: an automated figure of Santa Claus pokes out its tongue to lick a candy apple; hot dogs steam on a vendor's tray; ice-cream sundaes revolve on a turntable; a neon sign in a store window reads 'Photos', and beyond it conventional portraits of families and young soldiers in uniform are displayed on a wall; most bizarrely of all, a tiny plastic baby swims around in a pan of water.

These shots create a slightly disturbing feeling because, even though we are situated in the midst of a city whose noises we hear in the background, we see no people – only images, simulacra and automata, as if the film were foreshadowing the climactic fight in a mannequin factory. The dehumanised atmosphere is reinforced by a series of documentary shots depicting the façade of the Pleasure Land dance hall. Above a gaudy sign ('Couples Invited/Dancing Partners') is the painted image of a blonde with large breasts who faces right; over another ('Dancing Tonite/Hostesses') is a brunette who faces left. As Edward

Dimendberg has pointed out, these billboard images rhyme with the photos of male box-
ers we've seen in flyers at the beginning of the film. At the Pleasure Land box office, a man
smokes and sells tickets for a dollar, his face entirely hidden from view. Inside, the camera
tracks laterally across a large room in which we see tough-looking bouncers standing
against the wall and eccentric couples dancing to a hollow-sounding tune piped over a
loudspeaker. (This is the only occasion in the movie when Kubrick used a large group of
extras, who were recruited from his friends in Greenwich Village.) Cut to Gloria's dressing room, where we hear the distant music and see a make-up table and a pair of high-heel
shoes. Standing before a mirror in the smoky glare, Gloria removes her sweater to reveal a
black strapless bra. Cut to Davy's dressing room: his face and naked torso are being greased
by his fight trainer; Davy warms up by throwing a few punches at his manager's hands,
and we hear the crowd roaring outside.

    While Davy and Gloria, the two entertainers, prepare their bodies, Vince is seen alone
in his small office above the dance hall, drinking and smoking a big cigar. The lighting is
exceedingly noirish and the room decorated in surreal, unmotivated fashion with turn-of-
the-century theatrical posters and what looks like a weird advertisement for blue jeans.
(This is the first of many instances in his career when Kubrick will decorate the set with
fascinating kitsch. The two largest posters, barely glimpsed in this shot, depict violent
tableaux from stage melodramas; in one of them a figure is spreadeagled in front of a buzz
saw and in another a man stands with arms raised in front of a gigantic cannon.) Vince
looks through venetian blinds at the dance floor below, turns on a television set and switches
off the office lights. Grotesquely lit by the glare from the TV screen, he listens to an
announcer introducing a boxing match between 'two game boys' – Kid Rodriguez, 'unde-
feated in twenty-two professional encounters', and Davy Gordon, 'the veteran'. An insert of
the TV screen shows two fighters meeting in the ring to talk with the referee. (Kubrick
appears to have photographed an actual broadcast, not bothering to adjust the shutter
speed of his camera so as to eliminate television scan lines. One of the most popular shows
on the CBS network in the early 1950s was the Wednesday-night 'Pabst Blue Ribbon Fights',
which the broadcast resembles.) The announcer tells us that Davy Gordon, age twenty-
nine, is a clever boxer who has been 'plagued by a weak chin and the unlucky knack of
being at his worst for the big ones'.

    Cut to Vince, who stands by the office window, smiling dreamily. He goes downstairs
and pulls Gloria off the dance floor, roughing up her partner in the process. In the
moments that follow, Kubrick cross-cuts between Davy, who is beaten by Rodriguez, and
Gloria, who is embraced and pawed by Vince as he forces her to watch the fight on TV. The
fight itself is a cinematic *tour de force*, recreating many shots from the match Kubrick had
photographed for *Day of the Fight*, but adding subjective views from Davy's point of view as
he is repeatedly floored by his opponent. Less bloody than similar boxing sequences from
other films noir of the post-war era (*The Killers* [1946], *Body and Soul* [1947], *The Set Up*,
Champion), it nevertheless looks far more tough and authentic, in part because the two

actors are quick on their feet and seem to know something about boxing. The juxtaposition of the fight in the ring and the sexual grappling in Vince's office imbues everything with a distinctly sadomasochistic eroticism, revealing one of the sublimated meanings of boxing as entertainment.

The action between Gloria and Vince as they watch the fight is ambiguous, anticipating some of the perverse, decadent voluptuousness that Kubrick later created in one of the best moments in *Spartacus*, when a small group of Roman nobles and their wives are given a private viewing of a gladiatorial contest. There is also a subtle racial implication to the embrace between the gangster and the taxi-dancer, as if Kubrick were trying to create a frisson of forbidden sexuality. Here, as in *Fear and Desire*, Frank Silvera is cast in the role of a primitive, his somewhat African features placed in sharp contrast with Irene Kane's aristocratic blondness and extremely white skin, which is displayed by her backless dress. Vince takes her bare shoulders in his hands and points her towards the off-screen glow of the TV. Like the woman tied to the tree in *Fear and Desire*, she is both abject and possessed with a kind of sexual power over her captor. At first she seems puzzled, but as Vince silently gropes her, she begins to understand the reason for his excitement. After Davy is knocked down twice by Rodriguez, she looks frightened and yet somewhat aroused. Cut to the fight arena, where Davy goes down for the third and last time; as he is being helped to his corner

a voice from the crowd yells, 'Go on home, you bum! You're all through!' The TV announcer tells us that 'For Gordon tonight must have come as a bitter pill indeed.' Vince embraces Gloria and kisses her on the neck. Smiling slightly, she turns to look towards the flickering light of the TV. Vince smiles and so does she. As they kiss, Vince bends towards her hungrily, putting his hand behind her head, pressing her roughly to his mouth and turning her naked back to the camera. She responds, but her arms don't fully embrace him. Fade out to the rising sound of hot Latin jazz.

Davy and Gloria, already paralleled in several ways, have been humiliated at the same moment. Fade in to an eloquent hidden-camera shot of Times Square at night, showing Gloria in the distance, wearing her trenchcoat and crossing the street like a zombie. The camera moves from left to right, framing her at the bottom centre of the screen with her legs out of view. A forlorn figure backed by the cavernous city and clouds of steam rising from the street, she passes a sharply dressed man, perhaps an actual passerby, who stares briefly at her. Cut to Davy, who is shirtless in his darkened room, drinking a can of beer and brooding. When a light comes on across the way he moves to the window. The camera tracks forward to show his torso reflected in the glass. We hear music from a distant radio and in the next apartment we see Gloria, who seems desperate and a bit unsteady as she takes off her shoes and belt.

Davy's telephone rings again. A close-up of his profile shows him looking intently towards Gloria. He answers the phone and stands with his back to his dressing table, with Gloria reflected in the mirror behind him. The shot is filled with frames within the frame (the mirror, the various snapshots pasted to the mirror and the two windows), creating a sort of dark comedy of voyeurism: Davy is shirtless and Gloria is undressing, and Davy has to answer a call from his Uncle George. In the mirror, Gloria strips down to a black slip and steps out of view as Davy politely explains to his uncle that this isn't a good time to talk. As Davy hangs up, Gloria reappears in pyjamas and turns out her light. Romantic music can be heard from the distant radio. Davy winds his clock, turns off a lamp and stretches out on his bed in the cell-like room. Fade to black.

The next sequence, one of the most memorable in the film, depicts Davy's dream, although we learn that fact retroactively. A direct cut shows a negative image of a narrow, littered street containing a few parked cars in what looks like a desolate area of Soho. The camera, equipped with a wide-angle lens and positioned as if it were mounted atop a car, races down the empty street towards an infinite horizon, the buildings on either side sheering past at high speed. A jump-cut jerks us back to a previous spot and the camera continues to race forward, going nowhere. We hear tense music, a muffled voice from the invisible crowd at Davy's boxing match ('Go on home, bum!') and then a woman's scream. This is the first use of a 'tunnel' view that Kubrick would often employ, always with a riveting effect. The dream is both an expression of Davy's anxiety and a kind of sinister premonition, for the street we see is the same one where the climactic violence of the film will unfold.

Davy awakes to Gloria's scream, sees Vince shoving her and rushes across the apartment building's rooftop to find the stairway to her room. When he arrives, Vince has fled, and Davy can only ask Gloria what happened. 'Well,' she says, 'about an hour ago . . .'. Percussive Latin jazz rises on the soundtrack and a wavy dissolve marks a transition to a flashback, which opens with a tight, vivid close-up of Gloria, her face lit from below as she hovers beside her closed door and listens to Vince's knock. When Vince enters, he seems pathetically contrite yet still dangerous. We never learn what happened in his office but the implication is sexual assault. Gloria backs away, putting a table between the two of them. 'Go away,' she says, but Vince ignores her and whines, 'All my life I've always spoiled the things that meant the most to me . . . . If only you knew how low and worthless I feel!' Circling the table, he grasps her arms: 'I want to set you up right . . . Just tolerate me!' Kubrick cuts to a close-up of Gloria, breaking the 180-degree line to create a violent effect. 'To me you're just an old man,' she says. 'You smell bad.' When she threatens to scream, he tries to cover her mouth. The camera spins into a 'swish pan' reminiscent of *Citizen Kane* and the flashback ends. Davy tells Gloria, 'Don't think about it any more,' and promises to sit with her while she sleeps.

The film's love theme plays in the background as Gloria falls to sleep. Davy looks at a small doll suspended from her bedpost. Commentators usually describe the doll as a symbol of innocence but it has a distinctly strange look: tattered, wearing a sort of blond fright wig, it stares with open eyes and dangles from the bed like a hanged figure. Davy turns out a light and moves about Gloria's room, fingering the stockings and lingerie drying on a clothes line, smelling a bottle of perfume on a dressing table, reading a postcard, opening and shutting a music box and gazing at a pair of framed photographs. His interest in Gloria may be benign but it has a fetishistic and voyeuristic quality.

The remainder of the film observes the oldest of Hollywood formulas: boy meets girl, boy loses girl and boy gets girl. But all the characters have darkly 'psychological' motivations. Davy's curiosity about Gloria seems perverse, if only because of Kubrick's weird *mise en scène*. Gloria's difficulties with her love-life become apparent on the next day, when, during a sunny breakfast in her room, Davy asks, 'Who are those people in that picture over there, and how did you get mixed up with that dance-hall guy?' An insert shows the pair of framed photographs from the previous sequence – a swarthy and rather distinguished older man with thinning hair and a moustache and a ballet dancer in costume. For this shot Kubrick used photos of his own wife and her father. Significantly the male figure bears a certain resemblance to Frank Silvera in the role of Vince Rapallo.

Gloria identifies the two people as her father and her sister Iris, and explains that they have something to do with why she became involved with Vince. 'I never told anybody before,' she says and, in a lengthy monologue accompanied by a dream image of the sister performing a ballet, she reveals her secret life. Iris, it seems, was eight years her senior. 'She adored Daddy, and of course she was his favourite.' The father was a successful writer and the mother a great beauty; they 'were very happy. Then I was born and mother died on the same day.' As time passed, Iris grew to resemble her mother, and Gloria became increasingly jealous. When a rich man asked Iris to marry him and give up her career as a ballet dancer, she refused; but then her father became seriously ill and needed constant medical care. Iris married the rich suitor, gave up dancing, and sat by her father's bedside every day. 'I guess I hated her more than ever now,' Gloria says. When the father died, Iris went to his bedroom, put on his favourite record of one of her ballets, and committed suicide by cutting her wrists. 'She left me a note,' Gloria tells us. Then, a few days later, Gloria was passing Pleasure Land, where she saw a 'dancers wanted' sign. 'I don't know what possessed me. That depraved place. I kept thinking, at least Iris never had to dance like this . . . . Then I started to feel less unhappy.'

Gloria's story is filled with Freudian themes: sibling rivalry, guilt over the death of her sister and ambivalence towards the gangster who resembles her father. By dancing in the club, she finds expiation for her guilt and at the same time unconsciously 'wins' by parodying her sister's romantic relationship with Daddy. There may be a therapeutic value in her confession but she hardly seems ready for a relationship – especially with Davy, who comes from a working-class world about which she knows little other than her experience in the dance hall. Because Kubrick chose to cut a scene showing Davy and Gloria spending the day walking in the city, their attachment looks all the more hasty and questionable. After kissing Gloria only once (and grasping her hair in the same way Vince had done),

Davy declares his love. In a less threatening version of the same scene she had just played with Vince, she tries to move away from him. 'Love me? That's funny,' she says. She sits on the bed and he kneels at her feet. The scene ends with an image of night falling over Manhattan.

Back in his office, Vince is drinking heavily when a call from one of his underlings informs him that Gloria is quitting and coming to get her paycheque. On his desk is a book-leaf pair of framed photographs similar to the one on Gloria's dressing table, and the strange artwork on his walls seems to reflect his state of mind. He scowls at one image in particular – a cartoon showing a couple of turn-of-the-century vaudeville characters who appear to look back at him in mockery. Cut to an 'impossible' shot from the point of view of the picture. Vince hurls his glass of whisky at it. (Kubrick suspends a piece of glass in front of the camera so that the picture frame/camera lens seems to shatter.)

The subsequent action is standard melodrama, ironically inflected and skilfully shot and edited. Intending to leave for Seattle, Davy and Gloria go to Pleasure Land so that she can claim her pay. Davy plans to meet his manager and collect his earnings from the boxing match, but is momentarily drawn away when a drunken Shriner grabs his scarf and runs off with it. (The Shriner is played by David Vaughn, a friend of Kubrick and a trained dancer, who moves far too theatrically to convey a tourist on a bender.) Vince sends his goons to beat or kill Davy, but they end up killing the manager by mistake. Because Gloria can provide evidence of the murder, Vince kidnaps her and hides her in a loft on 24th Street, where the *mise en scène* is worthy of the theatrical posters in Vince's office: the blonde Gloria is tied to a chair on a raised platform while her dark guards play poker under a naked lightbulb. Davy rides to the rescue but Gloria's captors trick him and, for the second time in three days, he is knocked out. The episode is especially interesting for the way it subverts expectations: the hero fails in his quest and the heroine begs to return to the villain. 'Listen, Vinny,' Gloria says in a rational tone, 'don't kill me. I don't want to die. I'll do anything you say.' When Vince asks if she loves Davy, she replies, 'I don't know. I don't think so. I've only known him for two days.'

As he regains consciousness, Davy hears much of this and decides to save himself by diving out a second-storey window to the street below. Fleeing from Vince and one of his gunmen, he ends up in a storeroom full of mannequins, where he and Vince fight to the death with a spear and an axe. In its own low-budget way, this climactic action is worthy of comparison with the cinematic bravura at the ending of Welles's *The Lady from Shanghai*. Violence and suspense are mingled with a grotesque visual wit. When Davy enters the room to the sound of eerie music, he passes a row of nude female figures (one with its torso twisted awry from its legs), a row of male heads, a hand and the figure of a little girl; suddenly, a shadowy figure in the distance seems to come alive: a repairman working on the mannequins like a *demiurge*. When Vince enters close behind Davy and knocks out the repairman, Kubrick cuts to a shot of Davy hiding among the male heads, his profile pointed in the same direction as theirs. Later, as Vince and Davy flail away at one another like a couple of awkward gladiators, they become entangled with the mannequins and it becomes difficult to tell whether they are striking each other or the fake bodies.

The visual confusion between the characters and the mannequins not only heightens the degree of violence and suspense but also has a thematic significance. The mannequins share something with the strange doll in Gloria's room, with the plastic baby swimming around a pan of water on Times Square, with the lifeless photographic images in Davy's mirror, with the empty New York streets and with the characters themselves. As Dana Polan has pointed out, all the players in *Killer's Kiss* are 'either flat or awkwardly or overly histrionic, and this, plus the distancing provided by a quite disembodied tone in the clumsy post-synchronization, serves to make [the characters] somewhat dull'.[13] Far from being a flaw in the movie, however, the relatively flat characterisations and the zombie-like dialogue are consistent with Kubrick's tendency to place less emphasis on individuals than on what Polan calls 'social roles'. The film systematically overturns or deglamorises the stereotypes upon which the characters are based (the boxer has a glass jaw, the taxi-dancer comes from an artistic family with a blighted past, and the gangster is neurotically insecure), and at the same time it keeps the characters at an emotional distance, making them seem alienated and a bit robotic. Notice also that, while the characters are dehumanised, the dolls or mannequins are made spooky, as if they were possessed of spirit or mentality. This is perhaps Kubrick's ultimate joke, which he will complicate and enrich as his career progresses.

Still another dark joke arises from the fact that most of the mannequins are women. In the midst of their wild struggle, Gloria's rival lovers begin hurling female body parts at one another. At one point Davy picks up the entire body of a woman and throws it at Vince, who swings his axe and chops the body in half. Davy then picks up another woman's body and throws it, following up with a woman's torso and leg. Later, Davy pushes Vince down on a pile of nude female bodies, tries to spear him and misses, in the process getting his spear stuck in the lower half of a woman, which Vince swings at and chops apart. The battle becomes a symbolic comment on the jealous impulses of both men, but it also functions in a general way as a comment on the tendency of commercial modernity to fragment and fetishise the body parts of women. Kubrick depicts the men's struggle in a frightening, suspenseful fashion that also makes them look inept. At several points he uses wide shots that run for a fairly long time, so that we see the two combatants stumbling, floundering, falling and growing weary. Sweat and dust cling to their exhausted faces in close-ups, and when Davy finally manages to push Vince down and spear him, the action looks squalid rather than chivalric. Kubrick cuts from Vince's scream to a close-up of the head of one of the mannequins, lying upside down and lit from below like a figure in a horror movie. The scream and the image dissolve to a loud train whistle in Penn Station, returning us to the place where we began.

Several commentators, among them Alexander Walker and Thomas Allen Nelson, have compared *Killer's Kiss* to a fairy tale, which is a form of narrative that most Hollywood movies replicate on a structural level. The comparison is apt because the film gives us a story about a fair maiden who is rescued by a kind of knight errant from the clutches of an ogre. The tone Kubrick maintains throughout, however, is more appropriate to the sombre, perverse romanticism of surrealist fantasy. The ending, in which Gloria shows up at the last minute to join Davy at the train station, was no doubt conceived in an attempt to make *Killer's Kiss* a commercial venture and is the closest thing to a Hollywood conclusion in Kubrick's career – and yet it seems bizarre, because we've just seen the lovers betray each other. When Davy embraces Gloria, their pose resembles the two previous kissing scenes: the woman's face is turned from the camera and the man grasps her hair passionately. Gloria has no luggage, the departure of the train for Seattle has already been announced and there seems no place for the couple to go. Audiences can view the ending as conventionally happy or as a perfunctory conclusion to a genre movie whose real aims are more disturbingly dreamlike. In either case, with this project Kubrick proved his readiness to enter the truly professional phase of his career.

Notes

1. Quoted in Vincent LoBrutto, *Stanley Kubrick: A Biography* (New York: Da Capo Press, 1999), p. 91.
2. Paolo Cherchi Usai, 'Checkmating the General: Stanley Kubrick's *Fear and Desire,' Image* vol. 38, nos 1–2: p. 27.
3. See Erich Auerbach, 'Figura', in *Scenes from the Drama of European Literature* (New York: Meridian Books, 1959), pp. 11–76.
4. Norman Kagan, *The Cinema of Stanley Kubrick* (New York: Continuum, 1997), pp. 19–20.
5. Gilles Deleuze, *Cinema 2: The Time-Image,* trans. Hugh Tomlinson and Robert Galeta (Minneapolis: University of Minnesota Press, 1989), p. 205.
6. Jason Sperb, *The Kubrick Façade: Faces and Voices in the Films of Stanley Kubrick* (Lanham, MD: Scarecrow Press, 2006), p. 2. See also Jason Sperb, 'The Country of the Mind in Kubrick's *Fear and Desire*', *Film Criticism*, vol. 29 no. 1 (Autumn 2004), pp. 23–37.
7. Quoted in Kagan, *The Cinema of Stanley Kubrick*, p. 9.
8. Production Code Administration file on *Along Came a Spider*, Margaret Herrick Library, Academy of Motion Picture Arts and Sciences, Los Angeles.
9. Production Code Administration file on *Killer's Kiss*, Margaret Herrick Library, Motion Picture Academy of Arts and Sciences, Los Angeles.
10. Gavin Lambert, '*Killer's Kiss*', *Sight and Sound* vol. 25 no. 4 (Spring 1956), p. 198.
11. Edward Dimendberg, *Film Noir and the Spaces of Modernity* (Cambridge, MA: Harvard University Press, 2004), p. 144. All further references are to this edition, and page numbers are indicated in the text.
12. Maurice Rapf, 'A Talk with Stanley Kubrick about *2001*', in Gene D. Phillips (ed.), *Stanley Kubrick Interviews* (Jackson: University Press of Mississippi, 2001), p. 77.
13. Dana Polan, 'Materiality and Sociality in *Killer's Kiss*', in Mario Falsetto (ed.), *Perspectives on Stanley Kubrick* (New York: G. K. Hall, 1996), p. 93.

Part Three

KUBRICK, HARRIS, DOUGLAS

I. The Criminal and the Artist

French critics Raymond Borde and Etienne Chaumeton once argued that most examples of film noir are told more or less from the perspective of criminals or psychopaths. If we accept this argument, several of Kubrick's movies have something noir-like about them, including *Lolita*, *Dr. Strangelove*, *A Clockwork Orange* and *The Shining*. The list could be extended to *2001*, where parts of the action are viewed from the point of view of a homicidal computer, and to *Barry Lyndon*, whose eponymous hero grows up to become a rogue and a scoundrel. The most obvious case, however, is *The Killing*, which Kubrick regarded as his first truly professional film.

Soon after Kubrick and James Harris formed a partnership and set up an office on West 57th Street in New York, Harris went to a nearby bookstore and picked up a copy of Lionel White's *Clean Break*, a thriller about a race-track robbery, told from the point of view of the criminals, which he brought to Kubrick as a potential source for their first production. Part of the book's appeal for Kubrick no doubt lay in its setting at a sporting event but the plot was also an attraction because one of the directors he admired, John Huston, had recently made the most influential of all heist movies, *The Asphalt Jungle*. Both he and Harris were intrigued by the jazzy, non-chronological time scheme of White's narrative, which could be reproduced and even improved upon in a film. Harris quickly located White's agent and spent $10,000 for the motion-picture rights, in the process outmanoeuvring no less a personage than Frank Sinatra, who had been dithering over buying the novel for one of his own projects.

Lionel White had begun his career as a true-crime writer for the pulps and was good at creating suspenseful, 'cinematic' plots (a later film noir based on one of his novels is *The Money Trap* [1966], directed by Burt Kennedy). What Kubrick needed in addition, as his previous two films had shown, was someone who could provide vivid characters and pungent dialogue. To this end he had a brilliant idea: he suggested that Harris-Kubrick hire Jim Thompson, the darkest of all the *maudit* authors in the world of pulp crime fiction. Thompson's unsettling series of paperbacks for Lion Books – including *The Killer inside Me* (1952), *Savage Night* (1953) and *A Hell of a Woman* (1954) – are told from the point of view of psychopaths or disintegrating personalities, and are situated artistically somewhere in the subversive borderland between trash and the avant-garde; as Robert Polito has put it, all the Thompson crime novels are 'fueled by a lurid intelligence that bulldozes distinctions between sensational and serious culture. Like Weegee's photographs of spectacles and murders . . . [they] revel in their own shaky, contradictory status' (p. 4). This was precisely the sensibility that inspired *Killer's Kiss*, and it gives *The Killing* its distinctive tone.

In 1955, Kubrick and the alcoholic, forty-nine-year-old Thompson began work in New York on an adaptation of White's novel, initially entitled *Day of Violence* and then *Bed of Fear*. Kubrick wrote a treatment, breaking the action down into sequences and leaving Thompson to provide most of the dialogue. (Harris also made contributions.) Although Thompson would continue to work with Kubrick on later projects, he was reportedly apoplectic when he saw the credits for the completed movie, which listed Kubrick as the author of the screenplay and Thompson himself, in smaller print, as a secondary contributor. To anyone familiar with either Lionel White's novel or Thompson's fiction, this credit seems to understate Thompson's importance. Kubrick and Thompson obviously shared a black-comic viewpoint and an interest in sadomasochistic relationships, but the film's dialogue, especially in scenes involving the bickering married couple George and Sherry Peatty (Elisha Cook Jr and Marie Windsor), has the true Thompson ring:

GEORGE: I been kinda sick today. I keep getting pains in my stomach.

SHERRY: Maybe you've got a hole in it, George, do you suppose you have?

GEORGE: A hole in it? How would I get a hole in it?

SHERRY: How would you get a hole in your head? Fix me a drink, George, I'm beginning to get pains myself.

GEORGE: Sherry, can't I ever say anything at all without you joking about it?

SHERRY: Hurry up with that drink, George. The pains are getting worse.

The screenplay preserves the basic time scheme of the novel, which, like the movie, deals with ex-con Johnny Clay's attempt to organise a band of amateurs to help him pull off a $2-million robbery. ('I'm avoiding the one mistake that most thieves make,' Johnny explains in the book. 'These men, the ones who are in the deal with me – none of them are professional crooks. They all have jobs, they all live seemingly decent, normal lives. But they all have money problems and they all have larceny in them.') The film, however, pays less attention than White had done to Johnny's personal history and motivations, and it changes the novel's ending, in which Johnny is shot and killed by George Peatty. It also changes or eliminates certain of White's characters. In the novel, Marvin Unger is a court stenographer and an anal personality who is seething with class resentment and has no particular attachment to Johnny. Michael Henty (O'Reilly in the film) is a gambler who has both a wife and a daughter to support. George Peatty is a big man, and his wife, Sherry, is a diminutive vixen, who is having an affair with both the petty gangster Val Cannon and the corrupt cop Randy Kennan. (When Cannon discovers her knowledge of the impending race-track robbery, he beats the information out of her.) As in the case of most movie adaptations, the screenplay is more economical than the novel, eliminating minor characters, simplifying the story and quickening the pace of the action; at the same time, it amplifies and places greater emphasis on sexual motives – Unger's passion for Johnny, George's jealousy and sense of inferiority, Sherry's desire to hold on to a virile younger man – all of which threaten the success of the robbery. This stress on sexual desire accounts for the film's early title, *Bed of Fear*, and for the large number of scenes played on or around beds.

When the script was submitted for the approval of the Production Code Administration, the Hollywood censors overlooked its sexual innuendos, including the implied homosexuality of Marvin Ungar (Jay C. Flippen). The PCA wrote to Harris warning that the film should limit itself to firearms 'for which a license can be obtained', which meant that the race-track robbery could involve no automatic weapons. Kubrick wrote back, complaining that in Samuel Fuller's recent film, *The House of Bamboo* (1955), 'Robert Ryan uses a German P38 pistol, which is, as far as I know, a fully automatic weapon.' (In the completed film, Sterling Hayden uses a sawn-off shotgun with a machine-gun grip.) The censors were equally concerned because one of the robbers in the film is a policeman. Harris-Kubrick agreed to the PCA suggestion that the script should be read by Captain Stanley Sheldon of the LAPD for 'any suggestion he may have regarding the character'.[1] Whether or not Sheldon offered comments, nothing was changed, and one of the best jokes in the script remains in the film. As patrolman Kennan is about to leave for the race track on the day of the robbery, a woman in a housecoat comes running up, shouting 'Officer, oh thank heaven! Come quick! They're killing each other!' Kennan drives off, leaving the woman standing in the street. The only remaining censorship problem had to do with the word 'nigger', almost never heard in films, in a scene dealing with an altercation between a hired gunman and a black parking-lot attendant. Harris-Kubrick was told that the word could remain only if the attendant reacted to it in an overtly hostile manner.

Once PCA approval was obtained, Kubrick and his associates moved to Los Angeles for the filming. Kubrick's earlier, shoe-string productions had taught him virtually every craft involved in the making of motion pictures, but *The Killing*, despite its cheapness, gave him the invaluable assistance of professional technicians and an experienced Hollywood crew.

There were no problems with the sound recording and the camera was supplied with a dolly that Kubrick used impressively. The studio orchestra that performed Gerald Fried's driving, Stravinsky-esque jazz score included such musicians as André Previn, Pete Candoli and Shelly Manne. The only tension grew out of Kubrick's relationship with his director of photography, Lucien Ballard, who had previously worked with Josef von Sternberg and who later become Sam Peckinpah's favoured cameraman. Kubrick didn't belong to the cinematographers' union and wasn't allowed to photograph the film (except for a few hand-held shots), but he clashed with Ballard over camera lenses and *découpage*, always asserting final authority. At one point he completely rejected the location footage Ballard and his crew had shot at Bay Meadows race track in San Francisco and sent his friend and associate producer Alexander Singer to the track, where Singer single-handedly photographed a horse race using the same type of Eymo camera that he and Kubrick had employed in *Day of the Fight*.[2]

    The film offers plenty of evidence that Kubrick's photographic decisions were correct. As in most of his other work, he realistically motivates the lighting, but his realism usually results in a boldly exaggerated effect: Val Cannon (Vince Edwards) and Sherry Peatty face one another over a table lamp like figures in a horror movie; Mike O'Reilly (Joe Sawyer) leans forward under a lamp and we see every line of his face and every crinkle of his bent cigarette; the criminal gang gathers around a table lit by a single overhead bulb, and the black limbo around them prefigures the surreal 'War Room' in *Dr. Strangelove*. Kubrick also moves the camera in vivid fashion. Perhaps the most striking instances are the sequences involving George and Sherry, the first of which, running for over five minutes, is composed of only five shots, one of them a very brief close-up. In a fine analysis, Mario Falsetto has pointed out how the succession of long takes and leisurely movements across the room tends to 'efface the passage of time', providing the viewer with a feeling of real duration in a film that otherwise juggles the chronology and urgently moves from one place to another.[3] At other junctures, the motion of camera and characters is more sweeping and energetic. Near the end of the film, when the gang is waiting for Johnny to appear with the loot from the robbery, the camera moves restlessly around the room along with George Peatty, viewing him from a distance as he walks away and looks out a window, framing the whisky glass in his hand as he walks into the extreme foreground, and occasionally pausing to linger on other characters as he walks past them. In many other cases, the moving shots have an unusually ostentatious quality because Kubrick employs a wide-angle lens and a low camera level in conjunction with fairly rapid lateral or forward-backward tracking motions. The short lens, which Kubrick insisted upon in an early argument with Ballard, distorts both time and perspective; thus when Johnny Clay walks forward past a row of motel cabins, he looms slightly above us and seems to take unnaturally broad steps, like a giant striding across deep space. Shots of this sort are perfectly in keeping with the relentless march of the film's narration and the pulsing rhythm of Fried's music, helping to create an atmosphere of thrusting power.

Lateral movements of the camera, which become a motif in the film, have a similar quality, but their slightly weird look also has something to do with the way Kubrick treats objects or people in the extreme foreground. In the opening scene, we move first right and then left with Marvin Ungar as he walks past a background of race-track cashiers and isolated betters, while in the foreground, almost at the point of the picture-plane, motionless figures slide across the screen like the bars of a cage. These figures face the camera and look above it, as if studying the racing results posted on a wall; the camera seems to be inside the wall, viewing everything from an 'impossible' position similar to the one Kubrick often used in the static shots of *Killer's Kiss*. The same effect can be seen at later points. When Johnny Clay is introduced, the camera frames his hand opening a bottle of beer and then pans and tracks to the right as he steps back, turns and crosses the entire length of a three-room apartment, speaking to someone off screen as he moves past a shadowy foreground of window curtains, wall ornaments and walls between rooms. The basic technique dates back to at least the 1930s, when Hollywood films often created a kind of optical wipe by tracking with a character past a wall between two rooms of a set; in this case, however, partly because of the low camera level and the wide-angle lens, and partly because we slide past items of decor that seem to be attached to or lined up against a transparent fourth wall, the movement looks especially bizarre.

Such things are probably to be expected from a director who began his career as a photographer. More surprising is the unusually high calibre of the acting in the film. This was the first picture in which Kubrick had the benefit of an experienced cast, most of whom were often cast in film noir. Johnny Clay's touchingly insecure girlfriend Faye is played by Colleen Gray, who had appeared in *Kiss of Death*, *Nightmare Alley* (1947) and *Kansas City Confidential* (1952); the gambler-cop Randy Kennan is Ted de Corsia, who had often been cast as a heavy, most memorably in *The Lady from Shanghai* and *The Naked City*; the sad-faced gangster Leo is Jay Adler, who had worked in *Cry Danger* (1951), *Scandal Sheet* (1952), *99 River Street* (1953) and *Murder Is My Beat* (1955); the bartender Mike O'Reilly is Joe Sawyer, who had been a tough guy in *Gilda* (1946); the minor-league crook Val Cannon is Vince Edwards, who had acted handsome killers in *Rogue Cop* (1954) and *The Night Holds Terror* (1955); and Joe Piano, the owner of a cheap motel, is Tito Vuolo, who had impersonated mobsters or working-class Italians in *The Enforcer* (1951) and many other hardboiled films.

The names of most of these actors were unfamiliar to the public, but their faces had been seen so often in crime pictures that they immediately evoked vivid personalities. As I've already noted, they were joined by a couple of less familiar figures who greatly enhance the grotesque atmosphere: Kola Kwariani as Maurice, the strong man hired to distract race-track police, and Timothy Carey as Nikki, the sharpshooter hired to kill the lead horse in the Lansdowne Stakes. More centrally important are Sterling Hayden as Johnny, a slight variation on the character Hayden had played in *The Asphalt Jungle*; Marie Windsor as Sherry, a tough, sexy woman similar to the ones Windsor had embodied in *Force of Evil* (1948) and *The Narrow Margin* (1952); and the iconic Elisha Cook Jr as George, a homicidal little man of the sort Cook had created again and again following his indelible portrayal of Wilmer in *The Maltese Falcon* (1941). All three of these actors were typecast, and yet their performances were never better. Hayden, with his ham-sized fists, booming voice and sailor's gait (he was a former ship's captain and a lifelong sailor), lends an air of proletarian nobility to the leading role, but Kubrick seems to have encouraged him to behave in a less sentimental fashion than John Huston had done, understating the scenes in which he demonstrates kindness (as when he tells Joe Piano that his son Patsy is doing well at Alcatraz, or when he sits on Marvin Ungar's bed and wishes him goodbye), and emphasising his physical energy and strength of will. Windsor and Cook, meanwhile, play their roles on the knife-edge of absurdity, pushing slightly beyond realistic convention and into caricature.

At the most general level, the style of *The Killing* as a whole can be described in terms of a clash between the 'rational' qualities of its jigsaw-puzzle plot and the 'irrational' qualities of its pulp eroticism and black-comic absurdity. One of the places where this clash is most evident is in the relationship between the portentous narration and the decidedly grotesque *mise en scène*. The style of narration was quite familiar to audiences of the time, having been widely used in Louis de Rochement's documentary-like crime dramas at 20th Century-Fox in the years after World War II, and in radio and TV police-procedurals such as *Mr. District Attorney* and *Highway Patrol* in the 1950s. Jack Webb's just-the-facts narration of *Dragnet* is descended from the technique, but the particular vocal style in *The Killing* was associated above all with news or documentary announcers, who were chosen on the basis of their deep, authoritative voices and featureless enunciation. Kubrick's own *Day of the Fight* had employed *CBS News* announcer Douglas Edwards as its narrator, and the early scenes of *The Killing*, in which we see documentary race-track footage and hear a narrative voice, are very similar in feeling to that film. But Kubrick was also aware that such voices had been parodied in the 'News on the March' segment of *Citizen Kane*. Perhaps for that reason, his crime film, which manipulates time in a fashion that owes something to *Kane*, allows the tonal disparity between the narration and the dramatic action to create an ironic effect.

The nameless narrator of *The Killing* tells the story in the past tense and from an omniscient perspective, withholding at least one important piece of information (Randy Kennan's particular role in the heist) and ceasing his commentary at the point when the story reaches a double climax, with the killing of Sherry and the fiasco at the airport. On one occasion, he explains what a character is thinking: 'He began to feel as if he had as much effect on the final outcome of the operation as a single piece of a jumbled jigsaw puzzle has to its predetermined final design.' At a few other junctures, he tries to build suspense: 'At seven that morning, Johnny Clay began what might be the final day of his life.' In general, however, his function is simply to make it easier for us to follow the complicated time scheme. Everything we see transpires during a single week, but the plot is designed to follow an individual character's activity on a specific day and then jump backward or forward in time to follow another character on the same day.[4] To make sure that the audience is properly oriented, the narrator is aided on the day of the robbery by a public-address announcer at the race track, whom we hear making the same announcement of the Lansdowne Stakes at five different points, usually accompanied by the same footage of horses being led out to the starting gate. Viewers who are sufficiently attentive (or obsessive) can use these cues to try and fit together the pieces of the plot, but in so doing they will discover anomalies. Mario Falsetto has pointed out two manifest errors: Johnny Clay's farewell to Marvin Ungar in Marvin's apartment takes place 'at 7.00am', but in the next sequence the narrator says that Johnny arrived at the airport at 'exactly 7.00am'. The shoot-out between George Peatty and Val Cannon takes place shortly after 7.15pm, but in the next sequence the narrator says that Johnny arrived at Joe Piano's motel 'forty minutes before, at 6.25'.[5]

Was the normally well-organised Kubrick simply nodding when the pieces of the film were put together, or did he intend to suggest that the narration is unreliable? There's no completely satisfactory answer to the question, but I suspect he regarded the narration as a mere expository device and was inclined to subtly joke about its authority. The film obviously wants us to decipher a temporal puzzle, but its convoluted plot is only a clever variation on a clichéd set of genre conventions, aimed at satisfying our rational impulses while releasing a darker, more perverse energy. Much of the pleasure derives from the way an almost military plan for committing a robbery is presented as a dreamlike montage – a shattered form of storytelling that allows us to become absorbed in the fascinating, sometimes lurid, grace notes of particular images, settings and scenes.

As one minor example, notice something as commonplace as Joe Piano's motel, a real-life setting that nicely conveys a sense of rootless poverty in Los Angeles. As Johnny pulls up to the office, one of the nearby doors opens and an ordinary-looking woman who seems to be a prostitute walks out, followed by a man in work clothes. When Johnny enters his rude, clapboard cabin, a carpenter's notation, '78x09', is still chalked on the inside of the door. A similar rawness inflects the scenes involving Nikki, who has heavily lidded eyes, a grin that freezes into a rictus and a habit of speaking hipster slang through his teeth. 'Yeah, Pops,' he says to Johnny, 'you could take care of a whole roomful of people with that gun.' (Later in the film, a similar gun does just that.) When he and Johnny converse, we become aware of vividly contrasting rhythms: Nikki lazily strokes the puppy in his arms while Johnny delivers an unusually long speech at top speed and in near monotone, describing the entire plan and building to an absurdist climax: 'Suppose you do get picked up? What have you done? You've shot a horse. It isn't first-degree murder, in fact it isn't even murder – I don't know what it is. The best they could get you on would be inciting a riot or shooting horses out of season.'

Nikki's later interaction with a black parking-lot attendant is more disconcerting. The scene is designed to create a perverse, Hitchcock-style suspense, forcing us against our normal sympathies to root for the bad guy: we want Nikki to get rid of the attendant, who is an impediment to the robbery plan. The attendant, however, is a sympathetic black man acted by James Edwards, who had previously appeared in Stanley Kramer's *Home of the Brave* in which he plays a psychosomatically paralysed soldier who is shocked out of his paralysis by an Army psychologist who deliberately calls him 'nigger'. (Edwards also appeared as a boxer in Robert Wise's *The Set Up* and as a psychologically traumatised Korean War veteran in *The Manchurian Candidate* [1962].) Kubrick does everything to encourage our sympathy for him – he's a handsome young war veteran with a lame leg, who seems intelligent but whose only employment is a menial job. Nikki, on the other hand, is a smarmy, manipulative fellow who drives a sportscar and is bent on shooting a horse. When Nikki first tries to gain entrance to the closed lot, the attendant towers over him and looks excessively angry, as if he were neurotically asserting an ability to say no to a white man. In response, Nikki adopts the outrageous stratagem of pretending to be a fellow wounded veteran – a paraplegic, no less, who fought in the Battle of the Bulge – at the same moment stuffing money in the attendant's pocket. The attendant now becomes subservient, almost fawningly apologetic. First, he brings Nikki a programme for the race, then a horseshoe for luck. 'I sure do appreciate the way you treated me, Mister,' he says. His attempt to make conversation about the horses and the weather feels weakly motivated, annoying and even a little embarrassing. The combination of deference and obtuseness – plus the danger of the situation and the fact that the race is about to start – makes the audience even more anxious for him to go away. Nikki accomplishes this goal by dropping his mask of cordiality and calling the attendant 'nigger' – a word that threatens our engagement with the mechanisms of suspense. The attendant limps off and angrily throws the horseshoe to the ground, his gesture eventuating in poetic justice: after Nikki shoots Red Lightning, he backs his car over the horseshoe, gets a flat tyre and is shot by a policeman. Nevertheless, Nikki's insult and the attendant's slightly odd behaviour linger uncomfortably in the mind, making *The Killing* more slyly cruel in its humour than an ordinary thriller.

The scenes between George and Sherry are even more memorable, almost to the point where the film's subplot becomes more compelling than the robbery itself. A savage parody of marriage, their relationship is treated with deadpan solemnity. During the couple's first conversation, the calm gaze of the low-level camera and the temporal duration of the shots serve to intensify the perversity of the situation. The sequence is worth study because of the way it treats cinematic space, developing into a graceful dance between the camera and the actors. At the beginning, the narrator tells us with his customary stern seriousness that it was precisely 7.15pm when George arrived home. We see George entering a narrow hallway and putting down his lunchbox. As in the earlier shot when Johnny Clay walks across his apartment, the camera moves with the character as he crosses the room, passing a door frame, a lamp and various shadowed objects in the extreme foreground. (The sequence involving Johnny ended with a conversation between him and Fay near their bed; this was followed by a sequence showing Mike O'Reilly returning home and crossing his apartment to talk with his bedridden wife; now we come to George, who arrives home to find Sherry in bedclothes.)

Both George and the camera come to a stop as they arrive at Sherry, who reclines on a lounger in the foreground, leafing idly through a glossy magazine. To borrow the title of one of Jim Thompson's novels, she's a 'swell-looking babe' – a large, voluptuous presence exaggerated by the wide-angle lens and the low level of the shot. Wearing a low-cut sleeping gown and arranged in a pose that offers her ample bosom to the camera, she seems to have been lolling around all day, although she must have spent lots of time on her artificial lashes, lipstick and dyed blonde, permanent-waved hair. The apartment behind her is small – a double bed in the corner takes up most of the space – but more elaborately decorated than any other room in the film, indicating Sherry's need for domestic finery: we see flowered wallpaper, a parrot in a cage, a TV set, a pair of bed lamps with pagoda-shaped shades and a couple of framed Oriental prints hanging over the bed in a his-and-hers arrangement. Jazz music is playing softly on a radio. Sherry reacts with mild disgust when George bends down to kiss her on the cheek, and when he sits near her feet, she looks like a pulp-fiction

dominatrix (the ideal woman of George's fantasies). She speaks in a tone of weary contempt, without even looking up from the magazine. A potentially violent undercurrent runs beneath both characters' words, but Cook and Windsor play most of the scene in soft, intimate fashion, giving a subtextual weight to every line they speak. One more turn of the dramatic screw and we would be in Pinter or Albee country.

After mixing a drink and telling Sherry about a happily married couple he has noticed that day, George says 'I'm tired', and we cut to a new angle as he rises and crosses to the birdcage at the other side of the room. Sherry follows and when they stand facing one another, she looks six inches taller than him. She adopts a mock sweetness: 'You want me to call you Papa, isn't that it, George? And you want to call me Mamma.' At this point, the pace of the conversation and the level of anger rise slightly, the two actors briefly overlapping one another, the caged parrot (vaguely reminiscent of the cockatoo in *Citizen Kane*) squawking in counterpoint. 'You know all the answers,' George says in lame rebuke, and Sherry steps on his line. 'You go right ahead,' she says. 'Of course it might be the last words you ever say, but I'll try to kill you as painlessly as possible.' Ignoring her, George explains that he has to go out tonight. 'I don't suppose there's anything for dinner.' She crosses to the window, lights a cigarette and tells him sure there is, there's a whole elaborate menu, and it's all down at the grocery store.

Throughout, Windsor does an amusing job of letting us see how Sherry manipulates George by shifting from one character type to another. Depending on her needs, she can become a castrating vixen, a scorned woman, a temptress, and even a loving companion. 'Tell me something, will you, Sherry?' George asks. 'Tell me one thing. Why did you ever marry me?' Sherry frowns and finishes her drink, the ice tinkling in the glass. 'Oh, George,' she says in a patronising and self-pitying voice, 'when a man has to ask his wife a question like that, well, he just hadn't better, that's all.' She lounges on the edge of the bed and we cut to a low angle as George again sits near her feet. 'You used to love me,' he says, 'at least, you said you did.' She reminds him that he 'made a memorable statement too,' when he promised that they would become rich. 'Not that I really care about such things, you understand, as long as I have a big, handsome, intelligent brute like you.' George tells her that they're going to have money, 'hundreds of thousands'. At first Sherry is derisive: 'Of course you are, George. Did you put the right address on the envelope when you sent it to the North Pole?' Then she realises he's serious. He gets up and crosses in front of her, standing partly out of frame in the foreground, the glass in his hand visible at the right corner of the screen. Sherry looks up at him and for a moment the relative size of the two characters is reversed, so that George seems to dominate. 'You've never been a liar, George,' Sherry says, almost to herself. 'You don't have enough imagination to lie.'

In a brief, wordless close-up, George refuses to comment. Cut to a new angle, looking across the room from the vantage of Sherry's dressing table. 'I see,' she says. Giving a little flip to the silk handkerchief in her hand, she rises from the bed and flounces over to her dressing table, where she sits, turns on a lamp and begins combing her hair in the mirror. She's once again the largest figure in the frame. George meekly follows and sits behind her. Between them, in the distance, we can see the marriage bed and the two Oriental prints of a man and a woman. 'Sherry, Sherry, honey,' George softly pleads. 'Don't be so sore at me . . . . You know I'm crazy about you!' Sherry takes a mascara brush from a small case, spits on it and begins amplifying her already enormous lashes. 'Don't you be surprised if I'm not here when you get home,' she says in a pouting tone. 'Don't you be at all surprised.' Quietly, evenly, George warns her, 'You better be here, you hear me, Sherry? If I ever caught you with another man . . .' Sherry now transforms herself into a neglected wife: 'But why? You have no use for me . . . . You say one thing and then you do another.' George hesitates. 'Well, I could tell you a little bit about it, I guess, but you have to promise to keep it quiet.' Sherry turns to look at him, smiles and speaks in a honeyed, submissive tone: 'Why of course, darling.'

The image immediately dissolves to a close shot of a rumpled bed in the apartment of Sherry's lover, Val Cannon, a man she would probably describe as a 'big, handsome, intelligent brute'. Val wears a black muscle shirt and has apparently been entertaining another woman; in his presence, Sherry becomes a clingy, insecure girlfriend. After they make love (signified by a fade to black and a rising sound of bongo drums), we see her cuddled next to him on a couch, lit by a table lamp that brings out her age and vulnerability. We begin to realise that Sherry's previous scene with George is motivated by something more than a desire for money; she hopes to buy Val by showing him how to hijack the loot from the race-track robbery.

Every encounter between Sherry and George is governed by a barely repressed contest for power, but the two actors never allow this contest to eventuate in loud voices or violence. The inevitable explosion is saved for a point near the end of the film, when George bursts into a crowded room, firing a gun at Val and yelling 'The jerk's right here!' Val's shotgun goes off, leaving bodies strewn around like the devastated mannequins in *Killer's Kiss*. George is the only man left standing; mortally wounded, his face shredded with buckshot, he summons all his strength for a last confrontation with Sherry. Kubrick uses a hand-held camera to show George's subjective point of view as he stumbles out of the apartment. Then we see George from Johnny's point of view as he sprawls on the hood of Johnny's car and staggers across the road to his own vehicle. The two men drive off in opposite directions, barely avoiding the police.

George's final moments with Sherry have exactly the same black-comic tone as before. The sequence begins with a low-angle shot of Sherry, wearing a black slip and packing two bags on her unmade bed. Muted saxophone jazz comes from a radio. She hears someone enter, turns and calls out in the voice of a happy housewife, 'How'd it go, dear?' Seen from an even lower angle, George staggers through the door, his face and shirt bloody, a gun in his hand. He bumps into the caged parrot behind him, who squawks, 'Watch out! Pretty Polly!' In close-up, George speaks softly. 'Sherry! Why? Why did you do it?' Ignoring the blood and the gun, Sherry tries to conceal her fear with a ludicrously sweet reply. 'Do? Do what, dear? I don't know what you're talking about. I was just getting some clothes ready to go to the cleaners.' When George weaves and stares back at her, she pauses, drops the smile and shifts into a nagging tone that conceals an undercurrent of guilt. 'So you had to be stupid. You couldn't even play it smart when you had a gun pointed at you. Well, you better get smart and get out of here while you can still walk.' With his last breath, George says, 'I love, you, Sherry.' Not without some concern, she replies, 'George, you better go on and go. You look terrible.' The parrot squawks again and George shoots. With her dying words, Sherry once again attacks his masculinity: 'It isn't fair,' she says in a self-pitying whine as she grasps her stomach. 'I never had anybody but you. Not a real husband, just a bad joke without a punch line.'

Nothing ever changes for George and Sherry, nor for Johnny and Fay, who find themselves the victims of another 'bad joke' at the airport. Because of its dark, twist-of-fate conclusion, *The Killing* has often been treated by critics as a template for Kubrick's subsequent work, which usually involves a careful plan that goes disastrously awry. Among Kubrick's many commentators, Thomas Allen Nelson places the strongest emphasis on this theme, describing the failure of the robbery plan and the other failed schemes in later pictures in terms of a metaphysical conflict between order and contingency. Of course, the capture of Johnny Clay is determined in the last analysis by the Hollywood Production Code, which insisted that crime could not pay; even so, Kubrick chose to have the robbery foiled not by methodical police work but by the capricious winds of fortune. The closing scenes consist of nothing more than a quick series of ironic accidents: a suitcase with a weakened clasp; an officious airline attendant who insists that the suitcase is too large to be brought into the passenger compartment of an aeroplane; a rich old lady who baby-talks to her poodle and then allows the dog to dash across the airport runway; and an overloaded baggage cart that swerves to avoid the dog, tipping over the suitcase and scattering $100,000 into the swirling wind of a propeller. These events have more in common with the existentialist absurdity of John Huston's *Treasure of the Sierra Madre* (1945) than with the bloody climax of Lionel White's *Clean Break*, in which a jealous George Peatty hunts down Johnny Clay at the airport, shoots him and then accidentally runs into a moving propeller. In Kubrick's version, Johnny is shocked and numbed, as if he has glimpsed a cosmic truth. Like a hulking zombie, he is guided through the airport waiting room by the diminutive Fay, who tries unsuccessfully to hail a cab. 'Johnny,' she cries, 'you've got to run!' Johnny simply turns and looks at two plainclothes cops advancing towards him, their weapons drawn; 'Yeah,' he says in a dead voice. 'What's the difference?'

In my own view, the failure of the robbery has less to do with contingency than with the evident passions and weaknesses of several of the criminals – in particular the lack of intelligence and the combustible mixture of lust, greed and jealousy in the triangle created by George, Sherry and Val. The robbery develops alongside a criminal counterplot involving the unfaithful wife and her lover, and the gang's success is momentarily threatened by Marvin Ungar's love for Johnny, which causes Marvin to show up drunk at the track on a day when he is supposed to be out of sight. But even without these sexual complications, most people in the original audience knew that the criminals would never be allowed to get away with their loot. Maybe on some level the audience actually *wanted* the criminals to fail. Kubrick calls attention to that possibility in the film's most self-reflexive scene, which is staged in a chess club similar to the one Kubrick had belonged to in New York: Maurice, sounding like a film-noir version of Friedrich Nietzsche, tells Johnny that, 'In this life we have to be like everybody else – the perfect mediocrity, no better, no worse. I often thought that the gangster and the artist are the same in the eyes of the masses. They're admired and hero worshipped, but there is always present an underlying wish to see them destroyed at the peak of their glory.'

As if to undercut the somewhat pretentious effect of this statement, Johnny, who is Kubrick's *alter ego* in the sense that he masterminds a complex plot, gives a wry, nonsensical reply: 'Yeah, like the man said, life is like a glass of tea, huh?' An air of doomed inevitability nevertheless hovers about the film, the only question being in what particular ways the plan will go wrong. The seeds of destruction are planted quite early, in the scenes between George and Sherry, and the demands of the genre are satisfied by an overdetermined conflict between rational planning and primal emotion. This conflict is at the core of Kubrick's later films, though it's seldom dramatised more effectively than here, where the split between disciplined reason and wild instinct is starkly clear. Where *The Killing* is concerned, the criminal was required to be a failure, but the artist responsible for the film succeeded.

II. Ant Hill

There are vexed questions of authorship surrounding *Paths of Glory*, but everyone agrees that the film originated with Kubrick during his abortive stay at MGM in the mid-1950s, when he proposed to James Harris that they adapt a novel Kubrick remembered reading as a teenager in his father's library: Humphrey Cobb's *Paths of Glory* (1935), based on the true story of five French soldiers in World War I who were falsely accused of cowardice and shot by a firing squad. The novel had been inspired by a 1934 *New York Times* report of a recent French trial in which the two surviving widows of the soldiers were awarded approximately seven cents each in reparation; of no great literary importance, it nevertheless provided a harrowing account of trench warfare and a disturbing picture of how generals treated their troops as cannon fodder. Upon publication, it enjoyed a favourable critical reception in the US and spawned an unsuccessful 1938 Broadway theatrical adaptation by the well-known playwright and screenwriter Sidney Howard; by the 1950s, however, it was virtually forgotten. Kubrick believed it had cinematic possibilities and knew that, since it was unfamiliar to the contemporary audience, it could be easily acquired and freely adapted. He and Jim Thompson developed a script, which was later revised by Calder Willingham. As we've seen in an earlier chapter, however, MGM rejected the project. The film was ultimately financed by United Artists – this entirely because of Kirk Douglas, who, after reading the

Kubrick–Thompson–Willingham script, agreed to star in the picture on condition that Kubrick would direct other films for Douglas's production company.

Besides originating with Kubrick, the completed film is everywhere marked by Kubrick's stylistic and thematic preoccupations – among them a skilful deployment of wide-angle tracking shots, an ability to make a realistic world seem strange, an interest in the grotesque, and a fascination with the underlying irrationality of orderly, almost glamorous military action. World War I is a particularly apt subject for Kubrick because it was generated by a meaningless tangle of nationalist alliances and resulted in over 8 million deaths, most of which can be blamed on benighted politicians and incompetent generals, who arranged massive bombardments and short, suicidal charges across open ground. As literary historian Paul Fussel has pointed out in *The Great War and Modern Memory* (1997), one of the war's grisliest and most symptomatic events, the Battle of the Somme in 1916, known to ordinary troops as 'The Great Fuck-Up', was the largest and in many ways most senseless military engagement in human history. It began with a sustained, one-week shelling of German trenches from over 15,000 guns but, when the shelling stopped and the British charged, the outmanned Germans simply pulled their machine guns from deep, well-engineered tunnels and mowed them down. On that single day, 60,000 of the British were killed, and it was almost a week before 20,000 others who lay mortally wounded in no man's land stopped crying out for help.

André Breton derived the concept of 'black humour', which is central to Kubrick's work, from the writings of the proto-surrealist Jaques Vache, a soldier in the French army during World War I. It isn't surprising that *Paths of Glory* was greatly admired by another surrealist, Luis Buñuel, and was just as greatly disliked by the French government, which in 1958 was involved in the Algerian war. Through political pressure, the French managed to have the picture dropped from the Berlin Film Festival and banned from theatres in France and Switzerland for two decades. Their reasons were obvious. Like Cobb's novel, the film involves the French high command's attempt to achieve a 'breakthrough' by attacking a heavily fortified mound of dirt called the 'Ant Hill'. (The novel calls it the 'Pimple'.) The attack has no apparent strategic value and is supervised by a vain general, who has been led to believe it might result in a promotion. When the charge is stopped in its tracks, the general orders his artillery to fire upon his own troops. When his order is refused, he tries to have a large number of men shot by a firing squad on the grounds that 'only dead bodies would show the attack was impossible'. Ultimately, he agrees to have three non-commissioned soldiers chosen by their unit officers, tried in summary fashion and shot as examples. After the execution, the general and his immediate superior enjoy a breakfast of croissants in a luxurious chateau and congratulate themselves on how wonderfully the men died. In the last shot, the troops are ordered back to the trenches for another senseless battle.

Paths of Glory is quite different in tone from the most famous of the previous movies about World War I. *All Quiet on the Western Front* (1930) and *Grand Illusion* (1937) take a critical yet humanist approach to the war; the two versions of *The Dawn Patrol* (1930 and 1938) provide spectacular images of aerial combat waged in the spirit of a doomed aristocratic code; and *Sergeant York* (1941) offers populist and patriotic mythologising. To find something similar, we need to compare *Paths of Glory* with Robert Aldrich's *Attack* (1956), which concerns World War II, or with Kubrick's other war films. Here, as elsewhere, Kubrick underlines war's absurdity by making the two sides virtually indistinguishable from one another, as if he were trying to illustrate a famous line from Walt Kelly's *Pogo*, a 1950s' comic strip that satirised the McCarthy era: 'We have met the enemy and he is us.' From the beginning of his career until the end, on the rare occasions in his war pictures when soldiers come face to face with someone from behind enemy lines, that person is either a mirror image or a woman. In *Fear and Desire* and *Full Metal Jacket*, the woman is killed in disturbing fashion. Where *Paths of Glory* is concerned, the conflict is internecine and the enemy simply unseen, consisting of nothing more than lethal gunfire and bombardment emanating from the smoke and darkness at the other side of no man's land; the film deviates from Kubrick's usual pattern only in the sense that, at the conclusion, when the French encounter a female German captive, she becomes less an object of perverse desire and murderous anxiety than a sort of maternal figure, producing a flood of repressed nostalgia and a momentary dissolution of psychic and bodily armour.

In certain other ways, however, *Paths of Glory* is quite atypical of Kubrick – most notably in the sense that, aside from *Spartacus*, which also stars Kirk Douglas and which Kubrick later disowned, it is the only one of his pictures that centres on an admirable character with whom the audience can feel a comfortable identification. Colonel Dax, as portrayed by Douglas, is not only given more close-ups and point-of-view shots than anyone else in the movie, he is also a paragon of heroic virtue. A handsome and brave officer, he takes the front-line position in a deadly charge on the Ant Hill, picking his way through a withering storm of gunfire, weaving around massive casualties and returning to the trenches to try and rally a unit of troops that have remained behind. Before the war, Dax also happens to have been 'perhaps the foremost criminal lawyer in all France'. When corrupt generals select three innocent soldiers to be executed, he passionately and eloquently comes to the men's defence. Against impossible odds, he's never afraid to speak truth to power. Near the beginning of the film, he tells the general in command of the regiment that Samuel Johnson once described patriotism as 'the last refuge of scoundrels' and, at the end, he angrily denounces an even more important general in patented Kirk Douglas style, with the body and face contorted in righteous anger and the voice pitched somewhere between a sob and a shout: 'You're a degenerate, sadistic old man,' he says, 'and you can go to *hell* before I ever apologise to you again!'

In other words, for all its grimness and horror, *Paths of Glory* is also a star vehicle designed to give its audience the pleasures of melodrama – a form Kubrick usually avoided or treated ironically, in the manner of the film noir or the art film. I should pause here to explain that I use the term 'melodrama' to indicate a suspenseful, emotionally charged plot filled with action and last-minute rescues – a plot grounded in moral conflict, in which good usually but not necessarily wins. Melodrama of this sort is the cornerstone of classic Hollywood and of the liberal social problem picture with which Kirk Douglas was sometimes associated. Kubrick, a social pessimist by disposition, disliked it for reasons he articulated in an interview with Michel Ciment: 'Melodrama,' he said, 'uses all the problems of the world, and the difficulties and disasters which befall the characters, to demonstrate that the world is, after all, a benevolent and just place' (p. 163). *Paths of Glory* never goes that far, but it features a benevolent hero who battles evil, who witnesses the positive humanity of ordinary people and who survives to fight another day.

Some critics have argued that Dax is less than a hero because he remains a loyal officer of a corrupt regime. This may be one of the film's subtle ironies, but neither Humphrey Cobb's novel nor the theatrical adaptation by Sidney Howard give us such an upright and courageous character, and neither offer the same emotional consolations. Both earlier versions end abruptly, with the execution of the innocent soldiers (presented off-stage in the case of the play), and in neither does Dax play an especially significant role – at any rate, he doesn't lead an assault across no man's land, and he isn't the defence attorney at the court martial. Humphrey Cobb's depiction of the attack on the Pimple lacks even a vestige of heroic spectacle; when one of the officers climbs out of his trench to signal a charge, à la Douglas in the film, he is decapitated by machine-gun fire and his body falls on the men below. By contrast, the film gives Douglas an opportunity for derring-do and Kubrick the opportunity for bravura tracking and zooming shots across no man's land. It also creates the impression that the survivors in Douglas's unit might have reached the Ant Hill if not for the cowardice of Lieutenant Roget (Wayne Morris), who keeps his men in the trenches.

Surprisingly, the earliest, pre-Kirk Douglas version of the screenplay, which survives in Douglas's papers at the University of Wisconsin, was in at least one respect even more melodramatic. In his autobiography, *The Ragman's Son*, Douglas says that when he and the production crew arrived in Munich, he was given what he thought was a new script, revised by Kubrick with the help of Jim Thompson, containing numerous pages of cheap dialogue and ending with a last-minute reprieve of the three condemned soldiers: '[T]he general's car arrives screeching to halt the firing squad and he changes the men's death sentence to thirty days in the guardhouse. Then my character, Colonel Dax, goes off with the bad guy he has been fighting all through the movie . . . to have a drink, and the general puts his arm around my shoulder.' According to Douglas, when he confronted Harris and Kubrick about the revisions, Kubrick calmly replied, 'I want to make money.' Douglas threw the script across the room and launched into a tirade worthy of his film performances. 'We're going back to the original script,' he declared, 'or we're not making the picture.'[6]

The script that provoked this outburst is undated but signed by Kubrick and Thompson. It ends very much as Douglas says, but is somewhat morally ambiguous in that it makes the villain a bit less ruthless and the hero a bit more political. The last pages involve a conversation between Colonel Dax, who has more or less blackmailed the corps commander into saving the condemned men, and General Rousseau, the division commander who insisted upon the execution and has now been relieved of command (in the released film this character's name is General Mireau). Dax says that he has 'always had the greatest professional respect' for Rousseau, and that it will be 'a great loss to the army' if the general is cast aside. The two men fall silent and walk along together, until Rousseau asks, 'Which of us was on the side of the angels, I wonder?' Dax seems puzzled, and Rousseau explains:

> GEN. ROUSSEAU: Tyranny gave birth to the Magna Carta. Callousness and indifference to human welfare brought about the French Republic. And so on through History. It may be that progress comes really through a kind of challenge. And who is to say that if those men had been shot today, that it wouldn't have been a step towards the end of a certain kind of despotism in the army?
>
> COL. DAX: General, you have a very strange theory there. I am not at all sure I agree with you.
>
> GEN. ROUSSEAU: I'm not at all sure I agree with myself. You know, when they say that man is a rational animal, what they really mean is that he has a limitless ability to rationalize ... I am undoubtedly a very wicked man – but I don't feel wicked inside. Though, I suppose that's a prerequisite for being labeled truly wicked.
>
> COL. DAX: Labels are fine for tin cans, but not for people. I don't know, perhaps every man is as righteous as the circumstances of his life allow him to be.
>
> GEN. ROUSSEAU: That doesn't explain very much, Colonel.
>
> COL. DAX Perhaps there are no explanations . . . . I was just thinking of a conversation I had with a client of mine who was an Atheist. I asked him how he could possibly believe that Christianity was a failure – that it hadn't worked? Very simple, he said. It was never tried . . . .
>
> GEN. ROUSSEAU: Colonel, may I ask you to join me at the Chateau for some coffee?
>
> COL. DAX: I'd be very happy to, sir. I might even suggest something a little stronger, if it isn't too early for you.
>
> ROUSSEAU laughs and puts his arm around DAX's shoulder.
>
> GEN. ROUSSEAU: It isn't too early for me, Colonel. In fact, I'd say it was rather late.
>
> They walk away from the camera. The last fading strains of the band are heard.
>
> THE END [7]

If we look closely at the completed film, we can see how a 'happy' ending similar to this one might have been achieved even in the script Douglas preferred. Two scenes, neither of which is in the source novel or the play, are especially significant. On the eve of the execution, the artillery officer who had been ordered by General Mireau to fire on his own troops comes to Dax's room and says, 'I have something to tell you that may have a great bearing on the court martial.' In the next scene, Dax interrupts a party at the commanding officers' chateau and has a tense argument in the library with General Broulard. 'Oh, by the way,' Dax says towards the end of their confrontation, 'were you aware that General Mireau ordered his own battery to fire on his men?' This remark might have functioned as a dramatic *peripeteia*, enabling Dax to blackmail the high command into giving the three soldiers a nominal sentence in the guardhouse. As the film stands, however, our hero's last-minute effort comes to relatively little – Gerneral Broulard simply assumes that Dax is angling for Mireau's job.

What Douglas wanted, and what he got, was a film based on the second and third drafts of the script, which had undergone revisions by Calder Willingham. Shortly before his death in 1995, Willingham claimed that he was the author of '99%' of *Paths of Glory*; the completed script, he said, contained only two unimportant lines of dialogue by Kubrick and nothing by Jim Thompson (quoted in Polito, p. 405). Thompson's biographer, Robert Polito, has argued that Thompson was responsible for at least half of the movie, and the material retained from the early script I've quoted above supports his argument. It should also be noted that a great deal of the film's dialogue comes straight from Cobb's novel – including most of the big speeches in the trial scene, which Cobb writes in the form of a play. We may never sort out who contributed what to the screenplay, and Kubrick's reported motives for his attempt to change scripts are not convincing. Polito has offered the shrewd suggestion that Kubrick was playing 'ego chess' with Douglas, giving him an early draft in which Dax is a more politically expedient character, in order to make sure that the completed film wouldn't be compromised by further build-up of the star's role (pp. 404–5).

One thing is clear: the making of *Paths of Glory* involved a struggle between director and star. Douglas, who in print has called Kubrick 'a talented shit', portrays himself as the guardian of the film's integrity (p. 305). But Douglas also made sure that the film would be a proper vehicle for his stardom – even to the point of the unwritten rule that virtually every one of his pictures after his breakthrough role in *Champion* had to contain a scene in which he takes off his shirt. Sure enough, in his first scene in *Paths of Glory*, which has no equivalent in either the novel or the play, he is shown naked to the waist, washing his face from a basin of water in his underground bunker. Nearly all the major differences between the novel and the film can be accounted for by a need to build up Douglas's role, giving him plenty of melodramatic actions to perform. The emotionally shattering execution is one of the few places where his character is a marginal figure, witnessing a horror from the sidelines. After the execution, the film departs from the novel by creating two additional scenes – both written by Calder Willingham and used, according to Willingham, despite Kubrick's initial reservations – that give evidence of Colonel Dax's moral authority and of the innate goodness of humanity (neither of these scenes is in the final draft of the script).

Willingham claimed that during the production he argued with Kubrick that 'the stark brutality of ending the film with the execution of the soldiers would be intolerable to an audience and philosophically an empty statement as well' (quoted in Polito, p. 406). Kubrick ultimately agreed, even though the book and the play derived from the book had ended with the execution. In the first of Willingham's added scenes, General Broulard calls Dax to the chateau and allows him to witness General Mireau's humiliation. Mireau draws himself up to attention. 'So that's it!' he says. 'You're making me the goat – the only com-pletely innocent man in this whole affair!' He marches off in a huff, and Broulard offers the regimental commander's job to Dax, who abandons decorum and calls Broulard a degenerate. In the next scene, Dax stands at the window of a roadside café and witnesses his men as they first ogle and hoot at a captured German girl (Susanne Christian, later Christiane Kubrick) and then tearfully join her in singing '*Das Lied vom treuen Husaren*'.

In the last analysis, it might be said that the authorship of *Paths of Glory* has something to do with the tension between Kubrick, a dark satirist, and Douglas, a star whose flamboy-ant acting style and personal worldview were dependant upon melodramatic effects. Both men wanted to be the star, and in this case the clash between the auteur and the actor was reasonably productive. It should be remembered that Douglas was a sincere liberal whose films tend not only to highlight his stardom but also to communicate his social convictions. *Champion*, which gave him stardom, was a left-wing project whose producer was later black-listed; Douglas helped to break the blacklist by crediting Dalton Trumbo for *Spartacus*; and Douglas's personal favourite of all his Bryna productions was another liberal allegory, *Lonely are the Brave* (1962), also scripted by Trumbo. From the scripts of *Paths of Glory*, he and Kubrick fashioned a dark, in some ways melodramatic film that allows Douglas to function as the voice of liberal reason and humanism, a character who tempers Kubrick's harsh, trau-matic view of European history.

The credits for the completed film begin by announcing 'Bryna' production but also say that we are watching a 'Harris-Kubrick' production. Douglas comments wryly on this phenomenon in his autobiography: '[W]herever we went, Stanley made sure they stuck signs saying HARRIS-KUBRICK like FOR RENT signs . . . . It amused me . . . I'm surprised that he didn't want the signs to just say KUBRICK. It amused me less years later when Kubrick told people I was only an employee on *Paths of Glory*' (p. 250). For his own part, Kubrick never responded to Douglas. In an unpublished 1962 interview with Terry Southern, however, he admitted that during the production there was discussion about letting the soldiers escape execution: 'there were some people who said you've got to save the men, but of course it was out of the question . . . . it would just be pointless. Also, of course, it really happened.'[8]

Ultimately, Kubrick might be said to have won his battle for authorship, because *Paths of Glory* is not only a skilful adaptation but also a director's picture in which the total 'per-formance' – acting, photography, *mise en scène*, cutting – is at the heart of the narrative's power. The film greatly intensifies the dramatic force of the novel (and of Sidney Howard's unsuccessful stage version) by eliminating minor characters and paring down the action that leads up to the attack on the Ant Hill. In moving from page to screen, it also achieves a brilliant realisation of the novel's 'cinematic' elements, especially by virtue of Kubrick and cinematographer George Krause's naturalistic location photography and the sharp visual and aural contrasts Kubrick draws between the chateau where the generals man-age the war and the trenches where the war is fought.

Jonathan Rosenbaum has pointed out to me that the Schleissheim Palace just outside Munich where much of *Paths of Glory* was photographed is also a setting in Alain Resnais's *Last Year at Marienbad* (1961). The coincidence is especially interesting if one thinks of the *Marienbad*-like qualities of Kubrick's *The Shining*, which uses a Steadicam to explore the haunted corridors of a vast hotel. All three films depict upper-class intrigues amid the architecture of a decadent past – huge buildings made up of echoing spaces, luxurious furnishings and fascinating geometrical patterns. Where *Paths of Glory* is concerned, Kubrick was to some degree influenced by the elegant, *fin de siècle* settings in the films of Max Ophuls. According to actor Richard Anderson (Major Saint-Aubin in the film), on the first day of shooting Kubrick announced to the cast and crew that Ophuls had just died and that the moving-camera shots in the sequence they were about to perform would be dedicated to him (quoted in LoBrutto, p. 138). The sequence in question (written, according to Robert Polito, chiefly by Jim Thompson) is more dynamically and emphatically edited than a typical Ophuls movie, but it contains important moments when the camera dollies with the actors as they walk around a large room, engaging in a sort of perversely Ophulsian choreography. Kubrick makes excellent use of natural light and, in a style reminiscent of *Citizen Kane*, allows the room's sonic reverberation to make us feel the contrast between close-up and distant voices. The sequence is also noteworthy for the way the editing, camera movement and blocking of the actors help to signal the emotional undercurrents and shifts of tone in the conversation.

First we see a high-angle shot looking down from an immense ceiling as the tall, aristocratic General Mireau (George Macready) crosses a marbled floor to greet Broulard (Adolphe Menjou). 'Hel-lo, George!' Mireau says expansively, and we cut to an eye-level view, the camera moving left as the two men, their chests covered with medals, smile a little too broadly and walk along together, passing an indistinct background of imperial splendour. 'This is splendid! Superb!' says Broulard, his voice echoing off the walls. Mireau smiles modestly. 'Well,' he says, 'I try to create a pleasant atmosphere in which to work.' Broulard keeps up the flattery, almost to the point of suggesting that his compatriot is a little too comfortable: 'You've succeeded marvellously! I wish I had your taste in carpets and pictures!' The camera pans as he and Mireau approach a French-empire table and chairs, where Mireau stops, indicates a seat and turns, revealing a nasty duelling scar on his left cheek. 'You're much too kind, George, much too kind,' he says, his smile fading. 'I really haven't done much.'

A brief series of shot-reverse shots reveals the purpose of the visit: Broulard announces top-secret plans for 'something big', and Mireau, eyes gleaming, hands clasped almost prayerfully, intuits the attack on the Ant Hill. Broulard praises Mireau as a 'mindreader' and remarks, 'Paul, if there's one man in this army who can do this for me, it's you!' But Mireau resists, declaring that it would be 'out of the question' to expect his decimated and fatigued division to hold the Ant Hill, even in the unlikely event that they could capture it. Broulard rises and walks away from the table to a more authoritative position. 'Well, Paul,' he says,

looking back at the seated Mireau. 'There was something else I wanted to tell you; however, I'm sure you'll misunderstand my motives.' Mireau gets up expectantly and the camera dollies forward with him towards Broulard, who circles an eighteenth-century settee in the centre of the room. 'Talk around headquarters,' Broulard says, 'is that you are being considered for head of 12th Corps.' He takes Mireau's arm and they walk forward towards the camera, which dollies backward to keep them in frame. Broulard explains the need for a 'fighting general' as head of the Corps, and points out that Mireau's record is good enough for the promotion; he also implies that any refusal to attack the Ant Hill might have a bad effect on the impending promotion: 'No one would question your opinion – they'd simply get someone else to do the job.' The two men pause at a table, where Mireau, realising what is at stake, abstractedly pours himself a drink. Broulard pats him on the arm: 'So, you shouldn't let this influence your opinion, Paul.' Mireau suddenly becomes aware of what he is doing. 'Cognac?' he offers. 'No thanks, Paul,' Broulard says. 'Not before dinner.'

Broulard suavely takes a seat and a close-up shows him watching Mireau, who, in a wide shot, paces back and forth, his voice pitched like an orator: 'George, I'm responsible for the lives of 8,000 men . . . . The life of any one of those soldiers means more to me than all the stars and decorations and honours in France!' A reverse angle shows Broulard rising and walking into the distance at the other side of the room, where he pauses and turns, rather like a duellist aiming a shot, and raises his own voice: 'You think this attack is absolutely beyond the ability of your men at this time?' In a large close-up, Mireau smiles and speaks quietly: 'I didn't say that, George.' He walks forward, the camera dollying with him as he vigorously announces, 'Nothing is beyond those men, once their fighting spirit is aroused!' He takes Broulard's arm and they turn, walking back across the room, the camera following. They completely circle the settee and move towards the camera as Mireau asks for artillery and replacements to support the attack. Broulard replies, 'We'll see what we can do, if you're sure you can get along with what you have.' He pats Mireau on the back and reassures him, 'You are the man to take the Ant Hill!' The camera stops its movement as the two men turn again and walk off into the distance, where they become silhouetted and slightly conspiratorial figures. Daylight spills from the big windows behind them, leaving soft, long shadows on the marble floor, and their voices become distant echoes. 'When did you say you see this coming off?' Mireau asks. 'No later than the day after tomorrow,' Broulard answers. 'We just might do it!' Mireau says, driving his fist into his hand with a hollow-sounding smack that punctuates the end of the sequence.

The baroque chateau and the graceful movements of the camera have an ironic effect, as if they were illustrating Walter Benjamin's famous observation that every achievement of human culture is also a monument to barbarism. The irony is made explicit when a direct cut takes us to the Ant Hill, a meaningless, undistinguishable mound of dirt on the horizon of a wasteland, seen by an anonymous soldier through a slit in a trench. What follows is a reverse dolly of approximately a minute and a half's duration, showing General Mireau marching forward along the trench, visiting his troops. A litter containing a wounded solder is borne past as the general, followed closely by his fawning aide Saint-Aubin, moves briskly down the route, pausing occasionally in an attempt to inspire the regiment with fake bonhomie and pompous military clichés. The wide-angle lens and low camera level lend his movement force, and his peacock uniform makes a sharp contrast to the battle-weary men, some wearing bloody bandages, who stand at attention as he passes. The sky is grey; the dusty soldiers are cramped together along the dirt walls of the trench; and the cold air produces steam when people speak. Gerald Fried's non-diegetic music consists of nothing but a snare drum beating out an ominous march. In the background, we hear the intermittent sounds of machine-gun fire and bursting shells, some of which strike near the lip of the trench, causing Mireau to flinch slightly, even though he is trying to present an image of confidence. (The bombardments owe their effectiveness to special-effects technician Erwin Lange, who used explosive devices to toss dirt and heavy, shrapnel-like shards of black cork high into the sky.) In an implausible but poetically appropriate coincidence, Mireau pauses near the three men who will later be chosen for execution. 'Hello there, soldier,' he says to Private Ferol (Tim Carey), 'ready to kill more Germans?' He asks if Ferol is married, and when he learns not, he shouts, 'I'll bet your mother's proud of you!' Next he stops at Corporal Paris (Ralph Meeker). 'Hello there, soldier,' he says, 'ready to kill more Germans? Working over your rifle, I see. It's a soldier's best friend – you be good to it, and it'll always be good to you!' At this point a huge explosion goes off, forcing Mireau to duck and keep on walking. After a long space, he arrives at a chubby, grinning sergeant who is standing next to Private Arnaud (Joe Turkel). 'Hello there, soldier,' he says again, 'ready to kill more Germans?'

The long take ends here, with a sudden close-up of the grinning sergeant, who is clearly mad. When Private Arnaud explains that the sergeant can't respond properly because he is shell-shocked, Mireau flies into a rage, slapping the sergeant with almost enough force to knock him down. (The scene would have reminded audiences in the 1950s of a much-publicised event of World War II, when General George Patton slapped a soldier in an army hospital.) 'There is no such thing as shell shock,' he announces, and orders the miscreant taken out of the unit. The general and his aide start off again, the camera following them. 'You were right, Sir,' Saint-Aubin says. 'That sort of thing could spread . . . . I'm convinced that these tours of yours have an incalculable effect on the men!' The camera punctuates the end of the sequence by halting and allowing the two officers to walk away just at the moment when a couple of exhausted soldiers enter from a trench to the right and walk toward us.

A bit later in the film, Kubrick returns to the same trench to show Colonel Dax preparing for the charge on the Ant Hill. This sequence, lasting approximately two minutes and consisting of eight cuts, constitutes one of the most impressive 'tunnel' images of Kubrick's

career – an iconic moment for both the film and the director, and clear evidence of Kubrick's ability to generate poetic or dramatic emotion through the power of photography and sound recording. Unlike General Mireau's similar walk, Dax's is shown from the character's subjective point of view. In the first shot, however, the camera seems to be showing us the scene independently of any character; we move straight down the trench, looking through a wide-angle lens from an eye-level position, while scores of dirty, unshaven men packed shoulder to shoulder on either side of the walkway gaze silently back at us. Kubrick takes his visual cue from the first page of Cobb's novel, which describes the soldiers as having a 'grayish', 'constipated' look. Everything is in shades of grey – the overcast sky, the wooden pallets at the base of the trench and the massed figures covered with a chalky powder that makes them resemble statuary. A great many of the men are smoking cigarettes or pipes while an incessant artillery bombardment goes off around them. Amid the overwhelming noise, smoke and dirt, the soldiers (played by a German police unit) are sharply individuated, their fatigued faces and grubby uniforms arrayed in a line that leads off to infinity.

A reverse shot shows Dax walking forward, the wide-angle camera retreating before him as he grimly passes among his men, ignoring a bomb blast that makes everyone else duck. The bombardment increases – rushing, high-pitched sounds, followed by shattering explosions that arrive with increasing regularity. At least twenty-five blasts go off during the

two-minute sequence: a distant shell, then two close shells, then three bunched together, then another, and another, and another, until the soundtrack is filled with whooshing, shrieking and concussion. In one of the point-of-view shots, Dax sees the troops lean hard against the trench, hunched and turning their faces away. In the penultimate shot, the camera moves through a cloud of smoke in which only a few ghostly figures are visible, as if it were journeying into the underworld.

Prior to the assault, we hear General Mireau argue that troops under his command are expected to 'absorb bullets and shrapnel, and by doing so make it possible for others to get through'. He estimates that 5 per cent will be killed by their own artillery ('a very generous allowance'), 10 per cent in no man's land and 50 per cent in taking and holding the hill. In the actual assault, it looks as if nearly all the men in Dax's unit are killed. The attack opens with a lofty crane shot of the battlefield as the troops surge out of their trench like swarming maggots on a rotted surface. Against a cacophony of machine-gun fire, explosions and yells, Dax repeatedly blows a whistle to summon his men forward. Kubrick uses multiple cameras to photograph the action, but most of the sequence involves two types of reframing: steady tracking shots from left to right, in which the troops scurry in wave-like oscillation across shell holes and mounds of dirt, and hand-held shots (operated by Kubrick himself) that zoom in and out on Dax as he leads the charge. The bodies of dead and wounded soon litter the field, and a bomb lands squarely on one of the corpses, apparently blowing it to smithereens.

The remainder of the film, which is paced more slowly, is devoted to the ritual killing of three more men amid the baroque stairways, ballrooms and gardens of the chateau. Kubrick stages the trial scene in a palatial, relatively empty room with a chessboard pattern on the floor, where marching feet and judicial rhetoric are given minatory reverberation. General Mireau lolls elegantly across a sofa on the sideline; Saint-Aubin, the prosecuting officer, paces back and forth and smirks at the proceedings; and the three accused men are lined up on chairs facing an impatient, irritated chief judge (Peter Capell). The drama arises not from any doubt about the outcome, but from the breathtaking ease with which standards of evidence are dismissed, and from the kinetic effects of photography and editing. Telephoto close-ups of the lawyers and judges alternate with extreme wide-angle shots of the accused soldiers, who, when they are called forward to testify, seem to be standing at attention in a crazy-house.

As usual in Hollywood movies with foreign settings, most of the cast in *Paths of Glory* speaks in American accents, but the villains have trained voices and 'European' enunciation. By all accounts, Kubrick seldom supplied his players with specific notes or keys to interpretation; when the film was completed, however, he left instructions for dubbing the actor's voices into foreign languages. Where Kirk Douglas was concerned, he wanted to keep the actor's innate emotionalism somewhat in check, and to make it clear that Colonel Dax is loyal to the army: 'Be careful not to let Dax wear his heart on his sleeve. Despite the conflict with his commanding officers he is always a soldier; *and never let him indulge in*

self pity, or, for that matter, never let him break his heart over the injustice being done to his men' (Kubrick's emphasis). Douglas's antagonist, George Macready, had often been cast as a supercilious aristocrat and a man we love to hate (most memorably as Balin, the fascist villain in *Gilda*), but Kubrick tried to keep him from seeming too melodramatically evil: 'Extremely dignified, superb diction, *strong*, aristocratic. In his own mind, general Mireau is never, even for a moment, aware of the selfish motives that seem to guide his actions . . . . He is proud of his rank and very ambitious but *he is not a scheming villain. The job here is to play him as sympathetically as possible and to make us believe he always means what he says*, no matter how cliché-ridden it may sound, and no matter how blatantly cruel and selfish it may seem' (Kubrick's emphasis). As the more calculating General Broulard, Adolph Menjou, who had recently been a prominent right-wing witness in the HUAC investigations into communists in Hollywood, had other qualities to offer. An urbane star in silent movies directed by Chaplin, Lubitsch and Griffith, Menjou later proved to be especially good at rapid-fire dialogue (see *The Front Page* [1930], *Stage Door* [1937] and one of Kubrick's favourite films, *Roxie Hart* [1942]). Kubrick may have wanted to exploit Menjou's recent political activities, but the actor's continental charm and distinctive voice were even more important: 'Strong, perfect pronunciation, as close as possible to Menjou's own voice, which is something rather unique and special. Intellectual but warm. He has a

Machiavellian brilliance which he hides in a cloak of warmth and friendliness. *When he is warm and friendly, he must really be warm and friendly. We must never feel he is pretending to be warm* . . . . He means what he says about doing things for the good of the war. *Don't help the audience hate him*' (Kubrick's emphasis).

About the minor players, Kubrick had equally interesting things to say. Wayne Morris, who plays the cowardly Lieutenant Roget, was a veteran of Warner Bros. in the 1930s and 1940s; a handsome, Nordic type, he never quite achieved stardom, perhaps because his voice lacked authority. Kubrick realised that Morris's slight whine made him perfect for the role: 'A voice that a big man should have but revealing its insecurity as subtl[y] as possible. Middle-class, average education. . . . He is not mean, he is weak. He is the kind of man who tries to get along in life by being a "nice guy"'. For other players, the instructions were brief but explicit. On the inimitable Timothy Carey as Ferol: 'He has a quality that is really unique and almost impossible to duplicate. The biggest danger with him . . . is overdoing the thing. Favor the too normal rather than the too abnormal.' On Joe Turkel as Arnaud: 'Lower-class but not back-gutter slang . . . . Don't let him get too self righteous either. At the court martial [he] feels a bit guilty despite the unfairness of his being there.' On Ralph Meeker as Paris: 'Strong, manly, middle class, a good soldier.' And, finally, on Emile Meyer, unforgettable in that same year as the sadistic cop in *Sweet Smell of Success*, who was cast against type as Father Dupree: 'Try and match his *lower-class, rough voice*. It's a pleasant relief from the stereotype priest.'[9]

These notes demonstrate Kubrick's close attention to social class. Alexander Walker has even gone so far as to argue that Kubrick was making a movie about 'war as the continuation of class struggle'.[10] It should be pointed out, however, that the film is more liberal than revolutionary in its political spirit: Dax, the most heroic and morally upright figure, is a member of the officer class and Corporal Paris, the most capable of the three condemned soldiers, attended the same school and has the same background as the lieutenant who selects him for execution. To be sure, class divisions are everywhere apparent, and the film's satire is aimed directly at the military hierarchy. (When Dax volunteers to be executed in place of his men, Broulard immediately replies, 'This is not a question of officers!') Even so, the most vivid conflicts are dramatised in the arguments between Dax and the two generals. There are also class implications of a debatable, stereotypical sort in the different reactions of the three condemned men to their executions. Private Ferol, played with customary drollery by Carey, is a slow-witted reprobate and lumpen-proletarian chosen to stand trial because he is deemed a 'social undesirable' ('Me?' he says. 'A social undesirable?'). On the eve of the execution, he eagerly chews on a roast duck sent by General Mireau, then spits it out when he thinks it might be drugged. When Corporal Paris mutters that a cockroach crawling across the floor of the barn will be alive tomorrow and will have 'more contact with my wife and child than I will', Ferol purses his lips, reaches off screen to bash the cockroach and wryly announces, 'Now you got the edge on him.' But when a priest arrives to announce that there will be no reprieve, Ferol begins sobbing like a child. As he is led to execution (in a wide-angle subjective shot similar to Dax's journey down the trench), he threatens to upset the 'dignity' of the occasion by clutching a set of prayer beads and whimpering, 'Why do I have to die? Why don't they die?' For his part, the working-class Private Arnaud becomes drunk and tries to attack the priest, only to be punched by Corporal Paris and driven backward into a post that cracks his skull; unconscious, he's carried to execution on a stretcher and pinched awake for the firing squad. It is Paris, the somewhat more educated and socially well-placed figure, who manages to salvage his dignity, though it could be argued that he becomes a sort of collaborator in the spectacle of execution. At first, he cringes and begs pathetically for his life, but then he accepts the last rites and marches stoically to his death, refusing a blindfold from his apologetic former schoolmate.

The execution scene, played against the background of the chateau and its formal grounds, gains emotional impact not only from Kubrick's manipulation of space, but also from his deliberate pacing. Although the sequence is skilfully edited, it gives the impression that events are unfolding in real time; the camera advances inexorably towards the three stakes where the men will be positioned and shot, its passage lengthened by the wide-angle lens. And the visually elongated, elaborately drawn-out ceremony – which involves a parade-ground full of soldiers, a row of decorated officers and numerous reporters from the newspapers – looks grotesquely overblown in relation to the three pathetic figures who are being executed. The spectacular background helps to reinforce the central irony of Humphrey Cobb's novel, which takes its title from a line in Thomas Gray's 'Elegy in a Country Churchyard': 'The paths of glory lead but to the grave.' But when the killing happens, Kubrick gives the audience nowhere to look except at the executed men; capital punishment in all its remorseless efficiency and crude brutality is faced square on, without distant architecture or picturesque embellishment.

Calder Willingham may have been correct in arguing that audiences needed some kind of relief after the trauma of the execution, but the effectiveness of the film's last scenes has more to do with the director's taste than with the writing itself. When the captured German girl melts the hearts of a rowdy band of French infantrymen, everything could easily have descended into sentimentality. Kubrick avoids this danger by virtue of *typage*, naturalistic lighting and the skilful way he modulates from a mood of barbaric carnival to a mood of love and grief. The tavern owner (Jerry Hauser) introduces the girl in the style of a borsht-belt comic, but her halting, amateurish singing, plus the montage of individual figures in the audience, gives the scene a rough-hewn authenticity. Using mostly non-professionals from the area around Munich, Kubrick shows an array of faces – a handsome but rather sadistic-looking fellow who shouts 'louder', a pale-skinned boy, a grey-bearded older man, a student, a peasant, all gradually moved to tearful humming. The song is Frantzen-Gustav Gerdes's 'The Faithful Hussar', a 'folkish' tune from the '*Befreiungskriege*' of the early nineteenth century, when Napoleon's army occupied the Rhineland. It can still be heard in southern Germany during the February carnival; it speaks of love and death during war, and resonates ironically with the bloody history of the region, which extended into World War I:

Es war einmal ein treue Husar
Der liebt sein Mäedchen ein ganzes Jahr . . .
Und als man ihm de Botschaft bracht,
Das sein Liebchen im Sterben lag,
Da liess er all sein Hab und Gut
Und elite seinem Hertzliebchen zu.
Ach, bitte Mutter bring ein Licht
Mein Liebchen stirbt.

(There was once a faithful hussar/ Who loved his girl all year long . . ./ And when he was brought the news/ That his sweetheart lay dying,/ He left all his goods behind/ And rushed to his heart's true love./ Oh please, Mother, bring a light,/ My sweetheart is going to die.)

This song seems all the more ironic when Colonel Dax, after listening to it, is informed that his troops have been ordered back into action. As he walks into his quarters and closes the door in the face of the camera, Gerald Fried's non-diegetic score picks up Gerdes's sweet melody, orchestrating it as military march. The absurd war goes on and the film ends with the survivors returning to their original roles. I suspect that what most people remember about the picture as a whole is not so much the heroism of Colonel Dax as the brilliant photographic *grisalle* of trench warfare, the execution of three soldiers in the name of patriotic honour, and the brief interlude of nostalgia before the barbaric system asserts itself again. This may have been the director's plan from the beginning and the reason why critics have given relatively little attention to the film's production history, its relationship to a relatively unknown novel and its underlying political tensions.

III. Dolores, Lady of Pain

Vladimir Nabokov's *Lolita*, the story of a European paedophile's obsession with a pre-pubescent American girl (or, as the paedophile puts it, the story of an 'enchanted traveler' who finds himself 'in the possession and thralldom of a nymphet')[11], was first published in the United States in 1958 by G. P. Putnam's Sons, and has since become such a canonical work that the controversy surrounding its original appearance may be difficult to appreciate. Kingsley Amis, the author of *Lucky Jim* and other celebrated comic novels about sex, wrote in the British journal *The Spectator* that Nabokov's book was 'thoroughly bad in both senses: bad as a work of art, that is, and morally bad'. *Lolita* was denounced in the British parliament, banned in the UK, banned twice in France (where it had originally been published by the Olympia Press, a purveyor of what Billy Wilder once described as the sort of books you can read with one hand) and attacked as 'repulsive' and 'disgusting' by Orville Prescott in *The New York Times*. Before G. P. Putnam's took a chance with the novel, most American publishers had rejected it outright. Simon & Schuster reportedly turned it down because Mrs Schuster refused to have her name on 'that dirty book'. Even James Laughlin of New Directions, a press that specialised in avant-garde literature, refused to publish it. (Laughlin claimed it might reflect badly on Nabokov's wife and son.)[12]

But *Lolita* also had important defenders among the most distinguished literary figures of the day. Upon its original European publication, Graham Greene selected it as one of the best books of the year. When it appeared in the US, Lionel Trilling praised it as a story about romantic love, not about the mere sex he associated with another recent book, the best-selling Kinsey report. So intense were the public reactions for and against the book that it became a blockbuster success, selling 3 million hardback copies of its first US edition, remaining number one on the best-seller list for fifty-six weeks and quickly being translated into fifteen languages. At the height of the craze, unauthorised Lolita dolls were being sold as toys in Italy.

Nabokov was surprised by his good fortune. As he later boasted, he had dared to write about one of at least three themes that were virtually taboo in American publishing, the other two being 'a Negro-White marriage which is a complete and glorious success resulting in lots of children and grandchildren' and 'the total atheist who lives a happy and useful life, and dies in his sleep at the age of 106' (p. 314). His book even attracted the interest of Hollywood, where it fell into the hands of Stanley Kubrick, a director well suited to bring it to the screen. Nabokov and Kubrick had a number of traits in common, including an

intense aestheticism, a love of chess and a taste for dark humour. When Kubrick and James
Harris read the novel just prior to its publication, they immediately acquired the film rights
and began the struggle to create a script that would satisfy censors.

In 1958, Geoffrey Shurlock of the Production Code Administration sent Warner Bros.,
the studio that expressed interest in financing the picture, a memo summarising an apparently satisfactory discussion he had held with Harris and Kubrick. According to Shurlock,
they had suggested having Humbert Humbert and Lolita Haze marry one another in 'some
state like Kentucky or Tennessee', so that the film would involve 'humor arising from the
problems of a mature man married to a gum-chewing teenager'. They also assured Shurlock
that they wanted to prevent 'any objectionable sex flavor' and thereby prevent 'another
Baby Doll uproar'.[13] Shurlock was referring to Elia Kazan's 1956 film, adapted from a
Tennessee Williams story, which told the story of a triangle between a middle-aged southerner, his child bride and his business rival; the picture starred the young Carroll Baker as
a thumb-sucking adolescent who liked to sleep in a baby's crib. It had earned a much-
publicised condemnation from the Legion of Decency, but suggested a way of transforming Nabokov's outrageous plot into something 'legal'. (A similar suggestion had already
been offered by Humbert Humbert in the novel, who argues in his defence that 'in some
of the United States', a tradition is preserved of allowing a girl to marry at twelve [p. 135]).

In 1959, Harris and Kubrick approached Nabokov through his agent, Irving 'Swifty'
Lazarr, about the possibility of having the author himself write a screenplay for the film.
Their initial discussions proved unsuccessful, in part because they were still convinced
that, to get *Lolita* past the censors, they would have to convert it into a story about a middle-aged man who secretly marries a teenager. When Nabokov declined the invitation,
Kubrick assigned the project to Calder Willingham, who drafted a script that Kubrick
rejected. Meanwhile, Nabokov travelled to Europe, where he began to have second thoughts
about the screenplay. By this time, Harris-Kubrick had given up on the deal with Warner and
formed a new arrangement with Seven Arts in England, where, if they used a mostly British
cast and crew, they could enjoy tax advantages and a certain distance from Hollywood's
usual ways of doing business. When Kubrick wired Nabokov, pleading that he reconsider
and showing more willingness to battle the censors, Nabokov accepted the assignment.

By the summer of 1960, Nabokov completed a 400-page script, sacrificing nothing and
even adding a few scenes he had omitted from the novel. As a result of an agreement he
made with Kubrick, he was allowed to publish a shortened version of this screenplay in
1974, long after the movie had played in theatres. According to Richard Corliss's excellent
BFI monograph on the film, the published version of Nabokov's script is much revised
from the original and may even contain ideas from Kubrick; nevertheless, Corliss estimates
that its running time would have been approximately four hours, whereas Kubrick's more
radically shortened movie, paced in a characteristically slow style, runs 152 minutes. The
published script has the same flashback structure as the film, but not the elaborate opening dialogue between Humbert Humbert and Claire Quilty; it preserves the form of the

novel by giving us two narrators – Dr John Ray, a quack psychologist who lectures to the audience, and Humbert, who is seen writing his memoirs in prison – and it gives us Humbert's full history leading up to his meeting with Dolores/ Dolly/ Lo/ Lolita Haze – the death of his mother, his childhood sexual experience with Annabel, his ludicrous marriage and divorce in Paris, his growing obsession with young girls, his theory of nymphets (delivered in the form of a crazed lecture on the 'divine' Edgar Allan Poe to a woman's literary club in America), his brief incarceration in an asylum and his arrival in Ramsdale to work as a French tutor for young Virginia McCoo. All the major incidents of the novel are dramatised, including Humbert's abortive attempt to murder Charlotte Haze while swimming in Our Glass Lake and his extended journey across America with the captive Lolita. At one point Nabokov even writes a cameo appearance for himself, in the role of a lepidopterist whom Humbert asks for directions.

The Nabokov screenplay is not only lengthy but also in some ways formally adventurous, making use of Fellini-esque dream images and other deliberately anti-realistic effects. When Humbert's mother is struck by lightning, 'Her graceful specter floats up above the black cliffs holding a parasol and blowing kisses to her husband and child.' When Dr John Ray narrates the story of Humbert's first marriage, he sounds like a bystander watching a movie he can't control: 'I think the cab driver ought to have turned left here. Oh, well, he can take the next cross street.' And when Humbert reads aloud from Charlotte's letter confessing her love, he appears before us in a variety of guises: 'In one SHOT, he is dressed as a gowned professor, in another as a routine Hamlet, in a third, as a dilapidated Poe.' Nabokov also does very little to bowdlerise the sex in the novel. When Humbert and Lolita sleep overnight at the Enchanted Hunters Hotel (inhabited by a Mr Swoon, a Dr Love and a Bliss family), Lolita leans seductively over his recumbent figure (we can see only his twitching big toe) and proposes that they experiment with 'a game lots of kids play nowadays':

> HUMBERT: (faintly) I never played that game.
> LOLITA: Like me to show you?
> HUMBERT: If it's not too dangerous. If it's not too difficult. If it's not too – *Ah, mon Dieu!*

Dismayed by the length of this script (James Harris quipped, 'You couldn't make it. You couldn't *lift* it.'), Kubrick and Harris effusively complimented the author and, with Kubrick's assistance, Harris quietly set about doing much of the cutting, rewriting and coping with censors in both Britain and America. In December 1960, after several months of revision, Kubrick submitted the revised script to John Trevelyan, OBE, Secretary of the British Board of Film Censors, who argued that the subject matter was unsuitable for comic treatment. 'We can see the possibility of an acceptable film on this book,' Trevelyan wrote, 'if it had the mood of Greek Tragedy.' Trevelyan was particularly upset by 'the juxtaposition of lavatory noises and sexual situations' and by the double-entendre dialogue, as in a speech by a frantic schoolteacher named 'Miss Pratt': 'And just yesterday, she wrote a most obscene four-letter word which our Doctor Cutler tells me is low-Mexican for urinal with her lip-stick on some health pamphlets!'[14]

One month later, James Harris sent the script to Martin Quigley, publisher of *Motion Picture Daily* and one of the original designers of the Hollywood PCA, having deleted most of Nabokov's descriptive language or 'interpretive material relating to characters and incidents', which Quigley had previously found 'highly objectionable' and conducive of 'a most distasteful odor'. Among various other concerns, Quigley insisted that the girl in the film be portrayed as not less than fifteen years' old. Both he and Geoffrey Shurlock were specific about lines of dialogue they wanted removed, including 'Because you took her at an age when lads play with erector sets'. Harris responded with a masterfully diplomatic letter addressing nearly all of the issues raised by Quigley and Shurlock. Much would be done, he assured them, in scenes such as the high-school dance, to make Lolita look fifteen or older; the 'erector set' line would be removed; care would be taken to assure that the murder of Quilty would not look excessively brutal; and in the seduction scene at the Enchanted Hunters Hotel, 'We will avoid any criticisms by having Lolita wear a heavy flannel, long-sleeved, high-necked, full-length nightgown and Humbert not only in pajamas, but bathrobe as well.'[15] These promises were kept. Lolita looks like a sophisticated senior at the high-school dance, Quilty's death is discreetly shielded from view by a Gainsborough-like painting and Lolita and Humbert are properly buttoned up when they share a bedroom in the hotel. Only the first half of the sentence about the erector set makes it into the film: in the midst of reading aloud from Humbert Humbert's poetic denunciation of him, Claire Quilty comes to 'Because you took her at an age when young lads', and Humbert snatches the paper from his hand. 'Why'd you take it away, Mister?' Quilty asks in a country-hick voice. 'It's gittin kinda smutty there!'

The development of the script involved the jettisoning of nearly a third of the incidents in the novel and repeated concessions to the censors. After Shurlock and Quigley viewed the film in August 1961, they wanted to cut Charlotte Haze's reference to a 'limp noodle', as well as numerous sounds of grunting from a closed bathroom door. Harris agreed to make the changes 'so far as technical matters permit'. (The limp noodle remains; the toilet sounds are reduced to a few ambiguous murmurs when Humbert hides in the bathroom to write in his diary, and to a single loud flush when Charlotte exhibits the house to her prospective lodger: 'We still have that good old-fashioned crank plumbing,' she says. 'Should appeal to a European.') Despite these changes, the resulting film, distributed by MGM, belonged in company with several A-list pictures of the late 1950s and early 1960s that appeared slightly scandalous; it was given an 'A' or 'adult' Certificate by the MPAA, an 'X' by the British Board of Censors and it was initially condemned by the Legion of Decency, which relented only when ads for the film were captioned 'For persons over eighteen only'. (J. Lee Thompson's *Cape Fear*, starring Robert Mitchum as a sadistic ex-con who preys upon a pre-teen girl in tight shorts, was released in the same year as *Lolita*, but seems to have escaped age restrictions everywhere except in Berlin.) Nevertheless, on 24 March 1961, shortly before the picture opened, *Variety* reported that a British group calling itself 'Christian Action' was attempting to have *Lolita* banned because it might be 'seen by people suffering from the same perversion ... and might, therefore, do great harm, perhaps even leading to rape and murder, which would otherwise not have occurred'.

This was one occasion when the screenplay credit on the finished movie, which listed Nabokov as the sole writer, was an underestimation of Kubrick's contribution, although the characteristically modest Harris had done a great deal of the work. When Nabokov attended the New York premiere in 1962, 'as eager and innocent as the fans who peered into my car hoping to glimpse James Mason but finding only the placid profile of a stand-in for Hitchcock', he saw that 'only ragged odds and ends of my script had been used' (*Screenplay*, xii). He praised many aspects of the film (his contract prevented him from speaking against it) and told *The Paris Review* in 1967 that he regarded Kubrick's 'borrowings' sufficient to 'justify my legal position as author of the script'.[16] For their part, Kubrick and Harris must have been happy to obtain the cultural capital that Nabokov's name bestowed upon the project. Even so, many critics were disappointed. *Time* said that *Lolita* was 'the saddest and most important victim of the current reckless adaptation fad' (22 June 1962) and *Newsweek* described it as a 'negotiated settlement' with the novel (18 June 1962). Outside the US, both *Sight and Sound* and *Cahiers du cinéma* published negative reviews.

Subsequent commentators have typically compared the film unfavourably with the novel, not only because it leaves out a good deal of illicit sex, but also because its style is 'illusionistic', lacking cinematic equivalents for Nabokov's self-reflexivity, allusiveness, narrative complexity and Joycean word-play. The best examples of this argument can be found in Richard Corliss's BFI monograph on *Lolita* and in Robert Stam's *Literature through Film: Realism, Magic, and the Art of Adaptation*. Stam is particularly good at pinpointing signs of what he calls the director's 'aesthetic failure of nerve' and 'consequent incapacity to create a filmic equivalent to the novel's self-flaunting artificiality'.[17] On the other hand, as Stam points out, something can also be said for Kubrick's relative self-effacement, which makes the film 'more pleasurable on a second viewing. Lovers of the Nabokov novel can forget the literary qualities of the book to better appreciate the film's specifically cinematic pleasures: its fine-tuned performances and subtle *mise en scène*' (p. 235). Surprisingly, the positive qualities Stam mentions were also admired upon the original release of the film by none other than Jean-Luc Godard, the least illusionistic of directors, who was pleased by the fact that *Lolita* was less cinematically 'show-offy' than Kubrick's previous work. Godard had thought little of *The Killing*, but he praised *Lolita* as a 'simple, lucid film, precisely written, which reveals America and American sex ... and proves Kubrick need not abandon the cinema'.[18]

Kubrick and Harris had, in fact, deliberately set out to keep the film 'simple'. Their aim was to create a respectable and largely straightforward production that would both perpetuate and, in some ways, parody the well-made Hollywood romantic comedy. Much was done to give the film a slick look and sound. Kubrick asked British photographer Oswald Morris to borrow from the US a set of lenses that MGM had used in the 1950s, which gave the studio's black-and-white imagery a glossy sheen (as one example of what these lenses did for the polished look of MGM film noir, see *The People against O'Hara*, directed by John Sturges in 1951). When Bernard Herrmann turned down an offer to compose the music (on the grounds that James Harris's brother had written a theme song for the picture), Kubrick and Harris commissioned Nelson Riddle, the arranger of Frank Sinatra's famous albums in the 1950s and 1960s, to compose a lush, romantic score. Kubrick favoured a conventional editing style (see, for example, the game of 'Roman Ping Pong' between Humbert and Quilty, which starts with an establishing shot and then ping-pongs from shot to reverse shot),[19] and he confined his elaborate, Ophulsian tracking and craning effects to the early scenes in the Haze household, where the camera moves up and down the staircase, glides past walls à la *The Killing* and at one point (involving a masked cut) seems to travel down through the floor of an upstairs bedroom to the kitchen below. The resulting film eased the studio's nervousness about the novel's sensational subject matter and at the same time achieved a blend of sophistication and kitsch that captures some of Nabokov's most important effects.

The plush but ironically inflected style is established immediately in the credit sequence (designed by the British firm of Chambers and Partners), which uses elegant white lettering over the glowing image of a girl's pointed, naked foot, held in the palm of a man's manicured but slightly hairy hand. As the man gently places bits of cotton between the girl's toes and begins painting her nails, Riddle's orchestration of the 'Lolita' theme, featuring a plangent, yearning piano, floods the soundtrack like the score of an old-fashioned woman's melodrama. The theme was written by Bob Harris and, at one point, it had a title and lyrics that would have pushed it more blatantly into the realm of satire. Kubrick and Harris commissioned the aging but still prolific Hollywood songsmith Sammy Cahn (who, when someone once asked him which came first, the words or the music, famously replied, 'the cheque') to pen the following, perhaps wisely omitted, verses:

'Never Before-Never Again'

Chorus (with great warmth):
Never before-never again,
One trembling kiss, told me this,
There and then.
Ours was a love as timeless as time,
As bright as a star, as warm as a rhyme.
Let others search for a dream, my search is through.
I have no need of a dream, I have you.
Sighing together, feasting or fasting,

> Not just for now, but ever and lasting.
> In all this world of women and men,
> Never before and never again!!!
> Never before and never again,
> No love like ours, not ever again!!!

No doubt these schmaltzy lyrics were commissioned because the novel is deeply, even lov-ingly preoccupied with kitsch, or with what the Russians call *poshlust*, and it makes numerous jokes about American pop music. Alfred Appel Jr, the editor of *The Annotated* Lolita, lists sev-eral hit recordings of the period between 1947 and 1952 that are mentioned in Nabokov's text: Sammy Kaye ('I'm Laughing on the Outside but Crying on the Inside'), Eddie Fisher ('My Heart Cries for You'), Tony Bennett ('Because of You') and Patti Page ('Detour' and 'Tennessee Waltz'). Kubrick, who almost single-handedly invented the 'compilation' score for his subsequent movies, missed a good opportunity to use some of these recordings for *Lolita*. Even better, he could have used equivalent material from the years when the film was made – this was, after all, the era of Chubby Checker and 'The Twist'. He does better with allusions to movies. The novel, which is set mostly in 1947, contains an ironically appropriate reference to two of the many films noirs released that year: *Brute Force* and *Possessed*; Kubrick alludes to a scene in Fritz Lang's *Scarlet Street* (1945), in which Edward G. Robinson paints Joan Bennett's toenails, and he includes an actual clip from a horror film, which we shall note momentarily.

The style and tone of the film presented one kind of problem and the plot another. Like any movie adaptation of a novel, *Lolita* needed to condense or cut a good deal of its source material in order to conform to the length requirements of a feature film; at the same time, because this particular novel was well known and admired, there was a pressure to deliver something akin to what Nabokov's readers expected to see. Fortunately, Nabokov's plot contains three distinct 'acts', much like the well-made drama or boy-meets-girl screenplay. Act I: paedophile meets nymphet and marries her widowed mother in order to be close to her. Act II: when mother accidentally dies, paedophile has sex with nymphet, travels across country with her in the role of stepfather and suffers horribly when she is stolen away by another man. Act III: after several years paedophile finds his lost love, unsuccessfully pleads with her to leave the man she has married and murders the man who stole her. The film pre-serves this basic structure. The most serious loss is at the beginning. The opening scenes 'hook' us with a tunnel shot of a station wagon moving down a foggy road, a comically surreal murder in a Xanadu-like castle and a flashback to a plane arriving in New York; nevertheless, in deference to the censorship code, the film omits Humbert's account of his childhood sex with Annabel and his life as a paedophile before his arrival in Ramsdale. Kubrick originally intended to show a montage of Humbert's involvement with a series of nymphets but, under pressure from the censors, he cut these scenes, leaving the theme of paedophilia implicit and allowing at least some viewers to think of the film as a dark comedy about a middle-aged academic who is besotted with a teenager.

The other major cuts came from the second act of the novel, in which Humbert and Lolita take a couple of lengthy cross-country tours in the Haze automobile, aptly named 'Melmoth'. The film elides most of this material, in the process eliminating sordid details of Humbert's treatment of his child captive and sacrificing Nabokov's panoramic view of America. *Lolita* might have been a trip to rival *2001*, documenting a felon's marathon westward trek through an array of motels and curio shops; but to do the job properly it would have needed at least another hour of screen time during which not much happens to advance the plot. Kubrick contented himself with brief but nicely photographed views of highways, main streets and houses that he and his second-unit crew photographed in a score of locations in the eastern US and in the western desert. A great deal of this footage appears in skilfully engineered process-screen images viewed from within Humbert's car. We see almost nothing from the point of view of the driver; the countryside is mere background to Humbert's attempts to cope with Lolita, who munches potato chips and makes teenaged comments ('Oh, did you see that? A squashed cat!' 'Have you seen any of those, you know, those foreign films? . . . I don't like 'um.'). As a result, the film has a more claustrophobic feeling than the novel.

David Thomson has severely criticised this hot-house atmosphere, remarking that Nabokov's 'love story to America was ruinously shot in England' (p. 408). It seems to me, however, that the film actually gains something from being produced in the UK. The wit and pleasure of Nabokov's vision of America (which he described in his own commentary on the novel as a theatrical 'set' and a 'fantastic and personal' world [p. 315]) derive from the way the details of suburban Americana are mediated through a European sensibility. In roughly analogous fashion, the British craft workers and actors who constituted at least 80 per cent of the total personnel on *Lolita* mediate Kubrick's New York sensibility, creating an intangible but entirely appropriate air of America seen through a foreign lens. Along similar lines, it seems to me that in many cases Kubrick's decision to omit explicit sexual information and slightly de-eroticise the novel amounts to a virtue rather than a failing. Because Nabokov's medium was entirely words, he could render fleshly detail without creating the pornographic effect that photography almost inevitably produces. (This thesis can be tested by viewing Adrian Lyne's soft-core 1997 adaptation of the novel, in which the nymphet is indistinguishable from a Victoria's Secret model.) Even so, Nabokov had disappointed many of his Olympia Press readers by rendering his erotic scenes in a playful, elaborately literary style – a strategy quite different from the pornographic novel, in which, as he explained, sex should grow in intensity and perversity as the narrative proceeds, and 'Style, structure, and imagery should never distract the reader from his tepid lust' (p. 313). Kubrick and Harris understood this principle and saw no need to linger over Humbert's voyeuristic appreciation of little girls. As Harris has said, 'being explicit was never of any interest to us',[20] especially since virtually everyone who went to the movie already knew that the novel was about paedophilia; indeed, I suspect that some of the people who complained about the film's unfaithfulness to the novel were merely disappointed that it wasn't as sexy as they imagined it could be.

Still other trimming was to the film's advantage. The Nabokov screenplay, for example, takes nearly fourteen pages to go from the point when Humbert first sees Lolita to the point when he chaperones her high-school dance; these pages contain a few 'cinematic' devices, including a comic dream sequence, but they also contain a great deal of dialogue and business that retards the action. Kubrick accomplishes everything in four short, relatively wordless sequences. When the love-stricken Humbert seals the deal to rent a room in the Haze household, we cut from a soft-focus, glamour-girl close-up of the bikinied Lolita in her feathery sunhat, half-smiling in a knowing fashion and surrounded by an aureole of light, to a harsh close-up of a horror-movie mummy (Christopher Lee in *The Curse of Frankenstein* [1957]) who rips the bandages from his face to reveal decaying flesh. Cut to Humbert, seated between Charlotte and Lolita at a drive-in theatre where the horror movie is playing. Each of the frightened women takes one of Humbert's hands. He eludes the mother's grasp so as to better comfort the daughter. Charlotte places her gloved hand atop his, which is atop Lolita's, thus creating a perverse pyramid. Humbert releases Lolita and awkwardly crosses his arms. Fade out. Fade in to a bored Humbert teaching Charlotte how to play chess. Lo comes downstairs in a granny gown, gives her mom a resentful look and a perfunctory goodnight kiss, and then pauses to give Humbert a subtly sexy peck on the cheek; as Lo exits, Humbert takes Charlotte's queen, remarking, 'It had to happen sometime.' Fade out. Fade in to a close-up of Humbert peering over the edge of a book while on the soundtrack we hear bubblegum music and Lolita's voice counting 'thirty one, thirty two, thirty three...' Zoom out to show voyeuristic Humbert in a bathrobe, sunning in the

backyard and enjoying the sight of Lolita practising the hula hoop. Charlotte tiptoes into the scene wearing Capri pants and a straw hat and takes a flash picture of Humbert that startles him and causes Lolita to drop the hoop. She beams at Humbert: 'See how relaxed you're getting?'

These segments are remarkable for the way that they amusingly condense Nabokov's characterisations and themes. They clearly establish the triangle of desire that motivates the action, showing us Charlotte's pathetic aggressiveness, Lolita's pleasure in her new-found sex appeal and Humbert's mix of urbanity and naiveté. By cutting from girl to monster, they give us not only a grotesque shock effect but also a concise expression of the way Humbert in the novel sees himself as both a romantic swain and a guilt-ridden degenerate. ('The beastly and the beautiful merged at one point,' he tells his readers, 'and it is that borderline I would like to fix' [p. 135]). They provide mounting evidence of the rampant sexuality underlying Ramsdale's suburban propriety, and they repeatedly dramatise the masochistic encounter between European aestheticism and American vulgarity that is at the heart of the novel. The bikini and the sunglasses, the saccharine but sexy tune from the portable radio, the drive-in movie, the hula hoop, the awkward chess game – all these details reinforce the satire. Meanwhile, Charlotte's snobbish gentility and Humbert's baffled fascination with an apotheosis of American pop are demonstrated in the simplest, most comic terms.

As might be expected, Harris and Kubrick spent a good deal of time and generated publicity in searching for the girl they cast as Lolita. Given the fact that Hollywood has been preoccupied with child-women since the days of Lillian Gish and Mary Pickford and that US visual culture and advertising since the 1950s has been increasingly devoted to images of sexy children (Kirsten Dunst in *Interview with the Vampire* [1994], the Olsen twins on TV and Britney Spears in her pre-adolescence are only a few examples from the *fin de siècle*), it might seem that there would have been many candidates for the job. The novel, however, is quite explicit about matters that the nation preferred to deny or treat coyly, and any screen incarnation of the title character required an actor of talent as well as charm. Kubrick and Harris passed over the brilliant Tuesday Weld, who had played carnal teenagers in several movies of the 1950s but was approaching twenty at the time when *Lolita* went into production. With Nabokov's approval, they selected Sue Lyon, a dyed blonde fourteen-year-old whose previous experience consisted of playing a few bit roles on television and winning the title of 'Miss Smile' from the Los Angeles County Dental Association. When the film began shooting, Lyon was just young enough to qualify as a nymphet under the terms set by the novel: 'Between the age limits of nine and fourteen' (p. 16). Her inexperience as an actor and the slightly artificial look of her hair and make-up, especially at the high-school dance and at the Enchanted Hunters Hotel, where the film bows to censorship by trying to make her look older, are in some ways beneficial, adding to what Humbert describes as 'a mixture of tender, dreamy childishness and a kind of eerie vulgarity'. Without doubt her most eerily artificial scene is the one in Humbert's living room at Beardsley, where she behaves like a cross between a frustrated, bored wife and an angry, sulking child while wearing tarty make-up and a flimsy costume for her role as a wood nymph in Quilty's school play, *The Hunted Enchanters*. Even when she is assisted by editing and other tricks, however, she has an extremely difficult role, requiring oscillations between bratty teenager and bemused temptress, provincial dope and cynical sophisticate, innocent victim and crafty manipulator – sometimes within the same sequence. She also has the problem of aging into a married and pregnant young woman by the end of the film. If she never fascinates the audience in the way she fascinates Humbert, she at least achieves sexy moments and tricky emotional transitions – an achievement that probably owes both to her native skill and to Kubrick's coaching.

As Charlotte Haze, Shelley Winters is physically different from the woman in the novel, who is described by Humbert as 'a weak solution of Marlene Dietrich' (p. 37). She nevertheless gives a vivid caricature of the female type that Humbert finds most revolting: 'a big-breasted and practically brainless *baba*' (p. 26). Her job, as Richard Corliss observes, is 'to make a strong, bad impression, then get off ' (p. 42). At this point in her career she was well suited to the task, having specialised in lower-class blondes who are murdered halfway through the picture – by Ronald Colman in *A Double Life* (1947), by Montgomery Clift in *A Place in the Sun* (1952) and, most memorably, by Robert Mitchum in *Night of the Hunter* (1955). Her deeper value to these films and to *Lolita*, however, lies in her ability to appear both annoying and touching. When she sashays around waving a cigarette-holder while describing her spare room as a 'semi-studio affair . . . very male', and when she announces that West Ramsdale is a 'culturally advanced' community 'with lots of good *Anglo* Dutch and *Anglo* Scotch stock', she seems ludicrously vulgar. In other scenes she makes the audience wince not only at but *for* Charlotte. Her bedroom conversations with Humbert represent some of the novel's ability to shift suddenly from comedy into pain and, in the cleverly written scene (not from the novel) in which Charlotte soliloquises to the ashes of her late husband Harold – 'the soul of integrity' who tried to commit suicide and who, in a photograph, scowls down at her bed – she manages to elicit a degree of compassion alongside the satire.

The most important figure in the cast is of course James Mason, who was always Kubrick's first choice for Humbert. A romantic heart-throb of the 1940s and early 1950s who contributed both sex appeal and an aura of intelligence to films directed by Carol Reed, Max Ophuls and Joseph Mankiewicz, Mason was a versatile performer who could play both troubled characters (*A Star Is Born* [1954], *Bigger than Life* [1956]) and amusing villains (*20,000 Leagues under the Sea* [1954], *North by Northwest* [1959]). Because he was British, he helped fulfil the national quota that Harris-Kubrick needed in order to obtain financing for the picture. He looked sufficiently like the character in Nabokov's novel, who describes himself as 'despite *mes malheurs*, an exceptionally handsome male; slow moving, tall, with soft dark hair and a gloomy but all the more seductive cast of demeanor' (p. 25), and his voice was perfect – suave, possessing a velvet musical

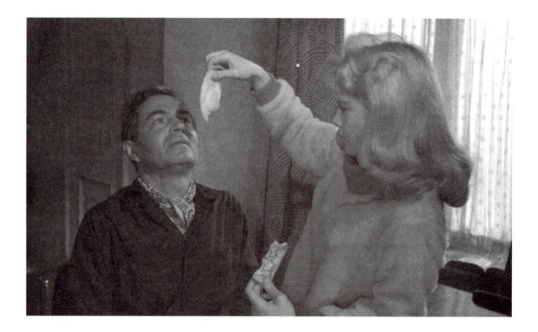

quality suitable for both the polished diction of an aesthete and the 'fancy prose style' of
a murderer (p. 9).

By any standard, this is one of the finest performances in Mason's distinguished career.
Nearly all the comedy and sometimes painful emotional effects arise out of Humbert's
struggle to maintain his *savoir faire*. As a vengeful lover, he confronts Quilty garbed in a
dashing, fur-trimmed topcoat and bearing a pistol and a poem, but is repeatedly thrown
off balance by his opponent's lightning wit and chameleon-like behaviour. As a prospective lodger trapped in Charlotte's house, he backs away from her relentless advances and
tries to keep his smile from becoming a grimace. As a chaperone at the high-school dance,
he sits awkwardly on a folding chair, balancing a cup of punch in one hand and a slice of
cake in the other, while Charlotte and the partner-swapping Farlows (Jerry Stovin and
Diana Decker) stand over him and discuss ways of getting Lolita out of the house. As
Charlotte's 'glamour date', he is forced to drink pink champagne and participate in a
clumsy cha-cha. As her would-be murderer, he snaps open a revolver and spills the bullets
on the floor. As Lolita's instructor in the art of verse, he is made to behave like a trained
seal while biting a fried egg. As her seducer, he arrives at a motel during a police convention and ends up sleeping on a collapsed cot. His one moment of relaxation is after
Charlotte's accidental death, when he reclines in a hot bath, pie-eyed from a day of booz-
ing, with a glass of whisky balanced on the floating tendrils of his hairy chest. In the midst
of his steamy stupor, he learns from the Farlows that Charlotte had only one kidney and
might not have lived much longer, and he unwittingly manoeuvres the weaselly, bow-tied

Frederick Beal (James Dyrenforth), who is seated on a nearby toilet lid, into paying for her funeral. In all other cases his plans fail. His discomfort mounts as the film progresses, producing a facial twitch, a nasty-sounding head cold and, finally, a dull pain in the arm that portends a heart attack.

Throughout everything, Mason conveys a blend of refinement, ineptitude and romantic agony, all the while allowing us to see Humbert's the dark shadow of his obsession and his ignorance of a modernised world. One of his finest moments, cleverly staged by Kubrick, is the dramatic peripeteia that transforms Humbert from a lovesick swain into a gleeful monster. The episode begins with a hirsute Humbert rising from his bed, donning a silken dressing gown and peering unhappily out of a window as Lolita prepares to board the family stationwagon for her summer trip to 'Camp Climax'. Seen from his point of view, she looks up and tells her mother, 'I'll be right back.' In a crane shot, she dashes into the house wearing a white dress and high heels, her petticoats billowing, and runs up the stairway to the sound of Nelson Riddle's music. A maudlin piano breaks through the orchestration at the moment when she arrives on the landing and embraces Humbert. In close-up, she says, 'I guess I won't be seeing you again, huh?' Humbert nods and tragically replies, 'I shall be moving on.' Lolita smiles. 'I guess this is goodbye.' She winks at him. 'Don't forget me,' she says cheerfully, and runs off. The piano launches into the 'Lolita' theme and, from a slightly low angle, we see Humbert forlornly gazing down over the balcony. The camera rises and cranes in to a closer view of his misery as he leans over and watches her go; then it follows him as he turns and wanders into her room, where, surrounded by her girlish possessions (including a magazine ad tacked to the wall featuring a photo of Claire Quilty), he sits on her bed, buries his head in her pillow and weeps.

It's as if we were watching a Douglas Sirk picture with the gender roles reversed, so that a 'feminised' man suffers for love. (Actually, Sirk himself once directed such a film: *There's Always Tomorrow* [1956].) At the lowest point of Humbert's despair, however, the hand of the family's black maid (Isobel Lucas) enters the frame to give him a letter from Charlotte. Sitting on the edge of the bed and sniffling, he reads aloud in a congested, contemptuous voice: 'Last Sunday in church, my dear one, when I asked the Lord what to do about it, I was told to act as I am acting now . . . . Go, scram, *departez*! . . . The fact that you are remaining would mean only one thing [Humbert begins to smile through his tears, relishing Charlotte's clichés and hypocritical piety, and then he gives a deep, delighted chuckle]: that you want me as much as I do you, as a lifelong mate [more laughter] . . . . Goodbye, dear one! Pray for me [laughter], if you ever pray!' Triumphantly, the unshaven, evil-looking Humbert tosses his head back and lapses into diabolic laughter. He drops blissfully onto Lolita's pillow and continues to laugh as the camera pans over to the magazine image of Quilty endorsing Drone cigarettes, the brand with the 'real, true taste'.

The casting of Claire Quilty was Kubrick's most radical choice. An ubiquitous presence in the novel, Quilty is often alluded to but is fully recognisable only retrospectively, after Humbert discovers his identity and tracks him to his gothic lair. His big scene comes at the end of the book, when he appears for the first time as himself – a fantastically decadent character who frustrates Humbert's revenge. A grotesque struggle breaks out between Quilty and Humbert, who tells his prospective readers from 'the first years of 2000 AD' that they shouldn't expect the 'ox-stunning fisticuffs' of a Western movie: 'He and I were two large dummies, stuffed with dirty cotton and rags. It was a silent, soft, formless tussle on the part of two literati, one of whom was utterly disorganised by a drug while the other was handicapped by a heart condition and too much gin' (p. 299). At the climax of the battle Humbert repeatedly shoots Quilty, who shivers, squirms and complains in a fake British accent as he retreats upstairs. Humbert is amazed: 'I was injecting spurts of energy into the poor fellow,' he remarks, 'as if the bullets had been capsules wherein a heady elixir danced' (p. 303).

Because Kubrick places his version of this scene at the beginning of the film, the screen Quilty achieves a greater presence and is always recognisable in whatever guise he adopts. His function as Humbert's *doppelgänger* also becomes more immediately apparent. Nabokov had designed the two 'literati' as mirror opposites. Humbert is a romantic and a masochist – a civilised, anachronistic, alienated European who is excited by the philistine Lolita and enslaved by his emotions to such a degree that he becomes a servant to his captive. He makes her sandwiches ('loaded with mayonnaise, just the way you like it'), paints her toenails, buys her presents, does all the housework and ludicrously tries to supervise her education by taking her to museums and offering her a copy of *A Portrait of the Artist as a Young Man*. Always out of his element, he never stops desiring his young charge, even when she grows older and gets pregnant. Quilty, on the other hand, is a cynic and a sadist

– a writer of American television shows and Hollywood films ('I got fifty-two successful scenarios to my credit') who easily makes a conquest of Lolita. He whisks her off to his castle, tries to force her to act in pornographic 'art' movies, and then casually tosses her aside. The master of every situation, he enjoys humiliating Humbert and makes wisecracks even when he is being shot to death.

To play this evil twin, Kubrick chose impersonator Peter Sellers, who had acted in numerous British comedy films, including *The Ladykillers* (1955) and *I'm All Right, Jack* (1959), but who was even better known in England for his wildly irreverent collaborations with Spike Milligan on BBC radio's surreal *The Goon Show*. Kubrick and Sellers shared a bizarre comic sensibility and Kubrick especially admired Sellers's improvisatory skills, which had the effect of a jazz musician riffing on a basic melody. Much of the dialogue Sellers speaks in the film was, in fact, scripted – his most important lines in the opening scene, for example, come straight from the novel – but Kubrick also encouraged him to invent speeches and bits of business, sometimes as the camera was rolling. The film shifts into a slightly different mode whenever he appears, abandoning realistic illusion to create something rather like a vaudeville show or a speciality act. Although Sellers had the ability to subsume his personality into whichever voices or mannerisms he adopted (by all accounts his off-screen character was almost as blank as 'Chance', the childlike idiot he portrays in *Being There* [1979]), in *Lolita* he usually seems to be 'himself' – that is, a comedian who does funny impersonations. At the high-school dance he's such a cool jitterbug – in contrast to Humbert, who can barely keep time by clapping his hands – that he virtually stands still, snapping his fingers and glancing at his watch as he twirls the wildly Bohemian Vivian Darkbloom (Marianne Stone). When Charlotte whispers in his ear to remind him of an afternoon they once spent together, he looks straight down her neckline and smirks, 'Did I do that?' Then he breaks into alliterative, literary-hipster talk, slyly alluding to Algernon Charles Swinburne's decadent poem, 'Dolores, Our Lady of Pain': 'Lissen, din't you have a daughter? Din't you have a daughter with a lovely name? Yeah, a lovely, what was it now, a lovely, lilting, lyrical name? . . . Lolita! Yes, that's right. Diminutive of Dolores, "the tears and the roses" . . .'. Later, when he and Vivian arrive at the Enchanted Hunters Hotel, Kubrick photographs him with a cartoon-like wide-angle lens. His exchange of innuendo with Mr Swine, the hotel clerk, sounds less like Nabokov than like a sketch from *The Goon Show*:

SWINE: Maybe you could use me sometime.

QUILTY: Yeah, maybe I could use you.

SWINE: I swim, play tennis, lift weights. Gets rid of the excess energy. What do you do with your excess energy?

QUILTY (looking at Vivian, who wears a shiny black raincoat): We do a lot of things with my excess energy . . . . She's a yellow belt. I'm a green belt. That's the way nature made it. What happens is, she throws me all over the place.

SWINE: She throws you all over the place?

QUILTY: . . . She sweeps my ankles out from under me and I go down with one helluva bang.
I sort of lay there in pain but I really love it . . . . I lay there hovering between
consciousness and unconsciousness.

Sellers's American accent was reportedly based on Norman Granz, a celebrated Los Angeles jazz promoter, but Richard Corliss has noted that he actually sounds more like Lenny Bruce. I suspect that at times he was also imitating Stanley Kubrick. After all, Claire Quilty is a film director of sorts – at any rate he's a fellow who has experience in Hollywood and who wants to put Lolita in a movie. His first words to Humbert are a reference to Kubrick's recently completed *Spartacus* ('Come ta free the slaves or sumpthin?'), and his first action is to challenge Humbert to a game of ping-pong, which was one of Kubrick's favourite forms of recreation. In several of his appearances he wears a 35mm still camera strapped around his neck, much like the one Kubrick can be seen wearing in behind-the-scenes publicity shots taken during the production of the film. ('Go and get some Type-A Kodachrome,' he instructs his assistant at one point, using a distinct Bronx accent.) Although he's a far more dapper fellow than Kubrick, he has the same aura of New York artistic-ness, and his female companion is a comic stereotype of the sort of Greenwich Village women Kubrick knew in his youth.

As the plot develops, Kubrick allows Sellers to engage in increasingly flamboyant *schtik*. Such moments are roughly equivalent to passages in Nabokov's novel when everything tips over into farcical absurdity – as when Humbert daydreams about sneaking into Camp Q and visiting Lolita disguised as 'a somber old-fashioned girl, gawking Mlle Humbert' (p. 66). First, Sellers masquerades as a nervous, slightly effeminate delegate to the police convention who keeps his back to Humbert on the dark veranda of the Enchanted Hunters: 'Maybe you think I think you look suspicious, me being a policeman and everything . . . . I look suspicious myself. A lot of people think I'm suspicious, especially when I stand around on street corners. One of our own boys picked me up last week . . . . I said to myself when I saw you, I said, there's a guy with the most *normal* looking face I ever saw in my life . . . . It's great to see a normal face, 'cause I'm a normal guy. Be great for two normal guys like us to get together and talk about world events in a normal sort of way.' Then he appears as 'Dr. Zemf, ze Beardsly High School pzychiatrist', a sort of ur-Strangelove in thick eye-glasses, who sits in the darkness of Humbert's parlour, disguised with an obviously fake moustache, puffing Drone cigarettes and speaking in a stage-German accent: 'Vell, Doktor Humbarts, to *you* she's still za liddle girl vat iz cradled in za arms. But to zoze boys over zere at Beardsly High she's a lovely girl, you know, mit, mit, mit, mit der *schving*! . . . All ze time she iz chewing ziz gum! Und she hass private jokes of her own, vich no one under-stands zo zey can't enjoy zem mit her!'

In an interview with Terry Southern before the making of *Dr. Strangelove*, Kubrick remarked that he had treated these scenes as 'comic nightmare' à la Kafka, and that he was 'very pleased' because they opened 'an avenue ... of telling certain types of stories in ways that haven't yet been explored in movies' (p. 3). There had certainly been cinematic precedents for such effects – Kubrick seems to have overlooked Welles's adaptation of *The Trial*, released in the same year as *Lolita*, which provides a much more thoroughgoing exploration of nightmarish humour – but *Lolita*'s particular mingling of grotesque caricature, deadpan realism and 'forbidden' sexual implication was quite rare in movies before the 1960s. Sellers's impersonations, moreover, are only a part of the film's shifting, unusually complex emotional tone. Its comedy ranges from the somewhat dubious slapstick of the scene in which Humbert and the aged hotel porter Tom (John Harrison) try to open a bedroom cot while Lolita is sleeping, to a number of minor and more subtle forms of visual wit, such as the moment when Lolita toys with a sculpture of a hand holding a quill pen while she is interrogating her mother about Claire Quilty. At another extreme, the film blends satire with pain and pathos. Consider the scene in which the feverishly ill Humbert, wild with grief and anger because Lolita has run away, is wrestled to the floor by hospital attendants; as Greg Jenkins has pointed out, this action is much more elaborately dramatised than in the novel, making Humbert appear 'overpowered and utterly humbled' and giving him a poignant exit line as he gets to his feet, tries to regain his dignity, and slowly walks off: 'She didn't by any chance leave a message for me? No, I suppose not.' [21]

After Humbert's forlorn exit, we leap over four years of the story and roughly twenty pages of the novel to arrive at the climactic, equally pathetic recognition scene. Humbert receives a subliterate 'Dear Dad' letter from Lolita: 'How's everything?' she asks. 'I'm going

to have a baby. I'm going nuts because we don't have enough to pay our debts and get out of here. Please send us a check.' Arming himself with a pistol, he drives to what appears to be a working-class district in a small city (the exteriors were shot in Albany, New York), where he finds Lolita married to Richard T. 'Dick' Schiller (Gary Cockrell). Humbert's expensive garb and upper-class manner are in vivid contrast to the shabby surroundings and with Lolita herself, who is bespectacled, blue-jeaned and great with child. When the partly deaf Dick (his hearing aid is a nice touch) opens a can of beer and steps out into the tiny backyard with his friend Bill (Roland Brand), Lolita explains how she ran away with Claire Quilty, her special lover, whom she describes as a 'genius' with a 'beautiful Japanese-Oriental philosophy of life'. She shows no resentment for the sordid way Quilty treated her, nor any emotional attachment to Humbert, who grasps her wrists and pleads with her to abandon her marriage and return to him. The idea is 'crazy', she says; she wants only to go off to Alaska and have the baby with her gentle but unremarkable husband. Broken-hearted, sobbing uncontrollably, Humbert releases Lolita and gives her cash, a cheque and the mortgage profits from her mother's house. As he makes a swift, grief-stricken departure, she apologises for 'cheating'. That's the 'way things are', she tells him, and calls out, 'Let's keep in touch.'

Kubrick explained to Terry Southern that he spent a full twelve days shooting this scene, trying to achieve the effect of a 'disparity' and 'incongruity' between Humbert, who is 'still emotionally involved', and Lolita, who is 'simply embarrassed' (p. 5). He believed it was the crucial moment in the novel, showing the metamorphosis of Humbert's desire for the nymphet into something like love for the grown woman – the point at which 'the

surface of comedy' was penetrated to disclose a 'tragic romance' (p. 7). He agreed with Lionel Trilling's description of Nabokov's novel as a modern love story in the tradition of such classic predecessors as *Romeo and Juliet*, *Anna Karenina* and *Madame Bovary*, all of which involve illicit passion of one kind or another; and he told Southern that he especially admired the way Nabokov had refrained from revealing his authorial approval or disapproval of the relationship between Humbert and Lolita. 'In fact,' he said, 'it isn't until the very end, when Humbert sees her again four years later, and she's no longer by any stretch of the definition a nymphet, that the really genuine and selfless love he has for her is revealed' (p. 2).

If indeed the novel and the film are about love, they treat the theme ironically, as if playing a black-comic variation on Proust's notion that love is never equal. All the intertwined passions in the story – Charlotte Haze's desire for Humbert, Lolita's for Quilty and Humbert's for Lolita – are wildly inappropriate, destined to arrive at the moment when the lover will be rejected. Nowhere is this sense of 'disparity' and 'incongruity' more evident than in the penultimate scene, when all the signs of class, age and emotion are marshalled to indicate how much Humbert's love for Lolita extends across a chasm of difference, transcending even sexual desire. Perhaps, as Lolita says, that's just the 'way things are'. Love begins as erotic attraction for an out-of-reach or forbidden object, but is always in danger of becoming hopeless idealism, somehow both admirable and absurd.

To my knowledge, no one has ever claimed that the Harris-Kubrick adaptation of *Lolita* is as artistically impressive as Nabokov's novel, nor has anyone ever offered a compelling reason why any film can or should exactly reproduce a literary text. But given the fact that Kubrick and Harris set out to evoke certain qualities they admired in one of the twentieth century's most brilliant works of fiction, it seems worthwhile to conclude with a sort of balance-sheet of their successes and shortcomings. The film effectively conveys the blend of romantic masochism and social alienation that underlies not only Humbert's obsession with Lolita but also some of the screen's great love stories, including what seems to me a better film, Ophuls's *Letter from an Unknown Woman* (1948). Its satire of philistine America is less complex than Nabokov's, lacking his particular mixture of lofty amusement and affection; but it's more pointed and relevant, less mingled with sentiment and moralising, than what we find in a superficially similar film like Sam Mendes's *American Beauty* (2000), in which the leading male is treated as a kind of heroic rebel, free of criminal impulses. Unfortunately, however, Kubrick's *Lolita* shies away from the darkest irony at the heart of the novel: the fact that Humbert is both an idealist and an abuser of children. As a result, we have too little indication of Humbert's potential for violence or his occasional spasms of guilt, and almost no sense of why Lolita might prefer to be married to Dick Schiller. (In the novel, Humbert notes, 'It had become gradually clear to my conventional Lolita during our singular and bestial cohabitation that even the most miserable of family lives was better than the parody of incest, which, in the long run, was the best I could offer the waif' [p.287].)

Another important aspect of the novel is missing or attenuated in the film. Nabokov's ultimate subject is the transcendent value of art itself, which provides him with the only justification for writing the book and the only consolation for the folly, cruelty and mortality he observes. 'I see nothing for the treatment of my misery,' Humbert tells the readers of his confessions, 'but the melancholy and very local palliative of articulate art' (p. 283). The novel informs us that Humbert died of heart failure in 1952 and that Lolita died not long afterward while giving birth to her stillborn child. The film omits the last of these events and has no equivalent for the novel's moving last lines, which might be read as the voice of Nabokov himself, speaking through Humbert: 'I am thinking of aurochs and angels, the secret of durable pigments, prophetic sonnets, the refuge of art. And this is the only immortality you and I may share, my Lolita' (p. 309). This final meditation not only creates one of the novel's most poignant effects, but also gives force and substance to Nabokov's gorgeous prose and self-reflexive literary gamesmanship. Lacking an equivalent degree of artistic virtuosity (and perhaps thinking such things would be too rarified for the movie audience), the film makes the art theme less explicit; in place of Humbert's valedictory, it gives us bullet holes penetrating the 'durable pigments' of a painting. (A continuity error causes the painting to change places: in the opening of the film it sits at the bottom of the stairway and in the closing at the top.) The painting is nevertheless an appropriate image with which to conclude the film, because Kubrick is no less an aesthete than Nabokov. Here and in most of his subsequent work, the only recompense he offers his audience for pain and death is the somewhat detached beauty of his cinematic craft.

Notes

1. All quotations in this paragraph are from correspondence in the Production Code Administration files, Margaret Herrick Library, Academy of Motion Picture Arts and Sciences, Los Angeles.

2. Other significant contributors to the film included Kubrick's wife, Ruth Sobotka, who was the art director, and Betty Steinberg, who worked with Kubrick as the editor.

3. Mario Falsetto (ed.), *Stanley Kubrick: A Narrative and Stylistic Analysis*, 2nd edn (Westport, CT: Praeger, 2001), p. 25. All further quotations are from this edition, and page numbers are given in parentheses.

4. As far as I'm aware, no previous movie had been organised in quite this way. Quentin Tarantino's *Reservoir Dogs* (1992), which is influenced by *The Killing*, employs an even more complicated time scheme without the aid of a narrator.

5. See Falsetto, *Stanley Kubrick*, pp. 4–5. To his two examples I would add a third, which is much less obvious and might be an error in my own calculations. The narrator tells us that Nikki is killed at 4.24, less than a minute after he shoots Red Lightning. At virtually the same moment, according to a later scene, Johnny is in the race-track locker room taking a shotgun from a box of flowers. But as Johnny opens the box, the announcer on the race-track public-address system tells us that Red Lightning has just fallen.

6. Kirk Douglas, *The Ragman's Son* (New York: Pocket Books, 1989), p. 249.

7. *Paths of Glory*, screenplay by Stanley Kubrick and Jim Thompson (undated), Kirk Douglas collection, Wisconsin Center for Film and Theater Research.

8. 'Terry Southern's Interview with Stanley Kubrick', ‹www.terrysouthern.com/archive/SKint.htm›, p. 3.

9. Production file on *Paths of Glory*, Lilly Library, Indiana University.

10. Alexander Walker, Sybil Taylor and Ulrich Rachti, *Stanley Kubrick, Director* (New York: W.W. Norton & Company, 1999), p. 69.

11. Vladimir Nabokov, *Lolita* (New York: Second Vintage International Edition, 1997), p. 166. All further references are to this edition, and page numbers are indicated in the text.

12. Quotations in this paragraph come from the clippings file on *Lolita* in the Margaret Herrick Library of the Motion Picture Academy, Los Angeles.

13. Memo dated 11 September 1958, in the Production Code Administration files, Margaret Herrick Library, Los Angeles.

14. Quotations in this paragraph are from correspondence in the Production Code Administration files, Margaret Herrick Library, Los Angeles.

15. All quotations in this paragraph are from correspondence in the Production Code Administration files, Margaret Herrick Library, Los Angeles.

16. Quoted in Alfred Appel Jr (ed.), *The Annotated* Lolita (New York: Vintage Books, 1991), p. 354.

17. Robert Stam, *Literature through Film: Realism, Magic, and the Art of Adaptation* (London: Blackwell, 2005), p. 233. Subsequent quotes are from this edition, and page numbers are indicated in the text.

18. Jean-Luc Godard, *Godard on Godard*, ed. and trans. Tom Milne (New York: Viking Press, 1972), p. 202.

19. The editing style was in part determined by the actors. Anthony Harvey, the editor of the film, has said that the scene between Peter Sellers and Shelley Winters at the high-school dance involved 'about sixty-five takes' because Winters kept forgetting her lines. Sellers's performance lost steam as the work wore on and, as a result, Harvey, had to use an over-the-shoulder editing style that took the best moments he could find from a multitude of shots. Harvey is quoted in Ed Sikov, *Mr. Strangelove: A Biography of Peter Sellers* (New York: Hyperion, 2002), p. 161.

20. James Harris, quoted in Gene D. Phillips and Rodney Hill (eds), *The Encyclopedia of Stanley Kubrick* (New York: Checkmark Books, 2002), p. 147.

21. Greg Jenkins, *Stanley Kubrick and the Art of Adaptation* (Jefferson, NC: McFarland Publishing, 1997), p. 65.

Part Four

STANLEY KUBRICK PRESENTS

I. Wargasm

On 15 November 1961, after *Lolita* was completed and he had returned to the US, Kubrick wrote to Anthony Harvey, his British editor, that 'even though I know NY very well having lived about 25 years of my life here, it seemed like a wonderland'. In the same letter he recommended two recent books on a subject with which he was increasingly preoccupied: Herman Kahn's *On Thermonuclear War* (1960) and Henry Kissinger's *The Necessity for Choice* (1961), both of which offered a rationale for the development of an atomic arsenal. The first volume, weighing in at 652 pages, had received a good deal of media attention and sold 30,000 copies in the previous year; the second helped to earn its author a position as an advisor for John F. Kennedy during the 1960 presidential election. Kubrick was deeply concerned about such matters. He had amassed a research library of over seventy books on nuclear war and was a regular reader of military magazines and the US Naval Institute's proceedings. '[T]he main thing,' he wrote to Harvey, 'is the immediate effects of a nuclear explosion, e.g. blast, heat, flying objects – then the short lived (two weeks maximum) deadly radioactivity that ensues . . . . Carbon 14, which effects [sic] you genetically, lasts 10,000 years without diminishing.'[1]

The novel Kubrick had been planning to adapt for his next film, Peter George's *Red Alert*, first published in Britain in 1958 under the pseudonym 'Peter Bryant' and entitled *Two Hours to Doom*, is a thriller reflecting the world's growing fear of nuclear apocalypse. A veteran of the Royal Air Force, George was an active member of the Campaign for Nuclear

Disarmament and his knowledge of strategic military planning was impressive enough to earn praise from Herman Kahn. In his novel, a rogue US general orders a B-52 bombing attack on Russia and then commits suicide rather than reveal the secret code that would enable higher authorities to abort the mission. The general believes that his action will save America from the Red menace, but, as the US president subsequently explains to the Pentagon, he could not be more wrong. The Soviets have buried dozens of cobalt and hydrogen bombs in the Ural Mountains; in the event of a surprise nuclear attack, the bombs will detonate, destroying the entire planet. As the Strategic Air Command speeds towards its targets, the US informs the Soviets of the impending attack. Soviet air defences, however, aren't sophisticated enough to ward off the approaching planes. At the last minute, a US Air Force officer notices that the dead general has scribbled the letters 'POE' (representing 'Peace on Earth') on a note pad, and deduces that some combination of these letters is the secret recall code. When the letters are broadcast to the bombing planes, the mission is successfully cut short. One plane, however, doesn't receive the recall. The 'Alabama Angel', piloted by the resolute Major Clint Brown, has been crippled by a Soviet rocket and can't receive radio transmissions. Even though Brown is wounded and dying, the bomber continues on course, ultimately crash-diving into a minor target and failing to create a full-scale hydrogen explosion. In the aftermath, the diplomatic skill of the US president helps to prevent retaliation by the Soviets. The brush with doomsday brings both governments nearer to peace on earth.

The novel is narrated in a quasi-documentary style that might have eventuated in a film quite similar to Sidney Lumet's *Fail-Safe* (1964), which went into production at the same time as Kubrick's picture under the auspices of the same distributor, Columbia Pictures. Kubrick hired George to collaborate with him on a screenplay; but from the time of his earliest conferences about the project with James Harris, he found it difficult to accept either the novel's optimistic conclusion or its bland seriousness. 'We started to get silly,' Harris recalled. '"What would happen in the War Room if everybody's hungry and they want the guy from the deli to come in and a waiter with an apron around him takes the sandwich order?" We started to giggle about it' (LoBrutto, p. 228). Harris believed it would be a mistake to bring this anarchic humour into the film (soon after he and Kubrick dissolved their partnership, he directed *The Bedford Incident*, a realistic drama dealing with themes similar to the Peter George novel), but Kubrick disagreed. By late 1962, he had made two crucial decisions: first, since it was by no means irrational to imagine that nuclear weapons could destroy the planet, he planned to show them doing exactly that; and second, given the absurdity of the arms race, he decided to transform George's story into a 'nightmare comedy' entitled *Dr. Strangelove or: How I Learned to Stop Worrying and Love the Bomb*, featuring Peter Sellers in the title role.

At Sellers's suggestion, Kubrick commissioned American novelist Terry Southern, author of *The Magic Christian* (1959), for a month's work helping him to add jokes to the script. Sellers himself added a good many more jokes through improvisation during filming. When *Dr. Strangelove* was released, many people assumed its humour derived chiefly from Southern, who was strongly associated with 1960s' counter-culture. Kubrick insisted that the satire was his own idea and that the order of script credits on the screen (himself first, George second and Southern third) was proper. At one point, he threatened legal action against MGM for advertising *The Loved One* (1964), an adaptation by Southern of a novel by Evelyn Waugh, as a film by 'the writer of *Dr. Strangelove*'. In fact, Kubrick deserves a good deal of credit, if only because he recognised how easily the basic elements of George's story could be tipped over into absurdity (it takes only a minor alteration, for instance, to transform 'Peace on Earth' into 'Purity of Essence'). Because of this strategy, combined with Kubrick's direction, *Dr. Strangelove* became a box-office hit and one of the most effective black comedies in film history. A risky commercial venture at the time of the Cuban missile crisis and the assassination of John F. Kennedy, it has never lost its edge and still looks refreshingly irreverent in today's world of global capitalism, nuclear proliferation and flag-waving militarism. (As I write these words, the George W. Bush administration is renewing and increasing US holdings of nuclear weapons.)

At the time when *Dr. Strangelove* was produced, Hollywood had long been involved in the nexus of profit interests that President Eisenhower dubbed 'the military-industrial complex'. During the Cold War, it was unusual to see any film about modern military hardware made without the active participation and endorsement of the armed services – an arrangement that allowed film-makers to obtain expensive equipment and the military to enhance its public relations. The credit sequences in war pictures invariably thanked some branch of the service and often listed the officers who were supplied as advisors. (The tradition is alive today in spectacular action movies such as Ridley Scott's *Black Hawk Down* [2001].) The US Strategic Air Command had encouraged and received particularly lavish screen treatment of this type. The most awe-inspiring example was Paramount's *Strategic Air Command* (1955), directed by Anthony Mann and starring Air Force Reserve Colonel James Stewart, which took colour, Vista Vision cameras directly inside the huge nuclear bombers and showed stunning aerial photography of mid-air refuelling techniques. That film was followed by Warner's colour and CinemaScope production of *Bombers B-52* (1957), which was virtually a recruitment film for the Air Force. In contrast, the black-and-white *Dr. Strangelove* lists no military advisors and inserts a crawl that precedes its credits, every line of which invites the viewer's knowing scepticism: 'It is the stated position of the US Air Force that their safeguards would prevent the occurrence of such events as are depicted in this film. Furthermore, it should be noted that none of the characters portrayed in this film are meant to represent any real persons living or dead.'

Despite or perhaps because of its cheeky approach, *Dr. Strangelove* became the most popular film in America for seventeen straight weeks. It won a New York Film Critics Award for Kubrick, but not before it had prompted a remarkably large and contentious response from critics and intellectuals. Pauline Kael and Andrew Sarris gave it mixed reviews,[2] *Sight and Sound* panned it and several of the established newspaper critics were downright offended.

Phillip K. Scheuer of the *Los Angeles Times* described it as 'snide' and 'dangerous', and argued that '[its] villains are not funny per se – especially when there are no good guys around to off-set them' (2 January 1964). Bosley Crowther of *The New York Times* admitted that it was 'cleverly written and most skillfully directed and played', but found it 'a bit too contemptuous of our defense establishment for my comfort and taste' (2 January 1964). Two weeks later, after a series of pro and con letters about the film began to appear in the New York papers, Crowther wrote a follow-up review in which he pronounced *Strangelove* 'malefic and sick', 'close to being irresponsible', 'a rather flagrant indulgence of free speech', 'defeatist and destructive of morale' and 'foolish and hysterical'. Not only was it a 'dangerous indulgence' of 'extreme anxieties', but also a misrepresentation of the US defence system 'based on military and political flaws that are so fanciful and unsupported by any evidence that they are beyond belief' (16 February 1964).

Soon afterward, the respected cultural critic Lewis Mumford came to Kubrick's defence in a lengthy letter to *The New York Times*, in which he accused Crowther of having failed to understand *Dr. Strangelove*'s satiric method and 'the soundness of its morals'. 'It is not this film that is sick,' he wrote.

> [W]hat is sick is our supposedly moral, democratic country which allowed this policy [of nuclear warfare] to be formulated and implemented without even the pretense of open public debate.... This film is the first break in the catatonic Cold-War trance that has so long held our country in its rigid grip.' (1 March 1964)

Of all the film's US admirers, however, theatre critic and director Robert Brustein gave the most persuasive explanation of its power. Writing in the *New York Review of Books*, Brustein contended that *Dr. Strangelove* 'may well be the most courageous movie ever made', in part because it 'pays absolutely no deference at all to the expectations of its audience' and creates 'the kind of total theater that Antonin Artaud would have admired'. In contrast to the 'weary meanderings of Resnais, Fellini, and Antonioni', who seemed to Brustein by the mid-1960s to be 'inexorably closing in on the spiritual lassitude of certain melancholy French or Italian aristocrats', Kubrick had made a picture that was 'fun' – enjoyable 'for the way it exploits the exciting narrative conventions of the Hollywood war movie ... and even more, for the way it turns these conventions upside down'. What was arrestingly new, Brustein argued, was the film's 'wry, mordant, destructive, and, at the same time, cheerful, unmoralistic tone'. This tone had 'rumbled a little bit under the conventional noises of *The Manchurian Candidate*', but here it exploded to the surface; if the film managed to remain open, it might even 'knock the block off every ideologue in the country'.[3]

The iconoclastic attitude Brustein was describing could be detected elsewhere in America in the 1950s and early 1960s – in Nabokov's *Lolita*, in Joseph Heller's *Catch-22*, in pulp fiction by Jim Thompson and Charles Willeford, in the early issues of *Mad* comics, in Lenny Bruce's nightclub act and even in certain episodes of Alfred Hitchcock's television show. But the sheer popularity of Kubrick's Juvenalian satire was unexpected. Far from being harmed by negative reviews or picketed by right-wing bullies, the film prospered. Perhaps because of its gleeful, totalising cynicism, it especially appealed to young people (Elvis Presley was said to be one of its biggest fans). Without actually planning it, Kubrick had moved ahead of the cultural curve, tapping into a youth audience that would sustain him over the next decade no matter what the critics said.

Both the opponents and the defenders of *Dr. Strangelove* assumed that Kubrick had taken great liberties with military and political truth. Even Brustein argued that the film was 'based less on verifiable facts than on unconscious terrors' (p. 137). What should have been apparent and has become increasingly clear is that much of it was derived without exaggeration from government practice and public discourse. There was in fact a 'fail-safe' system used by the Strategic Air Command, who adopted 'Peace Is Our Profession' as its motto and who kept at least a dozen armed B-52s always on airborne alert; there was a 'Go Code' by which the planes could be ordered to attack and a real-life general who was itching for a pre-emptive strike against the Russians; there was a procedure approved by the president to transfer war powers in case he was killed in a nuclear attack, and a plan for underground shelters where selected prominent people could survive and propagate; there was even a paranoid fear among right-wing Americans that socialists were turning the population into zombies by putting fluoride into their drinking water. Neither the Pentagon nor the White House had a surreal 'War Room' of the sort imagined by Kubrick and set designer Ken Adam, but when Ronald Reagan was elected president he logically assumed such a place existed and asked to see it.

Audiences of the time were certainly aware that various characters in *Strangelove* are based on actual persons, or at least on well-known political positions: President Merkin Muffley (Sellers) physically resembles Adlai Stevenson, the liberal Democrat who, after losing a presidential election to Dwight Eisenhower, became US ambassador to the United Nations under JFK; and General Jack D. Ripper (Sterling Hayden) could hardly fail to remind viewers of Curtis LeMay, the gun-toting, cigar-chewing general who headed the Strategic Air Command and later became Air Force chief of staff. As for Dr Strangelove (Sellers again), he is usually said to be an amalgam of several figures: Edward Teller, the right-wing scientist who falsely led others to believe that he had created the hydrogen bomb and later spearheaded the vast military stockpiling of nuclear weapons; Wernher von Braun, the jet-propulsion expert who worked first for the Nazis and then for the US (a wag once remarked that Braun's autobiography, entitled *I Aim at the Stars*, should have been called 'I Aim at the Stars but I Hit London'); and Henry Kissinger, the foreign-policy guru who would later become Richard Nixon's secretary of state.

Strangelove's accent sounds a bit like Kissinger's but, according to Sellers, it was actually based on the voice of Weegee, who was hired by Kubrick as a still photographer for the film. Kissinger's *The Necessity for Choice*, which Kubrick had recommended to Anthony Harvey, is nevertheless particularly relevant to the characterisation. The book opens with a lengthy chapter on the strategy of nuclear deterrence (a word Strangelove speaks with cruel relish), in which Kissinger feeds anxieties about the 'missile gap' between the US and the Soviet Union and the 'gap between our deterrent policy and the strategy for fighting a war'.[4] At one point Kissinger remarks, 'Ten million casualties may be unacceptable when a country can avoid any by maintaining the peace. But they may be seen to be the lesser of two evils when the country concerned believes it must either launch an attack or receive a blow that may eliminate its striking force and produce a hundred million casualties' (p. 17). Repeatedly he emphasises that the threat of nuclear war can work only so long as 'no doubts could arise about the willingness to resort to it' (p. 14).

The public personality who probably bore the strongest resemblance to Dr Strangelove, however, was the aforementioned Herman Kahn, a leading strategic planner with the RAND Corporation (called the BLAND Corporation in the film). Kubrick had become so interested in Kahn's *On Thermonuclear War* that he cultivated a sort of friendship with the author and constantly picked his brain for information about nuclear strategy. (When the film appeared, Kahn asked Kubrick for royalties, and Kubrick is said to have replied, 'It doesn't work that way.'[5]) A great deal of the film's nutty logic and language was inspired by Kahn, who had coined the term 'Doomsday Machine' and at the same time argued that there was less danger from radioactivity than people imagined. A charismatic lecturer, he spoke with a German accent and theorised about nuclear war on the grounds that it was not only conceivable but also winnable. He also contributed significantly to the widespread US belief that there was a 'missile gap' between the two superpowers; his statistical evidence in support of this claim was derived from wildly exaggerated Army intelligence, but it was convincing enough to the public that Jack Kennedy was able to use it to his advantage during the 1960 presidential election. On top of all this, Kahn was a leading proponent of the importance of bomb shelters and mineshafts in any survival strategy. When someone once asked him what people would eat in such places, Kahn, who was hugely fat, quipped, 'I personally intend to live with the chef at Lindy's who really understands sour cream herring and other quite storable delicacies' (quoted in Menand, p. 96). He was so confident of his plans that his book could well have been subtitled *How I Learned to Stop Worrying and Love the Bomb*.

In the film, Kahn's language is placed more or less directly into the mouths of Strangelove and his chief US ally, General Buck Turgidson (George C. Scott). When Turgidson tells the president that the US ought to strike Russia first in order to have a choice between 'two admittedly regrettable but nevertheless distinguishable post-war environments – one where you get 20 million people killed and the other where you get 150 million killed', his argument comes straight out of *On Thermonuclear War*, which contains a chart labelled 'Tragic but Distinguishable Postwar States'. And when Strangelove reassures the president that, far from being grief-stricken and envious of the dead, the underground survivors of nuclear attack will feel 'a spirit of bold curiosity for the adventure ahead', he is echoing Kahn's chapter on mineshafts, entitled 'Will Survivors Envy the

Dead?', which optimistically predicts 'a renewed vigor among the population with a zeal-ous, almost religious dedication to reconstruction'.[6]

Some of Kahn's early readers were anti-nuclear advocates and pacifists who thought he had made the best possible case for dismantling the atomic arsenal; in fact, however, he was a statistician whose baggy monster of a book is filled with charts that support ever greater investment in bombs and bomb shelters. His is precisely the style of thinking that the film satirises. When Buck Turgidson refers to the Air Force's 'human reliability tests' and clutches to his breast a batch of top-secret folders labelled 'Megadeaths', he is speaking Kahn's language. Instrumental rationality, which helped to design the Nazi death camps in World War II, also lies behind Strangelove's gleeful presentation of his final solution in the closing scenes:

> STRANGELOVE [seen from a low, wide-angle perspective, silhouetted against the Big Board as he spins his wheelchair around, grins and stiffly cocks his head]: I would not rule out za chance to preserve a nucleus of human specimens. [Cut to a telephoto shot as he wheels toward us out of the shadow.] It would be quite easy, heh, heh, at za bottom of some of our deeper mineshafts.
> PRESIDENT: How long would you have to stay down there?
> STRANGELOVE [in close up]: Vell, let's see now. [He reaches into his coat with his gloved right hand and extracts a calculator. His left hand struggles to pull it free from the glove.] Cobalt Thorium G . . . . [He calculates] I would think, possibly one hundred years.
> PRESIDENT: You mean people could actually stay down there for a hundred years?
> STRANGELOVE [seen from a low angle, with the Soviet Ambassador and others gathered around, as he shouts triumphantly.] *IT VOULD NOT BE DIFFICULT, MEIN FUHRER!* [Twisting grotesquely in the chair, he grins and tries to speak in a normal voice.] . . . Heh, heh, I'm sorry, Mr. President . . . . Animals could be bred and *SLAUGHTERED* . . . .
> PRESIDENT [thoughtfully]: I would hate to have to decide who stays up and who goes down.
> STRANGELOVE [fighting to control his right arm, which drops toward the floor and nearly drags him off the side of the chair]: It could easily be accomplished with a computer!

Kahn may have provided another of the film's satiric targets when he reportedly said that the military proponents of the strategy of overwhelming force were dreaming of a 'war-gasm' (quoted in Menand, p. 95). This idea motivates virtually everything in *Dr. Strangelove*, from the opening credits, which show a distinctly phallic refuelling rod being inserted into a B-52 as 'Try a Little Tenderness' plays on the soundtrack, to the astonishing climax, when Major Kong exultantly straddles a nuclear bomb that looks like a huge phallus. Throughout, nuclear war is a hard-on for the men who wage it. (The qualified exceptions are Merkin Muffley and Lionel Mandrake, both of whom are made to seem feminine and ineffectual.) Phallic symbols are everywhere – sometimes a cigar is just a cigar, but not when General Ripper smokes it – and the competition to possess a bigger weapon than the other guy makes the characters look like little boys suffering from locker-room anxiety. The only woman in the film, Buck Turgidson's bikinied 'secretary' (Tracy Reed, stepdaughter of director Carol Reed), who can also be glimpsed in a *Playboy* centrefold with a copy of *Foreign Affairs* spread across her derriere, is an emblem of the way sex and war are linked, and of the way women in general are valued by warrior males. 'Of course it isn't only physical,' Buck whispers over the phone when she calls him in the War Room. 'I deeply respect you as a human being!' In the mineshaft utopia envisaged by Strangelove, there will be ten such women for every man. But sexually attractive women are also a threat. Jack Ripper orders the bombing mission because during the 'physical act of love' he suffers 'a profound sense of fatigue, a feeling of emptiness'. Women sense his 'power' but are attempting to deprive him of 'essence', in much the same way as the 'post-war Commie conspiracy' is attempting to destroy his 'fluids'. Only through death can he and the other warriors achieve potency. The theme is summed up at the end, when Kong's bomb goes off and Strangelove rises from his wheelchair like a mummy from its tomb. Standing erect in a spotlight, he is astonished by his own virility: 'Sir, I have a plan,' he says, then looks down at his legs and shouts, '*MEIN FÜHRER!* I CAN WALK!' As he clumsily steps forward, we cut to a montage of mushroom clouds bursting in orgasmic release.

In a more general fashion, as Robert Brustein observed, *Dr. Strangelove* also satirises the conventions of the Hollywood war movie: the planning sessions among the generals, the lightning strike to capture an important base, the intrepid bombing plane manned by a cross-section of American ethnicities and social types, and so on. All this action is superbly edited by Anthony Harvey and Kubrick, who greatly revised the original picture in the cutting room in order to achieve comic timing and dramatic tension; aside from the effective uses of direct cuts between major sequences, however, the film is utterly classical in construction, building suspense with cinematic techniques as old as D. W. Griffith. It establishes a deadline, initiates a chase and methodically cross-cuts between a few important locales. The B-52 keeps advancing towards its goal despite every impediment, always to the sound of a drumbeat and the stirring melody of 'When Johnny Comes Marching Home'. The audience is made to hover somewhere between rooting for the US and contemplating it in horror. Everything is insane, but the old-fashioned elements of the chase film are so skilfully executed that we may find ourselves falling into the same emotional trap as Buck Turgidson, who is momentarily carried away by the individual 'initiative' of Kong's aircraft.

The clever parody of Hollywood nicely supports the film's cheerful assault on what the exasperated Captain Mandrake (Sellers) calls America's 'flay-mouthed way of life'. *Dr. Strangelove* makes fun of every nationality in sight, including the Russians, the British and the Germans, but there can be no doubt that its primary target is the world's most powerful nation – not only its Hollywood entertainment, but also its fundamentalist religion (the crew of the B-52 is given miniature copies of a 'combination Rooshan phrase book and Bible') and worship of capitalism (a Coca-Cola machine becomes a subversive instance of product placement).

These iconoclastic jokes would never have been so effective if not for the brilliant design and direction of the film. One of Kubrick's most important decisions was to treat the comic material with solemnity, in a style that resembles a cross between a documentary and a noirish suspense movie. His major deviation from this strategy was a sequence that he cut from the picture after the first preview: a custard-pie fight in the War Room. The sequence survives in the British Film Institute archives,[7] and would make an interesting 'extra' for a DVD edition of the film. According to Ed Sikov, who has described it in detail, the action is initiated when the doomsday device goes off, causing Strangelove to fall from his chair and roll about on the floor. President Muffley demands that Soviet ambassador de Sadesky be strip-searched 'in view of the tininess of your equipment'. Buck Turgidson insists that the ambassador's 'seven bodily orifices' be examined. In response, de Sadesky snatches a pie from the banquet table and hurls it at Turgidson, who ducks, only to have it strike the President. Holding the wounded leader in his arms like a *pietà* Turgidson shouts, 'Gentlemen, our beloved President has been infamously struck down by a pie in the prime of life! Are we going to let that happen? Massive retaliation!' A fast-motion pie fight ensues, scored to silent-movie music. Characters climb atop tables and swing from the overhead lights; Turgidson sits atop somebody's shoulders, stuffing pie in his mouth between throws, and the circular conference table becomes a sort of boxing ring filled with white cream. Eventually, Strangelove fires off a gun and shouts, 'Ve must stop zis childish game! Zere is *Verk* to do!' The other characters sit around on the floor and play with the custard cream like children building sandcastles. 'I think their minds have snepped from the strain,' Strangelove announces. Soon afterward, we cut to the montage of nuclear bombs exploding as Vera Lynn sings 'We'll Meet Again'. (At an early stage of the production, Kubrick planned to have the lyrics to the song appear on screen with a bouncing ball.)

The pie fight seems like something from a Richard Lester movie or perhaps a Monty Python routine. Terry Southern later said that the studio was dead set against it. Kubrick withdrew it because it seemed not to fit with the tone of the rest of the film and because the assassination of President Kennedy just prior to the release of *Dr. Strangelove* made the joke about the president being 'struck down by a pie in the prime of life' sound inappropriate. His decision was undoubtedly correct, because the film achieves its best effects by avoiding pure slapstick and maintaining a relatively straight-faced style. Throughout, it manages a delicate balance of expressive, realistic and comic codes, playing its exaggerations off against ostensibly 'serious' techniques such as source lighting and sets with ceilings. Its wide-angle, low-key shots, sometimes illuminated with a single lamp against a black limbo, are reminiscent of Welles, especially in the smoky, fluorescent scenes in Ripper's office and in the expressionistic War Room, where a circle of light above the huge round table creates the impression of a ring of energy expanding out from a nuclear explosion.

By contrast, parts of the film are shot in pure cinéma vérité style. The battle of Burpleson Air Force Base is photographed by Kubrick himself under what appears to be newsreel

conditions, using a hand-held 16mm camera equipped with a telephoto lens. (One of the base defenders indirectly comments on the authenticity of the images: 'You've sure got to hand it to those Commies . . . . Those trucks look like the real thing!') Kubrick also operated a hand-held camera for the rapidly edited sequences inside Kong's B-52, which involve lots of panning and zooming and produce lens flare when the camera shoots directly at light bulbs. (The Air Force was troubled that the film might have used spies to unearth classified information about military aircraft, but the instrument panels and technology were copied straight from aviation magazines.) Here and elsewhere the soundtrack adds to the feeling of realism: everything in the B-52 is heard through the tinny earphones of the pilot and crew, and in the War Room the quality of volume and reverb shifts with the camera angles. But of course the film also deviates from realism in obvious ways. The title and credits announce a stylised, satiric purpose, which is reinforced early on when Peter Sellers appears wearing a fake nose and a guardsman's moustache. (Informed by his superior that a shooting war has commenced, he replies, 'Oh, Hell! Are the Russians involved, Sir?') The exterior shots of Kong's B-52 are accomplished with models – skilfully executed by the British designer Wally Veevers, who later worked on *2001*, but nevertheless recognisable as artifice. And the music score, which is Kubrick's first use of pre-existing recordings, comments derisively on the action; like Brecht's theatre, it puts the audience in the position of critical observers rather than emotionally absorbed witnesses.

The most intriguing affective quality of the film is the sustained tension or dialectic between realistic suspense and outrageous satire, as if we were being pulled into emotional involvement only to be pushed back with a joke. A good example of this tension can be seen when Lionel Mandrake rushes into Jack Ripper's office to let him hear an innocuous broadcast from a portable radio, thus proving that the world isn't under nuclear attack. Sellers portrays Mandrake as a parody of British reserve, but Kubrick gives the sequence a noir-like mood, viewing most of the action in a long take and deep focus with an unmoving camera positioned at some distance behind Ripper's desk. A wide-angle lens brings the ceiling and walls into view and dramatically elongates the shadowy room, which is illuminated chiefly by a fluorescent lamp above Ripper's head. Everything is played at a sombre, deliberate pace that involves many pauses in the dialogue. After Mandrake enters and demonstrates that the radio is playing ordinary music, Ripper, a big, imposing man, silently rises from the desk, walks the length of the room and locks the door in the distance. 'The Officers' Exchange Program does not give you any special prerogatives to change my orders,' he says to Mandrake. He returns to his desk, sits with his back to us, clips the end off a cigar and lights it. 'My orders are going to stand.' Mandrake pauses to absorb this command and then, in a polite, David Niven accent, tells Ripper that this seems 'rather an odd way of looking at it'. Ripper responds patronisingly: 'Now why don't you take it easy, Group Captain. Make me a drink of grain alcohol and rain water and help yourself to whatever you'd like.' A long pause follows. Mandrake primly comes to attention, clicks his heels and salutes: 'General Ripper, Sir, as a member of Her Majesty's Air Force, it is my clear duty under the present circumstances to issue the recall upon my own authority.' He crisply executes an about face, walks to the door in the distance, tries to open it and finds it locked. Then he tries another door, which is also locked. 'I told you to take it easy,' Ripper says. 'I'm the only person who knows the three-letter code.' Mandrake marches forward and stands rigidly in front of the desk: 'Then I must insist, Sir, that you give them to me!'

At this point, the long take ends with a sudden cut to a huge, intimidating close-up of Ripper's face. In the previous shot he was seen from the middle distance and from the back; now he looms above us, viewed with a telephoto against a black limbo, his sinister visage lit by the lamp above his head. Photographer Gilbert Taylor uses an additional light to give a mad gleam to Ripper's dark eyes. We see an insert of his hand reaching into his desk and taking out a pearl-handled .45. A medium close-up shows Mandrake's astonished, comic reaction: 'Do I take it, Sir, that you are threatening a brother officer with a gun?' Cut to a close-up of Ripper from an even lower angle, his broad chest covered with ribbons, his thick cigar jutting out of his mouth. He puffs the cigar and speaks slowly in a grim tone, building to a wacko climax without ever dropping his intensity and seriousness:

RIPPER: A decision is being made by the President [puff] and the Joint Chiefs of Staff in the
    War Room at the Pentagon. And when they realize there is no possibility of recalling the

Wing, there will be only one course of action open. [Pause] Total commitment! [Long pause] Mandrake, do you recall what Clemenceau once said about war? He said that war was too important to be left to the Generals. When he said that [pause] he might have been right. But today [pause] war is too important to be left to the politicians! They have neither the time, the training, nor the inclination for strategic thought. [Long pause, takes cigar out of mouth, blows smoke] I can no longer sit back and allow Communist infiltration, Communist indoctrination, Communist subversion, and the International Communist Conspiracy [pause] to sap and impurify [pause] all our precious bodily fluids!

Sterling Hayden, a stranger to comedy, told interviewers that he was terrified during the shooting of this scene because of his respect for Kubrick and the other actors; a slight uneasiness can be sensed in his performance, but it combines with his thick-set, commanding presence to make him look all the more menacing. He dominates his scenes with Sellers, who plays Mandrake as a somewhat slow-witted twit attempting to maintain a stiff upper lip. One of Sellers's best comic moments in the role comes when he sits on the edge of a couch and silently, methodically folds and unfolds a chewing-gum wrapper, trying to maintain his calm as the madman Ripper sits down next to him, throws a big arm over his shoulder, and asks, 'Mandrake, have you ever seen a commie drink a glass of water?'

Despite the fact that the film allows Sellers to display a range of accents, he never seems to be the star, perhaps because two of the three characters he plays are comparatively rational. Mandrake is a self-effacing fellow even when he tells Ripper what it was like to be tortured by the Japanese: 'It was just their way of having fun, the swine. Strange thing is they make such bloody good cameras.' When Colonel 'Bat' Guano (played by the ever-reliable Keenan Wynn, who was once singled out by James Agee as among the best Hollywood actors of his generation) accuses him of being a 'deviated prevert' who wants to commit 'preversions' in Ripper's bathroom, he responds with sputtering but civilised outrage.

According to Ed Sikov, Sellers intended to portray President Muffley in a more theatrically effeminate style, but Kubrick toned the performance down so that we see only a trace of the original conception, in the form of a nose spray and handkerchief. Sellers's one chance for broad comedy in the presidential role is the telephone conversation with Premier Kissov, a partly improvised scene that resembles the routines made popular during the period by comic recording artists such as Bob Newhart and Shelly Berman:

> MUFFLEY: Dimitri, could you turn the music down just a little? [Pause] You're coming through fine. I'm coming through fine, too, eh? Well, it's good that you're fine and I'm fine. It's great to be fine. Well, now, Dimitri, you know how we've always talked about the possibility of something going wrong with the bomb? The *bomb*, Dimitri. Well, now, what happened is, one of our base commanders, well, he went a little funny in the head, and he went and did a silly thing. [Pause] Well, I'll tell you what he did. He ordered his planes [pause] to attack your country. Let me finish, Dimitri. Well, listen, how do you think *I* feel about it? Why do you think I'm calling you? *Of course* I like to speak to you! I'm just calling you up to tell you something terrible has happened. Of course it's a friendly call! Listen; if it wasn't friendly you probably wouldn't even have got it!

By far the most important contribution Sellers makes is in his unforgettable interpretation of the title character, a performance Kubrick photographed with three cameras in order to be sure not to miss any of its improvised moments. Strangelove doesn't assume centre stage until more than halfway into the picture, when he sweeps out from the War Room conference table and glides across the polished floor in his wheelchair. He wears an elegant black suit and sports a wavy blond pompadour that peaks at a crazy angle. His body is grotesquely twisted and everything about him is governed by a comic principle I've described in another book as 'expressive incoherence': his legs are dead and his torso alive; his eyes, gazing wildly out from a pair of sunglasses, are mismatched with his frozen grin; he tends to speak through clenched teeth; and his black-gloved right hand is in systematic rebellion against his ungloved left hand.[8] In his first close-up, he struggles to free a cigarette from the steely fingers of the glove and strains to keep his nasal, high-pitched speech under control. Now and then his mask of condescending politeness drops away and he involuntarily shouts key words as if he were Hitler on a podium:

Mr President, the technology required [for the doomsday device] is within the means of even the smallest nuclear power. It requires only the *VILL* to do so . . . . That's the whole idea of zis machine, you know. *DETERRENCE* is the art of producing in the mind of the enemy [pause] the *FEAR* of attack . . . . The automated device rules out *HUMAN MEDDLING*!

It was Kubrick who suggested that Strangelove should wear the black glove. Kubrick was probably thinking of Rotwang, the mad scientist in Fritz Lang's *Metropolis*, but Sellers improved on the idea by giving the gloved arm an independent life. It expresses Strangelove's storm-trooper instincts and keeps bursting through his every attempt to restrain it. At the climax of the film, it declares all-out war. First, it tries to take control of the wheelchair, but the left hand beats it back, striking it savagely again and again until it goes limp and forces Strangelove to slump rightward in exhaustion. From a tilted posture, Strangelove tries to explain sweetly to the president that the survivors of nuclear war won't feel despair. 'There vill be no shocking memories,' he says. Then his Nazi self begins to take over, promising that 'the prevailing emotion vill be one of nostalgia for those left behind, combined with *A SPIRIT OF BOLD CURIOSITY FOR THE ADVENTURE AHEAD!*' Suddenly the right hand jumps up in a Nazi salute. The left hand grabs it by the wrist, pulls it into his lap and starts beating it into submission. It jumps up and socks him in the jaw. He bites it, and his left hand struggles massively to push it back down. It grabs him by the neck and starts choking him. Eventually, the attack subsides, at almost the same moment when Strangelove regains his ability to walk and the world ends.

Sellers was also supposed to play the role of Major Kong, but he had difficulty finding a proper accent and injured himself when he tried to manoeuvre around the set of the B-52. Amazingly, Kubrick is said to have offered the part to John Wayne, whose response was predictably negative. He then approached Dan Blocker, one of the stars of TV's *Bonanza* and a Kennedy-era liberal, whose agent volubly refused on the grounds that the film was 'too pinko'.[9] Fortunately for posterity, Slim Pickens took the job. Pickens had previously done excellent work as a villainous sheriff's deputy in *One-Eyed Jacks*, a film Kubrick was briefly involved with, and he brings to *Dr. Strangelove* a similar feeling of violence underlying a slack-jawed, folksy exterior – a characterisation he would later play for even broader comedy in Mel Brooks's *Blazing Saddles* (1974). An ex-rodeo cowboy, Pickens may have inspired Kubrick to invent the famous image of Kong riding the bomb. The power of that shot derives in part from its audiovisual construction (Kong's scream echoes weirdly through the sound of a chill wind; the earth seems to rush up to meet the bomb at the last moment, and the explosion is rendered by cutting directly to white silence), but also from Pickens's ability to straddle the weapon with authority and yell 'Ya-hoo' with true cowboy zeal. Elsewhere he speaks his lines in an authentic western twang and he keeps a straight face while delivering some of the funniest speeches in the movie (written, one suspects,

by the Texas-born Terry Southern). Informed that 'Wing Attack Plan R' has been ordered, he responds, 'Well, I've been to one World's Fair, a picnic and a rodeo, and that's the stupidest thing I ever heard comin' out a set of earphones!' Realising the order is no joke, he then becomes patriotic, maudlin, and devious:

> KONG [putting on his cowboy hat]: Well, boys, I reckon this is it. Nukler combat with the Rooskies! . . . Now, look, boys, I ain't much of a hand at makin' speeches, but I got a pretty fair idea that something dog-goned important's goin' on back there. Now I got a fair idea the kind of personal emotions that some of you fellas may be thinking. Heck, I guess you wouldn't even be human be-ins if you didn't have some pretty strong personal feelin's about nukler combat . . . . Remember one thing. The folks back home is counting on you, and by golly we ain't about to let 'em down! Tell you somethin' else. If this thing turns out to be half as important as I figure it just might be, I'd say that you're all in line for important promotions and personal citations when this thing is all over. That goes for *ever last one of you*, regardless of your race, color, or your creed!

Despite all this, George C. Scott almost steals the picture. His achievement is surprising not only because he was associated with serious drama but also because we can easily imagine another kind of actor in the role of Buck Turgidson. As the name implies, the character is a blowhard politician and Pentagon bureaucrat who brims over with fake machismo, whereas Scott, who later gave a celebrated performance as George Patton, has a commanding physical presence – a burly chest, a broken nose and a gravelly voice capable of delivering lines in resonant, Shakespearian tones. Scott's natural face is something of a caricature, but one more suited to a tough guy or a crafty knave – Richard III, perhaps – than to a fool. And yet, as Roger Ebert has observed, his 'duet for voice and facial expression' rivals Jerry Lewis or Jim Carrey for sheer comic plasticity, and his performance is all the while 'hidden in plain view' by a complete emotional sincerity.[10]

Scott was unhappy because Kubrick chose takes in which the actor was mugging outrageously. But Turgidson, like Strangelove and Kong, lifts the darkly amusing film into moments of energetic absurdity. At one point, gesturing ostentatiously as he moves across the polished floor of the War Room, he slips, does a back flip and rises to his feet to finish his line – an accidental fall that Kubrick chose to preserve for the sake of its sheer goofiness. In his first scene, a long take in a mirrored bedroom, he enters like a figure in a cartoon. First, we hear his raspy voice coming from the toilet, relaying a message to his secretary, who has another officer on the phone ('Tell him to call whatshisname, Ripper! Grumble, grumble. I have to think of everything!'). Then he emerges into view from the distance, sporting a military crew-cut, an open Hawaiian shirt and Bermuda under-shorts. He takes the phone and stands bearing his slightly paunchy torso with pride: 'Fred? Buck,' he announces. 'What's cookin' on the Threat Board?' Hearing the news, he frowns, thinks a moment and postures grandly. 'Tell you what you better do, old buddy,' he says, and punctuates the statement by loudly slapping his stomach – one of the film's most inspired gestures, immediately conveying the character's braggadocio and dumb-ass self-confidence.

In the War Room, Turgidson's behaviour oscillates wildly. Sometimes he's a gung-ho leader who feels superior to the president, and sometimes a sheepish little boy who ducks his head and stuffs chewing gum in his mouth. He gets most of his laughs from the stress he puts on certain words and from the way his face and attitude keep rapidly changing. Concluding his pompous report on 'Operation Dropkick', he suddenly becomes chastened and insecure: 'Now it *appears* that the order *called* for the planes to [awkward pause] attack their targets inside Russia.' President Muffley scowls and says that he is the only person who can issue such orders. 'That's right, Sir,' Turgidson replies, putting a stick of gum in his mouth. 'And although I *hate* to judge before all the facts are in, it's beginning to look like General Ripper exceeded his authority.' When Muffley points out that the 'human reliability tests' assured him there was no possibility of such things happening, Turgidson assumes an air of haughty politeness: 'I don't think it's quite *fair* to condemn the whole program because of a single slip-up, Sir!' The president says he is 'less and less interested' in Turgidson's opinions, and we see a low-angle view of Turgidson frowning sulkily and sticking more gum in his mouth. Soon afterward, however, Turgidson launches into a cocky, full-voiced lecture, explaining to the president that the Russians 'are going to go absolutely ape' when the US bombers strike. Forgetting that he learned of Ripper's actions while sitting on the toilet, he leans forward and grins conspiratorially from beneath heavy eyebrows: 'Now, *if*, on the *other hand*, we were to launch an all-out and co-ordinated attack, we stand a damn good chance of catching them with their pants down!'

When Muffley announces his plans to confer with the Russians, Turgidson is loudly dismayed. Squinting mightily, he cries, 'Am I to understand that the *Russian Ambassador* is being admitted entrance to the *War Room?*' Bug-eyed, he gathers his statistical reports protectively into his arms: 'He'll see everything! He'll see the Big Board!' When it appears that the discovery of the recall code has ended the threat, he climbs atop a chair, whistles for silence and calls for a 'short prayer of thanks'. He looks up and shouts '*Lord*' in a commanding voice, but just then somebody announces that one plane has ignored the recall. Suddenly he squints. 'Mr President,' he says, 'I'm beginning to smell a big fat commie rat!' As the president confers with Premier Kissov on the phone, Turgidson puts one hand atop his head and looks frightened and stupid. When the President turns and asks if there's any chance of one plane getting through, Turgidson's stunned expression gives way to intense gum-chewing and gleeful enjoyment. 'Mr President,' he says ardently, 'if I may be permitted to speak freely, the Ruskie talks big, but frankly we think he's short of know-how. You just can't expect a bunch of *ignorant peons* to understand a machine like some of our boys! You take your average Ruskie and we all know how much guts he's got. Hell, look at all them the Nazzies killed and they still wouldn't quit!' Lowering his voice, he explains that guts count for nothing because if the pilot is 'really sharp, he can barrel that baby in

so low …'. Suddenly he's overcome with excitement. 'Hee hee,' he giggles, spreading his arms like wings. 'You oughta see it sometime, it's a pleasure! A *BIG* plane like a B-52! *VA-ROOM*, jet exhaust frying chickens in the barnyard! *HA, HA*! Have we got a chance? *Hell yes*!' Then he recognises what he's saying and executes one of the most exaggerated double-takes in the history of screen comedy – face drooping, eyes bulging, one hand over his mouth in embarrassment.

This moment of comic recognition is deeply symptomatic of the film as a whole. In bold fashion, it mimics Kubrick's overall strategy of pulling the audience up short, creating laughs that stop in the throat and suspense that suddenly turns silly. As in Kong's lethal ride on the bomb and Strangelove's rise from the wheelchair, Turgidson's 'wargasm' is cut short by death, but without the swooning towards darkness that characterises the 'little death' of sexual climax. Here as elsewhere, the military-industrial complex and the masculine libido are directly and disturbingly linked to a regime of frustrated and destructive sexuality: as Freud suggests in *Civilization and Its Discontents*, war is love. Turgidson's double-take might even be described as *coitus interruptus*. For Kong and Strangelove, the effect is more like the instantaneous transformation of Eros into Thanatos; the world stops before it can register even a shudder of anticipation, leaving behind only the frightening beauty of nuclear clouds and a pervasive feeling of savage, Swiftian indignation. In *Dr. Strangelove*, Kubrick had arrived at the pure black-comic style towards which he had been gravitating since the beginning of his career; it became the lodestone of his artistic temperament, but seldom again achieved such a powerful blending of zestful iconoclasm, misanthropic satire and unexpected horror.

II. Beyond the Stars

Kubrick's next and most ambitious project was released in 1968, one of the most traumatic years in US history: Martin Luther King and Robert Kennedy were assassinated, the Tet offensive broke out in Vietnam and protesting students were shot by National Guard troops at Kent State University. A short time earlier, just as the youth rebellion was turning violent and the forces of repression were gathering against it, Kubrick moved permanently to England and began making an elaborate, apparently apolitical studio film about the distant future and outer space. Now that the millennium has passed, we're in a good position to ask how much *2001: A Space Odyssey* reflects the time when it was made and how much it got wrong about the years to come.

Despite its flickering video screens and 'keyboards' integrated into the sleeves of space-suits, the film doesn't foresee the digital revolution and its miniaturised effects on computers. (Its astronauts use futuristic fountain pens and ordinary clipboards when they write.) It underestimates the degree to which spaceships can be automated and it overesti-mates the progress of Artificial Intelligence. And yet its vision of space travel, extrapolated from NASA's activities in the late 1960s, remains well within the realm of possibility. We've long employed a space shuttle – albeit of a less luxurious kind than the Pan-Am *Orion* in the film, which has TV screens mounted at the back of the seats, somewhat like the large passenger aircraft of today. The only reason why we don't have space stations and human space exploration beyond the moon landing is that the earth's major political pow-ers decided such things would have insufficient military and commercial value and that computerised rockets and cameras could do the job for scientific purposes. *2001* therefore feels most dated not at the technological but at the social and political level. It doesn't pre-dict the end of the Cold War, and its space travellers, apart from a small contingent of female Russian scientists and one member of the US group at the space station, are white males. One of the most obviously 1960s-ish images it contains, aside from the psychedelic effects in the concluding episode (reminiscent of Richard Avedon's colour-saturated photographs of the Beatles and exactly contemporary with Alfred Jenson's abstract paint-ings of cosmic energy), are the pretty young flight attendants and receptionists (the film calls them 'girls') who serve Dr Heywood Floyd (William Sylvester) on his journey to the moon.

2001 also shows its age in a more indirect fashion. Originally conceived for the Cinerama process, Kubrick's production was fully in keeping with the modernist project of fusing art and technology and was intended to suggest the future of cinema itself. In some ways typical of the Cinerama features that preceded it, all of which, as John Belton observes, were based on themes of nationalism and spectacular travel,[11] it used the 'engulfing' quality

of its 1:2.20 Super Panavision format in especially effective ways and developed new techniques that promised to transform the look of movies in general. Kubrick and Tom Howard
designed and patented a large-scale front-projection system for the scenes in Africa and
outer space; Douglas Trumbull created a 'slit-scan' device for the climactic light show; and
Wally Veevers and a small army of large-scale model-builders manufactured an illusion of
spacecraft that has never been surpassed. (The models, designed in part by Christiane
Kubrick, were built on a much larger scale than usual, which allowed for realistic details.)
Kubrick was among the first directors (along with Jerry Lewis) to use closed-circuit TV in
order to see certain sequences as they were being photographed, and he and his photographer, Geoffrey Unsworth, devised a way of using Polaroid snapshots to check the
effectiveness of colour and lighting schemes. He also created an elaborate filing or code system to enable him to follow closely the more than 250 special-effects scenes, most of which
involve a matte technology that took as much as ten separate steps to complete. The irony
of all this is that Cinerama died off almost as soon as the film appeared and nearly all the
'advanced' devices Kubrick had perfected were eventually replaced by computers. *2001*'s
crystalline, deep-focus imagery and state-of-the-art special effects have never lost their
power to evoke wonder; indeed the film seems to me a far more spectacular achievement
than any of the digitalised blockbusters of the early twenty-first century. It is, however, a
profoundly theatrical and *photographic* experience (even the astronauts in the film use film
rather than video cameras), which is nowadays mediated for most viewers through the new
technology of DVDs, TV screens and home theatre systems.

As Volker Fischer has pointed out, one reason why the spacesuits, instrument panels
and interior designs of the film have retained their futuristic fascination is that Kubrick
and his many designers achieved a sort of continuation of twentieth-century modernity,
projecting the utopian 'white modernism' of Le Corbusier and the Bauhaus into the distant future.[12] This quality of the film is especially evident in the sequences involving the
Pan-Am shuttle, the Hilton Lounge in Space Station Five, the *Aries B* spacecraft and the
giant centrifuge or gerbil-cage that houses the astronauts on the Discovery mission. The
red-orange lounge chairs in the space station are the Pop-Art creations of French designer
Olivier Morgue and the flight-attendant costumes were inspired by André Coureges, Mary
Quant and Vidal Sassoon; but even though these elements are redolent of the 1960s, they
create a believable 'future-ness' by emphasising streamlining and avoiding the retro or
dystopian styles so typical of postmodern space operas. Significantly, the only retro design
in the film is the strange apartment or hotel room that astronaut Bowman (Keir Dullea)
encounters at the end of his journey; an obviously modern room with new plumbing fix-
tures and lights emanating from translucent panels in the floor, its furnishings and decor
are reminiscent of the eighteenth century – the age of Enlightenment.

The story of how this unusual and highly influential film was made has been told in
several books, among them Vincent LoBrutto's biography of Kubrick; Jerome Angel's anthology, *The Making of Kubrick's* 2001; and Carolyn Geduld's *Filmguide to* 2001: A Space Odyssey

(a text that Kubrick admired). Selections from the Angel and Geduld books can be found in Stephanie Schwam's more recent collection, *The Making of* 2001: *A Space Odyssey*. For my own purposes, a brief summary of the production history, accompanied by a couple of details that haven't been discussed elsewhere, will be sufficient.

The project might be said to have originated in the mid-1950s, when Kubrick first began thinking about an outer space movie. He was particularly attracted to the perennial sci-fi theme of extra-terrestrial intelligence, and at one point during the planning of *Dr. Strangelove*, he thought of a scene in which visitors from another galaxy would discover a dead earth. Even without the space aliens, *Strangelove* won a 'Hugo' award for the best science-fiction film of 1964 and may have prompted Kubrick to approach the genre more directly. The Kennedy-era space-race with the Soviets was nearing the point at which men would soon be on the moon, creating considerable public interest in a film about the topic. Kubrick therefore determined to make a realistic, scientifically accurate picture that would take advantage of the 'special event' nature of movie production during the period. To that end he commissioned Arthur C. Clarke, one of the most respected writers of science fiction in the English-speaking world, to help him develop a screenplay.

An amateur palaeontologist and astronomer, Clarke possessed considerable scientific knowledge and imagination; he arrived independently at important ideas about space travel, such as the space shuttle and the centrifugal space station that generates its own gravity, and he was privy to NASA's long-range planning throughout the 1960s. He was best known for his philosophical novel *Childhood's End* and his speculative non-fiction book *Profiles of the Future*; but Kubrick proposed to start the screenplay with ideas from Clarke's short fiction – chiefly from a nine-page story entitled 'The Sentinel', which origi- nally appeared in print under a slightly different title in 1951. 'The Sentinel' concerns a 1996 expedition to the moon that uncovers a pyramid-shaped artefact surrounded by an invisible shield, emitting a radio signal or 'fire alarm' of its discovery by earthlings. From this seed, Clarke wrote a sort of 'novelisation' of a yet-to-be-filmed movie epic.

Like much of Clarke's work, the original version of the story, entitled 'Journey beyond the Stars', owed a considerable debt to the British philosopher and science-fiction author Olaf Stapledon (1886–1950), who had written novels about mutated supermen, alien intelligences and biological evolution across immense scales of time and space; Stapledon's *Star Maker* (1937), for example, covers billions of years, ranging from the point at which the cosmos is formed until the point at which the last galaxy dies and the universe reaches 'complete physical quiescence'.[13] 'Journey beyond the Stars' wasn't so expansive, but its story-time and spatial dimensions easily dwarfed other movies. The February 1965 version of the screenplay, co-authored with Kubrick, begins when prehistoric apes discover a 'crystal cube' emitting images that teach them what an off-screen narrator describes as 'the awesome and brilliant concept of using natural weapons as artificial tools'. The weapons enable the apes to convert from passive vegetarians into killers who eat other animals, at which point the plot jumps forward 4 million years to 2001, when the earth is plagued by over-population and the proliferation of nuclear bombs. Another crystal cube is discovered by astronauts on the moon, and a mission is formed to track its radio signals. There is no computer like HAL in this version, and at the end astronaut Bowman finds himself held for observation in an odd hotel room designed like the rooms he has seen on old TV shows. A telephone rings, and the voice of a space alien speaks to him. Bowman later meets the aliens, who 'walk upright, have two arms and legs, but seem made of shiny metal. They are naked but have no sign of sex, and the heads are utterly inhuman, with two huge, faceted eyes and a small, curled-up trunk where the nose should be.'[14]

At roughly this point, Kubrick hired Harry Lange and Frederick Ordway, both of whom had worked with NASA, to act as consultants on the film. He and Clarke also conferred with science writer Carl Sagan and managed to engage additional design help not only from NASA but also from IBM, Honeywell, Boeing, Bell Telephone, RCA and General Electric in exchange for putting some of their logos on screen. (The film treats commercial 'tie-ins' ironically, even while it gains in technological plausibility from the imaginations of the corporate designers.) By the end of August 1965, the revised screenplay was entitled *2001: A Space Odyssey*. In this version, the opening scenes are slightly elaborated, with the narrator making the theory of human development more explicit. We are told that the creation of a tool-weapon by an ape named 'Moonwatcher' caused him to feel 'the first faint twinges of a new and potent emotion – the urge to kill. He had taken his first steps toward humanity'. The plot leaps forward to 2001, and the rather garrulous narrator explains that human civilisation has reached 'utter perfection of the weapon', with hundreds of nuclear bombs in orbit around the earth and twenty-seven nations belonging to the nuclear club. 'There had been no deliberate or accidental use of nuclear weapons since World War II,' the narrator says, 'and some people felt secure in this knowledge. But to others, the situation seemed comparable to an airline with a perfect safety record; it showed admirable care and skill but no one could expect it to last forever.'[15] A computer named HAL appears in this draft (in an earlier, intermediate draft, the computer was female and named Athena), but Bowman is able to reprogramme the computer when it causes trouble.

The December 1965 shooting script contains more new material, including a scene in which Heywood Floyd uses a credit card and a 'Vision Shopper' to purchase an African bush-baby for his daughter. The US party on the moon has a conversation about the meaning of the object they've discovered (now a monolith), which seems to have been left by 'something, presumably from the stars'. HAL begins to resemble the computer we see in the completed film, but his dialogue isn't as effective. An elaborate communication between Bowman and the earth explains why HAL went bad: he was programmed to lie about the purpose of the mission, and direct questions about it led to a conflict with his equally strong programming to tell the truth. 'Faced with this dilemma,' we are told, 'he developed, for want of a better description, neurotic symptoms.' This version abandons the possibly hokey-looking aliens and opts instead for a mysterious, quasi-spiritual effect – the script speaks of cosmic 'machine entities' that have the ability to 'store knowledge in the structure of space itself, and to preserve their thoughts for eternity in frozen lattices of light'. These advanced beings have become 'creatures of radiation, free at last from the tyranny of matter'.[16]

Kubrick made further changes after he began shooting the film that December at Shepperton Studios near London and at Borehamwood, where the Vickers Engineering company constructed a giant Ferris wheel for the scenes aboard the Discovery centrifuge. *2001* went a year beyond its original production schedule because of the complexity of its special effects. During the editing Kubrick eliminated a few scenes and became so enamoured of the 'needle drops' of classical recordings he had used for temporary music that he decided to abandon an original score he had commissioned from composer Alex North. His eclectic choice of music – consisting of passages from Richard Strauss's *Also Sprach Zarathustra*, Johann Strauss's *Blue Danube*, Aram Khachaturyan's *Gayaneh* and György Ligeti's *Atmosphères*, *Requiem* and *Lux Aeterna* – would eventually become one of the film's most widely discussed features. There was nothing especially new about the practice of using well-known concert works in film soundtracks but, as Michel Chion has pointed out, the music in *2001* is 'rarely mixed with sound effects, more rarely still with dialogue; it refuses to meld or make common cause with other soundtrack elements'.[17] It seems on prominent display, which may explain why the opening motif from *Zarathustra* became an instant popular hit and has been parodied in countless later movies and TV commercials.

For once, Kubrick made a film that encountered no requests for cuts or revisions from Hollywood censors. The Production Code Administration report on *2001*'s content was virtually free of notations, although under the heading of 'Crime' the report's author made a puzzled entry: 'The computer causes the death of several members of the crew???'[18] The censor's bafflement was nothing compared to the reactions of many in the audience at the MGM preview in March 1968, who found *2001* utterly enigmatic, lacking in suspense and dramatic momentum. Michelangelo Antonioni's equally enigmatic *Blow-Up* had been a success for MGM in the previous year, but it hadn't cost as much and offered plenty of compensating sex in swinging London. The Kubrick film features little more than futuristic hardware and invisible aliens; there are no star actors or sex (Vanessa Redgrave had famously taken off her shirt in *Blow-Up*); almost two-thirds of the picture has no dialogue; and only about thirty minutes involves characters who are placed in jeopardy.

This situation wasn't helped by Kubrick's decision to render the extra-terrestrial intelligence invisible and to shroud the ending in mystery. The strange conclusion to the film, however, was consistent with a strategy he employed throughout post-production. He repeatedly stripped away the visible or audible manifestations of the film's scientific armature, making the meaning of events implicit, ambiguous and as much mythical as rational. (While working on the script, he and Clarke consulted popular scientific writings such as Louis Leakey's *Adam's Ancestors*, Robert Audrey's *African Genesis* and Carl Sagan and I. S. Shklovskii's *Intelligent Life in the Universe*; but they also read Joseph Campbell's *Hero with a Thousand Faces*, an exercise in Jungian mythology that may have influenced the slightly New Age spirituality of the film's climatic episode.) He had originally planned to begin *2001* with a black-and-white, Academy-ratio documentary in which twenty scientists and a Jewish theologian spoke about such topics as space travel, Artificial Intelligence and the possibility of life on other worlds; his assistant, Roger Caras, filmed the interviews, but they were never exhibited, in part because of their length.[19] At some point late in the production, Kubrick also cut the extensive off-screen narration – an uncharacteristic move given that nearly all his other films have narrators. As a result, the audience is unaware of certain details that were strongly emphasised in the script; for example, the famous match cut from a bone weapon flung in the air to an orbiting space vehicle was originally supposed to be accompanied by narration explaining that the object we see orbiting the earth is a nuclear bomb. The absence of narration further obscured what was intended to be one of the film's principal ironies: nuclear energy is required to propel the Discovery mission to Jupiter.

The studio's uneasiness about *2001* was reinforced by the majority of the New York critics after the official opening. Judith Christ in *New York Magazine* and Stanley Kaufman in the *New Republic* wrote negative reviews. Hollis Alpert in the *Saturday Review* complained that Kubrick had made his audience feel more concern for HAL than for the humans. *Time* said that *2001* was overlong and that Kubrick and Clarke had ignored 'such old-fashioned elements as character and conflict' (19 April 1968). *Newsweek* reported that 'the director's attempt to show the boredom of interplanetary flight becomes a crashing bore in its own right' (15 April 1968). The most savage review was by Pauline Kael in *Harper's*, who accused Kubrick of 'idiot solemnity' and 'big-shot show-business deep thinking'.[20] Andrew Sarris in the *Village Voice* was also against the film but, not long afterward, when *2001* began to draw huge crowds of the younger generation (it was advertised as 'The Ultimate Trip'), he jokingly confessed that he had revisited it 'under the influence of a smoked substance' and changed his mind. Explaining that the 'substance' was less potent than a 'vermouth cassis', he argued that Kubrick's film was no 'head movie' but 'a major work by a major artist . . . a parable of a future toward which metaphysical dread and mordant amusement tiptoe side by side'.[21]

The film's cosmic perspective, rigorous attention to technological design and rejection of conventional dramatic values had blinded most of the New York critical establishment to its special achievement. Kubrick's response was to cut nineteen minutes – a modest alteration, but any further revisions might have changed *2001* into a different kind of movie. As Mario Falsetto has remarked, the original 70mm presentation was intended to make audiences feel they were 'experiencing film for the first time' (p. 45). The youth audience and any viewer who attended for the sake of spectacle or in the spirit of what Tom Gunning has termed 'the cinema of attractions' were probably in a better position than the literary-minded critics to appreciate the unusual qualities of what she or he was seeing.[22] Certain sophisticated witnesses, however, were well attuned to the physical sensations *2001* created on the largest screens. Writing in *Film Comment*, Max Kosloff eloquently described how 'Every movement of the lens has a tangibly buoyant, decelerated grace.' Kubrick's boom and pan shots, Kosloff explained, 'wield the glance through circumferences mimed already by the curvature of the screen itself. Whether one is seated above or beneath this spectacle, one is brought almost physically toward its shifting gyre, hanging from it as if from some balcony on the solar system.'[23] In a lengthy essay in *Art Forum*, Annette Michelson argued that *2001* moved with the 'apparent absence of speed which one experiences only in the fastest of elevators, or jet planes', and that it impelled its viewers 'to rediscover the space and dimensions of the body as a theatre of consciousness'.[24]

David Lean's *Lawrence of Arabia* (1962), which contains a match-cut from a close-up of a burning match to a wide shot of the sun rising over sand dunes, creates panoramas almost as sublime as the ones in *2001*; what makes the Kubrick picture unique is the way it slows time in relation to the vastness of space. In the opening section, titled 'The Dawn of Man', one tableau follows another in quite leisurely fashion, the sheer immensity of the Super-Panavision screen retarding the forward march of narrative. The stillness and the diurnal rhythm of light from the sky begin to evoke a mood of anxious anticipation, like a held breath, until the serenity is disrupted by brief spasms of shock and surprise: a skeleton dried by the sun; a leopard attacking a tapir; a group of peaceful, vegetarian apes chased away from a water-hole by a screaming, marauding band of rival apes; a black monolith appearing out of nowhere, its surreal presence backed by Ligeti's ultra-modern music. When an astral alignment above the monolith (earth, sun, moon, in reverse-angle relationship to the shot that opened the film) leads to the slow dawning of consciousness and intelligence in one of the apes (named 'Moonwatcher' in Clarke's novel, and played here by Daniel Richter) we see him picking up a bone with slow-witted curiosity and toying lightly with it. To the music of Strauss's *Zarathustra*, he becomes a weapon bearer, a killer and a meat eater. In slow motion he fells a tapir. After disposing of the rival apes around the water-hole, he exultantly tosses his bone weapon into the air; and as it revolves in slow

motion, a somewhat technically awkward but conceptually dazzling match-cut elides
thousands of years, showing a spacecraft silently orbiting the earth. After a moment of
quietness, like another held breath, we hear the opening strains of *The Blue Danube* and
watch a series of other spacecraft floating through the heavens.

Once aloft, no other big-budget science-fiction film has ever been paced so slowly, as
if it were mesmerised by the sheer phenomenology of minimalist, methodical actions
played off against a disorienting widescreen background. Andrei Tarkovsky's *Solaris* (1972),
which is clearly influenced by *2001*, is sometimes equally slow, but less devoted to special
effects and more concerned with the psychology of characters. Kubrick's film is directly
about perception in outer space, which it explores in radical fashion while maintaining
some of the elemental pleasures of narrative. Unlike any of the Hollywood science-fiction
movies it influenced – among them the *Star Wars* and *Star Trek* franchises and Brian
DePalma's *Mission to Mars* (2000) – it never makes us feel as if we were rocketing away from
earth at high speed or whizzing around in jet aircraft. Beginning with the charming *ballet
mechanique* of Floyd's journeys to the space station and the moon, we encounter everything
in calmly measured fashion, witnessing spectacular new technology and vast feats of
mechanical engineering but at the same time gradually losing our bearings in the immensity of the universe. At certain junctures, especially in the section titled 'Jupiter Mission:
18 months later', time stands still and we don't know which way is up. The Discovery spacecraft is supposedly hurtling towards Jupiter, but it seems to be lumbering slowly through
starry blackness; inside, it revolves, so that when astronaut Poole (Gary Lockwood) jogs
down a corridor lined with what look like coffins or sarcophagi, he goes nowhere. The
only moments of acceleration are during Bowman's aborted attempt to rescue Poole, when
the astronaut's body and his inoperable 'pod' go spinning off into eternity, and in Bowman's
climactic journey towards 'Jupiter and beyond the Infinite'. In the latter case, however, the

film seems to be representing a journey *inward* to a new state of consciousness. Once Bowman arrives in the interplanetary holding room, everything slows again and all logic of time and space is suspended. In one shot we see Bowman's subjective point of view from inside his pod, but a few shots later we return to that same angle and look towards the spacesuited Bowman as he stands outside. When we cut from a long shot to a close-up of Bowman, he has grown inexplicably older. As he explores a bathroom, he hears something off screen; a subjective travelling shot shows him moving towards the bedroom, where he encounters an aged version of himself wearing a silk dressing gown. We see his astonished reaction, followed by a reverse shot of what he sees – but when we return to the initial angle, his young self has disappeared.

These systematic disorientations and reversals of values throw into relief the film's 'poetic' or musical strategies, especially its tendency to communicate through rhymes and motifs. Thomas Allen Nelson has described many of *2001*'s recurring patterns in detail, emphasising how they create 'a world that not only ascends into space and descends into time, but collapses from within in gestures of reflexive mockery as it expands outward toward implied realms of the imagination' (p. 116). The echoes between the first and second parts of the film are particularly evident: both apes and men are makers of weapons, both are organised in rival clans and both gather excitedly around a black monolith. Like the apes, the men spend most of their lives sleeping and eating. When Heywood Floyd reaches out to touch the mysterious object on the moon, he repeats the tentative gesture of the lead ape in 'The Dawn of Man'; and when the other astronauts gather around the Tyco monolith for a sort of tourist photo, they resemble their simian forebears. Elsewhere we find other doublings and repetitions: two human birthdays are celebrated, two virtually indistinguishable astronauts oversee the Discovery and we are told that HAL has a twin on earth. As the film proceeds, men increasingly resemble machines and machines appear vaguely biological. (Kubrick told an interviewer that it was common for NASA engineers to 'talk about machines as being sexy'.)[25] This is true not only of HAL, who is arguably the most emotional character and whose brain is filled with blood-red cells, but also of the Aries B, which looks like a giant head with gleaming jack-o-lantern eyes; the Discovery, which is shaped like a strange insect or deep-sea creature; the space-pods, which have arms and opposable 'fingers'; and the spacesuited astronauts, who emerge from their pods like colourful bugs breaking out of cocoons. Carolyn Geduld has observed that space travel in *2001* is also filled with a kind of 'abstract uterine imagery', especially in the scenes involving the astronauts emerging from the pods and in the shot in which Bowman blasts himself through the red-lit tunnel of the 'mother' ship's emergency air lock (pp. 55–8).

The journey-and-return pattern of Bowman's space odyssey is echoed in various circular rhythms and images: the stewardess who walks up and around walls, the turning space station, the orbiting satellites, the revolving room in the Discovery and the rotating spheres of the heavens. There is also a prominent motif of eyes and vision: HAL's gleaming red 'pupil' sees everything aboard the Discovery (our first view of an astronaut is a reflection

in HAL's eye), and Keir Dullea has particularly intense, ice-blue eyes. In this last regard, notice that the first parts of the film are quite sparing of point-of-view shots; when the lead ape awakes in the morning and reacts to something off screen, Kubrick cuts to a long-distance panorama rather than a subjective angle to reveal the monolith. The most intense subjective shots in the middle section belong to HAL, who sees the world in extreme wide-angle or, when he reads lips, telephoto perspective. Bowman's climactic journey through the star-gate, however, is completely subjective, seen from the vantage of a single blinking eye; and in the last shot, the foetus in the heavens turns its enormous eyes on us.

One of the more obvious thematic motifs of the film has to do with the disparity between technology and culture – thus the apes 'speak' in grunts and snarls and the astronauts in banalities or simple commands. The few dialogue scenes nevertheless have a humorous and

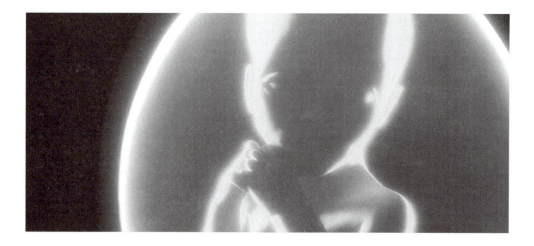

fairly complicated subtext of barely concealed emotion, signalled by long pauses and an air of strained politeness. The result is an effect that was becoming increasingly typical of Kubrick – an occasionally suspenseful but humorous banality. The two 'birthday' conversations, first between Floyd and 'Squirt' (Vivian Kubrick) and then between Poole and his parents, are awkward, somewhat emotionless attempts to achieve intimacy via television; but the cleverly acted and edited exchanges at the space station between Dr Floyd and Dr Smyslov (Leonard Rossiter) and later aboard the Discovery between Bowman and HAL (Douglas Rain) are emotionally freighted and rich with implication.

The former sequence is shot for the most part with the camera at some distance from the players. First we see Smyslov and three women seated around a table speaking Russian in conspiratorial tones; one of the women looks at her watch, and as Floyd approaches everyone breaks into broad smiles. Floyd responds formulaically to ritual greetings and introductions. ('You're looking wonderful.' 'Oh, I've heard a lot about you.' 'Well, how's Gregor?' 'Be sure to give him my regards.') Refusing a drink but agreeing to Smyslov's insistent offer of his own chair, Floyd sits back in relaxed fashion and crosses his legs while Smyslov pulls up another chair and leans forward. The three women fall silent when they learn Floyd is on his way to the Clavius base. 'Doctor Floyd,' Smyslov says with prissy exactitude, 'I hope you won't think I'm being too inquisitive, but perhaps you can clear up the great big mystery of what's been going on up there.' After a long pause and a slight diminution of his smile, Floyd quietly replies, 'I'm afraid I don't know what you mean.' Smyslov presses the issue, keeping his sharp features focused intently on the American, remarking that 'some extremely odd things have been happening' and that 'there's going to be a bit of a row about it'. Floyd repeatedly claims ignorance ('Oh, really?' 'Oh, I see.' 'Oh, that does sound odd.'), all the while maintaining a level gaze and a quiet demeanour. Smyslov leans forward a bit more and speaks in a hushed voice: 'Dr Floyd, at the risk of pressing . . . May

I ask you a straightforward question?' When Floyd replies 'Yes, certainly', the Russian tells him about 'reliable intelligence reports' of an epidemic on Clavius: 'Is this, in fact, what has happened?' Another long pause, during which Floyd gazes straight at Smyslov and we hear nothing but the ambient sound of generators and machines: 'I'm sorry, Dr Smyslov,' Floyd says, his face registering a slight discomfort beneath its calm, 'but I'm really not at liberty to discuss this with you.'

The personal dynamics and even some of the language in this scene are echoed in the later conversation between Bowman and HAL, which begins when Bowman walks past with sketches in his hand and HAL asks to see them. In this case the interaction is shot mostly in close-ups. 'That's a very nice rendering, Dave,' the computer says. 'I think you've improved a great deal.' As in the earlier encounter between Floyd and Smyslov, both speakers behave politely but one is excessively reserved and the other is loquacious and prissy (Pauline Kael describes HAL as gay – it's more accurate to say that he's androgynous, bearing traces of the female computer in the earliest scripts). The more active speaker begins pressing for information while the other tries with mixed success to maintain a mask of calm; the dialogue is filled with pregnant pauses, during which we hear the ambient sound of the ship's generators or equipment:

HAL: By the way, do you mind if I ask you a personal question?

DAVE: No, not at all.

HAL [A slight quaver]: Well, forgive me for being so inquisitive, but during the past few weeks I've wondered whether you might be having second thoughts about the mission.

DAVE [Blankly, after a pause]: How do you mean?

HAL: Well, it's rather difficult to define. Perhaps I'm just projecting my own concern about it. [Pause] I know I've never completely freed myself of the suspicion [slight note of irritation] that there are some extremely odd things about this mission. [Pause] I know you'll agree there's some truth in what I say.

DAVE [Pause]: Well, that's rather difficult to say.

HAL: You don't mind my talking about it, do you, Dave?

DAVE [Blankly, after a pause]: No, not at all.

HAL: Well, certainly no one could have been unaware of the strange stories floating around before we left. [Pause] Rumors about something being dug up. [Pause, during which we see DAVE's unresponsive face, his eyes blinking.] I never gave these stories much credence, but particularly in view of some of the other things that have happened I find them difficult to put out of mind. For instance, the way all our preparations were kept under such tight security. And the melodramatic touch of putting Professors Hunter, Kimball, and Kaminsky aboard already under hibernation after four months of separate training.

DAVE [Flatly, with a blank face]: You're working up your crew psychology report.

HAL: Of course I am. Sorry about this. I know it's a bit silly. [Pause] Just a moment. [Pause] I've just picked up a fault in the AE 35 unit.

Part of the fascination of the acting in this tense and amusing scene lies in the frequent pauses and the sustained counterpoint between calm statements and 'hidden' emotions. Keir Dullea's performance is almost entirely in his eyes, which are lit from slightly below, betraying a subtext of steely resolve or perhaps hostility, together with a mounting uneasiness about the direction of the conversation. (Despite the assurance Bowman has previously given a BBC interviewer that everything is harmonious aboard the Discovery, he seems to dislike and distrust HAL.) Douglas Rain's performance, on the other hand, is completely in his dreamy voice and fastidious enunciation, which is inflected with a good many emotional nuances – not only 'pride', as the BBC interviewer has observed, but also superciliousness, condescension and anger masked by a rather affected attitude of genteel self-deprecation.

Michel Chion, who has written at length about HAL in terms of what he calls an 'acous-metre' (a disembodied voice that seems to know everything) and an 'I-voice' (a voice that resonates from a subjective space), notes that HAL's speeches are 'closely miked, with no spatial indices or reverb', whereas Bowman's and Poole's are 'reflected off walls inside the ship' (p. 102) – hence the computer seems especially soulful and uncanny. Notice also that the astronauts are laconic and the computer verbose. As the uneasy subjects of HAL's panoptic gaze, Bowman and Poole hold their one important conversation in secret. Even when Bowman confronts HAL in the full knowledge that the computer plans to leave him stranded outside the ship, he keeps his fury under control and issues crisp military orders. In the final, darkly humorous yet somehow sad and brutal confrontation between man and machine, Bowman is virtually silent; the lobotomy in the blood-red 'brain room' is conducted to the sound of the astronaut's heavy, machine-filtered breathing and the computer's nervous, full-voiced prattle:

> HAL: Just what do you think you're doing, Dave? . . . Dave . . . I really think I'm entitled to an answer to that question . . . . I know everything hasn't been quite right with me, but I can assure you now, very confidentially, that it's going to be all right again . . . . I feel much better now, I really do . . . . Look, Dave . . . I can see you're really upset about this . . . . I honestly think you ought to sit down calmly, take a stress pill, and think things over . . . . I want to help you. Dave, stop . . . . Stop, will you . . . Stop, Dave . . . . Will you stop, Dave? I'm afraid . . . . I'm afraid, Dave.

Elsewhere, and in spite of its relative paucity of verbal cues, *2001* manages to create a rich variety of tonal effects, ranging from the awe-inspiring opening and closing scenes to the satiric imagery of the space travellers. At one extreme, we have the monolith that symbolises non-human technology and intelligence – dark, totemic, impervious, reflective of light, both Freudian and Jungian, suggesting both ultra-modernism and monumental force – and at the other, a series of playful symbols, including a one-eyed computer reminiscent of Homer's Cyclops and a space shuttle that enters its docking platform like a joke from

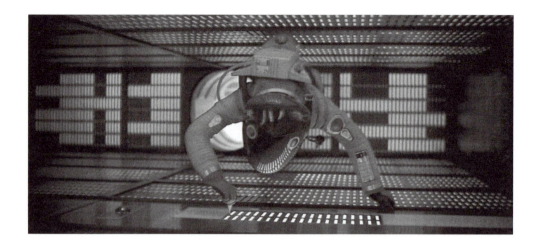

Dr. Strangelove. Unfortunately, the film doesn't always succeed in the effects it aims to pro-duce: the mimes and dancers who wear specially designed ape costumes are impressively realistic, certainly more so than the equivalent figures in *Planet of the Apes* (1968), but even so they look like actors in ape costumes (particularly when one of them holds a real-life baby chimp). The light show near the end is occasionally stunning, but Pauline Kael was correct to argue that the non-narrative avant-garde had already done such things more powerfully. Kubrick is at his best in the middle sections and in the bizarre concluding scenes, where he manages to combine philosophical and scientific speculation with eerie suspense, black humour with cosmic wonder.

The scenes involving HAL are so dramatically interesting and scientifically provoca-tive that they've prompted an entire book – *HAL's Legacy:* 2001*'s Computer as Dream and Reality* – in which scientists specialising in Artificial Intelligence attempt to answer funda-mental questions. Is it possible to make a foolproof computer? How do computers learn to understand human speech? How do they 'see'? Could they have emotions? When they kill, who is to blame?[26] These portions of the film also contain some of Kubrick's most impressive audiovisual effects. The agonisingly slow attempt to rescue Poole, for exam-ple, begins with the sound of methodical spacesuited breathing and computer noises and ends with complete silence. (Kubrick and Godard are among the few directors of the period to experiment with turning off *all* sound, including the ambient track, though Kubrick does it in the service of realism and Godard in the interest of self-reflexivity.) The image of Poole's body spiralling away into an utterly soundless void is both a frightening event and a chilling comment on human insignificance, a death touched by what George Toles has aptly described as 'veiled' melancholy (p. 149).

Kubrick's mid-course decision to cut most of the film's explanatory verbiage and to emphasise its oneiric and mysterious aspects was not such a radical change of plans as it

might seem for, at their extremes, scientific speculations about the nature of the universe are similar to the stories told by myth and religion. One of the reasons why *2001* remains a compelling film – and a more interesting work of art than Arthur C. Clarke's published novelisation – is its ability to fuse scientific vision with an equally strong feeling for the metaphysical, the eerie and the unexplained. Nevertheless, in interviews, Kubrick was insistent that he had tried to achieve what he called 'a *scientific* definition of God'.[27] The necessary and sufficient conditions for deity, he explained, are omniscience and omnipotence. Thus HAL, who sees every part of the Discovery and controls nearly all of the ship's technical functions, could be described as a sort of Benthamite god; and the transfigured astronaut or Odysseus who returns to earth as a foetus is certainly a kind of god in relation to ordinary humans. The film's ultimate god is, of course, the mysterious intelligence who created the monolith and intervened in human evolution. *2001*'s narrative of human history is not quite Darwinian and certainly not Judaeo-Christian; instead, in secular fashion, it posits a science-fiction version of what religious fundamentalists in the US at the beginning of the twenty-first century like to call 'intelligent design'.

One might also argue that the film has a Nietzschean view of history and civilisation. Kubrick uses Richard Wagner in the opening and closing not only to make us feel awe, but also to point us towards Nietzsche's *Thus Spake Zarathustra*, a few lines from which could have served as *2001*'s epigraph:

Man is something that is to be surpassed. What have ye done to surpass man?...

Once were ye apes, and yet even man is more of an ape than any of the apes. Even the wisest among you is only a disharmony and hybrid of plant and phantom. But do I bid you to become plants and phantoms?

Lo, I teach you the Superman![28]

Near the end of the film, when astronaut Bowman looks down at the broken shards of a crystal glass on the floor, the curious tilt of his head echoes the earlier scene of the ape looking down at a pile of bones in the sand: a monumental discovery is at hand, but it feels like an Eternal Return. And when the Superman finally arrives in the form of a foetus from outer space, we witness a revolutionary cycle governed by the same forces we've seen in the past.

Kubrick originally intended to show the child looking towards earth and exploding the nuclear satellites with the force of will, destroying civilisation as we know it. He changed his mind because he didn't want to repeat the ending of *Dr. Strangelove*. Nevertheless, it seems doubtful that he viewed the development of 'higher' life forms as a necessary advance in morality or peacefulness. The film suggests that every leap forward, every moment of mastery over nature, involves a kind of murder. At this level, Kubrick has something roughly in common with a satirist like Thorsten Veblen, who maintained that primitive social organisation is always peaceable (much like the apes in the film's opening) and that civilisation is grounded in predatory barbarism and patriarchy. In the futuristic world of *2001*, productive intelligence, creativity and advanced engineering are still to a great extent supported by private property and male aggression. The only way out of this cycle is a move towards the superhuman or non-human – but, according to the film, machine intelligence also harbours murderous instincts.

To these paradoxes we can add several others. Kubrick's production is in some respects a speculative documentary and in others a kind of dream or allegory: George Toles reads it brilliantly as a fairy tale in which a computer, resembling a 'belated modernist', is weighed down with the 'afflictions and burdens of consciousness that the humans have left behind' (p. 161). The film can be viewed as a Hollywood spectacle and as the most expensive art movie ever made, with an open-ended, ambiguous conclusion that Andrew Sarris initially described as 'Instant Ingmar'.[29] As I've previously indicated, it's both the ultimate in futurist cinema and a film that transcends the utopian/dystopian distinction upon which futurism depends. No wonder commentators have been sharply divided over its ultimate significance. Is the non-human intelligence represented by the black monolith a benign force or a malign joke? Is the baby in the heavens a saviour or a devil child? Is the film humanist or anti-humanist, optimistic or pessimistic? Andrew Walker says that *2001* is 'buoyed up with hope' and Raymond Durgnat calls it a film noir.[30] Marvin Minskey, one of the founders of the field of Artificial Intelligence and a consultant on *2001*, says in an interview that the film synthesises the different temperaments of Clarke and Kubrick: '[T]he last scene is due to Clarke, based on his story 'Childhood's End.' Nevertheless I think that both [authors] are quite mystical, in a way. Kubrick's vision seemed to be that humans are doomed, whereas Clarke's is that humans are moving on to a better stage of evolution' (Stork, p. 23). In an intriguing essay, critic Carl Freedman tries to explain these contradictions or inner tensions from a different angle, maintaining that *2001* re-invents science-fiction cinema and, at the same time, 'views with the most cogent skepticism the very tenability of the genre that it exemplifies'. According to Freedman, the special effects in science-fiction movies have nearly always been implicitly authoritarian or Wagnerian in their aims, in contrast with a film like Godard's *Alphaville*, which is relatively free of special effects. Certain films, such as Robert Wise's *The Day the Earth Stood Still* (1951) and Ridley Scott's *Blade Runner* (1982), tend to mix special effects with what Freedman calls 'literary' and 'psychological' elements in order to develop a critical point of view. The paradox of the highly Wagnerian *2001* is that, while it avoids the 'literary' and 'grants to special effects an aesthetic hegemony unsurpassed in the whole range of science-fiction cinema', it maintains a critical edge by making the banality of human life one of its central themes. For Freedman, 'in spite of its strategic avoidance of politics, *2001* conveys authentic utopian energy in its glimpse of a spiritual richness that may rescue humanity from the bureaucratic pettiness of a Heywood Floyd or his Russian counterparts'.[31]

One of the issues raised by the ending of the film, however, is whether humanity needs to be 'rescued' or whether it needs to evolve into something else. The great achievement of *2001* seems to me its ability to keep this question floating in the air, somewhere between a longing for utopia and a deep suspicion of utopia. George Toles captures the feeling exactly when he notes that the Star Child, who seems larger than the earth, 'gazes like a fledgling predator on a world it has nearly outgrown', but at the same time represents a spirit of metamorphosis and resurrection: 'our fears of old age and dying are addressed, then magically alleviated' (p. 156). The ultimate irony of the film is that the humanoid foetus in the heavens is partly the child of what the script describes as 'creatures of radiation, free at last from the tyranny of matter'. In this regard, *2001* becomes unexpectedly prophetic. To understand why, we need only remember that I began by listing a few things Kubrick and Clarke didn't foresee. The most revolutionary scientific development that might have been mentioned is the mapping of the human genome, which made rapid progress at the turn of the twenty-first century. Even though *2001* doesn't predict this event, it gives us a vision of what the deep knowledge of biology leads us towards. Writing in 2005, the scientific futurist Ray Kurzweil predicted that, because computers can now read the genome, we are facing the immanent arrival of a computerised 'non-biological intelligence' that will fuse with the human body and engineer something new, strange and theoretically immortal.[32] Kubrick imagined just such a future, in the form of an evolutionary epic of outer space. As we shall see at a later point, he planned to return to the topic at the end of the century, in an earth-bound film, *A. I. Artificial Intelligence*, which appeared posthumously under the direction of Steven Spielberg. A fitting memorial, *A. I.* confronts the inevitability of human death, a theme that haunts all of Kubrick's work, by imagining the death of the species and the survival of pure intelligence.

III. A Professional Piece of Sinny

As we've seen, Kubrick's original plan was to follow *2001* with a dialectically opposite movie – an early nineteenth-century epic dealing with the life of Napoleon. For reasons

already explained, he was forced to abandon that picture. Eventually, he formed an agreement with Warner Bros. to adapt Anthony Burgess's 1962 novel, *A Clockwork Orange*, which
could be transformed into another film about the future, this time without special effects.
The novel had been brought to his attention by Terry Southern during the making of
Dr. Strangelove, but at first Kubrick seems to have paid little attention to it. Southern
purchased the movie rights for a relatively small sum and, through his lawyer, tried unsuccessfully to interest the Rolling Stones and Ken Russell in a screen version. Meanwhile,
Kubrick read the book more closely and recognised its potential. He bought the rights for
a higher price than Southern had paid (none of which went to Burgess) and decided to
write the screenplay himself.

Made at the height of England's influence on fashion design and international pop culture, *A Clockwork Orange* turned out to be Kubrick's only film about modern British society.
(Although it may be significant that the Vera Lynn song at the end of *Dr. Strangelove* derives
from British popular culture, and that the television broadcasts viewed by the US astronauts in *2001* originate from the BBC.) Ironically, it set off a firestorm of protest from British
conservatives and was banned by the British Board of Film Censors, who restricted it to a
limited run. In the US, where a ratings system had recently been introduced, the initial
release was given an X. Three years earlier, the first runs of John Schlesinger's Academy
Award-winning *Midnight Cowboy* and Sam Peckinpah's *The Wild Bunch* had also received
X ratings, but *A Clockwork Orange* was far more troublesome – a black comedy in the mode
of *Dr. Strangelove*, filled with explicit sex and horrific violence. *The Detroit News* and other
papers in America refused to advertise it on the grounds of the X, and it was shown in only
one London theatre during 1972. Kubrick briefly withdrew it from circulation and removed
about thirty seconds of footage in order to obtain an R rating in the US (the Americans
were more concerned with the sex scenes than the violence), but the British press, who
were themselves satirised in the film, would not let the controversy die. The tabloids
claimed that *A Clockwork Orange* had prompted copy-cat murders in England, and Kubrick
began to receive anonymous death threats in the mail. His response was to forbid exhibition of the film anywhere in Great Britain, where he owned the distribution rights.
A Clockwork Orange was not given an authorised showing in England until after his death,
and even today it's the Kubrick movie least likely to be shown on US cable TV. (In 2006,
the mass-circulation news magazine *Entertainment Weekly* listed it as the second most controversial film of all time, just after Mel Gibson's *The Passion of the Christ*.)

Kubrick won the New York Film Critics Award for the picture, but many influential
critics in the US took a strong dislike to it. Andrew Sarris called it boring and pretentious
(*The Village Voice*, 30 December 1971, p. 49), David Denby said it was decadent and nihilistic (*Atlantic*, March 1972, p. 100) and Pauline Kael claimed it had been designed in such a
way as to enable viewers to enjoy scenes of rapes and beatings (*The New Yorker*, 1 January
1972, p. 50). In *The New York Times* and other forums, the film's aesthetic, moral and political effects were widely debated. Was it art or pornography? Was it an important satire

or an immoral, misogynistic and misanthropic fraud? Was it right-wing or liberal? The public couldn't decide and, as the controversy grew, Kubrick himself gave somewhat different statements about his intentions. In an interview for *Take One*, he said the film was intentionally dreamlike and, like dreams, demanded 'a suspension of moral judgment' (May–June 1971, p. 28); but in a later interview for *Positif*, he said it was about the moral/philosophical question of the freedom to choose between good and evil (June 1972, pp. 23–31).

As Janet Staiger has pointed out, Kubrick's different remarks and the wildly conflicted cultural responses to the film were historically conditioned.[33] The sexual revolutions of the 1960s had produced changing and often contradictory definitions of pornography and obscenity, thus making *A Clockwork Orange* 'available' for different readings by different audiences. Initially discussed within the discursive framework of art cinema, it later became a cult favourite. Staiger suggests that it was probably viewed in certain contexts as camp for gay males – indeed the androgynous David Bowie, a 'glam rock' superstar in the 1980s, referred to it repeatedly in his concerts.

Anthony Burgess, who was at the time regarded as one of the most talented novelists of his generation, was ambivalent about the adaptation. (At Kubrick's suggestion, he later wrote *Napoleon Symphony* [1974]; and in the 1980s he adapted two musical versions of *A Clockwork Orange* for the British stage, one of which made fun of Kubrick.) A prolific author and critic, Burgess was also a musician and linguist who, despite the fact that he wrote several screenplays, was condescending towards the movies. Much of his fiction shows his extensive knowledge of orchestral music, which he occasionally composed, as well as his indebtedness to James Joyce, about whom he wrote two books. Born a Catholic, he was intensely preoccupied with the religious problem of the relation between original sin and free will; at the time when *A Clockwork Orange* was filmed, however, he said that the book was a relatively minor exploration of his favoured theme – a sub-par, Orwellian dystopia written in haste during a period when he was suffering from a potentially deadly illness. The novel expresses a Tory attitude towards modern England (where its initial publication was poorly received) and was partly an attempt to 'exorcise' memories of his first wife, who, as a result of being sexually assaulted during World War II by four US Army deserters, had lost the child with which she was pregnant (LoBrutto, p. 336). Symptomatic of the moral panic over the 'youth problem' and 'juvenile delinquency' in the decades after the war, it projects the violence of the Teddy Boys and the Mods and Rockers into the 1980s, imagining a world of boy rapists and their ineffectual victims, all of whom are governed by a soulless and hypocritical socialism of both the right and the left.

Burgess's literary reputation went into decline after his death (in his later years he sounded increasingly bitter and reactionary about high taxes and pop culture), and yet most critics today would disagree with his somewhat dismissive judgment of his writing in *A Clockwork Orange*. Despite its many depressing qualities, the novel is an energetic narrative and a bravura linguistic accomplishment. The story is told in the first person by a narcissistic and sadistic teenager named Alex (in the film he gives his full name as 'Alexander DeLarge', but a montage of newspaper headlines names him 'Alexander Burgess'), who speaks 'Nadsat', his word for 'teen'. Most of Alex's patois derives from Slavic and is intended by Burgess to suggest a dreary socialist future, but it also makes use of Cockney and Elizabethan English: 'How art thou, thou globby bottle of stinking chip-oil? Come and get one in the yarbles, if you have any yarbles, you eunuch jelly, thou.'[34] Loaded with puns, portmanteau words and other forms of verbal play, it sometimes resembles a light version of the invented language in Joyce's *Finnegans Wake*: 'You will have little desire to slooshy all the cally and horrible razkazz of the shock that sent my dad beating his brused and krovvy rockers against unfair like Bog in his Heaven, and my mum squaring her rot for owwwww owwwww owwwww in her mother's grief at her only child and son of her bosom like letting everybody down real horrorshow' (p. 61). As Colin Burrow has pointed out, this language makes readers of the novel 'look inside the mechanics of their own understanding, and use their grasp of syntax and whatever ghosts of etymological understanding they might have as a means of construing the sense of individual words from their context'.[35] The overall effect is ironically comic and poetic, providing a kind of screen or filter for descriptions of ghastly violence and making Alex seem slyly charming and inventive even when he acts like a monster.

Underlying Burgess's social satire is both a religious theme and an art theme. Very much like T. S. Eliot and Graham Greene, Burgess is a critic of modernity who believes in sin and seems to prefer a remorseless, knowing sinner to a secular humanist or a social worker. He accepts the conservative Christian teaching that all human beings are imperfect or 'fallen' – but fortunately so, because they can choose to be redeemed by the grace of God. Given this teaching, anyone who deliberately joins the Devil's party with a full knowledge of sin is closer to God, and hence to humanity and salvation, than is a mere atheist. Consider the murderous Alex, who tells us that he believes in God, but that he belongs to the Devil's 'shop':

> [B]adness is of the self, the one, the you or me on our oddy knockies, and that badness is made by old Bog or God and is his great pride and radosty. But the not-self cannot have the bad, meaning they of the government and the judges and the schools cannot allow the bad because they cannot allow the self. And is not our modern history, my brothers, the story of brave malenky selves fighting these big machines? I am serious with you, my brothers, over this . . . . what I do I do because I like to do. (p. 34)

Burgess wants us to recoil in horror when Alex savagely beats up old codgers and rapes children, but he also wants us to feel contempt for 'Mr Alexander', Alex's victim and ironic namesake, who, like Alex, has written a book entitled *A Clockwork Orange*. Alexander's book is a Rousseau-like disquisition on the natural goodness of humanity; it rails against the government's attempt to treat humans as machines, but at the same time argues that the common folk need to be 'prodded' into an acceptance of liberty. A godless liberal, Alexander is no more admirable in Burgess's eyes than the equally godless Minister of the Interior, who subjects Alex to Pavlovian mind-control. Alex achieves a qualified, ironic victory over both of these men. He and his gang destroy the first draft of Alexander's book, beat the author almost to death and gang-rape his young wife before his eyes. The 'Minister of the Interior or Inferior', as Alex calls him, escapes physical punishment but in the end is forced by liberal politicians to reverse the 'Lodovico treatment' and tacitly support Alex's crimes. The only significant character exempted from retribution of some kind is the alcoholic and perhaps homosexual priest or 'charley' in the state prison, who objects in the name of God to the government's mind-control experiment, and who resigns from his job when Alex is turned into a meek robot.

The novel's art theme reinforces its religious theme and, given Burgess's implicit attitude towards high art versus commercial art, is equally paradoxical and conservative. Alex's passionate love for Beethoven, Mozart, Handel and fictional contemporaries such as 'Claudius Birdman', 'Friedrich Gitterfenster' and 'Anthony Plautus' is intended by Burgess as a sign that the young killer is closer to the angels than are the social engineers and agents of the state who try to control him. The point is not that art equals 'goodness' (an idea Alex derides) but that it rises out of the wellsprings of human consciousness and is capable of expressing not only atavistic cruelty but also spiritual longing and exaltation. Perhaps, as Peter J. Rabinowitz has argued, Burgess believed that classical German music is somehow evil,[36] but the novel also suggests that Beethoven achieves the highest levels of the demonic sublime. For Alex, the 'glorious 9th' functions as a Dionysian rite, feeding sadistic fantasies and inducing erotic ecstasy. For the well-adjusted citizens of the modern state, on the other hand, no music can be said to have mythic or quasi-religious qualities, whether for good or evil; it's either kitsch (exemplified in the novel by 'Johnny Zhivago', Stash Kroh', 'Id Molotov' and other pop stars that Alex, like Burgess, despises) or utilitarian – a 'mood enhancer', as the inventor of the Lodovico treatment says of Beethoven. Burgess drives the point home when the government mind-control experiment destroys Alex's ability to listen to Beethoven alongside his ability to commit violent acts. Significantly, Alex also loses his taste for the Bible, which he once enjoyed for its stories of violence and sex. Humanity dies along with evil and, as Mr Alexander puts it, 'Music and the sexual act, literature and art, all must be a source now not of pleasure but of pain' (p. 122).

Its political strangeness aside, *A Clockwork Orange* was a relatively inexpensive book to adapt as a film, and it no doubt interested Kubrick for several aesthetic and ideological reasons: it offered a gripping narrative in three easily recognisable 'acts'; it satirised instrumental rationality; it indirectly commented on the relation between humans, puppets and machines; it depicted a disturbingly aggressive male sexuality; and it provided still another example of the criminal-as-artist theme Kubrick had previously explored in *The Killing* and *Lolita*. He said that he was particularly drawn to the fairy-tale quality of the second half of the story, with its many coincidences and dramatic ironies, which pushed the boundaries of narrative realism and parodied sentimental conventions, opening up many possibilities for a surrealistic, black-comic approach. Besides all this, he knew the project would enable him to induce a crisis of sympathy or judgment. Alex may be appalling, but he is utterly forthright about his crimes and repeatedly addresses us, his readers, as 'my brothers' (Burgess's sly way of alluding to Baudelaire's and Eliot's '*hypocrite lecteur, mon semblable, mon frere*'). Kubrick told interviewers that he was intrigued with this sort of honest, charismatic villainy, which reminded him of a famous character in Shakespeare:

> Alex makes no attempt to deceive himself or the audience as to his total corruption and wickedness. He is the very personification of evil. On the other hand, he has winning qualities: his total candor, his wit, his intelligence and his energy; these are attractive qualities and ones, I might add, which he shares with Richard III. (Phillips, *Stanley Kubrick Interviews*, p. 128)

The difference is that Richard III is a melodramatic figure who suffers fit punishment at the end of the play. Shakespeare's audience might thrill to Richard's forthright evil, but they leave the theatre with their sense of moral superiority confirmed and with a comforting feeling that justice and order have triumphed. Kubrick's version of *A Clockwork Orange* offers no such escape hatch. Alex is the only attractive character and is in approximately the same condition at the end of the film as he was at the beginning. Indeed, the most striking difference between the film and the novel is that Kubrick omits Burgess's rather comforting conclusion, in which Alex begins to reform. The original British edition of the novel was structured in three parts of seven chapters each; in the last chapter (the twenty-first, a symbolic number) Alex loses interest in ultra-violence, prefers German *Lieder* to Beethoven and daydreams about marriage and fatherhood. The last pages of the British edition also extend the implications of the novel's 'clockwork' metaphor: Alex compares himself as a youth to one of the 'toys you viddy being sold in the streets, like little chellovecks made out of tin and with a spring inside ... it ittys in a straight line and bangs straight into things bang bang and it cannot help what it is doing. Being young is like being one of these malenky machines' (p. 148). He imagines that his son will have the same problem, as will his son's son – but instead of moving in a straight mechanical line, they will eventually become part of God's turning universe: 'And so it would itty on to like the end of the world, round and round and round, like some bolshy gigantic like chelloveck, like old Bog Himself ... turning and turning and turning a vonny grahzny orange in his gigantic rookers' (p. 148).

Kubrick was unaware of this ending when he set out to adapt the novel. His source was the first US edition, which omitted Burgess's last chapter because an executive at W. W. Norton thought it anticlimactic and inconsistent. Kubrick insisted that even had he known about the different editions he would have closed the screenplay as he did. His film is reasonably faithful to the original novel's penultimate chapter, but it also has something in common with *Dr. Strangelove*, in that it concludes abruptly and ironically, with the maimed body of a villain brought back to virile life. It also shifts the emphasis from the religious to the political, making the ostensibly 'free' Alex into a paradoxical agent of the state. We see the proto-fascist Alex (Malcolm McDowell) encased in a cast and recuperating in a private hospital room, where the conservative Minister of the Interior (Anthony Sharp) personally feeds him a meal and allows him to listen to Beethoven on a giant stereo. Alex seems to mock the situation. Like a young bird in its nest, he opens his mouth wide and chews with broad, lip-smacking movements. Happily posing for press photos, he cuddles next to the minister and gives a thumbs-up sign. Then he becomes hypnotised by the music. The last image of the film, often described inaccurately in critical writings, represents his fantasy as he listens to Beethoven. In Burgess's novel, he imagines himself running lightly through the world and lashing out with his switchblade; but in the film, he lies nude on a ground of white feathers or snow, enjoying a slow-motion version of 'the old in-out' with a beautiful young woman who is wearing little but long black gloves and a black choker. The woman sits astride him and seems to be enjoying the occasion as much as he. This is the only image in the film of intense mutual pleasure in sex (the earlier 'orgy' in Alex's room, shot in fast motion to an electronic version of the 'William Tell Overture', is perfunctory by comparison), but ultimately it amounts to nothing more than Alex's imaginary and quite decadent view of himself as a performer or theatrical character. His sexual acrobatics are observed and applauded by a small crowd of ladies and gentlemen representing the British Establishment, all of whom are dressed in Edwardian finery, as if they had just returned from Ascot or perhaps from the set of *My Fair Lady*. On the soundtrack, Alex's voice declares, 'I was cured alright!'

In most other respects, Kubrick's film delivers something close to the total experience of the novel without seeming a slavish translation. Burgess grumbled that the work of adaptation consisted of nothing more than the director – whom he nicknamed 'The Thieving Magpie' – walking onto the set with a copy of the novel and using it to improvise scenes with the actors.[37] This description of Kubrick's methods wasn't entirely incorrect, but it belies the fact that the completed film is both formally rigorous and slightly different from its source. Shocking as the screen version may be, it considerably and necessarily lightens the amount of violence Burgess had described: it eliminates several beatings, transforms Alex's rape of a pair of ten-year-old girls into an afternoon of playful sex with a couple of teenagers, changes the Cat Lady from a pathetic old woman into an upper-class anorexic and makes the prison a much more comfortable place than Burgess had done. In addition, it drastically reduces the amount of 'Nasdat'. Kubrick retains the all-important first-person narration and direct address to the audience, and just enough of the original word-play to reveal the touch of the poet in little Alex, or what Nabokov would have called called 'the fancy prose style' of a killer (in the novel Alex is aware of Shelley and Rimbaud). Throughout, Alex's sadism is leavened with wit and his sexuality made lyrical by virtue of his language. This is true not only of his narration ('The Durango-95 purred away real horrorshow – a nice warm vibraty feeling all through your guttiwuts') but also of his dialogue ('What you got back home, little sister, to play your fuzzy warbles on? I bet you got little save pitiful portable picnic players. Hear angel trumpets and devil trombones. You are invited.').

Alex in the novel is fifteen years old when he kills the Cat Lady and seventeen at the end of his story. To play the character, Kubrick chose an older actor: twenty-eight-year-old Malcolm McDowell, who, as a result of his performance in Lindsay Anderson's *If* (1968), was strongly associated in the public mind with youthful rebellion. Given his boyish good looks, McDowell is reasonably convincing as a teenaged thug, but he lacks the dancer's movements Kubrick wanted for the scenes of violence. Kubrick assists him and also gives us a cinematic correlative for the novel's stylised descriptions of mayhem and sex by using a good deal of montage, music and fast- or slow-motion photography. In every other way, however, McDowell delivers one of the most impressive and unusual performances in modern cinema. The physical demands of his role are considerable. He submitted to being strapped into a straitjacket with his eyelids clamped open for the Lodovico treatment, and injured his eyes in the process. In the long take in which he is beaten by Dim (Warren Clarke), his head is held under water for more than forty seconds. The role also requires a mastery of voice and accent and a subtle control of emotional tone. Alex is a theatrical personality and a picaresque rogue who finds himself in widely different dramatic situations; as a result, McDowell plays him broadly, in a comic style that employs more volume and ostensive gesture than is usual for movies. Some of his scenes are pure slapstick, as when he passes out and his face lands in a plate of spaghetti; others are intimidating expressions of sadistic evil, as in the powerful opening shot, in which he stares back at us, head slightly bowed and right eye adorned with extravagant, razor-sharp lashes (McDowell himself contributed the idea for the eye make-up). Always a performer, he wears several masks and costumes, slipping easily from devil to angel, monster to clown, poet to scamp, seducer to victim, con-man to dupe. McDowell plays these different personae with charm, humour and élan, leaving such a mark on the role that anyone who reads the novel after seeing the film will have difficulty keeping him out of the mind's eye.

McDowell's performance aside, Kubrick's version of *A Clockwork Orange* is fraught with problems of emotional affect and intellectual import. Interestingly, he attenuates the novel's religious theme but leaves it in place. It's difficult to say how seriously he took Burgess's paradoxical Christian ideology. For most viewers, it might seem he is merely satirising religion – for example, when he uses montage to animate four identical ceramic figures of Christ, their penises on show, making them dance like bloody chorus boys while Alex listens to Beethoven and masturbates; or when he parodies DeMille in order to show Alex's fantasies of the stories in the Bible. Throughout, he represents Christ as a source of sexual fantasy or erotic energy – as in the obscene drawings that cover the biblical mural in the lobby of Alex's apartment building, in the daydream in which Alex becomes a Roman soldier on the road to Calvary, and in the scene of Alex being carried like a *pietà* in the arms of Mr Alexander's muscle-builder bodyguard. In one sense, however, these details are fully consonant with Burgess's notion that humanity is both carnal and spiritual, and with the novel's emphasis on sin: insofar as the novel is concerned, Alex is a potentially satanic character, not an atheist. Thus, in the film the dancing Jesuses have a place of honour in his bedroom alongside his picture of Beethoven, and he keeps a carving of the crucified Christ next to the pin-ups in his jail cell.

Something equally complicated and confusing is going on in the film's other references to religion. As in Burgess, the prison chaplain is depicted as a closeted homosexual who delivers a sermon vaguely reminiscent of the hellfire priest in Joyce's *A Portrait of the Artist as a Young Man*. But the chaplain also makes a passionate speech about moral freedom of choice. A somewhat dubious man of God, he becomes the bearer of what Kubrick claimed was the film's message: 'Although he is partially concealed behind a satirical disguise,' Kubrick told Michel Ciment, 'the prison chaplain, played by Godfrey Quigley, is the moral voice of the film . . . . A very delicate balance had to be achieved in Godfrey's performance between his somewhat comical image and the important ideas he is called upon to express' (p. 149). The 'delicate balance' presumably amounts to a sophisticated rhetorical strategy that asks the audience to make a distinction between the personal attributes of a character and the moral or ethical position the character represents. It should be noted, however, that in its attempt to avoid demagoguery by creating a split between sympathy and judgment, Kubrick's film must surmount problems that Burgess never had to confront. Every event in the novel is mediated through Alex's unreliable narration and by an implied author who fills the text with an indirect discourse on good and evil; the film, on the other hand, elides some of the religious discourse and shows us a world that 'exists' in front of the camera, independent of Alex's distorted point of view.

Kubrick tries to approximate the subjective quality of the novel by keeping a fair amount of Alex's first-person narration and by heightening or exaggerating the performances and *mise en scène* in ways that seem appropriate to an overheated, adolescent imagination. In the novel, for example, Alex is preoccupied with women who have big breasts ('horrorshow groodies'), and the film has a mammary obsession almost equal to Russ Meyer's. But in the film things are not simply told but shown, so that they seem to confirm Alex's judgments of the adult world. There are, in addition, a few scenes in the film that Alex doesn't witness and a number of subjective shots from the viewpoints of other characters – as when Mr Alexander looks up from the floor to 'viddy' Alex's masked face and huge, penis-shaped false nose. Given this technique, the film's stereotypes or grotesques take on an independent, objective quality and it becomes difficult to regard anyone as a voice of moral truth. We have no values to cling to other than what Kubrick described as Alex's candour, wit, intelligence and energy. Hence, for many viewers the film seems to express a kind of radical libertarianism based on a deep-seated contempt for human civilisation; it loads the deck against every adult, implies that official society is as violent and ruthless as the criminals it aims to suppress, and appears to endorse the 'free' expression of Alex's sadism over any kind of religious and secular 'law and order'. Because it views everything in a satiric light, it never conveys the idealism that somewhat redeems the darkness of Burgess's novel.

I shall have more to say about the political theme in a moment. Where the novel's art theme is concerned, Kubrick's medium works somewhat more to his advantage, although even here the film has a somewhat confusing effect, as if a playful view of Pop Art were being subjected to a kind of undertow of highbrow conservatism. Kubrick had become famous for the use of classical music in *2001* (an LP of that film's score is prominently displayed in the record-store scene), and the Burgess novel gave him many opportunities to exploit the technique again. He features a Deutsche Grammophon recording of Beethoven's 9th, but also hires Walter/Wendy Carlos to perform a version on a Moog synthesiser for the film-within-the-film. In many other places, he completely ignores the musical suggestions offered by Burgess. In the novel Alex inclines mainly towards classical German composers and moderns such as Benjamin Britten and Arnold Schoenberg. Kubrick tilts the soundtrack in a more eclectic and popular direction, using Purcell, Rossini, Elgar and Rimskii-Korsakov to comment ironically on the action and give it 'mood enhancing' theatrical vivacity. In the record store he shows album covers that feature the fictional pop stars from the novel, but one of his striking omissions is a rock-style equivalent for the music British teens actually listened to in the 1970s. Kubrick seems as isolated from this music as Burgess was. His score is chiefly devoted to well-known classics that signify Alex's 'artistic' proclivities, plus a single piece of pop-culture kitsch, Erica Eigen's 'I Want to Marry a Lighthouse Keeper', which is presumably intended to suggest the bad taste of Alex's parents and their young boarder.

In a slightly different musical category is 'Singin' in the Rain', an older and more charming standard that Alex performs twice. Malcolm McDowell began singing it during rehearsal, when Kubrick asked him to improvise a dance movement for Alex's assault on

Mr and Mrs Alexander. Originally composed by Arthur Freed and Nacio Herb Brown for MGM's first all-talking picture, it was used in several later musicals at that studio, until Gene Kelly's version in *Singin' in the Rain* (1952) transformed it into an iconic moment. As soon as Kubrick heard McDowell improvising to the tune, he acquired permission to use it; he even plays the original Kelly recording over the closing credits, as if to comment on Alex's glee-ful announcement of his 'cure'. This decision might seem to run somewhat against the grain of the novel, since Alex as created by Burgess is contemptuous of mass culture and more likely to sing or hum something from the classical repertoire. 'Singin' in the Rain' neverthe-less has a deeply shocking effect, quite different from the ironic use of 'Try a Little Tenderness' and 'We'll Meet Again' in *Dr. Strangelove*. It stylises and heightens the horror of the beating and rape, but it also functions as an attack on mass culture and a leering assault on a great Hollywood film. It's as if Kubrick wants to administer a kind of Lodovico treat-ment for cinephiles, many of whom, like me, can never again witness the joyful Gene Kelly number without feeling queasiness coupled with resentment of *A Clockwork Orange*'s smug appropriation of the song. (Presumably some viewers of the film feel an equivalent sacri-lege has been committed with regard to Beethoven.)

The production design serves to further elaborate the theme of the degradation of art under modernity. Kubrick's three previous films had been shot almost entirely in a studio, but in this case he used carefully selected locations in and around London in ways that establish continuity between the present and the imaginary future. The graffiti-covered housing block where Alex lives ('municipal flatblock 18a Linear North'), the panoptic prison where he is incarcerated ('Staja No. 84F') and the cold institution where he under-goes treatment ('Lodovico Medical Facility') are 'played' by actual buildings, all of them representing the dark side of *2001*'s white modernism. The record store and the pub are likewise real places, as are the wealthy homes in the countryside, although the domestic interiors were extensively redecorated by production designer John Barry and art direc-tors Russell Hagg and Peter Shields. One of the most interesting qualities of these interiors is the degree to which paintings and sculptures are constantly on show. Fine art has no importance in the novel but in the film it can be seen everywhere, contributing to the film's aura of sexuality and demonstrating the ways in which art, kitsch and pornography have become increasingly 'democratised' and indistinguishable from one another.

In the future, Kubrick told Michel Ciment, 'erotic art will eventually become popular art, and just as you now buy African wildlife paintings in Woolworth's, you may one day buy erotica' (p. 162). We first become aware of this phenomenon in the set design for the Korova Milk Bar, which features a series of female nudes sculpted by Liz Moore, who also designed the Star Child in *2001*. Parodies of the fetish 'furniture' of 1960s' sculptor Allen Jones, the nudes look like skinny fashion models or department-store mannequins posed in submissive positions and endowed with dark eye sockets, prominent breasts, big hair and elaborately detailed genitalia. A roughly similar blend of pornography and artistic-ness can be seen in the trendy decor at the Cat Lady's house. In the novel this woman is

an elderly recluse, but in the film she becomes a rich, anorexic Bohemian who wears leotards, works out on a weight machine and collects eroticised Pop Art – including a large sculpture of a penis, resembling the work of Hans Arp, which fascinates and amuses Alex. ('Don't touch it,' the Cat Lady cries. 'It's a very important work of art!') When Alex assaults

her with the penis, his violence is conveyed expressionistically through a rapid montage of her cartoon-like, sadomasochistic paintings. The Pop-Art sensibility extends as well to the tiny apartment where Alex and his parents live, which has candy-coloured wallpaper and several paintings of a dark-skinned female with large eyes and prominent breasts. The

realistic style of the paintings marks them as working-class kitsch, in keeping with the 'lighthouse keeper' song, but in the last analysis such distinctions of taste are difficult to maintain. Almost the entire world of the film is filled with 'postmodern' ironies, such as the neon 'HOME' sign outside Mr Alexander's house. (Perhaps significantly, the Alexander interior is the only domestic space that seems free from Pop Art. Kubrick stages the gang rape of Mrs Alexander against the background of a large, rather pastoral oil painting by Christiane Kubrick.)

The film's costumes, created by Italian designer Milena Canonero, also establish a connection between the present and the future, at the same time commenting on the intensely fashionable nature of youth subcultures and their resultant commodification. The suits and uniforms worn by agents of the state are virtually indistinguishable from the ones that were being worn in England at the time of the film's release, and Alex's Droog outfit – white shirt and trousers, cuff ornaments shaped like bloody eyeballs, gentleman's black bowler hat, combat boots, suspenders, boxer's protective codpiece and truncheon-cane with a concealed knife in the handle – is vaguely suggestive of the skinheads of the late 1960s. At the record store, Alex wears a hugely exaggerated version of the 'New Edwardian' look that was popular on Carnaby Street in the era of 'swinging London'. The more he uses costumes to emphasise his sexual attributes – eyelashes, cane, codpiece, tight trousers, shoulder-padded Edwardian coat – the more androgynous he becomes. When the state takes control of his body and mind, he reverts to the plain blue suit of normative masculinity. At this point, even 'Em and Pee', his frightened parents, are more flamboyantly dressed than he, and more in tune with the fashion industry's cult of youth: the father wears the brightly coloured shirt, wide tie and broad lapels that were the height of male fashion in the 1970s, and the mother sports a go-go miniskirt, boots and metallic-coloured wig (earlier in the film we see a young waitress in a pub wearing the same costume).

The symptomatic art form of modernity is, of course, the cinema, or the 'sinny', as Alex calls it; hence the scenes in which the Lodovico treatment is administered are both a self-reflexive critique of the film we are watching and, at least potentially, an inoculation of the film against critical attack. Ironically, these scenes are highly dependent on language from the novel. At first, Alex is forced to watch the sort of things we've witnessed in the first third of the movie – 'a very good, professional piece of sinny, like it was done in Hollywood', in which young men in Droog costumes conduct beatings and rapes. The violence is realistic and accompanied by plenty of 'our dear old friend, the red, red vino . . . like it's put out by the same big firm'. For the most part, however, we don't hear the sounds and Alex's narration alienates us from the images. As cinematic opium mingles with drugs, Alex begins to experience an artificially induced nausea similar to that an ordinary audience might feel while watching the first half of A Clockwork Orange, except that Alex is strapped down and can't close his eyes or 'get out of the line of fire of this picture'. On the next day, he is shown Nazi propoganda accompanied by an electronic version of Beethoven's 9th. Kubrick could have shown us images of the death camps, but instead chose the sort

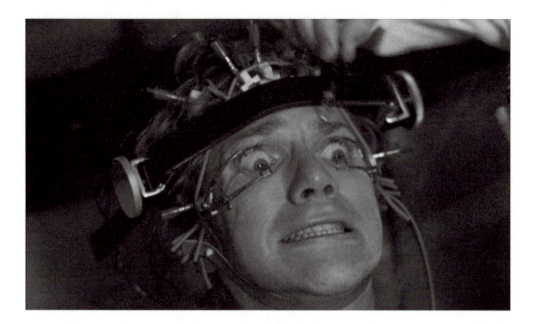

of thing with which Alex might identify: newsreel images of Hitler strutting on a parade ground followed by shots of a Nazi *Blitzkrieg*. Beethoven and proto-fascist barbarism, which were already linked in previous scenes, are now explicitly joined, and Alex's reaction is a pathetic plea: 'Stop it! . . . Please! I beg you! It's a *sin*!'

Quite apart from its philosophical or ideological implications, *A Clockwork Orange* is unquestionably a 'professional piece of sinny', containing brilliant examples of photography, staging and cutting. Among the more ostentatious photographic effects it employs is the zoom lens, which had come into widespread use in the 1960s, especially in the documentary-style French New Wave pictures and on television, where zooming provided a cheap substitute for tracking shots. Kubrick is one of the few directors who used the device systematically to create a stylistic motif. (Another was Robert Altman, who, like Kubrick, also made use of wireless microphones that could be attached to the actors' clothing.) His particular use of the zoom involves an unusually slow, stately movement from an extreme close-up to a wide shot, resulting in a gradual 'reveal'. The most obvious examples in *A Clockwork Orange* are the famous opening shot of the Korova Milk Bar and the later shot in which Mr Alexander torments Alex by playing a recording of Beethoven's 9th. Sometimes Kubrick reverses the process, moving towards the close-up, but in either case he creates the effect of a still image or tableau – a deliberately pictorial composition that he eventually brought to powerful expression in *Barry Lyndon*. Another, somewhat less obvious photographic technique of the film involves Kubrick's discovery of an easier and more stable way of holding the lightweight Arriflex camera. Notice the scene in which Alex stumbles through the rain at night to Mr Alexander's front door – a hand-held travelling shot over uneven terrain, resembling the Steadicam shots Kubrick would later employ in *The Shining*. (John Alcott, Kubrick's director of photography on *A Clockwork Orange* and most of his late pictures, once remarked that Kubrick was the only person he knew who could give the Arriflex such a smooth, gliding motion.[38])

Kubrick's previous work was grounded in a long-take, wide-angle aesthetic, especially when he found ways to photograph characters walking down a corridor or moving around a room; but in this period he became quite flexible, freely mixing sequences that depend on sustained shots with sequences that depend on editing. Alex's encounter with two girls in a record store is staged in a single, unbroken shot that roams through the shop and views everything through an extreme fisheye lens; his conversation with the prison priest is photographed in a wide-angle tracking shot in which the two characters walk down a tunnel-like corridor of library books; his bedroom interview with Mr Deltoid (Aubrey Morris) is composed of two alternating, wide-angle set-ups at some distance from the characters; and his 'interrogation' by three policemen consists of seven set-ups, half of them telephoto close-ups, with an establishing shot at the end of the sequence.

In many places, Kubrick and his editor, Bill Butler, illustrate how cutting can either support or work in counterpoint with the intense, sometimes radically slow acting style that had become a hallmark of Kubrick's films. Consider the spaghetti-eating scene in Mr Alexander's house, which offers one way of dealing with the complicated problem of staging action around a dinner table. (As David Bordwell has shown, this is a problem almost every director has faced at one time or another.[39]) The scene can be divided into two sequences: in the first, the wheelchair-bound Mr Alexander (Patrick Magee) and his bodyguard sit close to Alex at a circular glass table, watching him eat; and in the second, two additional characters join the group and take up the whole space around the table. The first sequence uses only 180 degrees of the room, and the second uses the full 360 degrees; together, they employ almost twenty camera set-ups or changes of perspective, leaping from low level to high level, from long shot to intense close-up, from wide angle to telephoto. Despite the busy *découpage*, however, the tempo seems almost lugubrious. Mr Alexander is weirdly overwrought – scowling, squinting, speaking with great deliberation and almost screaming certain words: '*Food* alright?' 'I'm pleased you appreciate good wine. Have another *glass*.' 'My *wife* used to do everything for me . . . . she's *dead*.' As Alex becomes more and more uneasy, the pace of the cutting increases; but the odd style of acting (Magee chews scenery and the other players behave naturalistically) creates an unusual mood – both emphatic and excessively drawn out, both sombre and ridiculous.

Magee's bizarre performance has something in common with George C. Scott's comic mugging in *Dr. Strangelove* and Peter Sellers's wild impersonations in *Lolita*, but it's less funny, more truly grotesque. Isolated instances of this sort of behaviour can be seen in all of Kubrick's later films, producing a disconcerting, off-key effect that critics sometimes find annoying or humourless. Kevin Jackson, for example, writes that the performance Kubrick 'extorts' from Magee is a 'crime against the art of acting', and that Aubrey Morris's portrayal of Deltoid – a 'crotch-grabbing' homosexual who accidentally drinks from a glass containing dentures – is, at best, worthy of a 1970's British sitcom (p. 26). There can be no doubt, however, that Kubrick wanted just this sort of frantic exaggeration. From the time of *Lolita* he tried to achieve a kind of surrealistic discontinuity or incoherence of perform-ance styles, allowing his films to lurch suddenly from naturalism into absurdity. He takes deliberate risks with the acting – as in the implausibly slow-paced, almost loony scene in which Alex returns home and confronts his parents, or in the lip-smacking enjoyment with which Alex eats dinner in the closing scene.

    A Clockwork Orange is, of course, equally risky in other ways. It not only tests the lim-its of the censorship code but also expresses a quite pessimistic view of society, depicting it as based on nothing more than innate, predatory violence and rationalised, utilitarian coercion (another expression of the man-as-killer-ape theme in *2001*). Unlike *Dr. Strangelove*, it can't be embraced by the political left, even though it provoked outraged responses from some conservatives. It does, however, imply a certain kind of radical politics, which are difficult to label. Theodor Adorno would probably turn in his grave at the suggestion, but Kubrick's adaptation of Burgess is in many ways like an argument by Adorno. The film shares Adorno's late-romantic devotion to Beethoven, his relentlessly satiric attitude towards socialism and fascism, his disdain for bureaucrats, his derisive response to kitsch and his despair over Enlightenment rationality. Kubrick's savage treatment of reification and alienation under modernity isn't far from what one finds in the famous 'Culture Industry' chapter of Adorno and Max Horkheimer's *Dialectic of Enlightenment*. Equally sig-nificant, his treatment of sex roughly corresponds to that book's chapter on the Marquis de Sade ('Enlightenment as Morality'), which argues that Sade's libertinism was merely a log-ical development in the history of the liberal bourgeois subject – a disavowal of religious superstition, a 'busy pursuit of pleasure' and an extension of reason, efficiency and social organisation into the realm of the senses. Horkheimer and Adorno quote with satiric rel-ish the words of the Prince in Sade's *120 Days of Sodom*, who sounds a good deal like both the Minister of the Interior and Mr Alexander in *A Clockwork Orange*: 'The people must be freed from the fear of a future Hell. But that chimerical fear must be replaced by penal laws of enormous severity, which apply, of course, only to the people, since they alone cause unrest in the state.' The government 'must possess the means to exterminate the people, should it fear them, or to increase their numbers, should it consider that necessary.' It may grant the people 'the widest, most criminal license,' except of course when they turn against the government.[40]

    Devoid of utopian impulses, *A Clockwork Orange* derives some of its politics from Anthony Burgess's debatable (and unprovable) notion that there is an Alex in all of us. It is, however, much less interested in religion than Burgess; its pessimism sounds a bit more like certain members of the Frankfurt School, offering little more than aestheticism as a defence against modernity. Where politics are concerned, we should also remember that, at the time the film was made, the western world as a whole was growing more violent and nasty. In the US, the carnage in Vietnam could be seen on the evening news; the Manson family had recently confirmed the worst conservative fears that hippies were devils; and US Vice-President Spiro Agnew was making appeals to the right-wing 'silent majority' about the need to establish 'law and order' (i.e., the need to suppress potentially revolutionary street demonstrations against war and social inequality). Near the beginning of the picture, in a scene taken directly from Burgess's 1962 novel, a homeless old alcoholic (Paul Farrell) bemoans the fact that there are 'men on the moon, and men spinning around the earth and there's not no attention paid to law and order no more'. This accurately expresses the regressive political atmosphere of 1971, when the youth rebellion of the previous decade was becoming perverse and increasingly commodified. *A Clockwork Orange* at least has the virtue of being a deliberately harsh and provocative vision of its times. The relative darkness of 1970s' cinema would soon give way to Ronald Reagan's 'Morning in America' and, in the brave new world of entertainment that followed, Hollywood would avoid producing any film as unrelentingly disturbing as this.

IV. Duellist

A Clockwork Orange was both a *succès de scandale* and one of Warner's most profitable releases of the 1970s, securing Kubrick's relationship with the studio and enabling him to return to his long-deferred idea of filming an historical epic to rival *2001*'s epic of the future. Because his Napoleon project remained too complex and costly, he briefly considered an adaptation of William Makepeace Thackeray's *Vanity Fair* (1847–8), which had been filmed three times in Hollywood, but not since the 1930s. Subtitled *A Novel without a Hero*, Thackeray's satiric narrative offered a panorama of middle- and upper-class struggles for power in early nineteenth-century England, and it probably had special interest for Kubrick because its anti-heroine, Becky Sharp, is explicitly compared with Napoleon – indeed, Becky's downfall coincides with the Battle of Waterloo, and the story as a whole ends in 1830, shortly after Napoleon's death at St Helena. Kubrick nevertheless decided that *Vanity Fair* was too difficult to compress into a three-hour film and instead turned his attention to Thackeray's earliest work of fiction, *The Luck of Barry Lyndon: A Romance of the Last Century*, which was first published as a magazine serial in 1844 and then revised and reissued in a single volume in 1856 under the title *The Memoirs of Barry Lyndon, Esq., of the Republic of Ireland*. This novel tells the story of an eighteenth-century Irish rake, loosely based on an actual historical character from the lower levels of the Anglo-Irish gentry, who seduces his way into the British aristocracy but comes to a bad end; little known outside the academy, it was a relatively minor fiction that could be freely adapted, and was in the public domain. In 1973, on the strength of an outline that concealed the title of the novel and the names of its characters, Kubrick convinced Warner to finance a film version. For the next two years, he set about making *Barry Lyndon*, one of the most remarkable and unorthodox costume pictures ever produced, and one of his most impressive artistic achievements.

Barry Lyndon won several technical awards from the Motion Picture Academy and its first impression on most viewers is one of breathtaking photographic beauty. Its distinctive visual qualities were determined first of all by Kubrick's long-standing interest in realistic, available-light photography. During his work on the Napoleon project, he had become excited by the idea of making an historical film set in a period before the invention of electric power, using as little motion-picture lighting equipment as possible. He also wanted to shoot in real historical locations, somewhat in the manner of the chateau sequences of *Paths of Glory*, avoiding studio sets and modern interpretations of historical costumes – in other words, he wanted to make a film antithetical to *Spartacus*. His motivation was aesthetic and intellectual, but he tried to convince studio executives that a quasi-documentary approach would save money. In 1968, he spelled out his intentions in a memo to potential investors in the proposed film about Napoleon:

> I plan to shoot all interiors of the film on location, instead of building sets, as has always been previously done in big budget epic films. Very great savings of money together with an increase of quality can be achieved . . . . Because of the new fast photographic lenses we intend to employ, very little lighting equipment will have to be used, depending instead on ordinary window light, which incidentally will look more beautiful and realistic than ordinary light.[41]

At roughly the same time, Kubrick shot 468 metres of colour test sequences showing a young man lit by candlelight; but ordinary camera lenses, combined with the relatively

low film speeds of the period, produced unsatisfactory results. By the time of *Barry Lyndon*, he was able to obtain an f 0.7 Zeiss lens that had been developed by NASA for lunar photography. He commissioned Ed di Giulio of Cinema Products Corporation to engineer an old Mitchell camera from the Warner studio so that it would accept three different focal lengths of the Zeiss lens and, with this equipment, photographer John Alcott was able to shoot the candlelit, golden interiors we see at various junctures in the film. Alcott often used booster lights, reflectors and various other types of equipment for the daylight interiors, but always in a fashion that imitates the effect of natural light. For the daylight exteriors, which were shot mostly in Ireland and England, he and Kubrick favoured an Arriflex camera, but eschewed diffusion filters. The landscape images, beginning with the opening shot of a distant pistol duel, have an almost tactile clarity and an exquisite sensitivity to changing patterns of air, clouds and sunlight.

Part of the fascination of the film lies in its documentation of castles, country estates and enormous rooms where we hear shoes clattering on wooden floors and view tapestry and leather-bound books in the light from high windows. The production achieved its air of authenticity not only by virtue of location shooting in Britain and second-unit photography in Germany, but also through minute historical research into every aspect of eighteenth-century life, including clothing, wigs, face powder, military hardware, playing cards, magical paraphernalia, shaving equipment and even such unseen matters as toothbrushes and contraceptives. Kubrick's rage for reality, however, was counterbalanced and even contradicted by an intense aesthetic historicism, which gives his film a quite unreal, painterly effect. He composed many of the shots to resemble images by eighteenth-century

artists such as Hogarth, Reynolds, Chardin, Watteau, Fragonard, Zoffany, Stubbs and Chodowiecki, and he insisted that production designer Ken Adam use these artists for inspiration. He filled the sets with eighteenth-century artefacts and frequently posed the costumed actors and extras as nearly still figures, arranging them in patterns suggested by genre or landscape paintings. (The ex-fashion model Marisa Berenson, who plays Lady Lyndon, and who hardly speaks a word, looks as if she had stepped out of a Gainsborough portrait.) In these and other respects, the film seems to acknowledge that the past is always mediated by historical discourse and artistic representation.[42] The ordinary Hollywood costume picture, which Kubrick regarded as unrealistic, usually assumes that history can be faithfully reproduced; the ostensibly more accurate *Barry Lyndon*, on the other hand, resembles what Fredric Jameson describes as a pastiche – in this case a detailed imitation of landscapes, architecture, and art, intended to evoke 'eighteenth-century-ness'.[43]

The film's painterly feeling is intensified by its exceptionally slow, stately pace and tendency to subordinate action to ritual. Kubrick draws out conversations and domestic scenes to the point where they take on the quality of *temps morts*; he dwells upon formal entertainments or state occasions; he requires most of the actors – especially Berenson and Ryan O'Neal, who plays Barry – to maintain highly controlled masks of social decorum; and he builds very quietly to the few scenes involving emotional outbursts and paroxysms of violence. Baldly summarised, Barry's life is filled with adventure, especially in the first half of the film: he fights a duel for the woman he loves and is sent away from home; he is robbed by highwaymen; he enlists in the British Army and survives a grim battle; he escapes from his unit by stealing a uniform and horse from a homosexual officer; he spends a

romantic evening with a young German mother whose husband is away at war; he meets a unit of the Prussian Army and poses as an officer on a mission; his imposture is quickly discovered and he is forced to become a foot soldier; during a battle he saves the life of his commanding officer; as reward, he is taken to Potsdam and assigned to spy on the activities of an Irish gambler; finally, he and the gambler become comrades, escape the Prussians, and live the life of itinerant cardsharps. All this picaresque activity, however, is presented in an extremely leisurely fashion and in an unvarying pace, almost as if it were a series of brilliantly colourful tableaux.

In the second half of the film, after Barry marries an aristocrat and settles into domestic life, things slow even more. The mannered dialogue suggests eighteenth-century neo-classicism, and is spoken with heavy pauses to mark the punctuation. For example, the following simple conversation between the young Lord Bullingdon (Dominic Savage) and Reverend Runt (Murray Melvin), is played at such a calm, steady rhythm and with such regulated silences that it could be written out as lines of verse:

RUNT: My Lord Bullingdon, you seem particularly glum today. / You should be happy that
    your mother has been married.
BULLINGDON: Not in this way, / and not in such haste, / and certainly not to this man.
RUNT: Do you not like your new father?
BULLINGDON: Not very much. / He seems to me little more than a common opportunist. /
    I don't think he loves my mother at all. / And it hurts me very much to see her make such
    a fool of herself.

In keeping with this stylised retardation, Kubrick's most striking camera effect, which becomes a motif, is a long, slow zoom out from a significant detail to a wide shot composed like a painting. The many zoom shots, together with the various long-distance views of gardens, estates and landscapes, are compelling not only for their beauty and sense of the eighteenth-century picturesque, but also because they register minimal movements within the stillness: the stirring of leaves in the wind, the ripple of water, a dog turning its head, a distant human figure aiming a pistol. Significantly, the zoom isn't a camera movement, but an alteration of the focal length of the lens, which creates a very different impression from Kubrick's signature tracking shots: in *Barry Lyndon* the image often looks flat but then slowly widens and takes on the depth of an illusionist painting. Frequently Kubrick will start a sequence with a zoom outward into an establishing shot, which he dissects with conventional close-ups and shot-reverse shots. Ralf Michael Fischer has persuasively analysed this technique in terms of dialectic between painting and motion pictures, or between a pre-photographic historical period and the present day. As Fischer puts it, 'Kubrick wishes to establish whether he can use moving pictures to visualize an age that did not know photography. Therefore, and this has often been ignored, *Barry Lyndon* develops into an exciting oscillation between cinematic and painterly/graphic representation strategies.'[44]

It follows that the technique makes viewers more than usually aware of stillness versus passing time. As in *2001*, but by a slightly different means, motion is slowed and a feeling of transience creeps into the images, as if a clock were ticking behind the still, orderly compositions. The live-action painterly effects are sometimes poignant in their beauty, suggesting that the past is both inaccessible (except through art) and dead. This implication is reinforced at the dramatic level; the passage of time is increasingly freighted with sadness and death, and people eventually take on a ghostly appearance. Something similar happens at the purely cinematic level, with the steady replacement of one image by another. Very few historical films (Welles's *Magnificent Ambersons* and John Ford's Westerns are good examples, though imbued with a nostalgia that Kubrick rejects) give us such a powerfully self-conscious sense of the motion picture as a temporal medium – an experience unlike a painting in the sense that a series of apparently substantial compositions as evanescent as a beam of light pass through the projector, each of them disappearing and 'dying' along with the world they represent.

In other ways, *Barry Lyndon* is deliberately anachronistic. Consider Kubrick's use of hand-held, *cinéma vérité* effects for scenes of violence, including the boxing match between Barry and a fellow soldier, Barry's attack on Lord Bullingdon during a concert and Lady Lyndon's attempted suicide. Consider also the music score. Once again Kubrick draws from the classical repertoire, this time commissioning Leonard Rosenman to select, arrange and conduct several of the orchestral pieces. (Rosenman won the Academy Award, but he told an American Film Institute seminar that he thought the film was 'incredibly long and boring' and that Kubrick's continual replaying of a passage from Handel's 'Sarabande' made a 'mess' of the music.)[45] The score favours the baroque over the neo-classical, featuring, among others, Handel, Bach, Mozart and Vivaldi; but it also gives us a modernised version of 'Sarabande' and makes considerable use both of Schubert, a nineteenth-century composer, and the Chieftains, a twentieth-century group that plays updated renditions of traditional Irish tunes. Much the same thing could be said of the many allusions to paintings. Eighteenth-century artists dominate, but certain images seem to be inspired by the nature scenes of the proto-romantic John Constable (1776–1837) and by the candlelit interiors of Adolph Menzel (1815–1905), a nineteenth-century painter of historical subjects.[46]

Whether or not Kubrick intended us to notice these anachronisms, they have an interesting relationship to Thackeray's novel, which is already a pastiche. A great admirer of Henry Fielding, Thackeray had written a picaresque, satiric, self-reflexive narrative, in imitation of eighteenth-century literary conventions. The book claims to be an autobiography, somewhat in the vein of Casanova's more jaw-droppingly adventurous and socially corrosive *Memoirs*, written by Barry from debtor's prison and addressed to his mother; and the manuscript is 'edited' by 'G. S. Fitz-Boodle', a man-of-the-world persona Thackeray frequently adopted for his magazine publications. Some of Fitz-Boodle's footnotes and editorial interventions were cut when *Barry Lyndon* was issued as a novel, but he remained a presence, functioning rather like a Victorian moralist who points out Barry's unreliability and the general wickedness of the eighteenth century. In the concluding pages, he steps forward to summarise Barry's life after being tossed out of Castle Lyndon and to inform us (in lines Thackeray wrote a few years before the Irish potato famine) that 'the thrifty, cleanly, orderly, loyal peasantry of Ireland . . . still entertain the stranger with stories of the daring, and the deviltry, and the wickedness, and the fall of Barry Lyndon'.[47] In other words, like Kubrick's film, *The Memoirs of Barry Lyndon* is a self-conscious experiment in historical fiction, creating an eighteenth-century world but viewing it through the lens of a later period.

There are, in addition, other ways in which Thackeray and Kubrick might be said to have a deep-structural relationship. Thackeray originally wanted to be a painter and was keenly interested in visual art; in fact, he drew illustrations for the first edition of *Vanity Fair*, which he subtitled *Pen and Pencil Sketches of English Society*. Essentially a caricaturist, he once described the people in his novels as 'puppets'. (At one point Barry remarks, 'I can hardly believe myself to have been any thing but a puppet in the hands of Fate' [p. 42].) In the magazine version of *Barry Lyndon*, he expressed strong admiration for the satires of William Hogarth, whose most famous work – 'A Rake's Progress' and 'Marriage à la Mode' – takes the form of image sequences that tell a story. Kubrick is, of course, also a caricaturist and satirist, and he often treats his characters as puppets. His film uses every opportunity to juxtapose ravishingly beautiful figures with satirical stereotypes that might have stepped out of an illustrated novel. Some of the most memorable moments involve character actors who introduce a grotesque quality into a serenely gorgeous *mise en scène*: Murray Melvin as Reverend Runt, the sly, effeminate cleric who owes his living to the Lyndons and barely contains his disapproval when he reads the marriage vows to Barry;

Patrick Magee as the Chevalier de Balibari, the decadent, aging gambler whose fancy wig, heavy make-up and eye patch make him look like a figure at a Halloween party; and most of all Leonard Rossiter as Captain Quinn, whose preening, cock-of-the-walk behaviour when he leads troops on a parade ground and dances an Irish jig with Nora Brady (Gay Hamilton) is as bizarrely funny as anything in *Dr. Strangelove*.

All this is not to suggest that Kubrick was striving to preserve the spirit of the novel. On the contrary, the film utterly transforms its source. The greater part of Thackeray's *The Memoirs of Barry Lyndon* is narrated by Barry, whose eventful life, filled with characters that the film omits, is told in a loose, digressive fashion. A handsome and clever fellow, Barry is also a boastful, loquacious scoundrel who calmly admits to beating his wife and probably lies about his more spectacular adventures. His wife is a vulgar woman of no great beauty, and yet she's a difficult conquest; she has lovers of her own and divorces Barry when she can no longer tolerate his behaviour. Kubrick's film is exactly the opposite in all these respects: it has an omniscient narrator and a unified, carefully patterned plot with a three-act structure; it depicts Barry as a quiet, inarticulate man who speaks in a soft Irish accent and seems to feel a certain guilt after he cheats on his wife; and it portrays Lady Lyndon as a fragile, melancholic beauty, easily seduced by Barry, who must be 'rescued' from the marriage.

Equally significant, the film's tone is different from the novel. Thackeray gives us a sometimes shocking but basically humorous tale written by a stage-Irish cad; the attitude of the implied author towards the characters is darker and more judgmental than Fielding's in *Tom Jones*, but the narrative has a rollicking atmosphere. Whether or not the original viewers of Kubrick's film were aware of this, they probably expected something swift, amusing and romantic, more in the vein of Tony Richardson's highly successful 1963 adaptation of *Tom Jones* (which today looks dated compared to *Barry Lyndon*). Instead, they were given a slow-paced film that builds towards a tragic dénouement, dealing with a relatively sympathetic social outsider who is observed from a godlike perspective. Even when Kubrick takes language directly from the novel, he often moves it into new contexts, making it seem less breezy, more serious. To choose a particularly significant example: in the early pages of Thackeray's first chapter, Barry explains how he and his ancestors were cheated out of their supposedly aristocratic pedigree and how his father, 'Roaring Harry Barry', died a natural death of dissipation while attending the Chester horse races; he then brushes the family history aside in order to move on to his more immediate concerns: 'It was in the reign of George III that the above-named personages lived and quarreled; good or bad, handsome or ugly, rich or poor, they are all equal now; and do not the Sunday papers and the courts of law supply us every week with more novel and interesting slander?'(p. 6) Kubrick appropriates, edits and slightly revises the first two sentences in these lines, placing them in a title card at the end of the picture, where they become the ultimate authorial comment, grimly philosophical in tone, on death as the great leveller: 'It was in the reign of George III that the aforesaid personages lived and quarreled; good or bad, handsome or ugly, rich or poor they are all equal now.'

Much of the tone of the film derives from Kubrick's decision to drop the novel's first-person narration and put its language into the mouth of a godlike narrator, beautifully played by Michael Hordern, who addresses us more in the fashion of nineteenth-century realism than in the archly playful style of a Fielding. Pauline Kael was annoyed by this device, in particular by the way the narrator sometimes tells us in advance what's going to happen; and, given the fact that many critics and film-makers have attacked movie narrators in general as 'un-cinematic', Kael probably wasn't alone.[48] (There's an interesting connection between arguments against narration in movies and strictures against 'telling' vs 'showing' in novels; the latter were thoroughly debunked by Wayne Booth in *The Rhetoric of Fiction* [1950], and the former have been effectively criticised by Sarah Kosloff in *Invisible Storytellers* [1998].) Most subsequent commentators, however, find the narration in *Barry Lyndon* unusually effective. Mario Falsetto describes Hordern's voice as a sort of aristocratic character, not always perfectly reliable, who represents 'an individuated, privileged point of view' (p. 100). But for all his urbanity and individuality, this narrator expresses many opinions that Thackeray had given to Barry, and as a result he doesn't always seem to be speaking for the ruling class. When he says, 'It would take a great philosopher and historian to explain the causes of the famous Seven Years War,' he sounds more knowingly ironic than Barry in the novel; and when he remarks that the war was the product of kings 'doing their murderous work in the world,' his judgment is more authoritative by virtue of its relative objectivity.

Among his many functions, the narrator helps to create the effect of premodernist fiction by putting us at a distance from the characters and offering commentary on their motives. Sometimes his remarks are in counterpoint with what we see, as in the first scene between Barry and Nora Brady; sometimes they make explicit what the image suggests, as when Lord Bullingdon is introduced as 'a melancholy little boy, much attached to his mother'; and sometimes they inform us of things not shown, as when we learn that the young German *Frau* with whom Barry enjoys an evening of sex has been enjoyed by other soldiers. Repeatedly, as in the traditional realist novel, the lofty, cosmopolitan narrator invites us to think of the diegetic world as co-terminus with the world we inhabit as readers/viewers; thus he speaks in maxims or truisms ('No lad with freedom and twenty guineas can be unhappy'), and he encourages us to draw on our own wisdom in making judgments (the 'young love' speech at the beginning of the film is a good example of the latter strategy; it's partly ironic and partly meant to draw us into a kind of paternalistic sympathy with Barry).[49]

Occasionally, the narrator also makes us aware of the art of storytelling itself. My favourite example occurs during Barry's seduction of Lady Lyndon, when the narrator appears be joking about Kubrick's glacial pacing of the action. In the novel, Barry's sexual conquest involves a great deal of busy effort; in the film, it occurs at first sight but almost in slow motion. Schubert plays in the background as Lady Lyndon and Barry exchange long, meaningful glances across a candlelit gambling table; she excuses herself, walks outside and stands in the moonlight, her breasts rising and falling in anticipation. Barry follows and approaches very slowly. She turns to face him. He takes her hands, gazes longingly into her eyes and kisses her delicately but ardently. This wordless, moonlit seduction takes almost a minute and forty seconds of screen time. Kubrick ends it by cutting directly from blue moonlight to daylight on a lake, where the red sail of a boat crosses gracefully from left to right and a second boat, bearing the two lovers, moves towards us. 'To make a long story short,' the narrator says, 'six hours after they met, her Ladyship was in love.'

The narrator isn't simply a wit who provides exposition and passes judgment. He plays a very important role in maintaining the audience's sympathy for the central character, even when that character behaves foolishly or cruelly. When the narrator explains Barry's sudden emotional outburst upon first meeting the Chevalier, he's almost like a barrister defending a client charged with ludicrous or self-serving behaviour; and when he tells us that 'Barry had his faults, but no man could say of him that he was not a good and tender father', he's more convincing than the boastful first-person narrator of the novel. One of his most important functions is his foreshadowing of the action, as when he tells us that an accident will soon take Barry out of military service with the Prussians, or when he introduces a lady who 'will henceforth play an important role in the story'. By giving us more information than the characters possess, he creates suspense and an air of inevitability. This effect is especially powerful during a scene in which we see Barry instructing his son Bryan in the art of fencing. The narrator comments, 'It is impossible to convey what high hopes he had for the boy; and he indulged in a thousand fond anticipations as to his future success and figure in the world. But fate had determined that he should leave none

of his race behind him, and that he should finish his life poor, lonely and childless.' Suddenly, in the midst of a sunlit, cheerful action, the whole outcome of the picture is foretold and an aura of pathos surrounds Barry. The image of young Bryan proudly brandishing a wooden sword takes on a painful, fleeting quality, like a happy memory clouded by the portent of disaster.

The narrative structure of the film is equally interesting. *Barry Lyndon* condenses its source, eliminating incidents and characters; but Kubrick also adds new material, in the process achieving a greater formal refinement and thematic coherence. For example, the pistol duel that kills Barry's father in the beginning is clearly intended to 'rhyme' with the pistol duel between Barry and Lord Bullingdon (Leon Vitali) near the end of the picture, and both scenes are Kubrick's invention. In the editorial coda to the novel, Fitz-Boodle summarises Barry's life after the Lyndon marriage and simply notes in passing that Bullingdon tracked Barry to the spa at Bath and 'administered to him a tremendous castigation in the Pump-room' (p. 225). Kubrick makes duels a prominent motif throughout: we're given three pistol duels, a fencing duel, a practice swordfight between Barry and his son and a bare-knuckle boxing match. The fencing and the fist fight require strength and skill, but the pistol duels are largely wars of nerves, similar in some ways to the film's most spectacular representation of military combat, in which men bearing rifles and dressed in colourful uniforms march straight into the face of opposing gunfire.

The film also has a motif of card playing, a contest more open to chance, guile or deception. The erotic card-game between Barry and Nora at the beginning rhymes with the desolate game between the legless Barry and his mother at the end, and in the middle we're given several scenes of Barry and the Chevalier cheating at cards. In a fine analysis of this structure, Marvin D'Lugo has argued that *Barry Lyndon* has a 'ludic' view of society, and that the card-game is more significant than the duel in representing the underlying contest to acquire money and power:

> Though the menace of physical aggression and violence embodied in the duel and its grander version, the battle, seem dramatically at the center of events, it is ... the card game, in which the adversaries struggle with fortunes and not lives, where the true spirit of this world is made manifest.[50]

Without denying that economic forces are at the centre of everything we see and that certain of the card-games involve money, I would argue differently. The outcome of the all various contests is predetermined by the class system, so that games are seldom equal. Duels, moreover, are at the social centre of the action. They may be less obviously economic than the card games, but are more completely gendered and more strongly grounded in social privilege. No matter how much skill is involved or what weapons are used, every variation of the trial at arms provides Kubrick with a stark means of illuminating the ironies and hypocrisies of the British squirearchy.

As an admirer of Max Ophuls, Kubrick could not have failed to recognise that duels have both theatrical value and considerable historic and cultural meaning. (He was also an admirer of Howard Hughes's *Hell's Angels* [1930], which contains a silhouetted pistol duel viewed from a great distance, rather like the one at the beginning of *Barry Lyndon*.) He seems aware that the elaborate rituals and regulations of eighteenth-century duels were vestigial remnants of Europe's feudal society, in which church-administered duels were fought for judicial purposes; no longer fully legitimate in the 'Age of Reason', they nevertheless continued to be supported by an ideology of chivalric virtue and manly 'honour'. In theory, they were supposed to be fought by members of the ruling class, not by peasants or shopkeepers. Kubrick puts great weight on their aristocratic quality: the combatants are described as 'gentlemen' and a formal ceremony, watched over by a referee and 'seconds', positions them as equals who are expected to show grace under pressure. He also depicts a boxing match, which might seem to represent the opposite end of the social scale. (He shoots this match with a low-level, hand-held camera and Foley effects reminiscent of the fight in *Killer's Kiss*; Ryan O'Neal, who had once been a boxer, helps make the action look realistic, but the big fellow who loses to O'Neal keeps swinging haymakers two feet over the star's head.) Interestingly, however, boxing assumed its modern form during the mid-eighteenth century, when Jack Broughton invented a skill-based, largely spectator sport guided by 'Broughton's rules'. At the time there were boxing academies in London in which young gentlemen could learn fisticuffs alongside fencing. Like duelling, boxing was presided over by a referee and, even though it sometimes had a kind of proletarian aura, its standards of conduct were established by the upper class.

The principal irony of the film is that Barry, an Irish *arriviste* who is looked upon with barely concealed contempt by the British lords, exhibits manly virtue in every sort of duel, even the boxing match, which he wins through skilled manoeuvre rather than brute strength, as if he had attended a gentleman's training school. In a sense he's more aristocratic than the aristocrats. His victories on the duelling field, however, take him only so far, since the duel, like warfare and gambling, is at bottom a predatory and barbaric mechanism ruled by hereditary money and power. A social outsider can't truly win (at least not in pre-Napoleonic Europe), no matter how much he masters the rules of the game. Barry and the Chevalier can rig the cards, but even when they cheat they earn relatively little. Barry can seduce Sir Charles Lyndon's wife ('Let those laugh that win,' he tells the dying lord), but he never gains a title from the Lyndon family. The same is true in the case of the supposed 'fair play' of armed battle: unbeknown to Barry, his pistol duel with the blustering, cowardly Captain Quinn is faked so that Nora Brady will be able to marry a British man of property. Near the end of the film, when Barry, devastated by his son's death, gallantly shoots a bullet into the ground and allows the terrified Lord Bullingdon to live, Bullingdon doesn't return the gesture.

The climactic duel with Bullingdon is milked for suspense and played in such slow fashion that it threatens to tip into absurdity (it's amusingly parodied in *Cheech and Chong's The Corsican Brothers* [1984]). Kubrick stages it in what he described to Michel Ciment as a 'tithe barn which also happened to have a lot of pigeons nesting in the rafters . . . . The sound of the pigeons added something to this, and, if it were a comedy, we could have had

further evidence of the pigeons' (p. 175). The atmosphere is vaguely religious, with light streaming through crucifix-shaped windows and white doves fluttering in the roof, as if Kubrick wanted to suggest the medieval origins of European duelling; and the slow pacing is justified by the fact that this particular confrontation represents the dramatic culmination of the film in both social and sexual terms: Barry and Bullingdon are a dual or tandem characterisation – rivals not only for what the latter calls a 'great family estate', but also for the possession of Lady Bullingdon.

This is another great difference between the film and the novel. In Thackeray, the Lady isn't especially interested in her son, but Barry repeatedly makes affectionate comments about his own mother, whom he describes as 'Lady Barry'. Thackeray often wrote about young men who are attached to their mothers (the theme reached its fullest expression in *Henry Esmond* [1852], his most brilliant pastiche of eighteenth-century fiction), but Kubrick pushes the mother–son relationship into more obviously Freudian territory, just as he had intended to do in his film about Napoleon. In the process, he greatly heightens the tension between Barry and his unlikely nemesis, bringing the two figures face to face in an over-determined duel. The result is a sharpening and condensation of the film's leading themes. The first half of Kubrick's *Barry Lyndon* is a picaresque narrative, but the second half zeroes in on what William Stephenson calls a 'tragedy of manners', featuring a pair of mother's boys who can be viewed as mirror images or ironic doubles, but who represent fundamentally different social types.

In one corner we have Redmond Barry, who, at an early age, loses his virile father in somewhat romantic fashion. Barry forms a strong bond with his mother (Marie Kean) based on their mutual affection and shared conviction that their shabby-genteel family has been deprived of its proper place in society. The mother takes no lovers, even though she's voluptuous and sexually attractive in a matronly, rather earthy way; instead she devotes herself to Barry's welfare and ultimately goads and instructs him in his attempts to achieve ascendancy over the Lyndons. Her son grows up to be a strong, handsome, vigorously heterosexual male who believes that his father was equally strong and who never faces a rival for his mother's attention. When Barry has a son by Lady Lyndon, Mrs Barry tucks the child into bed at night and sits nearby as Barry tells him adventurous bedtime stories. A tough, resilient woman, she becomes Barry's only trusted ally, and she's his single companion at the end, just as she was at the beginning.

In the other corner we have Bullingdon, who also loses his father at an early age. But Bullingdon's father is aged and emasculated – another of Kubrick's paralysed or wheelchair-bound males. Even before Sir Charles Lyndon's death, the son and his exceptionally beautiful young mother form what the narrator suggests is an excessively close attachment; she's a delicate, lonely woman, imprisoned in a dynastic marriage, prone to nervous 'distraction', and he's an equally melancholy youth, unable to resolve an Oedipal conflict that (as conventional Freudian theory would have it) thwarts his ability to achieve normative heterosexuality. When Bullingdon grows up to become a slight, 'feminine' young man, he faces a virile,

opportunistic rival for his mother's affection and a competitor for his patrimony. At the lavish birthday party for Barry's son, we see Barry and Mrs Barry laughing heartily at a magic show, while on the opposite side of the screen the fully grown Bullingdon sits languidly at Lady Lyndon's feet and holds her hand like an aestheticised child/lover.

In Bullingdon's eyes, Barry is not only an Irish adventurer who mistreats Lady Lyndon and lavishly spends her money, but also a 'manly' figure, frightening in his strength, who asserts a castrating power. More than once Barry whips Bullingdon's buttocks with a cane. Bullingdon retaliates by publicly denouncing Barry as a low-born adulterer; and in response, Barry attacks Bullingdon with animal fury. In the climactic duel, however, Bullingdon is able to score a primal victory. The outcome is clumsy and accidental and Barry is already a broken man; nevertheless, Barry suffers a symbolic castration. Legless, he's banished from Castle Lyndon, and Bullingdon recovers his old place beside his sad, lonely mother.

As I've already suggested, one result of these formal and substantive transformations of the novel is that Kubrick creates a much more sympathetic picture of the eponymous hero than Thackeray had done. Barry in the film is portrayed as a romantic young swain of considerable glamour and phallic power who discovers the underlying brutality of eighteenth-century Europe and is transformed by the experience into a ruffian, a trickster and a fortune hunter. It comes as a shock when, during a rich carriage ride with his new wife, he blows pipe smoke into her lovely face, but we know the sources of his cruelty. His inevitable downfall has less to do with his acquired ruthlessness than with his proud and mistaken belief that he rightly belongs to the ruling class. The death of his beloved son (a chip off the old block, in contrast to the effete child of the Lyndons), is also the death of what Barry presumes will be a dynasty. The film pulls out all the sentimental stops when the boy dies, treating his passing in the manner of Victorian fiction and any number of novels in which a similar event signals the fall of an aristocratic family (for two very different twentieth-century examples, see Evelyn Waugh's *A Handful of Dust* and Margaret Mitchell's *Gone with the Wind*). But Barry has never been an aristocrat insofar as the British are concerned. Despite his skill and nerve as a duellist, despite his extravagant campaign to buy his way into a title, he remains a colonial subject who is easily duped, conscripted and exiled. He seems always aware at some level of his outsider status. His tears during the protracted death-bed scene with Bryan – a rare moment of full-out pathos in a Kubrick film – are similar to those he sheds when his friend Captain Grogan (Godfrey Quigley) dies on the battlefield and when he first encounters the Chevalier de Balibari in Prussia. In all three cases, Barry weeps because of his intense love for his Irish countrymen and family, without whom he is completely alone.

Critics have generally undervalued Ryan O'Neal's portrayal of Barry. At the time the film appeared, he was a major Hollywood star (his tears in the saccharine but wildly popular *Love Story* [1970] are as copious as the ones in *Barry Lyndon*) but, despite or perhaps because of his box-office appeal, he was regarded as little more than a handsome leading man with a talent for light comedy. His open, innocent-looking face and sturdy, athletic build were ideal for the role in this particular film, and his off-screen reputation seemed to feed his performance – an ex Golden-Gloves fighter, he had a reputation as a Hollywood bad boy and was notorious for cheating on his wives with his leading ladies. His star image apart, however, he exhibits considerable range and subtlety. The character of Barry as Kubrick conceives him is courageous, resourceful, charming, but not highly intelligent or articulate. The social world he inhabits, whether as a common soldier, a gambler, or a wealthy husband, often requires him to be silent or to operate behind a mask. He and Lady Lyndon barely exchange words, and in some of his most important scenes with the other characters, he merely listens. For an actor, this sort of work is more difficult than it looks. O'Neal is on screen at nearly every moment of the lengthy film and must indicate different stages of Barry's life – the callow youth, the unscrupulous adventurer, the loving father and the tragic loner – chiefly through unspoken reactions and minimal facial expressions. He nicely conveys Barry's contradictory aspects – his quick temper and subdued cleverness, his cruelty and tenderness, his emotional shifts from pride to despair. His seduction of Lady Lyndon is convincingly romantic; his fury at Bullingdon in the concert scene is unnerving; and his awkwardness when he tries to behave like an aristocrat – as when he admires the 'the colour blue' in a painting or listens in smiling, eager silence to the conversation of a nobleman at a garden party – is perfectly calculated.

Our last view of this skilfully acted and many-faceted character is different in style from the rest of the film – a freeze frame in the manner of the French New Wave, showing him from behind as Mrs Barry assists him into a carriage.[51] One of his legs is amputated at the knee and he leans on a crutch. The relatively banal, almost snapshot-looking composition seems to enhance the atmosphere of desolation. Next we see a self-consciously beautiful, painterly shot of Lady Lyndon in her gilded cage at Castle Lyndon: gaunt, almost sepulchral, barely having survived her attempted suicide after the death of Bryan, she sits in the pale light of a window, hovered over by her son and her retainers, and signs a bank draft with a quill pen. An insert shows that she is paying Barry an annuity of 500 guineas – a not inconsiderable gift. The attentive viewer will also notice that the date on the draft is 1789, the year of the French Revolution.

Much has been made of the date. Critics usually argue that Kubrick wanted to end the film by subtly announcing the advent of revolution and democracy. An equally strong motive might have been a desire to make the film resemble the novel, which is a story viewed in retrospect, from the other side of an historical divide. Whatever Kubrick's intention, it should be pointed out that his implicit attitude towards European society and politics is somewhat different from Thackeray's. (And in any case, the French Revolution and the Napoleonic era were highly prosperous years for the British landowning class.) The author of *The Memoirs of Barry Lyndon* and *Vanity Fair* was a sort of anti-Dickens, critical of the eighteenth century but instinctively attracted to the pre-revolutionary world. His early fiction is contemptuous of the bourgeoisie, virtually oblivious of the peasants and working poor and unsympathetic towards social upstarts like Barry and Becky Sharp. He might admire the daring of his swashbuckling rogues, but he doesn't pity them when they meet disaster. Above all, he's against Napoleon. Late in *The Memoirs of Barry Lyndon*, when the aging narrator looks back on his adventures, we can almost hear Thackeray's voice breaking through the fiction: 'Yes, the old times were the times for *gentlemen*, before Buonaparte brutalized Europe with his swaggering Grenadiers, and was conquered in his turn by our shopkeepers and cheese-mongers of England here' (p. 99).

Thackeray and Kubrick are alike in their refusal to depict the eighteenth century as either an Age of Sensibility or an Age of Enlightenment (this last despite Kubrick's tendency to see the period in terms of elaborate manners and the suppression of emotion). Instead, they place emphasis on the harshness and brutality beneath the period's façade of aristocratic beauty. But Kubrick, a Jewish-American who eventually settled into a British country house, found it much easier to identify with a social outsider like Barry Lyndon, whom he depicts as an unwitting and unsuccessful rebel against his times. For roughly similar reasons, Kubrick identified with the Corsican upstart Napoleon, who gained ascendancy over France's old regime and became one of the founders of the modern world. Compared to Napoleon, Barry is an ordinary fellow, a soldier rather than a general, swept along by history; but in certain ways, Kubrick uses Barry's brief rise and fall as a foreshadowing of Napoleon's historically momentous adventures. I suspect that Kubrick's entire interest in the late eighteenth century is rooted in his desire to explore the conditions that give rise to Napoleon. I also suspect his reference to 1789 functions less as an optimistic tribute to democracy than as a portent of the Napoleonic era and a nod to a film he never made. Kubrick had intended to portray Napoleon as a tragic superman – both a dictator and a force of Enlightenment liberalism, worthy of being placed in structural relation to the killer ape and the Star Child in *2001*. He was unable to realise that ambition, but it became a kind of structuring absence in *Barry Lyndon* and one of the chief reasons why he was inspired to turn Thackeray's unruly novel into a film of such beauty, strangeness and emotional force.

V. Horrorshow

In 1975 Kubrick was among five directors that Warner approached for the upcoming production of *Network* (1976); he expressed interest, but screenwriter Paddy Chayefsky, who wanted to be the film's auteur, rejected him (LoBrutto, pp. 410–11). Perhaps because *Barry Lyndon* had encountered a lukewarm reception from the US press and was a relative disappointment at the box office, Kubrick next thought of something more commercial: a generic horror picture in the vein of *The Exorcist* (1973) and *The Omen* (1976), both of which had generated huge profits and contributed to a cycle of Hollywood pictures about grossout, supernatural terror. Given the noirish tenor of his previous work, horror was certainly not an unexpected theme for Kubrick to explore. He was unable to find a suitable property, however, until Warner's production chief, John Calley, sent him the page proofs of Stephen King's *The Shining*, which tells the story of a psychologically troubled family of three trapped in a huge, demonic hotel during a winter storm. King's popularity was on the rise (when it was published in 1977, the novel quickly shot to number eight on the US best-seller list), and for the leading role in the film adaptation Kubrick was able to attract a major star – Jack Nicholson, whom Kubrick had at one point considered to play Napoleon.

Kubrick rejected a screenplay that King himself had written, choosing instead to develop a script in collaboration with Diane Johnson, the author of, among other books, *The Shadow Knows* (1974), a psychological mystery novel Kubrick had at one point been interested in adapting. *The Shadow Knows* is the alternately sad, wryly amusing and frightening story of a divorced mother of four who lives with her children and nanny in a housing project and who fears that an unknown person wants to kill her. Like *The Shining*, it makes the reader wonder if the central character is mentally disturbed or truly in danger (ironically, 'The Shadow knows' is a line of dialogue in an early chapter of *The Shining*). Given its female point of view, it would have been an unusual project for Kubrick; but, as Diane Johnson herself once noted, her novel also has certain features in common with Arthur Schnitzler's *Traumnovella*, which later provided the basis for *Eyes Wide Shut*.[52]

The script Johnson and Kubrick ultimately wrote for *The Shining* differs from King's novel in several respects. It dispenses with most of the family's history before arriving at the hotel, it kills off the kindly hotel chef and it ends with the father freezing to death in a maze rather than dying in a fire that destroys the hotel. When the film was released, King publicly criticised it on the grounds that the tone was satiric and the depiction of the father almost completely unsympathetic. In an interview with *Playboy* magazine, he described Kubrick as 'a very cold man' who had 'great difficulty conceiving, even academically, of a supernatural world,' and who 'couldn't grasp the sheer inhuman evil of the Overlook Hotel'. He concluded that Kubrick had 'looked for evil in the characters and made the film into a domestic tragedy with only a few supernatural overtones'.[53] Leaving aside his remarks on Kubrick's personality, his description of the film was essentially correct. The novel is, in fact, much more extravagantly supernatural and animistic, and certainly more forgiving of the doomed, alcoholic father, whose last words to his son are 'Run away. Quick. And remember how much I love you.' (In 1996, King produced a bad adaptation of the novel in the form of a five-hour TV miniseries that featured King in a cameo role, wearing garish make-up and conducting a ghostly orchestra in the hotel; it ended in sentimental fashion, with the father's benign ghost appearing at his son's college graduation to declare paternal love.)

For all their differences, however, King and Kubrick were alike in thinking that *The Shining* provided what King described as 'a chance to blur the line between the supernatural and the psychotic'.[54] Kubrick said much the same thing in an interview with Michel Ciment, in which he emphasised the importance of King's plot:

> It seemed to strike an extraordinary balance between the psychological and the supernatural . . . . This allowed you to suspend your doubt of the supernatural until you were so thoroughly into the story that you could accept it almost without noticing . . . . The novel is by no means a serious literary work, but for the most part the plot is extremely well worked out . . . . I've never been able to decide whether the plot [in any film] is just a way of keeping people's attention while you do everything else, or whether the plot is really more important than anything else, perhaps communicating with us on an unconscious level which affects us in the way that myths once did. (p. 181)

The film maintains a balance between the psychological and the supernatural chiefly in the way it treats two characters: Jack Torrance (Nicholson), an alcoholic, would-be writer who has recently sworn off drinking and is reduced to doing menial work; and Jack's son, Danny (Danny Lloyd), a five-year-old who in the past has been the victim of a violent 'accident' at the hands of his drunken father. When Jack takes a job as the winter caretaker at the luxurious Overlook Hotel, he begins to experience what appear to be hallucinations and psychotic symptoms. By the end of the picture, however, we have no choice but to conclude that the ghosts who urge him to murder his wife and child are not simply in his mind. Danny, for his part, seems at first to be a disturbed little boy who suffers from horrific fantasies and a split personality; but early on, after he meets hotel chef Dick Halloran (Scatman Crothers), we suspect that he has a gift of 'shining' or ESP, which enables him to see directly into the hidden past and the traumatic future.

The is-this-happening-or-is-he-crazy quality that Kubrick tried to sustain for much of the film is precisely the quality that Tzvetan Todorov and other literary theorists have described as the 'fantastic'. According to Todorov, fantastic narrative isn't simply a story containing supernatural occurrences, but one that challenges the reader's ability to explain events as either imaginary or supernatural. He describes the form as follows (for the sake of readability I've refrained from entering 'sic' after the masculine pronouns):

> An inexplicable phenomenon occurs; to obey his determinist mentality, the reader finds himself obliged to choose between two solutions: either to reduce this phenomenon to known causes, to the natural order, describing the unwonted events as imaginary, or else to admit the existence of the supernatural and thereby to effect a modification in all the representations which form his image of the world. The fantastic lasts as long as this uncertainty lasts; once the reader opts for one solution or the other, he is in the realm of the uncanny or of the marvelous.[55]

Todorov's analysis suggests a continuum of effects involving three different ways of handling causal explanations in fiction: first is realism ('known causes'), then what Todorov's translator, Richard Howard, terms the uncanny (psychological causes, though it should be emphasised that Todorov isn't a Freudian and uses psychology in a more general sense) and, finally, the marvellous (supernatural causes). Two-thirds of the way down this range, at the point where the uncanny is on the verge of becoming the marvellous, we find what Todorov names the fantastic 'genre'. His exemplary text is Henry James's 'The Turn of the Screw', in which the uncertainty about how to explain events is never resolved – in other words, *pace* Edmund Wilson's famous interpretation of James's story, we never know whether the ghosts are real or figments of the governess-narrator's sexually repressed imagination.

Kubrick was always interested in grotesque combinations of the commonplace and the wildly satiric or fanciful, and he was instinctively drawn to any kind of story – Burgess's *A Clockwork Orange* and Schnitzler's *Traumnovella*, for example – that blurs the line between reality and dream or fairly tale. One of the interesting aspects of his adaptation of *The Shining*, however, is that it runs the entire range of narrative possibilities described by Todorov. An aura of weirdness or outright derangement haunts the film from the very start, but everything is motivated by the typically realistic situation of a 'nuclear' American family undergoing economic and psychological stress. The early scenes show us Jack's job interview with the corporate manager of the Overlook Hotel (Barry Nelson), a lunch-table conversation between Wendy (Shelley Duvall) and Danny, and a visit to Danny from a paediatrician (Anne Jackson). These and a few later scenes are so firmly grounded in down-at-heels, quotidian materials of domestic drama (the mother chain-smokes, the son eats a peanut-butter-and-jelly sandwich, a TV set plays in the background) and so inflected by touches of deadpan humour (the ash on the mother's cigarette keeps getting longer as she talks with the paediatrician) that, in 2005, a clever group of film-makers was able to construct a mock trailer for *The Shining*, choosing clips that make the picture look like a slightly whimsical family comedy.[56]

The early sequences also invoke the Freudian uncanny, which always depends upon a background of domestic realism: when Danny eats his sandwich, he speaks to 'Mrs Torrance'

in the gravelly voice of his apparently imaginary friend Tony, who 'lives' somewhere in his mouth; and when he brushes his teeth, he has a terrifying vision and an apparent seizure. As the plot develops, bizarre events proliferate (for most of the film, only Wendy seems immune from ghostly visitations) until we reach the point where it becomes difficult to decide whether or not we should suspend disbelief in the supernatural. When Jack walks into the Gold Ballroom and orders a drink from the satanic bartender, Lloyd (Joe Turkel), we reach a crisis of interpretation and enter the zone of the pure fantastic. Somewhat later, when Jack is set free from a food locker by the ghost of the former caretaker, we encounter the film's first unambiguously supernatural event (unless we want to assume on little evidence that Jack or somebody else is dreaming everything from here until the end) and we move into the zone of Todorov's 'marvellous'. The climactic scenes never entirely release their hold on realism or Freud, and some of the repeated images, such as the elevator of blood, retain an ambiguous status; but the film ends with a carnival of ghostly sadism and sexual decadence (chiefly homosexuality and a hint of bestiality), and with several allusions to myths and fairy tales.

Among the many commentators on *The Shining*, only Michel Ciment has noticed the degree to which the film can be understood in terms of what he, like Todorov, calls 'the genre of the fantastic', which for him constitutes a 'shock between what is real and what is imaginary' and a 'breach in the recognized order of things' (p. 125). Ciment argues that, for this reason, *The Shining* belongs in the same generic category as *2001*, and he points out a remarkable number of things that the two apparently unrelated films have in common: they both eschew off-screen narration in favour of intertitles (in *The Shining* the titles announce events or mark the passage of time in increasingly short intervals); they both use a mixture of modernist and romantic music (*The Shining* mingles Ligeti, Penderecki and Bartok with a '*Dies Irae*' derived from Berlioz's *Symphonie Fantastique*, which is orchestrated by Wendy Carlos and Rachel Elkind); they both take place inside large man-made structures controlled by non-human entities (the extremely large and fascinating sets for the two films were constructed at the same British studio); they both tell stories of characters who are trapped between a hostile outside world and a murderous figure on the inside who destroys their technical equipment; and, most significantly, 'In either film, the spectator is incapable of supplying a rational explanation for what [she or he] has witnessed' (p. 125).

Viewed in this light, a number of scenes in *The Shining* seem to echo *2001*. For example, the aerial photography at the beginning of the film bears a certain resemblance to the famous 'star gate'. Danny's wide-angle journey on his tricycle down the corridors of the Overlook, culminating in an astonished gaze into an impossible world, is not unlike Dave Bowman's climactic journey aboard the Discovery (at one juncture, Danny wears a sweater decorated with a NASA rocket ship). By the same token, the scene in which an ambiguously 'subjective' camera roams around the sickly green-and-purple room 237 in the Overlook, accompanied by the muffled sound of a heartbeat, is similar to Bowman's exploration of a mysterious, interstellar hotel suite. But when Ciment describes the two films as belonging to the same 'genre', he creates confusion, since we normally think of science fiction and gothic horror as distinct generic types. Fortunately, we have Rosemary Jackson's modification of Todorov's theory, which helps to clarify the situation. 'Fantastic narratives,' Jackson writes, 'confound elements of both the marvelous and the mimetic . . . . They pull the reader from the apparent familiarity and security of the known and everyday world . . . into a world whose improbabilities are closer to the realm normally associated with the marvelous.' The key to the fantastic has less to do with generic features than with the instability of the narrative's internal logic or rules of probability. It therefore becomes possible 'to suggest a definition of the fantastic as a *mode*, which then assumes different generic forms'.[57]

To explain the specific instability of the fantastic mode, Jackson appropriates the optical term 'paraxis', which is a region where refracted light rays seem to converge in the formation of an image – the region inside a camera obscura, for example, or in the reflected depth of a mirror. 'In this area,' she remarks, 'object and image seem to collide, but in fact neither object nor reconstituted image genuinely reside there: nothing does.' The paraxial area can serve as a metaphor for 'the spectral region of the fantastic, whose imaginary world is neither entirely "real" (object), nor entirely "unreal" (image), but is located somewhere indeterminately between the two' (p. 19). Interestingly, *The Shining* gives us several instances in which Kubrick, like many horror-movie directors before him, plays with this kind of spectral ambiguity. As Mario Falsetto has pointed out, there are several times in the film when we are unsure whether a shot is 'subjective' or 'objective'. A similar effect is created by the long tracking shot (somewhat reminiscent of *The Killing*) in which Jack walks down a hallway in the Overlook and enters the Gold Ballroom, where he encounters a large party: in a single movement, we travel from the 'real' into the 'unreal', with no clear boundary between the two and no way to determine if both are truly 'there'. Notice also that a dressing-table mirror in the Torrance family bedroom is used to create a sort of confusion between reality and image: when Wendy serves Jack his breakfast in bed, much of their conversation is photographed in the mirror, and the perspective is evident only because the writing on Jack's T-shirt is reversed; when Danny later sneaks into the bedroom to get his toy truck, we see Jack sitting on the edge of the bed in a sort of trance or depression, his image doubled by the mirror; and towards the end of the film, Wendy looks into the mirror and sees the hidden meaning of REDRUM, a word Danny has written backward on the bathroom door.

The genre, as opposed to the mode, of *The Shining* is gothic horror. Jackson contends that this type of fiction, which originated in Europe during the late eighteenth century, was developed in reaction against a dominant rationalism; for that reason, she believes the

gothic, like the grotesque, with which it participates, has often functioned as 'an art of estrangement' and a critique of 'capitalist and patriarchal orders' (pp. 175–6). Perhaps so; *The Shining* can certainly be read along those lines, and has been.[58] But as Robin Wood and others have pointed out, a good many horror films are ideologically reactionary.[59] In this regard, we should also recall that some gothic fiction tends to express a latent, romanticised nostalgia for a lost aristocratic world, symbolised by ruined castles and old dark houses. From Horace Walpole and Henry Maturin to Henry James and Daphne du Maurier, a certain kind of upper-class architecture has been essential to the spooky but fascinating *mise en scène* of ghost stories – indeed the very term 'gothic' derives from that architecture.

One of the clever aspects of *The Shining* is the way it updates the traditional style, eschewing gothic design and expressionistic lighting while at the same time emphasising the architectural splendour of a dead aristocracy. (The only place where Kubrick alludes to old-fashioned horror-movie lighting is the scene in which Jack has a conversation with the hotel's bartender; a row of soft lights along the bar illuminates the men's faces from below, giving them a demonic look.) The Overlook is a thoroughly modernist building modelled partly on the Timberline Lodge in Oregon and partly on art director Roy Walker's research into twentieth-century hotel architecture across America (the men's room in the bar is based on Frank Lloyd Wright's design for the Arizona Biltmore), but it's also a kind of castle perched atop a mountain. It has a high-ceilinged lobby, a dumb-waiter that Danny regards as a 'secret passage', a maze of haunted hallways and numerous locked rooms. In typical *moderne* style, it mixes streamlined materials with 'primitive' artefacts, in this case from native-American culture; indeed we learn from the hotel manager that the building sits atop what was once an Indian burial ground. One almost expects clichéd horror music to accompany this sort of information, but it turns out that the hotel is haunted not by Indians but by descendants of the white barbarians who destroyed the Indian culture – in particular by jazz-age sophisticates. As the manager tells Jack, the Overlook was 'one of the stopping places for the jet set before anyone knew what the jet set was'. All the 'best people' have stayed there, including four presidents and 'lots of movie stars'. In the lobby, a gallery of photos of the rich and famous from the old days (most of which Kubrick found in the Warner studio's archives) serves as a modern version of the spooky family portraits on the walls of gothic castles.

Nearly all the modern variants of gothic horror turn their haunted buildings into expressions of the characters' mental states – outward manifestations of individual isolation and unconscious sexual fears. In the Stephen King novel, the Overlook is both a psychological space and an organism with its own mind, complete with topiary shrubs in the grounds that come alive to menace the characters. Kubrick takes a more realistic approach, strongly emphasising the ways in which the building's luxury feeds Jack's resentment of his family and his fantasies of becoming a playboy author in the mould of Scott Fitzgerald. During his job interview, he seems to relish his surroundings and easily waves aside any concerns for Wendy and Danny. Twice in the early scenes, as the camera tracks around the hotel, we see him turn and look back at pretty girls who are leaving for the winter. Except for a few perfunctory endearments he addresses to Wendy in the presence of the hotel manager, he never shows affection for his mousy wife, and he never plays with his son, who spends a good deal of time watching TV. Jack becomes lively and sociable only when ghosts appear; they recognise him, call him 'sir', and, despite his flannel shirt and work boots, immediately accept his credit at the bar. In room 237, the classic locked chamber of spooky stories, always symbolic of sexual knowledge, he encounters a naked ghost in a bath (a twist on the shower scene in *Psycho*) who embodies all his desires and disgust for women; at first she's lithe and beautiful, but then she's an aging hag covered with oozing scabs. Not long afterward, in the blood-red toilet of the ballroom, he becomes the hotel's supreme 'caretaker', making direct contact with his feelings of white male supremacy and murderous rage.

Fredric Jameson has made the interesting point that Stephen King's novel depicts Jack as 'a writer of some minimal achievement and a classical American *poete maudit* whose talent is plagued and stimulated by alcoholism' (a sort of there-but-for-the-grace-of-God version of King himself), whereas the film depicts him as 'someone who would like to *be* a writer' (p. 93). As Jameson notes, Jack in the film certainly produces what the French would call 'du texte', but the result, depending on your point of view, is either the ultimate dada novel or an 'empty auto-referential statement' (p. 93). As a writer, Jack can only repeat himself – an appropriate action for a man who loves the storied, leisure-class atmosphere of the Overlook and who wants, as he tells Danny, to stay there 'for ever and ever and ever'. This obsession with the hotel gives a materialist spin to King's novel and to the conventions of occult or supernatural horror movies of the 1970s, transforming what Jameson calls their 'nostalgia for an absolute Evil' into nostalgia for the class certainties of 'the still Veblenesque social system in the 1920s' (p. 97). Here again the film invites comparison and contrast with *2001*. Like the Star Child at the end of the earlier film, Jack experiences Eternal Return, but with a vengeance; frozen inside the hotel maze, he becomes an emblem of 'repetition, with all its overtones of traumatic fixation and the death wish'. At the last moment, he's absorbed into a 1920s' photo on the lobby wall, where his spirit remains forever in 'the space of thralldom to the past' (p. 98).

But the Overlook isn't simply the physical manifestation of Jack's desires for wealth and fame; it's also an ironically domesticated space – a terrifying 'home' that makes the entire Torrance family feel what the novel calls 'cabin fever'. At this level, the film invites Freudian interpretation; and, in fact, when *The Shining* was released, Diane Johnson told interviewers that, as preparation for writing the screenplay, she and Kubrick had read Freud's essay, 'The Uncanny' (1919), which attempts to explain the sources of what Freud calls the 'common core of feeling . . . in certain things which lie within the field of what is frightening'.[60] In his essay, Freud notes that the German word *Unheimlich*, meaning 'unhomely', is akin to the English word 'uncanny', which has an Anglo-Saxon etymology meaning 'unknown' or 'unfamiliar'; he goes on, however, to argue that uncanny feelings, which we experience more strongly in art than in life, are stimulated not by strange or unearthly phenomena but by unconscious fears of a quite 'homely' kind, originating in the family and often expressing themselves as symbolic fantasies of castration at the hands of a father figure. Kubrick's film makes darkly humorous allusions to this theory. When the hotel manager shows the Torrance family their humble apartment in the staff quarters of the Overlook, Jack looks around the place with a slightly ironic grin and says, 'It's very homey.' Near the climax of the story, Jack bashes in the door of the apartment with a fire axe and calls out, 'Wendy? I'm home!'

Like King's novel, the film shifts its point of view from one member of the family to another; but it distributes the greater part of the subjective shots almost equally between Jack and Danny, maintaining a balance between two apparently Freudian perspectives. On the one hand, we have the father's narcissism, violent frustration and death wish; on the other, the son's latent sexual desires and emotional conflicts. From the latter viewpoint, the plot seems flagrantly Oedipal, dealing with a male child's struggle against a castrating father who, even though he is absent much of the time, inhibits full access to the mother. At one point, Danny and his mother watch Robert Mulligan's *Summer of '42* (1971) on TV, becoming absorbed in the scene of a beautiful older woman inviting a handsome boy into her kitchen; and, at the end of the movie, when Danny escapes the hedge

maze where Jack is trapped, he runs straight into Wendy's arms and kisses her on the lips.

In the interest of giving some of these events the atmosphere of a child's imagination, Johnson and Kubrick supplemented their reading of Freud with Bruno Bettelheim's *The Uses of Enchantment* (1973), a Freudian analysis of fairy tales, which argues that certain kinds of grisly stories provide children with therapeutic ways of dealing with primal anxieties. Thus, the film contains several references to fairy tales and violent cartoons such as 'Road Runner'. As she's shown around the Overlook, Wendy comments, 'This whole place is such an enormous maze I'll have to leave a trail of bread crumbs every time I come in.' Later, when things become menacing and violent, Jack resembles a half-sleeping giant that Danny fears to disturb in the bedroom, and he acts out the role of the big bad wolf ('little pigs, little pigs, let me come in') when he chops down a locked door to get at Wendy and Danny.

In one of the best commentaries on the film, William Paul discusses most of these details, but also makes the important point that *The Shining* uses Freud for revisionist ends. The most radical and disturbing aspect of the film is that Jack Torrance isn't, as Freudian analysis would have it, an imaginary menace or a fairy-tale monster created by a child's projected anxieties; he's a realistic character who despises his wife, who feels ambivalence towards his son and who actually becomes a crazed axe murderer. This situation is quite rare.

The villain in horror movies is usually a stepfather, as in *Night of the Hunter* (1955) and *The Stepfather* (1987); a mother, as in *Psycho* (1960) and *Mommie Dearest* (1981); or a demonic child, as in *The Exorcist* and *The Omen*. Significantly, Robin Wood's influential psychoanalytic theory of the horror film, which argues that the monster or the demonic 'other' represents a return of the repressed and a key to any individual film's ideological purpose, contains not a single example of a motion picture in which the monster is a white male patriarch.

One of the distinctive features of Steven King's fiction is that it contains several monstrous fathers or father figures. Kubrick's film seizes on this quality and, to a greater degree than King, locates the propensity towards evil in a father's psychology. Jack Torrance appears to be guided and assisted by ghosts but, at the ideological level, it hardly matters whether the ghosts are real or figments of his imagination; he's urged to do what he already wants to do. Furthermore, nearly all the ghosts who have speaking roles or significant scenes, including the sexual revellers we see near the end, are white males. (The exceptions are the Grady sisters, who are victims of their father, and the voiceless woman in the bath, who seems to have been a suicide.) Jack's male rage and the mainsprings of his violence are vividly revealed in his speech to Lloyd in the Gold Room – a frightening scene, but also a parody of a bar-fly's confession, played by Nicholson in a broad, squirming style. Tormented

by writer's block and guilt, Jack explains that he suffers from a 'white man's burden' caused by 'the old sperm bank upstairs':

> JACK: I never laid a hand on him, goddammit . . . . I wouldn't touch one hair on his god damned little head. I *love* the little sonofabitch. I'd do anything for him. Any fucking thing. That bitch! Long as I live she'll never let me forget what happened. [Pause] I did hurt him once, okay? It was an *accident*! Completely unintentional. Coulda happened to anybody. It was *three god damned years ago*! The little fucker had thrown all my papers over the floor. All I tried to do was pull him up! A momentary loss of muscular coordination!

An equally chilling moment comes when little Danny sits in his father's lap and asks, 'Dad, you would never hurt me and Mommy, would you?' In a dreamy tone, Jack replies, 'I love you, Danny. I love you more than anything in the *whole world*. I would *never* do anything to hurt you. You know that, don't you?' Here and elsewhere, as Paul argues, Kubrick 'redirects Freud's Oedipal drama to the original myth'.[61] Freud's version, as everybody knows, begins with Oedipus killing his father Laius at the crossroads; Paul reminds us, however, that the Greek myth begins earlier, with the parents abandoning the child and

the father mutilating his son by piercing his ankles and tying them together (hence the name Oedipus, which translates as 'swollen foot'). Freud seems to repress or conveniently ignore the incident of paternal abuse, but Kubrick faces it squarely, dramatising 'something so insistently repressed in Western culture, the hostility of the father toward his own son' (Paul, p. 344).

The film's play with the myths of psychoanalysis, as well as its uncanny emotional atmosphere, are reinforced by its visual design, which everywhere invokes the symbolic/allegorical implications of a maze: the aerial shots of the Torrance family Volkswagen travelling up a mountain towards the Overlook give the impression of a maze; a literal hedge maze is situated on the grounds of the Overlook; a model of the maze sits on a table inside the building; the numerous hotel hallways create a maze; and a maze pattern can be seen on the carpet where Danny plays with his toy truck. By virtue of this design, the film provides many opportunities for Kubrick's characteristic wide-angle tracking shots down tunnels or corridors, intensified here by sudden twists around corners to reveal new passageways. The idea for the twisting and turning probably had its origins in 1974, when Kubrick first saw test reels photographed by Garrett Brown's Steadicam, a gyroscopic device that maintains a stable image in hand-held or other kinds of previously impossible circumstances. When he came to make *The Shining*, Kubrick wanted the Steadicam to move at extremely low levels representing the viewpoint of a child, and he hired Brown to come to England as the camera's operator. Hence we have the exhilarating, amusing and suspenseful shot of Danny on his streamlined tricycle, pedalling furiously across the grand rooms and deserted hallways of the Overlook, his wheels alternately rumbling and muffling as he passes over floors and carpet. We travel along behind him, skimming just above the floor in his wake, fearing what we might see at the next turning. We also have the climactic chase sequence through the hedge maze, which cuts back and forth between the travelling viewpoints of Danny and his axe-wielding father (limping along incongruously as the 'swollen-foot' character), and culminates with a close-up of the father frozen in the snow. After the more-or-less subjective 'tunnel' shots that move swiftly down hedgerows and hotel corridors, the film concludes with an 'objective' camera movement reminiscent of Alain Resnais's *Last Year at Marienbad*, Michael Snow's *Wavelength* (1967) and a typical episode of Rod Serling's *Twilight Zone*. The eye of the camera slowly tracks, zooms and then cuts into the photo of Jack at a fourth-of-July party at the Overlook in the 1920s.

The image of Jack frozen inside the maze may be intended as an allusion to the Minotaur, as several critics have suggested, although this mythical creature (a half-man, half-bull who ate children) is said to have inhabited a labyrinth, not a maze. The labyrinth, some form of which exists in virtually every culture, is normally a circular pathway that spirals towards a centre; the maze, an equally familiar construction, is box-like, filled with dead ends and a bewildering array of passageways. You can't truly get lost in the average labyrinth, but the whole purpose of a maze is to trick you. The former is 'unicursal', leading in and out, a metaphor for an eternal return or a journey towards understanding; the latter is a puzzle, a metaphor for entrapment and death; hence *The Shining* makes an interesting contrast with Guillermo del Toro's *Pan's Labyrinth* (2006), which ends with a girl being pursued into a labyrinth by her evil stepfather. The two forms, however, sometimes become interchangeable, not only in critical writing (Michel Ciment refers to the hedge maze in *The Shining* as a labyrinth), but also in the Greek myth of the artist-technician Dedalus, who constructed a labyrinth, who was imprisoned there with his son Icarus and who built wings with which they could escape. Dedalus's labyrinth was designed to conceal the Minotaur, who demanded human sacrifice; Theseus entered the labyrinth to slay the monster and was helped by Ariadne, who gave him a ball of string to mark a way out. *The Shining* evokes several of these associations and, like the Greek myth, seems to combine the implications of labyrinth and maze. Christopher Hoile has remarked that, by the end of the film, several myths and fairy tales are bound up together: 'the father, son, and mother, who before isolation show the tensions psychoanalysis has identified with Laius, Oedipus, and Jocasta, once trapped in the Overlook Hotel take on a fairy-tale version of Minotaur, Theseus, and Ariadne or Ogre, Jack the Giant Killer, and the Ogre's kind wife'.[62]

In addition to Theseus and Jack the Giant Killer, the film (like the novel) alludes to Hansel and Gretel. All three stories involve cannibalism, a theme introduced early in *The Shining* by means of the Torrance family's conversation about the Donner party. The three stories also concern children or young men who cleverly manoeuvre through unfamiliar surroundings to defeat monstrous antagonists, just as Danny, aided by his mother, uses analytical skills and exploration of the hotel and its hedge maze to defeat his murderous father. For Danny, the maze/labyrinth leads to growth rather than death. William Paul has pointed out that the conclusion to the film is prefigured when Jack stands over a model of the maze and seems to look down at Wendy and Danny, who are exploring the actual maze outside. The overhead camera angle condenses the different possible meanings of 'overlook': it gives Jack a spectacular view and makes him seem an omnipotent 'overseer' or 'caretaker' (in an earlier scene, he tells Wendy that during his job interview he felt as if he 'knew what would be around every corner'); but it also 'overlooks' important lessons that can be learned at ground level (Paul, pp. 347–8). The focal and spectral ambiguity of the shot (Is it subjective or objective? Animated or photographed?) is appropriate to its double symbolic implication: it portends Jack's gradual descent into the imprisoning maze of his own mind, and at the same time his son's victory over a menacing environment.

Danny has an ally not only in Wendy but also in Halloran. During the writing of the film, Kubrick was unsure how to deal with these characters. In his notes on the screenplay, he observed that King had made Wendy 'strong and uncomplaining', and he asked himself, 'Why does she stay with [Jack]? Decide. Weakness? Physical? Love?'[63] In the end he took a satiric approach, dropping a good deal of dialogue that Diane Johnson had written for Wendy and transforming her from a relatively 'rounded' personality into a naive, almost laughably fragile and fearful character who clings to a troubled marriage. To play her, he chose Shelley Duvall, an eccentric performer best known for the off-beat comedy, sexiness and pathos she brought to several of Robert Altman's best films (she's a long-legged LA biker in *Nashville* [1975], a ditzy and fascinatingly weird young single in *Three Women* [1977] and the perfect Olive Oyl in *Popeye* [1980]). On the set, at least from what one sees in Vivian Kubrick's documentary about the making of *The Shining*, he treated Duvall with almost as much contempt as Jack treats Wendy, thereby contributing to the skittish quality of her performance. Some of her scenes were cut from the released film, but enough remain to make it clear that she's playing the sort of wife who might defer to Jack and at the same time drive him crazy. Her limp hair, string-bean body and trailer-park twang are an affront to Jack's sense of himself, and her timidity fuels his sadism. When she holds him at bay with a baseball bat, his elaborate condescension and darkly funny threats (he's a bit like an exasperated husband in a TV sitcom) tap into a vague irritation the audience has been encouraged to feel about Wendy, almost pushing the film into overt misogyny. Even so, Kubrick upsets our assumptions about the two characters. Despite Wendy's wilting anguish and horror-movie screaming, she subdues Jack fairly easily: she knocks him out, drags him into a storage room and locks him away for the winter; when he escapes and chops down her door, she nicks the back of his hand with a butcher knife and he runs away whimpering.

No such luck for Halloran, Jack's only victim and the subject of the film's only direct representation of grisly violence. In the novel, Halloran helps to defeat the forces of evil and becomes Danny's surrogate father. Kubrick and Johnson initially planned to invert this role, turning the gentle, affable chef into a secret ally of the hotel's ghosts, a killer who helps to murder the entire Torrance family. Instead they retained King's original conception of the character but killed him off to demonstrate Jack's ferocity and undercut the audience's expectations of a last-minute rescue. Pauline Kael was rightly disturbed about this strategy: 'The awful suspicion pops into the mind,' she wrote, 'that since we don't want Wendy or Danny hurt and there's no one else alive around for Jack to get at, he's given the black man.'[64] The only subsequent critic to discuss the issue in any detail is Dennis Bingham, who, in a long footnote to an essay on the critical reception of *The Shining*, points out that the theme of racial genocide is introduced early in the film, when we learn about the Indian burial ground beneath the Overlook; this detail reinforces Kubrick's Freudian approach to the story (Freud compared the unconscious history of the individual to the buried, archeological strata of historical sites), but also lends an air of primitivism to the film. According to Freud, primitive man, child and neurotic adult are alike in their propensity to animistic thinking. Halloran's conversation with Danny in the Overlook kitchen seems to imply a link between blackness and childlike animism, and therefore makes Halloran a kind of primitive. The situation isn't helped by the strange pictures of nude black women with big Afros on the walls of Halloran's Florida bedroom – pictures which, as Bingham remarks, resemble the kitschy art collected by Alex's family in *A Clockwork Orange*.

The film's treatment of Halloran originates with King, who more than once wrote about what Spike Lee describes as the 'magical Negro'. (See, for example, *The Green Mile.*) It might also be noted that Diane Johnson had written about un-supernatural black characters in *The Shadow Knows*, which is told from the point of view of a middle-class white woman.

Kubrick was perhaps aware of the 'magical' problem, and his plan to make Halloran into a killer might have been a subversive, if risky, way of treating it. But no matter which way Kubrick turned, he was likely to fall into a trap. When a working-class black character communicates with ghosts or demonstrates ESP in the context of a Freudian-inflected, supernatural story about white people, he can't avoid seeming like a product of racist imagination. Bingham argues that Kubrick, who wasn't a deliberate racist, may have wanted to treat the stereotype of black atavism ironically and somehow mixed it up with 'the satiric attitude toward the noble images of 1950s and 1960s white liberalism that moved him to cast James Earl Jones as Major Kong's bombardier in *Dr. Strangelove*'. If so, the joke doesn't work. Bingham concludes that 'Kubrick's confused attitude toward women is compounded with his confused attitude toward blacks: he seems not to have thought very much about either (perhaps the only modern issues he hasn't thought about very much).'[65]

Paradoxically, although the audience roots for Danny, Wendy and Halloran, Jack dominates the film. This is partly because the monster is always the most compelling character in a horror movie and partly because Jack is played by a gifted star performer. Nicholson's acting style in the latter part of the film, however, is almost camp – as when he puts his head through a hole in a door and shouts an improvised line, 'Heeere's Johnny!' In keeping with the mixed modes of *The Shining*, he begins as if he were working for Roman Polanski and ends as if he were working for Roger Corman. Richard T. Jameson has emphasised the way he boomerangs back and forth between character and star and between good acting and bad acting: 'Jack Nicholson plays Jack Nicholson playing Jack Torrance playing Jack Torrance as King of the Mountain.'[66] The result is a killer clown and a particularly evil Lord of Misrule, but also a somewhat pathetic bum-madman-bully, an inept actor who leers with Nicholson's trademark nasty grin, tries to behave like the rebellious inmate of a mental hospital in *One Flew over the Cuckoo's Nest* (1975) and flings crude insults like a parody of the oil rigger-artist in *Five Easy Pieces* (1970). In other words, Jack is a bad version of Nicholson, played cleverly by Jack Nicholson.

In interviews when the film was released (one of which can be seen in the Vivian Kubrick documentary), Nicholson recalled a conversation with Kubrick in which the director told him that actors try too hard to make the performance 'real', when 'real' isn't always interesting. This idea originates not with Kubrick but with Stanislavsky, the ultimate realist;[67] nevertheless, it serves as an appropriate motto for the unusual effects Kubrick seems to be trying to achieve. In film after film, his performers veer back and forth between realism and caricature; often the starring actor (James Mason in *Lolita*, Ryan O'Neal in *Barry Lyndon* and Tom Cruise in *Eyes Wide Shut*) is a straight man who works alongside bizarre supporting players, but sometimes the star gives a comically stylised performance. Nicholson obviously belongs in the second category. During his bar-room speech to Lloyd, he behaves like a homeless schizophrenic who has been given one great moment in the dramatic spotlight; when he comes to the phrase 'a momentary loss of muscular co-ordination', he mimics smallness and quietness, drawing out the words with embarrassingly broad sarcasm, whining and making big derisive gestures. During his later conversation in a men's room with a surreal English butler (Philip Stone, who had played subservient characters in Kubrick's two previous films), he seems like a vaudeville comic. 'What do they call you around here, Jeevsie?' he asks with elaborate cheerfulness. When the butler identifies himself as Delbert Grady, Nicholson does a double-take and arches his eyebrows: 'Uh,' he says, clearing his throat and grinning as if he wants to share his amusement with the audience, 'Mr Grady, haven't I seen you somewhere before?' Grady says no, but then weirdly claims that he has always been at the Overlook, where Jack has always been the 'caretaker'. In another crazy reversal, Grady adds that he had to 'correct' his family in order to fulfil his duties as caretaker. Then his mask of servility drops, revealing a steely disciplinarian who quietly but forcefully exhorts Jack to 'correct' his own family and do something about 'an outside party, a nigger, the nigger cook'. Nicholson pauses for a beat, lifts his eyebrows again, and asks, 'a *nigger*?' The reaction suggests that Jack's suppressed racism, already revealed in the earlier conversation with Lloyd, has been given a new outlet.

At several points, Nicholson conveys a barely contained violence – when he throws a tennis ball against the walls of the Overlook, for example – and his mouth and eyebrows work overtime when Jack enters his manic phases. The expressive extremes of his performance aren't to everyone's taste, and his dark portrait of fatherhood may be one of the reasons why *The Shining*, after a profitable opening, never achieved the ticket sales the studio expected. On the other hand, his work is very much in keeping with the conventions of popular horror, which usually mingles bloody terror with carnivalistic comedy. His anarchic jokes and repeated evocation of his star persona are so memorable that they potentially subvert the film (as scary monsters often do in more conservative pictures). In the last analysis, however, his portrayal is well suited to Kubrick's absurdist style. When the picture was released, Kubrick indicated that he wanted to make one of the most frightening movies of all time. If that was the case, he didn't succeed. What he made is an intellectualised, formally rigorous, genuinely disturbing satire of American paternity – a film that runs somewhat against the grain of King's novel and the horror-film cycle of its day. The satire is all the more troubling when Jack Torrance's misogyny, racism and bad-boy grin are enshrined in the hotel picture gallery, haunting the audience until the very end.

Notes

1. Stanley Kubrick, letter to Anthony Harvey, in Harvey's papers at the Lilly Library, Bloomington, Indiana.

2. Pauline Kael, who seemed never to have read Jonathan Swift, argued that *Dr. Strangelove* 'opened a new movie era' because 'it ridiculed *everything* and *everybody*' and 'concealed its own liberal pieties'. It was dangerous, she argued, because it didn't 'tell us how we are supposed to regain control'. As a result, the 'new generation enjoyed seeing the world as insane; they *literally* learned to stop worrying and love the bomb'. See *Kiss Kiss Bang Bang* (New York: Bantam, 1969), p. 78.

Andrew Sarris thought that *Dr. Strangelove* was 'not a bad movie by any standards', but that it was 'grossly overrated'. See *Confessions of a Cultist: On the Cinema 1955/1969* (New York: Simon & Schuster, 1970), pp. 119–22.

3. Robert Brustein, 'Out of This World', reprinted in Mario Falsetto (ed.), *Perspectives on Stanley Kubrick* (New York: G. K. Hall, 1996), pp. 136–40.

4. Henry Kissinger, *The Necessity for Choice: Prospects of American Foreign Policy* (New York: Harper & Brothers, 1961), p. 15. All other references are to this volume, and page numbers are indicated in the text.

5. Quoted by Louis Menand, 'Fat Man: Herman Kahn and the Nuclear Age', *The New Yorker* (27 June 2005), p. 96. All other references are to this article, and page numbers are indicated in the text. See also Sharon Ghamari-Tabrizi, *The Worlds of Herman Kahn* (Cambridge, MA: Harvard University Press, 2005).

6. The quotes in this and the previous paragraph are from Fred Kaplan, 'Truth Stranger than Strangelove', *The New York Times* (Sunday, 10 October 2004), p. 21. Almost twenty years after the release of the film and shortly before Kahn died, Kaplan asked him what he thought of *Strangelove*. Assuming that Kaplan was talking about the character and not the movie, Kahn replied, 'Strangelove wouldn't have lasted three weeks in the Pentagon. He was too creative.'

7. Ed Sikov, *Mr. Strangelove: A Biography of Peter Sellers* (New York: Hyperion, 2002), pp. 196–7.

8. See James Naremore, *Acting in the Cinema* (Berkeley: University of California Press, 1988), pp. 68–82.

9. Blocker's agent quoted by Billy Budd Vermillion, '*Dr. Strangelove*', in Gene D. Phillips and Rodney Hill (eds), *The Encyclopedia of Stanley Kubrick* (New York: Checkmark Books, 2002), p. 91.

10. Roger Ebert, *The Great Movies* (New York: Broadway Books, 2002), pp. 154–6.

11. John Belton, *Widescreen Cinema* (Cambridge, MA: Harvard University Press, 1992), pp. 89–92.

12. Volker Fischer, 'Designing the Future: On Pragmatic Forecasting in *2001: A Space Odyssey*', in Hans-Peter Reichmann and Ingeborg Flagge (eds), *Stanley Kubrick*, pp. 103–19.

13. Olaf Stapledon, *Last and First Men and Star Maker* (New York: Dover, 1968). I am grateful to Jonathan Rosenbaum for acquainting me with Stapledon's work.

14. Quotations in this paragraph are from the screenplay of 'Journey beyond the Stars' in the special collections department of the Margaret Herrick Library of the Motion Picture Academy, Los Angeles.

15. Quotations in this paragraph are from the 31 August 1965 screenplay of *2001* in the special collections department of the Margaret Herrick Library of the Motion Picture Academy, Los Angeles.

16. Quotations in this paragraph are from the 14 December 1965 shooting script of *2001: A Space Odyssey* in the special collections department of the Margaret Herrick Library of the Motion Picture Academy, Los Angeles.

17. Michel Chion, *Kubrick's Cinema Odyssey*, trans. Claudia Gorbman (London: BFI, 2001), p. 71.

18. Production Code Administration files, Margaret Herrick Library of the Motion Picture Academy, Los Angeles.

19. For an interesting description of the prologue and a discussion of scientific theories that interested Kubrick throughout his life, see Anthony Frewin, '*2001*: The Prologue that Nearly Was', in Reichmann and Flagge, *Stanley Kubrick*, pp. 129–35.

20. Kael's review is collected in Stephanie Schwam (ed.), *The Making of* 2001: A Space Odyssey (New York: Modern Library, 2000), pp. 144–6.

21. Andrew Sarris, 'Science Fiction: *The Forbin Project*', in *The Primal Screen: Essays on Film and Related Topics* (New York: Simon & Schuster, 1973), pp. 201–3.

22. See R. Barton Palmer, '*2001*: The Critical Reception and the Generation Gap', in Robert Kolker, (ed.), *Stanley Kubrick's* 2001: A Space Odyssey (New York: Oxford University Press, 2006), pp. 13–27. See also Tom Gunning, 'An Aesthetic of Astonishment', in Leo Braudy and Marshall Cohen (eds), *Film Theory and Criticism: Introductory Readings*, 5th edn (New York: Oxford University Press, 1999), pp. 818–30.

23. Max Kosloff, in Schwam, *The Making of* 2001, p. 180.

24. Annette Michelson, 'Bodies in Space: Film as Carnal Knowledge', in Schwam, *The Making of* 2001, pp. 212–15.

25. Charlie Kohler, 'Stanley Kubrick Raps', in Schwam, *The Making of* 2001, p. 247.

26. David G. Stork (ed.), *Hal's Legacy:* 2001's *Computer as Dream and Reality* (Cambridge, MA: MIT Press, 1997). All other references are to this edition, and page numbers are indicated in the text.

27. '*Playboy* Interview: Stanley Kubrick', in Schwam, *The Making of* 2001, pp. 274–5.

28. *Thus Spake Zarathustra*, trans. Thomas Common, in Willard Huntington Wright (ed.), *The Philosophy of Nietzsche* (New York: Modern Library, 1954), p. 6.

29. Andrew Sarris, *The American Cinema: Directors and Directions, 1929–1968* (New York: E. P. Dutton & Co., 1968), p. 196.

30. Alexander Walker, Sybil Taylor and Ulrich Rachti, *Stanley Kubrick, Director* (New York: W. W. Norton & Company, 1999), p. 162. Raymond Durgnat, 'Paint it Black: The Family Tree of Film Noir', *Film Comment* vol. 6 November 1974), p. 6.

31. Carl Freedman, 'Kubrick's *2001* and the Possibility of a Science-Fiction Cinema', *Science Fiction Studies* vol. 23 (1996), pp. 300–17.

32. Ray Kurzweil, *The Age of Spiritual Machines: When Computers Exceed Human* (London: Penguin, 2000).

33. Janet Staiger, 'The Cultural Productions of *A Clockwork Orange*', in Stuart Y. McDougal (ed.), *Stanley Kubrick's* A Clockwork Orange (New York: Cambridge University Press, 2003), pp. 37–60.

34. Anthony Burgess, *A Clockwork Orange* (London: Penguin Books, 1972), p. 16. All other citations are from this edition, and page numbers are indicated in the text.

35. Colin Burrow, 'Not Quite Nasty', *The London Review of Books* vol. 28 no. 3 (9 February 2006), p. 20.

36. Peter J. Rabinowitz, 'A Bird of Like Rarest Spun Heavenmetal,' in McDougal, *Stanley Kubrick's* A Clockwork Orange, pp. 109–30.

37. Kevin Jackson, 'Real Horrorshow: A Short Lexicon of Nasdat', *Sight and Sound* (September 1999), p. 27.

38. John Alcott, interviewed in Michel Ciment, *Kubrick: The Definitive Edition* (New York: Faber and Faber, 2001) p. 214.

39. David Bordwell, *Figures Traced in Light: On Cinematic Staging* (Berkeley: University of California Press, 2005), pp. 1–7.

40. Sade quoted by Max Horkheimer and Theodor Adorno, *Dialectic of Enlightenment: Philosophical Fragments*, ed. Gunzelin Schmid Noerr, trans. Edmund Jephcott (Stanford, CA: Stanford University Press, 2000), pp. 69–70.

41. Quoted in Eva-Maria Magel, 'The Best Movie (N)ever Made: Stanley Kubrick's Failed *Napoleon* Project', in Reichmann and Flagge, *Stanley Kubrick*, p. 159.

42. For a discussion of how Kubrick interprets the past through the present and at the same time makes us feel that the past is inaccessible, see William Stephenson, 'The Perception of "History" in Kubrick's *Barry Lyndon*', *Literature/Film Quarterly* vol. 9 no. 4 (1981), pp. 251–60.

43. Fredric Jameson uses 'pastiche' to describe *Barry Lyndon*, and tends to equate the technique with postmodernism. See 'Historicism in *The Shining*', in Jameson, *Signatures of the Visible* (New York: Routledge, 1990), pp. 91–2.

44. Ralf Michael Fischer, 'Pictures at an Exhibition? Allusions and Illusions in *Barry Lyndon*', in Reichmann and Flagge, *Stanley Kubrick*, pp. 169–83.

45. Rosenman quoted in Falsetto, *Perspectives on Stanley Kubrick*, pp. 404–5.

46. See Fischer, 'Pictures at an Exhibition?', pp. 176–7.

47. William Makepeace Thackeray, *The Luck of Barry Lyndon; a Romance of the Last Century*, ed. Edgar F. Harden (Ann Arbor: University of Michigan Press, 1999), p. 226. All other references are to this edition, and page numbers are given in the text.

48. Pauline Kael, 'Kubrick's Gilded Age', *The New Yorker* (29 December, 1975), p. 51. For a dissenting view, see Jonathan Rosenbaum, 'The Pluck of *Barry Lyndon*', *Film Comment* (March–April 1977), pp. 26–8.

49. Writers on the film have disagreed about whether the narrator is reliable or unreliable. See Mark Crispin Miller, 'Kubrick's Anti-Reading of *The Luck of Barry Lyndon*', in Falsetto, *Perspectives on Stanley Kubrick*, pp. 226–42. For a different view, see Sarah Kosloff, *Invisible Storytellers: Voice-Over Narration in American Film* (Berkeley: University of California Press, 1998).

50. Marvin D'Lugo, '*Barry Lyndon*: Kubrick on the Rules of the Game', *Explorations in National Cinemas, The 1977 Film Studies Annual: Part One* (Pleasantville, NY: Redgrave Publishing Company), p. 40.

51. Ryan O'Neal isn't the actor we see in this last shot; Kubrick uses an actual amputee who doubles for the star.

52. Diane Johnson's comments on her work with Kubrick in 'Writing *The Shining*', in Geoffrey Cocks, James Diedrick and Glenn Perusek (eds) *Depth of Field: Stanley Kubrick, Film, and the Uses of History* (Madison: University of Wisconsin Press, 2006), pp. 55–61. This essay describes a significant scene that Kubrick seems to have cut from the film for reasons of length: as in the novel, Jack discovers an old scrapbook containing fairy-tale plots and details that help him in his writing. The scrapbook is a 'gift' from the hotel ghosts, motivating Jack's sudden transition from deep depression to manic energy; it can be glimpsed sitting beside Jack's typewriter at one point in the release

version of the film. Other cuts from the original release print included a scene near the end in which we see Wendy and Danny recovering in a hospital. For detailed information on this and other trims, see *Monthly Film Bulletin* vol. 47 no. 562 (November 1980).

53. Stephen King quoted in Ursula Von Keitz, 'The Shining – Frozen Material: Stanley Kubrick's Adaptation of Stephen King's Novel', in Reichmann and Flagge, *Stanley Kubrick*, p. 187.

54. Stephen King, 'Introduction', *The Shining* (New York: Pocket Books, 2001), p. xvi. All further references are to this edition, and page numbers are indicated in the text.

55. Tzvetan Todorov, 'Henry James's Ghosts', in *The Poetics of Prose*, trans. Richard Howard (Ithaca, NY: Cornell University Press, 1977), p. 179. All further references are to this edition, and pages numbers are indicated in the text.

56. <www.liquidgeneration.com/content/a55hat.aspx?cid=1680>

57. Rosemary Jackson, *Fantasy: The Literature of Subversion* (London: Methuen, 1981), pp. 34–5. All further references are to this edition, and page numbers are indicated in the text.

58. See Michael Ryan and Douglas Kellner, *Camera Politica: The Politics and Ideology of Contemporary Hollywood Film* (Bloomington: Indiana University Press, 1990), pp. 172–8. See also David Cook, 'American Horror: *The Shining*', *Literature Film Quarterly* vol. 12 no. 1 (1984), pp. 2–5.

59. Robin Wood, 'American Nightmare: Horror in the 70s', in *Hollywood from Vietnam to Reagan* (New York: Columbia University Press, 1986), pp. 70–94.

60. Sigmund Freud, 'The Uncanny', in *The Standard Edition of the Complete Psychological Works of Sigmund Freud*, trans. James Strachey, vol. 17 (London: Hogarth Press, 1929), p. 226. All subsequent references are to this edition, and page numbers are indicated in the text.

61. William Paul, *Laughing/Screaming: Modern Hollywood Horror and Comedy* (New York: Columbia University Press, 1994), p. 343. All further references are to this volume, and page numbers are indicated in the text.

62. Christopher Hoile, 'The Uncanny and the Fairy Tale in Kubrick's *The Shining*', *Literature/Film Quarterly* vol. 12 no. 1 (1984), p. 8.

63. Quoted in Von Keitz, 'The Shining – Frozen Material, p. 190.

64. Pauline Kael, 'Devolution', in *Taking It All In* (New York: Holt, Rinehart, Winston, 1984), p. 6.

65. Dennis Bingham, 'The Displaced Auteur: A Reception History of *The Shining*', in Falsetto, *Perspectives on Stanley Kubrick*, pp. 304–5.

66. Richard T. Jameson, '*The Shining*', in Falsetto, *Perspectives on Stanley Kubrick*, p. 251.

67. 'I recall a comment recorded in a book called *Stanislavski Directs*, in which Stanislavski told an actor that he had the right understanding of the character, the right understanding of the text of the play, that what he was doing was completely believable, but that it was still no good because it wasn't interesting'. Kubrick interviewed in 1972 by Philip Stock and Penelope Huston in Gene D. Phillips (ed.), *Stanley Kubrick Interviews* (Jackson: University Press of Mississippi, 2001), p. 131.

Part Five

LATE KUBRICK

I. Warriors

Alan Dwan's *The Sands of Iwo Jima* (1949) stars John Wayne as a battle-scarred Marine sergeant who sacrifices himself for his unit and in doing so earns the respect of John Agar, a young recruit who had been trained by Wayne and who previously regarded Wayne as a heartless bully. The film ends with a sentimental tribute to the fallen Wayne and a re-creation of the famous *Life* magazine image of the Marines raising the US flag on Mount Suribachi. Like many American boys of my generation, I saw this movie in re-release when I was about eight years old. The tear-jerking plot, however, interested me not at all. I was fascinated with the combat scenes (some of which were made from newsreel footage) and especially with the military gear – the helmets, ammo belts, canteens, carbine rifles and machine guns. Afterward, I played war with other kids, imagining I was a Marine. I remember thinking that, if I owned a movie camera and the right military equipment, I could frame the action so as to screen out clothes lines, telephone poles and anything else that would interfere with my imaginary world. I suspect that Stanley Kubrick may have had a similar experience; in any case, his last war film deals with a generation of soldiers fighting in Vietnam who had seen Hollywood combat movies of the 1940s and 1950s, and who absorbed their warrior spirit.

The Vietnam War was a logical subject for Kubrick but, like most other Hollywood directors (with the exception of John Wayne), he waited until the war was over before he made a picture about it. In 1983, just prior to the success of Sylvester Stallone's reactionary *Rambo* series and towards the end of a cycle of darker films about Vietnam that included Michael Cimino's *The Deer Hunter* (1978), Francis Coppola's *Apocalypse Now* (1979) and Oliver Stone's *Platoon* (1986), Kubrick began work on an adaptation of Gustav Hasford's

spare, often surreal novel, *The Short-Timers* (1979), which is loosely based on Hasford's experience as a Marine newspaper correspondent and sometimes combatant during the Tet
offensive and the battle of Khe Sanh. Kubrick commissioned Michael Herr, the author of
Dispatches (1977), a much-admired collection of battlefield reports from the war, to help
write the screenplay and serve as associate producer. According to Herr, who had also written the voice-over narration for *Apocalypse Now*, Kubrick developed the treatment of the
film, which he entitled *Full Metal Jacket*, a term he found in gun magazines; Herr composed
the first draft of the script; and the two men collaborated on subsequent revisions.[1] Gustav
Hasford was consulted during the process and came to London to do some of the writing
but, even though the basic plot and a good deal of the language of his novel were used, he
contributed little new material.

The film was shot chiefly at Bessingbourn Barracks in Cambridgeshire, which 'played'
the US Marine training station at Parris Island, and at the disused Beckton Gasworks factory in East London, which art director Anton Furst designed to look like the bombed-out
city of Hue. (Unlike previous Vietnam movies, this one centres on urban combat; a few
palm trees were flown in from Spain to provide landscape, and aerial views of tropical
jungle were photographed by a second unit.) John Olson's *Life* magazine photos of
Hue influenced some of Furst's designs but, as Thomas Doherty has pointed out, the
film creates something more akin to a 'hallucinatory dreamscape, not a geographical
space'.[2] Shooting in primary locations began in 1985 and took slightly more than a year,
partly because of Kubrick's many retakes, but also because two of his principal actors,
Vincent D'Onofrio and Lee Ermey, were injured in separate accidents and needed time
to heal.

The completed film has an unorthodox, two-part structure, linked by the narration of
the leading character, Private Joker (Matthew Modine). The first part, which I've described
in some detail earlier in this book, expands on a relatively short section of the novel, treating daily life at a single Marine barracks in almost as detailed and documentary a fashion
as Frederick Wiseman's *Basic Training* (1971), at the same time telling the story of a conflict between a frightening drill instructor, Gunnery Sergeant Hartman (Ermey), and an
inept hillbilly recruit, Private Leonard Lawrence (D'Onofrio), whom Hartman dubs 'Gomer
Pyle'. The climax is staged in the barracks toilet: Pyle, clad in underwear and holding a
loaded rifle, lowers his head and gives the drill instructor a 1,000-yard stare; grinning and
sighing with feral pleasure, he murders Hartman and then commits suicide.

As critic Brad Stevens has noted, these killings resemble the violent Oedipal scenarios
in *A Clockwork Orange*, *Barry Lyndon* and *The Shining*, and as a result the film almost stops
cold.[3] Part two begins abruptly in Da Nang, where the camera follows a miniskirted prostitute as she sashays across a street to the music of Nancy Sinatra's 'These Boots Were Made
for Walking' and approaches Joker and a military photographer, Rafterman (Kevyn Major
Howard), at a sidewalk café. Joker has been assigned an alienating job writing newspaper
propaganda for the Marines and he takes a cynical but easygoing attitude towards the

Vietnamese hustlers and thieves who live off the American troops. Longing to see action, or, as he puts it, to be 'in the shit', he deliberately offends his smarmy editor (John Terry), who retaliates by sending him into the most dangerous zone of the Tet offensive. The film meanders in this section, not picking up steam until Joker reunites with his friend Cowboy (Arliss Howard) and joins the Lust Hog squad, who ultimately confront a deadly sniper in the ruins of Hue.

Bill Krohn has observed that the unexpected elimination of Hartman and Pyle, who were the only characters capable of sustaining a story, condemns us for a time to 'wander into regions bordering dangerously on nonsense'.[4] Kubrick told interviewers that he wanted to 'explode the narrative structure' (quoted in Krohn, p. 2) and, in the aftermath, he gives us not only fragmentation and aimlessness but also a mixture of styles or modes. The opening scenes of the second part, beginning with Joker's negotiation with the prostitute and extending to the point where he meets the Lust Hogs, are essentially realistic, if darkly absurdist. When the Lust Hogs approach Hue, however, the film makes an overtly self-reflexive, 'Brechtian' gesture: a TV crew executes a hand-held 'track' along the length of the squad (photographed by Kubrick's crew with a Steadicam), who joke about starring in 'Vietnam: The Movie', a Hollywood Western in which the 'gooks' play Indians. Next we're given a scene reminiscent of the psychological allegory in *Fear and Desire*: looking up from the subjective point of view of two US corpses on the ground, the camera pans around to individual members of the squad, who address the movie audience as if speaking to their fallen comrades. ('Goin' home now', 'Semper fi', 'Mean Marines', 'Go easy, bros', 'Better you than me', etc.) Then we return to activities of the TV crew: each member of the squad looks into Kubrick's camera, which stands in for the news camera, and responds to unheard questions from an interviewer. ('In Hue City, it's . . . you know, like what I thought a war was supposed to be; there's the enemy – kill 'em.' 'I don't think there's any question about it, I mean we're the best . . . . When the shit really hits the fan, who do they call?' 'Do I think America belongs in Vietnam? I know *I* belong in Vietnam.' 'Personally I think they don't want to be involved in this war . . . . They'd rather be alive than free, I guess. Poor dumb bastards.') Finally, as the squad enters Hue, we shift back into a more realistic mode and then into vivid expressionism when the sniper is discovered.

One consequence of the anti-classical narrative is that Joker seems less like the film's central consciousness than like a marginal observer who sometimes steps forward to take part in events. The character's somewhat recessive quality may also have to do with the casting of Matthew Modine, who lacks the movie-star charisma of Ryan O'Neal and Jack Nicholson. Kubrick said that Modine reminded him of a cross between Gary Cooper and Henry Fonda but, even if the intelligent young actor had brought a well-established star persona to the film, he would have found it difficult to assert himself. Joker is given few point-of-view shots and his sparse narration, which has been pruned down considerably from the original shooting script, doesn't begin until after the long opening sequence. We're given no psychological 'back-story' or personal information about him, or indeed about any of the other characters, most of whom, as in Hasford's novel, are known simply by their nicknames.

In part one Joker plays second-fiddle to the conflict between Hartman and Pyle, and in part two he seems feckless. He tells us that the Marines want 'killers, not robots', but he tends to move in unison with a group. His personality becomes interesting only in retrospect. As his name implies, he's a wild card with a shifting identity. 'Is that you, John Wayne?' he repeatedly asks himself. 'Is this me?' He both takes part in the Marine community and stands back to view it cynically. When the recruits sneak up on Pyle and attack him with bars of soap wrapped in towels, Joker strikes the last blow but then covers his eyes with shame. In Vietnam, he wears a peace symbol and yet has 'Born to Kill' written on his helmet (a detail taken from Herr's *Dispatches*). In his cynical interview with the American TV crew, he claims that he joined the Marines because 'I wanted to see exotic Vietnam, the jewel of Southeast Asia. I wanted to meet stimulating people of an ancient culture and kill them. I wanted to be the first kid on my block to get a confirmed kill.'

In this last regard, notice that Joker's adventures in part two have a certain affinity with Joseph Conrad's *Heart of Darkness*, which was the source of *Apocalypse Now*. Like Conrad's romantic but ineffectual Marlow, Joker narrates the story of his trip to an exotic country and his subsequent journey inward – geographically, psychologically and politically – during which he witnesses a series of imperialist barbarisms: he meets prostitutes and pimps; he is instructed to write fake stories about how the US is killing the enemy and winning hearts and minds; he takes a helicopter trip with a trigger-happy psychopath who fires cheerfully at peasants and, when asked how he can shoot down women and children, cracks one of the film's sickest jokes ('Easy – you just don't lead 'em so much!'); he sees a mass grave of Vietnamese villagers covered in lime and is informed by a smirking lieutenant that they were killed by the enemy; and he's lectured by a pompous US colonel who tells him, 'inside every gook there is an American trying to get out'. When the colonel asks him to explain the contradiction between the peace sign and the motto on the helmet, Joker replies, 'The duality of man. The Jungian thing, Sir.' At the end, he has an intimate experience of Jung's 'shadow' and Conrad's 'horror'. He comes face to face with the enemy and gets his confirmed kill – but it isn't the sort of thing he can joke about.

To achieve the odd shape of the film, Kubrick followed his usual procedure of making significant changes to the script during shooting and post-production. Lee Ermey's improvised obscenities were added, and a good deal of Joker's narration, much of it taken straight from the novel, was cut or shortened. By comparison with the film, the shooting script, written in a discursive style somewhere between a novel and a movie, is in some ways much more raw and disturbing. After Gunnery Sergeant Gerheim (Hartman in the film) punches, chokes and slaps a couple of his recruits, Joker's voice tells us, 'Beatings, we learn, are a routine element of life on Parris Island. And not that I'm-only-rough-on-'um-because-I-love-'um crap in Mr John Wayne's *The Sands of Iwo Jima*.'[5] During the Parris Island section, one of the recruits tries to commit suicide by cutting his wrist with a bayonet and Gerheim orders him to clean up the mess he has made. Pyle suffers truly sadistic humiliations: at one point Gerheim forces all the men in the barracks to pee in a toilet and then pushes Pyle's face into it; in another scene, Gerheim fits a Trojan condom with a hole in it over the mouth of a canteen and orders Pyle to suck milk through it at mealtimes – cut to the mess hall, where the other drill instructors make 'crude and derisory remarks' as Pyle nurses from the canteen. The most brutal moment of all, however, comes near the end of the script, just after Joker administers a *coup de grâce* by shooting a wounded female sniper at his feet:

> Sutton says, 'Joker, that's well done. You're hard.'
> Animal Mother spits. He takes a step, kneels, zips out his machete. With one powerful
>   blow he chops off her head.
> He picks the head up by its long black hair and holds it high. He laughs and says, 'Rest in
>   pieces, bitch.'
> Animal Mother laughs again. He walks around and sticks the bloody ball of gore into all
>   their faces. 'Hard? *Now* who's hard? Now who's hard, motherfuckers?'
> Animal Mother pauses, spits, throws the head into a ditch.
> He picks up his M-60 machine gun, lays it across his shoulders, struts over to Joker.
>   'Nobody shits on the Animal, motherfucker, nobody' (pp. 111–12).

In his diary of the production, Matthew Modine tells us that Kubrick spent gruelling hours shooting and re-shooting this particular scene, requiring Adam Baldwin, who plays Animal Mother, to throw a rubber head off screen to a crew member who caught it and saved it for the next take. 'The circle of actors around [Baldwin] agonizes with him,' Modine wrote. 'The mystery of the repetition is lost to us . . . . We're glad it's Adam and not us.'[6] When the scene was completed, however, Kubrick cut it from the film without informing Baldwin. He also cut a nude scene that he and Modine had invented: a Vietnamese prostitute (Papillon Soo Soo), was shown in post-coital conversation with Joker in the bedroom of a French Colonial house: 'Oh! Me want more boom boom,' the prostitute says. 'Me love you long time, G I. Me so hooooorny!' Joker lights two cigarettes and delivers a variation on Bette Davis's famous line in *Now, Voyager* (1942): 'My darling, we have the moon. Don't let's ask for the stars.'

In the shooting script, Joker has a much more active and potentially sympathetic role to play. (The same could be said of Joker in Hasford's novel.) During his helicopter ride to Hue, for example, he becomes so outraged at an Arvin captain and sergeant who are murdering prisoners that he machine-guns both of them. And at the end, he dies in almost heroic fashion while running through a hail of gunfire. His voice-over narration, italicised in the script, would have been accompanied by rapid cross-cutting between images of him as a man and as a boy:

JOKER, THE MARINE, RUNNING.

JOKER, *8 YEARS-OLD*, ARMED WITH A PLASTIC RIFLE, RUNNING IN A FIELD.

'Keep moving, keep moving, keep moving!!!'

People tell you what to do. Keep moving, keep moving, keep moving. If you stop moving, if you hesitate, your heart will stop beating. Your legs are machines winding you up like a mechanical toy.

JOKER, THE MARINE, RUNNING, FIRING HIS RIFLE.

JOKER, *THE 8 YEAR-OLD*, FIRING HIS TOY RIFLE.

You feel like you could run around the world. Now the asphalt is a trampoline and you are fast and graceful, a green jungle cat.

JOKER, THE MARINE, RUNNING.

JOKER, *THE 8 YEAR-OLD*, RUNNING.

Your feet take you up . . . up . . . over the rubble up . . . up . . . you're loving it . . . you're not human, you're an animal, you feel like a god . . . you scream: 'DIE! DIE! DIE, YOU MOTHERFUCKERS! DIE! DIE!'

JOKER, THE MARINE, IS RIDDLED WITH A BURST OF AUTOMATIC FIRE.

JOKER, *THE 8 YEAR-OLD*, CLUTCHES HIS CHEST IN MOCK AGONY AND STARTS TO CRUMPLE TO THE GROUND. HIS IMAGE WILL SLOW DOWN UNTIL WE HOLD ON A FROZEN FRAME, IN A POSE SOMETHING LIKE CAPA'S FAMOUS SPANISH CIVIL WAR PHOTOGRAPH OF A MAN WHO HAS JUST BEEN FATALLY SHOT BUT WHO IS FOREVER SUSPENDED IN MID-FALL BY THE CAMERA.

BUT THIS PICTURE IS OF AN *8 YEAR-OLD* BOY. (pp. 115–16)

In the script this sequence is followed by a brief scene at a military cemetery where Joker's father reads an A. E. Housman poem at his son's graveside. Michael Herr says that it was Kubrick's idea to conclude in this way and that, when Herr argued against it, Kubrick defended the idea passionately if somewhat jokingly: 'It's the death of the Hero. It'll be so powerful, so *moving* . . . . We've seen it in *Homer*, Michael' (Herr, p. 40). But during the filming Kubrick worried that Joker's death was sentimental. He repeatedly asked Matthew Modine what he thought, and was unresponsive when Modine said that he loved the way the script ended. Kubrick then asked several of the other actors to offer alternative endings and, when Modine derided their suggestions, Kubrick treated him coldly. Eventually, in frustration, Modine told Kubrick, 'You want to know what should happen? [Joker] should live. He should have to spend the rest of his life thinking about Pyle blowing his brains out.' According to Modine, Kubrick pondered a moment and said, 'That's the ending' (Modine, n.p.).

The ending Kubrick devised is vaguely similar to Hasford's novel, in which Joker and his decimated platoon simply 'hump back down the trail' after a bloody encounter with the enemy.[7] The last images of the film show Joker and a number of other Marines marching through a blasted nocturnal landscape, silhouetted against the burning city of Hue. Kubrick breaks the 180-degree rule, causing Joker's column to move first screen right and then screen left. 'We have nailed our names to the pages of history enough for today,' Joker's voice-over says. 'We hump down to the Perfume River to settle in for the night.' As they trudge along, the band of soldiers begins singing the marching song from Walt Disney's 'Mickey Mouse Club', occasionally imitating the voices of children. (In the shooting script, the song appears at a much earlier point.) Joker smiles as he sings, and again we hear his narration: 'My thoughts drift back to erect-nipple wet dreams about Mary Jane Rottencrotch and the great Homecoming Fuck Fantasy. I am so happy that I am alive . . . I'm in a world of shit, yes, but I'm alive. And I am not afraid.'

These last moments have been described by one writer as conveying a feeling of 'muted optimism'.[8] To me they seem intended to ironically convey Joker's relief and exhilaration at having survived combat, but they also have a good deal in common with the closing of *Dr. Strangelove*, in which a pop tune is sung over strangely beautiful images of apocalyptic destruction. Joker's smile is troubling, especially on the heels of his mercy killing of the female Vietnamese sniper. He may have survived a baptism of fire, but at some level he remains a child, speaking the catchphrases of the 'phony-tough and crazy-brave'. The ending also returns us to several of the film's more disturbing motifs. The Mickey Mouse Club song is the culminating instance of many ironic references to US pop culture, transforming the devastated Vietnamese landscape into a grotesque Disneyland. As Paula Willoquet-Maricondi has pointed out, the song's lyrics express a colonising impulse: 'Who is marching coast to coast and far across the sea? . . . Come along and sing this song and join our family.'[9] (Mickey Mouse is referenced in two earlier scenes: at the end of part one, Hartman storms into the latrine and shouts, 'What is this Mickey Mouse shit?' During the editorial conference for the Marine newspaper at the beginning of part two, a Mickey Mouse doll sits on the windowsill behind Joker.) Notice as well that we are once again in a 'world of shit', this time lit by glowing flames – an interesting comparison and contrast with the expressionistically designed, blue-lit toilet at the end of part one. Joker seems ambivalent about this world, wanting to be in it and yet recognising its threat to the protective 'full metal jacket' of hardened masculinity. It has something in common with Sergeant Hartman's earlier evocation of 'Mary Jane Rottencrotch', who is both desirable and foul.

The equation of war with shit isn't unusual. In *Rambo*, for instance, Sylvester Stallone immerses himself in a sewer so that he can evade the enemy. But, as I've already pointed out, Kubrick's film goes further in this direction. Its language is pervaded with excremental imagery, which is linked to women, queers and communists and set off against everything we see at Parris Island: the clean surfaces of the military barracks; the shaved young recruits; the obsessively polished toilet; and the well-oiled rifles that become sexy machines and substitutes for Mary Jane. (As Pyle goes slowly mad, he speaks to his rifle in loving tones: 'It's been swabbed and wiped. Everything is clean. Beautiful. So that it slides perfectly. Nice. Everything cleaned. Oiled. So that your action is beautiful. Smooth, Charlene.') I've also mentioned in passing that similar imagery features in Klaus Theweleit's *Male Fantasies*, an analysis of the fantasy life of proto-fascist soldiers in the German *Freicorps* of the 1920s. In making the connection I don't mean to suggest that Kubrick was influenced by Theweleit, whose work was published in German in 1977 and in English in 1987. My point is simply that Kubrick and Herr have an intuitive and critical grasp of a familiar warrior-male psychology, and that Theweleit can help us understand its workings.

A brief description of the first volume of *Male Fantasies* will help to clarify the point. Subtitled *Women, Floods, Bodies, History*, it provides an extensive analysis of popular literature, memoirs, diaries and propaganda by and about the men of the *Freicorps*, a volunteer private army of World War I veterans who engaged in domestic repression of organised labour and communism in the 1920s and early 1930s. In the course of his analysis, Theweleit generates what amounts to a full-scale psychological picture of a warrior caste. Throughout, he emphasises that the imaginative life of the *Freicorps* is filled with images of blood and shit, which are strongly associated with the 'Red flood' of communism. Consider Rudolf Herzog, a *Freicorps* novelist who equates the Rhineland separatist movements of the period with a 'wave of excrement' that 'rolled over the glorious cities of the Rhine, and when it paused and bubbled up, it was red with the blood of brothers' (p. 397). For Herzog and the other writers in question, the morass of slime and pulp carried along by the Red tide always has a female quality and needs to be combated with 'erections', which are represented by stalwart men and strong, hard weapons (p. 402). In fact, as Barbara Ehrenreich observes in her introduction to the US translation of *Male Fantasies*, the soldiers of the *Freicorps* are motivated less by how they feel about the Fatherland, communists, or Jews than about how they feel about women's bodies: '[The *Freicorps*'] hatred – or dread – of women cannot be explained with Freud's all-purpose Oedipal triangulation . . . . It is a dread, ultimately, of dissolution – of being swallowed, engulfed, annihilated. Women's bodies are the holes, swamps, pits of muck that can engulf' (p. xiii).

The women encountered by the *Freicorps* range from the relatively safe to the extremely dangerous: mothers and girls who are left behind when soldiers go to the front; 'white nurses' who serve on the battlefield; prostitutes who carry disease and can't be trusted; and – most threatening – 'Red women' who are armed with rifles and who face the soldiers in angry mobs or single combat. In one of the recurring scenes at the heart of *Freicorps* literature, a manly German soldier meets and kills a Red woman – a working-class communist who carries a rifle under her skirts like a penis substitute. Her death has sexual implications. Ehrenreich describes it as a 'brief moment of penetration – with bullet or knife', in which the soldier comes thrillingly close to the woman and the 'horror of dissolution', but then survives; he remains 'erect (and, we must imagine, clean and dry)', while she is a bloody mass. 'With her absent, the world becomes "safe" and male again' (p. xiv).

For anyone who has seen *Full Metal Jacket*, the relevance of the material discussed by Theweleit should be obvious. The action of the film is set in a metaphoric and sometimes literal world of blood and shit, and it climaxes with the killing of a 'Red woman'. (The shooting script, unlike the film, gives us all four types of women imagined by the *Freicorps*: in

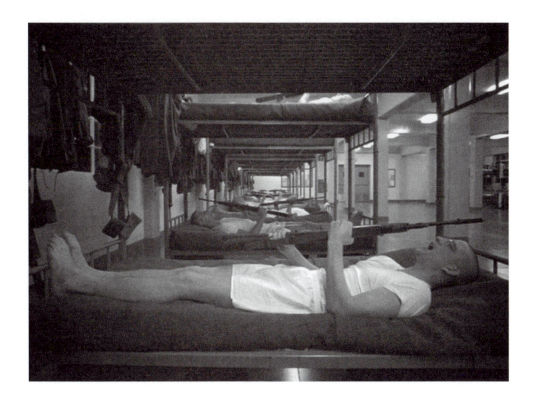

addition to 'Mary Jane Rottencrotch', two prostitutes and an armed communist, we have a brief sequence involving a couple of battlefield nurses.) The killing scene is especially significant because, during the first part of the film, Gunnery Sergeant Hartman orders the recruits to 'marry' their weapons of 'iron and wood', which have been given girls' names. Hartman explains that only the 'hard heart' kills, and he repeatedly inculcates physical hardness and steely determination as defences against softness, femininity and excrement. He also indoctrinates the troops to think of his 'beloved Corps' as the natural home of superb riflemen; in one of the most disconcertingly funny scenes, he boasts that two of history's most infamous snipers, Charles Whitman and Lee Harvey Oswald, 'showed what one motivated Marine and his rifle can do!' His training backfires, however, when the softest and flabbiest of his recruits becomes a talented shot and gets his revenge in a toilet. In a similar reversal, Joker and Cowboy face their greatest challenge when a talented young female sniper – a version of what the *Freicorps* called a *Flintenweiber* or 'rifle woman' – gets them in her gun sight.

Until this point, as in Kubrick's previous war films, the enemy has been nearly invisible: we've seen only a few silhouetted figures breaking through the perimeter of the base at Da Nang, plus the corpse of a North Vietnamese soldier. Also as in Kubrick's other pictures about war, the close encounter with the 'other' is with a female. She's photographed in

expressionist slow motion as she spins around from her hiding place to face Joker, whose gun jams. Rafterman, the most patriotically zealous of the young Marines, whom Joker has treated condescendingly, shoots her down. From Joker's point of view, we see her face in the bloody muck, writhing in an almost sexual fashion. She begs to be released from pain. Rafterman gloats and Animal Mother wants to 'let her rot', but Joker, after an appalled hesitation, puts her out of her misery. The other Marines interpret this action as an assertion of masculinity: 'Hard core, man,' one of them says, 'fucking hard core.' Next we see Joker marching away with his Mickey Mouse Club brethren, smiling and free of fear.[10]

Of course, the men in *Full Metal Jacket* are in some ways different from the proto-fascist ideologues in *Male Fantasies*. Most are provincial, poor and ill educated, and few seem to be motivated by appeals to Jesus and the USA. Rafterman claims to be fighting for 'a good cause', Animal Mother is engaged in 'slaughter' for the sake of 'poontang', Eightball is carried along by a confusing war and Joker enjoys the existential testing of his courage. Their repeated challenges to one another are like school-yard taunts or testosterone-driven displays of toughness in the midst of a brutal contest for survival. Notice as well that Joker's shooting of the rifle woman is an act of mercy, not the exultant violence against women imagined by the *Freicorps*. On the other hand, the US military, as represented by Hartman and every officer we see, is ruled by white Christian males and is a place where misogyny,

racism and ultra-nationalism are rules of the day. In this environment you can always indulge in a little hate speech as long as you maintain that the Corps is fair and that the uniform makes a brotherhood of the men who wear it. 'I am hard, but I am fair,' Hartman says at the beginning, 'I do not look down on niggers, Kikes, wops or greasers. Here you are all equally worthless!' The soldiers' enemies are 'gooks', but so are their ostensible allies. Even their 'beloved Corps' is internally fraught with racial tension. Thomas Doherty has nicely described the way contradictions are managed: 'the huge white grunt Animal Mother hassles and slurs his black comrade Eightball. But when Eightball lies wounded, stranded in an open field, it is Animal Mother who disobeys orders and makes a heroic rescue charge' (pp. 313–14).

In addition to exposing a kind of fascism at the heart of warrior male sexuality (as *Dr. Strangelove* had already done), *Full Metal Jacket* also satirises the culture industry's efforts at sustaining morale for the war. A major theme of the film is what Kubrick described as the US attempt to 'fine tune reality like an advertising agency' (Ciment, p. 243). Joker's editor wants stories with a 'weenie' – reports of American soldiers who 'give half their pay to buy gooks toothbrushes and deodorants' and of 'combat action that results in a kill'. The colonel who lectures to Joker speaks in the stale metaphors of advertising and business: 'What don't you get with the program? Why don't you jump on the team and come on in for the big win?' Lawrence Welk and Ann Margaret plan to entertain the Marines with schmaltz and sex; network TV visits the battlefield, blurring the boundary between war and show business; the action in Vietnam is played off against a background of American pop tunes (juxtaposed with an eerie score by Abigail Mead, the *nom de plume* of Vivian Kubrick); and in Da Nang even a petty thief gets into the act by imitating Bruce Lee.

The most significant cultural icon is John Wayne, the Hollywood hawk whose voice and name are evoked at several points. This motif has spectacular expression in the film's shooting script, in a scene taken from Hasford's novel: Joker and a group of Marines visit the 'Freedom PX Movie Theater' to watch Wayne's production of *The Green Berets* (1968), which Joker describes as 'a Hollywood soap opera about the love of guns'. As the film is screened, Joker comments in voice-over: 'We watch John Wayne leading the Green Beanies. John Wayne is a beautiful soldier, clean-shaven, sharply attired in tailored tiger-stripe jungle utilities, wearing boots that shine like black glass. Inspired by John Wayne, the fighting soldiers from the sky go hand-to-hand with all of the Victor Charlies in Southeast Asia' (pp. 39–40). The marines in the PX laugh uproariously at the film, especially at the Asian actor George Takei, who plays an Arvin officer in *The Green Berets* but who is most famous for playing Sulu in TV's *Star Trek.* When Takei says with great conviction, 'First kill . . . all stinking Cong . . . then go home,' one of the Marines shouts, 'You fuckin' asshole, *you* kill stinking Cong. I wanna go home *now*!'

The references to Wayne that remain in the film function as short-hand for the super-patriotic myths of cowboy masculinity and American triumphalism that were often purveyed by Hollywood in the years leading up to the US involvement in Vietnam. These same references also function to make *Full Metal Jacket* look authentic, edgy and honest in comparison with traditional combat movies. It's important to recognise, however, that despite Kubrick's sardonic portrayal of military conflict, not everyone has interpreted his film as an anti-war statement or 'used' it as a satire of proto-fascism in the US military. Samuel Fuller, no stranger to gritty war movies or indeed to war itself, angrily described *Full Metal Jacket* as a 'recruiting film' (quoted in Krohn, p. 1). An even more damaging description can be found in Anthony Swofford's memoir of combat, *Jarhead: A Marine's Chronicle of the Gulf War* (2003):

> Vietnam War films are all pro-war, no matter what the supposed message, what Kubrick or Coppola or Stone intended . . . . The magic brutality of the films celebrates the terrible and despicable beauty of [military] fighting skills. Fight, rape, war, pillage, burn. Filmic images of death and carnage are pornography for the military man.[11]

No one can predict all the perverse pleasures individual viewers might take from movies, and no director can ensure her or his film won't be enjoyed for reasons other than the ones intended. Even so, Swofford's observation and my own childhood experience lead me to ask whether Kubrick himself might love the masculine brutality he is satirising. This is a question many viewers have asked about *A Clockwork Orange*, and I think the answer is a qualified yes. Even though Kubrick was a nerdy-looking intellectual, he was a highly competitive fellow who was attracted to violent sports like boxing and football, and as an artist he gave careful attention to the phallic hardware of bombing planes and spacecraft. Michael Herr remembers that, during a break in working on the script of *Full Metal Jacket*, he and Kubrick took 'a few of Stanley's guns' to a local gun club and practised firing them (p. 42). In interviews, Kubrick was fond of a remark he attributed to Robert E. Lee: 'It is fortunate that war is so terrible or we should grow very fond of it.'[12] He clearly appreciated what Swofford calls the 'magic brutality' and 'terrible and despicable beauty' of combat, and he recognised a dirty little secret about young men in the military: there's a bit of Alex in even the best trained soldiers – a desire to '[f]ight, rape, war, pillage, and burn'.

I would argue, however, that Kubrick's ambivalence towards war isn't an artistic failing. Indeed the tension between the eroticism of warfare and the horror of warfare (symbolised by the peace emblem and the 'Born to Kill' motto) is precisely what makes *Full Metal Jacket* a compelling and disturbing film. This quality is especially evident in Lee Ermey's portrayal of Hartman, who is both hateful and charismatic, and who may have prompted Samuel Fuller's 'recruiting poster' comment. A Marine veteran and former DI who had been injured in combat during the Vietnam War, Ermey played a bit part in *Apocalypse Now* and worked as an advisor on that and several other films, including *Full Metal Jacket*. He wasn't originally cast in the role of Hartman, but his Marine Corps training sessions with the other players convinced Kubrick to use him. He's in sharp contrast with the sentimental, tough-love DIs in previous movies – especially with Louis Gossett Jr in *An Officer and a Gentleman* (1982), but more interestingly with Jack Webb in *The DI*, a film about a drill instructor who puts a spoiled, unwilling recruit through a kind of frat-house initiation and transforms him into a manly soldier. (Webb's *The DI* is explicitly referred to in Hasford's *The Short-Timers*.)

Ermey told reporters that his conception of the character was derived from 'the ten worst drill instructors I knew', who were combined to make 'the nastiest human being that could ever walk the earth'.[13] But Hartman became a less nasty fellow during the shooting, when Kubrick became enamoured of Ermey's improvisations. Ermey was no Peter Sellers, but he had a similar ability to crack the director up, and he contributed a good deal of brilliant profanity to the dialogue. His weird charm and grotesque wit assert themselves despite his wooden facial expression and his one-note performance, which consists mostly of abusive yelling. He's the most authentic-looking figure in the film, completely overshadowing Modine and D'Onofrio, whose work is more shaded and technically skilled. If, in spite of his almost cartoon-like sadism and jingoism, he can be seen as a character in a 'recruiting film', that may be because he has something in common with Alex in *A Clockwork Orange* and Jack in *The Shining*, who have a similarly seductive aura, and who invite us to laugh and thrill at cruelty. Ermey conveys the blend of military glamour and absurdist horror that lies at the core of the film, and this paradoxical quality seems to me an improvement over the purely monstrous drill sergeant that we find in the script. Hartman is bizarrely funny and, to some degree, admirably self-disciplined; his attractiveness, if one can call it that, may have prompted Kubrick to balance the dramatic scales by making Joker less active or heroic. As a result, Hartman is too fascinating to be truly hated and Joker too ineffectual to be fully sympathetic.

It would be difficult to conclude from all this that Kubrick approved of US policy in Vietnam or wanted to make the conflict seem tragic rather than criminally foolish. Kubrick's vision of military indoctrination and combat is distinctly unsentimental and unmelodramatic, especially compared with the patriotic distortions of *The Deer Hunter*, the operatic pretensions of *Apocalypse Now* and the emotional manipulations of *Platoon*. The action in the second half of the film is noticeably unspectacular, lacking the suspense we normally expect of the genre. Kubrick's refusal to pull heart-strings or arouse vengeful emotions is particularly evident in the way he stages a scene we've seen many times before in Hollywood war movies: the death of the hero's friend. In Hasford's novel, Joker kills the stranded Cowboy in order to stop the platoon from making suicidal attempts to save him. Kubrick is much less dramatic: Cowboy dies in Joker's arms and Joker bends his head to weep – but the camera is set at a distance and Joker is surrounded by so many figures that we hardly see him.

The most unusual aspect of the film is that it uses many familiar generic ingredients and yet never generates a lucid, conventionally unified plot with a forceful protagonist. The first part is a closet drama dealing with a failed ideological indoctrination and the second part a relatively aimless and sometimes emotionally flat series of episodes in ravaged Vietnam. Kubrick keeps the war-loving viewer off balance, waiting for a thrill that never comes. He does, however, offer the convulsive violence of two closures, the first staged in the blue latrine and the second in the flame-red factory. The emphasis in both cases is not on the heroic or pathetic sacrifices of US soldiers, but on the last, barely articulated expressions of two outsiders – an unmanly Marine and a teenage girl who use weapons of steel and wood, and whose deaths rebuke the warrior-male ethos.

II. Lovers

Twelve years went by before Kubrick's next and final film, a period when he worked with writers and designers on the development of two projects, *The Aryan Papers* and *A. I. Artificial Intelligence*, which, for reasons having to do with Warner's assessment of the market and Kubrick's own doubts about the scripts, were never brought to completion. In the end, he secured approval from Warner for *Eyes Wide Shut*, a modernised retelling of an erotic Arthur Schnitzler novella of 1925, scripted in collaboration with Frederic Raphael and starring Tom Cruise and Nicole Kidman, who were the most famous married couple in America. Kubrick died shortly after completing the lengthy production of the film; he probably didn't supervise the final sound mixing, and he had no opportunity to fine-tune the editing after the initial release. But *Eyes Wide Shut* is substantially what he aimed to accomplish and is a remarkable last testament.

Kubrick had been fascinated with the Schnitzler novella since at least 1968, when he asked his wife to read it. At about the same time, he briefly discussed with Terry Southern the possibility of making a sleek pornographic movie featuring major stars (Southern wrote *Blue Movie*, a novel about a Kubrick-like director who tries to make such a picture), and he told the potential backers of his Napoleon film that the central character would have a 'sex life worthy of Arthur Schnitzler' (quoted in LoBrutto, p. 322). Christiane Kubrick could easily have read the novella in its original German version, entitled *Traumnovella* ('Dream Story'), although Kubrick probably showed her the 1926 English translation by J. M. Q. Davies, entitled *Rhapsody*. The fact that he knew the text at all is an indication of his wide-ranging interests. By the middle of the twentieth century, Schnitzler, whose career began in the 1870s and lasted until 1931, seemed a bit dated as a writer, probably because most of his work was set in *fin de siècle* Vienna and involved characters who fought duels and spoke in formal language. Even in *Traumnovella*, in which the characters use telephones, the atmosphere is reminiscent of an earlier era. During the period between the 1890s and the 1920s, however, Schnitzler had been at the forefront of European literature. He was among the first novelists to employ internal monologue (in the third-person, free-indirect form known in Germany as *erlebte Rede*), and his writings were almost as sexually scandalous to their original audience as those of James Joyce or D. H. Lawrence.

Schnitzler's insights into bourgeois sexual psychology, most of which resulted from his personal experience as a medical student and self-confessed womaniser, attracted the interest of no less a contemporary than Sigmund Freud, who described Schnitzler as his 'double'. Schnitzler never returned the compliment, but he became part of an Austro-Hungarian cultural revolution that produced, in addition to Freud, Hugo Hofmannsthal, Gustav Klimt, Gustav Mahler, Karl Kraus and Arnold Schoenberg. The vibrant art world of 'Young Vienna' also influenced a later generation of film directors, including Fritz Lang, Otto Preminger and Billy Wilder. In fact, Schnitzler himself was a lover of movies. His diary, in addition to describing roughly 600 of his dreams, indicates that he saw at least three films a week in the late 1920s. His work was adapted by several film directors, including Cecil B. DeMille (*The Affairs of Anatol* [1921]), Paul Czinner (*Fraulein Else* [1929]) and Max Ophuls (*Liebeli* [1932] and *La Ronde* [1950]). G. W. Pabst was at one point interested in making a film based on *Traumnovella*, for which Schnitzler prepared an incomplete screenplay. (He believed the novella would make an interesting sound film without dialogue.) Finally, in 1969, *Traumnovella* was adapted for Austrian TV, directed by Wolfgang Glück.

Traumnovella differs from most European fiction of the previous two centuries in that it concerns fidelity rather than adultery. Its chief characters are Fredolin, a successful Jewish medical doctor in Vienna, and his decorative wife, Albertine. The couple has a 'flaxen-haired' little daughter and lives in bourgeois luxury, assisted by a maidservant. One evening at a fashionable masked ball, Fredolin is greeted warmly by two amorous young women while, at another place in the room, Albertine is almost seduced by a stranger 'whose blasé melancholy air and foreign-sounding – evidently Polish – accent had at first intrigued her'.[14] At home later that evening, the husband and wife fall into one another's arms 'with an ardor they had not experienced for quite some time' (p. 176). On the next evening, however, the memory of their 'missed opportunities' causes them to feel a 'need for mild revenge'; in the bedroom, they begin to confess 'scarcely admitted desires', exploring 'secret regions . . . towards which the irrational winds of fate might one day drive them, if only in their dreams' (p. 177). Albertine tells of an incident that occurred during their previous summer's vacation in Denmark, when she was so attracted to a passing naval officer that she would have been willing, had he asked, to run away with him. Fredolin recalls that on the last day of that same vacation, as he was walking near the sea-shore, he saw a naked girl of no more than fifteen with 'loose, flaxen hair', who looked at him with 'joy and abandon', leaving him on the point of swooning (p. 181).

On the heels of these troubling confessions, Fredolin is called away to meet with the family of a patient who has just died. For the rest of the evening he wanders the city, encountering sexual opportunities that he either rejects or is unable to seize: he hears a bizarre declaration of love from the dead patient's daughter; he is approached by a seventeen-year-old prostitute; he has a chance meeting with an old acquaintance who tells a fantastic story about playing piano blindfolded for a masked orgy; he makes a hasty visit to a costume shop where the proprietor acts as a pimp for his underage daughter; he travels by night to a mysterious estate where a secret password ('Denmark') gains him admission to the orgy; his masquerade is discovered and he is on the verge of being punished when a beautiful masked woman announces to the gathering that she will 'redeem' him; and he returns home to his marriage bed, where Albertine laughs in her sleep and, upon waking, explains that she has been dreaming of having sex with the Danish naval officer and a crowd of others while Fredolin was being crucified.

On the next day, Fredolin retraces his path through the city and tries to discover the identity of the beautiful woman who was ready to sacrifice herself for him. In a newspaper, he reads about the apparent suicide of 'Baroness D.', a lady of 'remarkable beauty' (p. 267) and fears this might be the woman at the orgy; he visits a mortuary to view her body but, when he sees the naked corpse, he realises that he can never know for certain who she is and perhaps doesn't want to know. Returning home in the evening, he finds Albertine asleep beside the mask he had worn to the orgy. When she wakes, he tearfully admits everything that has happened and asks what they should do. Albertine says they should both be grateful that 'we have safely emerged from these adventures – both from the real ones and from those we dreamed about' (p. 281). Before Fredolin can promise to be true forever, she places a finger over his lips and whispers, 'Never enquire into the future.' The story ends as the new day dawns and the couple's child is heard from a nearby room.

Although *Traumnovella* is a product of the *fin de siècle*'s 'dreamy' aestheticism, it also has certain affinities with well-known examples of high-modernist fiction. It occasionally resembles Kafka, partly because it introduces a note of perverse, unhealthy sexuality into an otherwise straightforward and rather polite narrative and partly because it blurs the boundaries between dreams, fantasies and reality. It also has a few things in common with James Joyce's most celebrated short story, 'The Dead' (1914), which, like *Traumnovella*, is told mostly from the point of view of a husband who learns that his beautiful wife once felt passionate desire for another man. Like Joyce, Schnitzler employs a free-associative 'inner speech' to reveal hidden aspects of the husband's character. In both stories the husbands are cautious men, clinging to respectability in a decadent or moribund society, who come to realise, in Schnitzler's words, that 'all this order, balance and security' are really 'an illusion and a lie' (p. 259). The two husbands are also subtly attracted to death. When Fredolin leaves his dead patient, he feels as if he has 'escaped, not so much from an experience as from some melancholy enchantment that must not gain power over him' (p. 193). When he visits the mortuary to view the naked body of the 'Baroness', he imagines that the corpse is trying to move and touch him and, as if 'drawn on by some enchantment', he bends down and almost kisses the dead woman on the lips (p. 276). The pull towards dissolution has something to do with Thanatos, but is also related to a more general insecurity and lack of moral courage in the face of social life. For example, when Fredolin first sets out to wander the nocturnal streets, he sees a homeless man sleeping on a park bench and struggles to avoid identification with him:

> What if I were to wake him, thought Fredolin, and give him money for a night's lodging? But what good would that do, he went on to reflect, I'd then have to provide for him tomorrow too, otherwise there would be no point and perhaps I would be suspected of some criminal association with him . . . . Why him, specifically? He asked himself, in Vienna alone there are thousands of such miserable souls. Supposing one were to start worrying about all of them – about the fates of all those unknown people! The dead man he had just left came into his mind, and with a shudder of revulsion he reflected how, in compliance with eternal laws, corruption and decay had already set to work in that emaciated body . . . . He was glad that he was still alive, that for him such ugly matters were still probably a long way off; glad that he was in his prime, that a charming and lovable woman was there at his disposal, and that he could have another one, many others, if he so desired. Such things might admittedly require more courage than he could muster; and he reflected that by eight o'clock tomorrow he would have to be back at the clinic. (pp. 193–4)

Whether or not Stanley Kubrick was aware of the similarities between Schnitzler and Joyce, he at one point considered setting his adaptation of *Traumnovella* in Dublin. Before that, he contemplated a black-comic version starring Steve Martin. Eventually he recognised the voyeuristic and commercial possibilities of giving the leading roles to major film stars who were married in real life. The participation of Cruise and Kidman also helped to confirm another of his ideas: the story could be moved to contemporary Manhattan. Kubrick strongly believed that Schnitzler's characters and themes would make sense in a late twentieth-century context. He was not alone in this conviction. At almost the same moment as the release of *Eyes Wide Shut*, and purely by coincidence, British playwright David Hare transformed Schnitzler's *Reigen* (1897) into a modern-day drama entitled *The Blue Room*; the London production starred Nicole Kidman, who, as in Kubrick's movie, appeared nude in some of her scenes.

By casting Cruise and Kidman, Kubrick invited the audience to speculate about their real-life relationship (their divorce not long after the release of the film fuelled even more speculation), but *Eyes Wide Shut* is also filled with 'inside' references to the director and several of the people close to him. The Manhattan apartment where the fictional married couple lives is loosely based on an apartment where Kubrick and his wife lived in the late 1960s. The paintings on the walls of the apartment are by Christiane Kubrick and Katharina Kubrick Hobbs, both of whom make cameo appearances as extras later in the film. The granny glasses and upswept hair Nicole Kidman wears in her domestic scenes bear a strong resemblance to the glasses and hair of Christiane Kubrick in photographs taken at the time when the film was made. The husband in the film watches pro football on TV, as Kubrick was fond of doing. When the wife watches TV, she sees *Blume in Love* (1973), a movie about the break-up of a marriage, directed by Paul Mazursky, who was an actor in Kubrick's *Fear and Desire*. When she wraps Christmas presents, we see her wrapping a boxed edition of Van Gogh's paintings much like the one Kubrick gave as a Christmas present to screen-writer Frederic Raphael during the making of the film. When the husband wanders the New York streets, he passes a storefront called 'Vitali's' – a reference to Leon Vitali, Bullingdon in *Barry Lyndon*, who plays a small role in this film and who worked as Kubrick's assistant on this and other pictures. There are also links to Kubrick's family history: his father, like the husband in the film, was a doctor, and his ancestors emigrated to America from Austria at about the time when Arthur Schnitzler was at the height of his fame. All these connec-tions may not constitute a full-fledged *film-à-clef*, but they provide a good deal of evidence to suggest that *Eyes Wide Shut* is Kubrick's most personal project. The result, as Jonathan Rosenbaum has observed, is 'personal filmmaking as well as dream poetry of the kind most movie commerce has ground underfoot'.[15]

Where the development of the screenplay was concerned, Kubrick's relationship with his co-writer appears to have been different from his previous collaborations – more distant and impersonal, at least if one can judge from Frederic Raphael's *Eyes Wide Open: A Memoir of Stanley Kubrick* (1999). A prolific author with a scholarly background, Raphael was no doubt hired for the job because he had written the screenplay for Stanley Donen's *Two for the Road* (1967), a realistic film about modern marriage. He made a few lunch-time visits to Kubrick's home but conducted most of the script conferences over the telephone, reluctantly sending Kubrick pages of work in progress via fax from various places in Europe. Kubrick made revisions to the first draft of the script, Raphael polished Kubrick's work and other changes were probably made by Kubrick during production. Although Raphael has described Kubrick as a 'genius', he seems to have felt a good deal of suspicion, resentment and intellectual defensiveness towards his employer, as if he and Kubrick were combatants in a chess match: 'If we sometimes acted like buddies,' he writes, 'there was between us an intimacy without commitment and, at times, heat without warmth.'[16]

Despite its subtitle, Raphael's memoir is chiefly about himself and needs to be used with caution, especially when it gives us lengthy, verbatim reports of his conversations with Kubrick in the form of a mock screenplay. Nevertheless, it contains some useful information. Raphael disliked the title *Eyes Wide Shut*, which was Kubrick's idea, and thought Schnitzler's treatment of sex would look dated if it were transposed without much change into the present day. He also thought – correctly – that an important issue in the novella was the married couple's Jewishness, a feature Schnitzler establishes early in the story, when several young men from a Viennese fencing fraternity deliberately bump against Fredolin in the street and make anti-Semitic remarks.[17] Kubrick insisted that the husband and wife should be a WASP couple, probably because he wanted to cast Cruise and Kidman. In the film they become Bill and Alice Harford, a surname created from the first and last names of Harrison Ford, a thoroughly middle-American star. Bill is abused in the street by American fraternity boys who call him a queer, and in a later scene a gay hotel clerk tries to flirt with him. As if to make things look even more Gentile, everybody in the film celebrates Christmas. I'm not sure what to make of the irony that the character who is coded as Jewish – Victor Ziegler (Sydney Pollack), Bill's super-wealthy patient – is also the most morally corrupt character.

Raphael initially tried to give Bill Harford a back-story, writing scenes in which we would see him in his student days and learn something about his relationship to his father. Later in the process Kubrick rejected these scenes and repeatedly asked Raphael to follow Schnitzler's 'beats', deviating as little as possible from the events in the original story. Most of the changes in the plot are relatively minor: for example, the party attended by the married couple is shown rather than reported upon; the husband's story about an encounter with a teenaged girl on the beach is eliminated; the husband doesn't pass a homeless man in the street; and the wife's passionate desire for the Danish officer seems to obsess the husband in the film a bit more than it obsesses Fredolin in the novella. The most significant change is the addition of an entirely new character – Victor Ziegler, an invention of Raphael's, who appears at the beginning and end, creating a slightly noirish aura and acting as a sinister *deus ex machina*.

Although the transformation of Schnitzler's characters into contemporary Manhattanites is cleverly achieved, the completed film often alludes to the Viennese origins of the story. The eclectic musical soundtrack includes '*Wein, Du Stadt meiner Träume*' by Rudolf Sieczynski. 'Sharkey's', the coffee shop where Bill Harford reads a newspaper with a minatory headline ('Lucky to Be Alive'), has frosted windowpanes, dark wooden furnishings and *fin de siècle* artwork reminiscent of the cafés in Schnitzler's world. The Beethoven opera *Fidelio*, which serves as a password to the masked orgy, had its premiere in Vienna in the

nineteenth century. A more prominent allusion can be seen in the dazzling curtain of gold lights decorating the ballroom at Ziegler's Christmas party – a reference to Gustav Klimt, a Viennese contemporary of Freud and Schnitzler, who began as a painter of bourgeois theatrical scenes but soon became what Carl Schorske describes as a 'psychological painter of women'.[18] A controversial figure in his lifetime, Klimt suffered a loss of patronage from official museum culture and evolved into a proto-modernist whose erotic images were characterised by a flat, golden luminescence and, in Schorske's words, a 'crystalline ornamentalism' (p. 264). Notice also that *Eyes Wide Shut* opens with 'Waltz # 2' from Dmitri Shostakovich's *Jazz Suite*, which, although written in the 1930s, evokes the sexy glamour of Viennese culture at the beginning of the twentieth century. As Claudia Gorbman has observed, the timbre of the saxophone passage conveys 'nostalgia or even melancholy', creating a slightly decadent, Old-World sense 'of texture, of history, of knowing' that seems at odds with the married couple we see in the film. (Because of its fullness and presence, we initially assume the Shostakovich music is non-diegetic, like *The Blue Danube* in *2001*; but Bill abruptly stops it by turning off a stereo.) Besides all this, Kubrick gives us a number of gracefully executed Steadicam shots of characters walking through rooms or dancing around ballrooms reminiscent of the films of Max Ophuls – a director who was born in Saärbrucken but who is usually regarded as quintessentially Viennese.

Like the novella, the film has an oneiric quality. Apart from a few stock shots of traffic on Manhattan streets, the city is vaguely like a stage setting, with street names that don't exist and a jazz club that looks like a nostalgic recreation of places Kubrick might have habituated in his youth. (Kubrick went to considerable lengths to achieve an accurate representation of New York, even hiring photographers to secretly snap pictures of people on Manhattan streets so that extras in the film could be garbed appropriately; but the subtle, deliberate unreality of the sets confused some of the film's original reviewers, who thought the director had been living abroad so long that he had forgotten what the city looked like.) Night-time scenes in the Harford apartment are designed and lit in a colour-coded, stylised manner: the golden bedroom is decorated with flaming-red drapes, and through an open doorway the adjacent rooms look mysteriously blue. The bedroom of the luxurious Park Avenue apartment where Bill goes to pay his respects to a dead man has a sickly, somewhat greenish quality; the secret orgy looks like a mixture of ancient ritual, Venetian carnival and perverse fairy tale; and the climactic conversation with Ziegler takes place around a strangely expressive, blood-red billiard table. Masks can be seen in several rooms, and the ubiquitous Christmas decorations take on a magical aura.

What gives the film an especially strange feeling, however, is the weird comedy of a few of the scenes, such as the ones involving the costumer and his daughter (Leelee Sobieski), plus

the associational or 'rhyming' relationship between certain events. Two beautiful models at Ziegler's party invite Bill to follow them to '[w]here the rainbow ends', and later Bill visits a shop named 'Rainbow Fashions' with a basement called 'Under the Rainbow'. During the party, a vaguely dangerous-looking associate of Ziegler calls Bill away from the two models and, during the Somerton orgy, an ominous man calls Bill away from a sexy masked woman. When Bill returns home from the orgy, where he was simply an observer of the action, Alice tells of a dream she's had in which she takes part in an orgy while he stands by and watches. Mandy, the naked call-girl who is saved by Bill early in the film, may or may not be the naked masked woman who saves Bill at the orgy and the naked woman whose body Bill later views at the morgue. (For the record, Mandy, the masked woman, and the woman in the morgue are played by two different actors – Abigail Good is the mysterious masked woman and Julienne Davis is Mandy and the woman in the morgue.)

These repetitions and transformations create a problem of interpretation similar to the one we've seen in *The Shining*. In the earlier film, we're constantly invited to ask: is this real or is he crazy? In *Eyes Wide Shut*, the question is only slightly different: is he awake or is he dreaming? Once again, we've entered the narrative mode of the uncanny as it verges on the fantastic. As previously, the story concerns a nuclear family and produces the spooky or eerie effects that Freud attributed to the intimate appeal of 'what is familiar and

agreeable' mixed with anxiety over 'what is concealed and kept out of sight' (pp. 224–5). Freud's essay on the uncanny was in fact written only a few years before Schnitzler's *Traumnovella*,[19] and Kubrick's film seems to emphasise the deep connection between the two texts, almost systematically touching upon the events and situations Freud had described as giving rise to uncanny feelings. Among these are the fear that a puppet, doll or lifeless body might become animate (as in the scenes involving the dead patient, the body in the morgue and the mannequins in Milich's shop); the fear of a mirror-image or *doppelgänger* (as in the two models at the party, the two prostitutes, the two dead bodies and the peculiar doubling effect that Michel Chion has noted in the scene of the grieving and neurotically love-struck daughter, in which the arrival of the daughter's fiancé is represented with exactly the same sequence of shots and movements that were used for the arrival of Bill Harford); and the fear of having one's eyes put out (in this case the purely metaphorical fear of having one's eyes wide shut – in Freudian terms, being symbolically castrated by a father-figure like Zeigler or a woman like Alice).

Freud also puts great stress on the uncanny effect of mysteriously recurring events, which he attributes to a neurotic 'repetition compulsion' and later analyses at length in *Beyond the Pleasure Principle* (1920). In the essay on the uncanny, he compares these recurrences with the 'helplessness experienced in some dream-states', and he gives an example from his personal experience:

> As I was walking, one hot summer afternoon, through the deserted streets of a provincial town in Italy, which was unknown to me, I found myself in a quarter of whose character I could not long remain in doubt. Nothing but painted women were to be seen in the windows of the small houses, and I hastened to leave the narrow street at the next turning. But after having wandered about for a time without enquiring my way, I suddenly found myself back in the same street ... I hurried away once more, only to arrive by a *detour* at the same place yet a third time. Now, however, a feeling overcame me which I can only describe as uncanny, and I was glad enough to find myself back at the piazza I had left a short while before, without any further voyages of discovery. (p. 237)

Freud's 'voyages of discovery' have something in common with Bill Harford's wanderings through New York, all of which return him uncannily to the same places, including the apartment of a prostitute. In one sense, Bill is an ironic version of Odysseus, experiencing dangerous adventures while Penelope remains at home; but he's also a Freudian everyman, led along by unrecognised wishes, confounded by the interpenetration of dreams and everyday life, neurotically repeating himself. Diane Johnson has described this psychological atmosphere perfectly: 'As in a dream, a texture of fears and wishes unfold – a lover waltzes away with one's wife, a patient's pretty daughter confesses her passion, a prostitute both beckons and threatens death, the erotic fantasies of men about little girls are made frighteningly specific. The wallet always has money in it ... .' The result, she concludes, is 'a ground plan of the male psyche, mapping the fear, desire, omnipresence of sex, preoccupation with death, the connection of death and Eros, the anxiety in men generated by female sexuality' (Cocks *et al.*, p. 61).

The feeling of eerie repetition also insinuates itself into the film's dialogue. During the development of the screenplay Kubrick emphasised to Raphael that the language should be plain to the point of minimalism. (Schnitzler's novella tends to report speech rather than giving it directly.) He particularly wanted to avoid the witty give-and-take associated with theatrical or cinematic depictions of middle-class sex – Neil Simon's *Plaza Suite* (1971), for example, and even Raphael's *Two for the Road*. As a result, most of the language in *Eyes Wide Shut* is utterly banal – a significant phenomenon given Kubrick's high regard for verbal stylists like Nabokov and Burgess and the obvious pleasure he takes in the elaborate formal locutions of *Barry Lyndon* or the flamboyant vulgarity of *Full Metal Jacket*. Even in *2001*, in which all the human characters speak in banalities or technocratic jargon, the HAL computer sounds almost eloquent. In *Eyes Wide Shut*, however, the speeches are usually so monosyllabic and quotidian that they constitute an anti-style. The qualified exceptions are the epigram that Alice's potential seducer borrows from Oscar Wilde ('Don't you think one of the charms of marriage is that it makes deception necessary for both parties?') and some of the longer speeches, such as Alice's story about the naval officer, her tearful recounting of her dream, and Ziegler's disquisition near the end of the film. But even these monologues are marked by hesitations and repeated words. The only artful touch, though at first it doesn't seem to be, is the extremely large number of what Michel Chion calls 'parroted' lines – instances when a character repeats what another character has just said.[20] In one crucial place, as Chion points out, a delayed parroting has an ironic effect: near the beginning of the film, Bill tells Mandy, the young woman who has nearly died of a drug overdose in Ziegler's bathroom, 'You're going to need some rehab. You know that, don't you?' And near the end, Ziegler tells Bill, 'Life goes on. It always does until it doesn't. But you know that, don't you?' The other repetitions are less weighty. A few of Chion's examples will suffice to reveal the pattern they create:

BILL: What did he want?
ALICE: What did he want? Oh ... what did he want?

DOMINO: Come inside with me?
BILL: Come inside with you?

MILICH: He moved to Chicago.
BILL: He moved to Chicago?

SALLY: HIV positive.
BILL: HIV positive?

ZIEGLER: I had you followed.
BILL: You had me followed?

BILL: What do you think we should do?
ALICE: What do I think we should do?

BILL: Forever?
ALICE: Forever?
BILL: Forever.

One might think that the actors would dislike this sort of thing, but I suspect they enjoyed it. In the jargon of professional linguistics, it enables them to demonstrate the 'performance' functions of language; they often convert simple declarative statements into questions, thus performing what the linguists describe as an 'illocutionary act', or they change a statement's inflection, performing a 'perlocutionary act'. (One of the most obvious instances of the latter technique is Alice's 'What did *he* want? Oh . . . what did he *want?*') Sometimes the repetitions achieve a kind of wit, as in the conversation between the slightly tipsy Alice and Sandor Szavost (Sky Dumont), who is one of the cinema's most aggressively seductive lounge lizards: 'My name is Sandor Szavost. I'm Hungarian.' 'My name is Alice Harford. I'm American.'

The repetitiousness induces a 'subtextual' style of acting, a tendency to communicate meanings chiefly through inflections, tones of voice, facial expressions or small gestures. Kubrick enhances this quality by giving the actors very little business to perform and seldom allowing them to walk around a room or execute complicated movements in relation to the camera. He paces everything in characteristically slow fashion and sometimes photographs simple actions (walking down a hall, crossing from A to B) in wide shots that create empty space and dead time. The effect is almost Antonioni-like, except that the framing is extremely precise and relatively little use is made of off-screen areas. With the notable exception of the Steadicam shots in the opening sequences and at the masked orgy, most scenes involve actors who face one another across a table, a desk or a small room.

A good example is Bill's conversation with a hotel desk clerk (Alan Cumming) who smiles, looks Bill up and down, rolls his eyes, flutters his hands and turns every line into a coy insinuation. A less comically ostentatious example is Bill's second visit to Domino's apartment, where he encounters Sally, Domino's attractive roommate (Fay Masterson). The conversation is filled with echoed lines and suggestive glances: 'So, do you have any idea when you expect Domino back?' 'No, I have no idea.' 'You have no idea?' 'Well, to be perfectly honest, she . . . she may not even be coming back.' 'She may not even be coming back?' At the beginning of this exchange, the two actors stand close together in the tiny room; an erotic charge passes between them and they smile or laugh each time they speak. By the time we reach 'She may not even be coming back', Bill is fondling Sally's breast.

'Well, umm . . . I, erh,' she murmurs, and Bill responds, 'You, erh.' Awkwardly, Sally finds her voice: 'I think some . . . something that I should tell you.' 'Really?' 'Yeah . . . but I don't know.' 'You don't know? What is it?' Forcing herself to break free, Sally asks Bill to sit down. A brief silence falls. Bill laughs softly. Sally's discomfort begins to show: 'Oh . . . I don't quite know how to say this.' Bill is still amused: 'You don't quite know how?' Sally grows serious, creating a beat-change in the emotional tenor of the conversation: 'I think it would be only fair to you, to let you know that, umm . . . [Domino] got the results of a blood test this morning and, erh . . . it was HIV positive.' Bill reacts quietly: 'HIV positive?' A longer silence descends. 'Well,' Bill says, and adopts his best bedside manner. 'I am very . . . very sorry to hear that.'

Within the film's deliberately narrow stylistic constraints, both Cruise and Kidman give impressive performances; but, even though the action is presented chiefly from Cruise's point of view and is almost entirely about masculine fantasy, Kidman makes the stronger immediate impression, contributing to the most complex female characterisation in Kubrick's career. (Not that it has much competition.) This is true despite the fact that, in traditional movie fashion, Kidman is offered up for the visual pleasure of the male audience. From the very beginning, in a temporally ambiguous shot, she sheds her party dress, revealing her coltish legs and beautifully shaped derrière for the eye of the camera. An obvious signifier of what Laura Mulvey has described as 'to-be-looked-at-ness', she over-shadows a gallery of young women with more voluptuous figures but less interesting or entirely masked features. Her porcelain skin and delicate lips connote propriety, and she plays the maternal scenes with convincing sweetness; but her red hair and vixen eyes connote sexual passion. She's a fantasy figure – the mother and the whore, a baby who, in the words of the Chris Isaak song, might 'do a bad, bad thing'. But she's also much more modern, independent and sympathetic than the equivalent character in Schnitzler's novella – a woman who might feel trapped and resentful in her marriage.

During the course of the film, Bill performs no household duties and Alice has no apparent purpose except to be decorative, wrap Christmas presents and help her daughter with schoolwork or the arts of beauty. (One of the toys her daughter wants to buy in the closing scene is a fairy-tale Barbie doll.) Everyone Alice meets, from her baby-sitter to Zeigler, compliments her on her beauty and says nothing else. When she explains to Sandor Szavost that the gallery where she once worked went broke and she's still looking for a job, Szavost is amused. 'Oh, what a shame!' he says, looking deep into her eyes. 'I have some friends in the art game. Perhaps they can be of help?' Then he tries to lure her upstairs, ostensibly to view Renaissance bronzes in Ziegler's private gallery. On the next day she reads newspaper ads, puts on a bra, combs her daughter's hair and prepares to go out (Job hunting? Shopping?). Kubrick cross-cuts between these scenes and Bill at his office, where, assisted by his female secretary and nurses, he examines a series of patients, including a bosomy young woman clad in bikini pants.

The film very swiftly establishes that Bill and Alice have been married for some time and that Bill takes her for granted. As they prepare to leave for the Christmas party, she sits on a toilet in their bathroom and urinates while he studies himself in a mirror. 'How do I look?' she asks. 'Perfect,' he replies, without glancing at her. Eyes wide shut, he leaves his ravishing wife alone at the party, never doubting her fidelity. Having no one to talk with, Alice drinks too much champagne and is pleased and amused by the flirtation that develops with Szavost. At home afterward she stands naked in front a mirror, wearing glasses and admiring her body as she moves seductively to music. Kidman expertly conveys the character's momentary pleasure in the power of her sexuality. As her husband embraces her, she looks away from him, into the mirror and almost into the camera, as if she were indulging her narcissism and at the same time offering herself to male viewers.

Kidman has nearly all the scenes in the film that showcase acting ability. She feigns two kinds of intoxication (champagne and marijuana) and delivers two monologues in different emotional registers (a vengeful confession of desire for another man and a tearful account of a sexual dream). Her most important scene is the one in which she tells Bill about the naval officer. First we see Alice studying herself wearily in the bathroom mirror, taking out a stash of marijuana and beginning to roll a joint. Cut to the bedroom, which is bathed in a golden light, again evoking Gustav Klimt. The camera zooms out from Alice, who reclines on the bed in sexy, pale lingerie, drawing deeply on the joint while Bill, in black boxer shorts, leans over her. Both characters are stoned, and Alice's resentments surface immediately. She asks if Bill happened to 'fuck' the two women she saw him with at the party. As an argument develops, Kubrick cuts to medium close-ups on every line of dialogue, then to a wide shot as Bill engages Alice in sex play and teases her about Szavost. When Bill says it's 'understandable' that another man would want to have sex with her, she becomes angry and moves to the other side of the room. In a series of shot-reverse shots we see Alice at full length and Bill seated on the bed. Alice's initial outburst seems almost comically excessive; she stands unsteadily, framed in a blue doorway in semi-transparent underclothes, her entire body on view. 'So,' she asks loudly, 'because I'm a beautiful woman, the only reason a man wants to talk to me is he wants to fuck me?' Faced with this evidence, it's difficult not to sympathise with Bill, whose woozy attempt to avoid a quarrel pushes him deeper into a hole: 'Well, I don't think it's quite that black and white,' he says lamely, 'but I think we both know what men are like.' Seizing on the point as if she were a lawyer, Alice reminds Bill that he chatted with two beautiful models at the party and that he examines beautiful women in his office every day. 'This pot is making you aggressive,' he says. 'I'm not *ar-gu-ing*,' she cries as she plops down drunkenly on a dressing-table stool, 'I'm just trying to find out where you're coming from!'

The sources of Alice's resentment have less to do with Bill's flirtations or her own missed sexual opportunities than with an understandable feeling of inequality in the relationship. She stands and begins pacing back and forth, the red drapes on the bedroom window subtly suggesting her passion and anger. After millions of years of evolution, she says, men 'stick it in every place they can', while for women marriage is supposed to be about 'security and commitment'. 'If you men only knew,' she taunts. When Bill tells her that he's sure of her faithfulness, she laughs uncontrollably and falls to her knees. The critic Christian Appelt has pointed out that, until this point, Kubrick's framing and staging has been meticulous but unobtrusive, but when Alice doubles up laughing we have the only visibly hand-held shot in the film: the camera quivers slightly, 'evoking the feeling that the foundations of the marriage have been shaken'.[21] Recovering her composure, Alice sits on the floor with her back to a radiator and begins telling him about the last summer in Cape Cod. A close-up frames her face in three-quarters profile and her expression takes on a sadistic quality as she slowly describes the moment when the naval officer glanced at her. 'I could hardly move,' she says quietly, giving stress to every syllable. Then she confesses that throughout the rest of that day, even while making love with Bill, the officer was never out of her mind. With almost ruthless conviction she says she 'was ready to give up everything', but then in a dreamy voice admits that her love for Bill also made her feel 'tender and sad'. When she discovered on the next day that the officer was gone, she found herself 'relieved'.

Four times during Alice's long speech, Kubrick cuts to large close-ups of Bill, who sits completely still. Despite everything that has been said about the Kuleshov effect and its ability to create meaning, Cruise's performance in these tightly framed shots is important. Motionless, gesture-less, he nevertheless conveys subtle gradations of emotion that Kubrick can use to chart the progress of Bill's feelings: a stunned, wounded look mixed with a slight frown of anger; a determined, stoic resistance to pain; a defeated glance downward, as if his bearings were gone; and, finally, as Alice mentions feeling 'tender and sad', a suggestion of tears. When Alice comes to the end of the story, Kubrick cuts to a more distant close-up that makes Bill seem isolated on the edge of the bed. Silence descends and the expression on Bill's face seems both hurt and resentfully angry. Suddenly, in time-honoured dramatic fashion, the telephone rings. Without changing the look on his face, Bill waits for three rings before he answers it.

Cruise's work in the film is consistently excellent but, as in this scene, relatively thankless. Most of the time he simply reacts quietly to what other people say and do. At Zeigler's Christmas party, where Bill tries to play the role of the successful young doctor, we glimpse the trademark energy and vitality of the Cruise persona – the action-hero intensity, the 1,000 kilowatt grin, the hearty back-slapping and hugs, and the sexual charisma. After Alice tells the story about the naval officer, however, Bill becomes a kind of sleepwalker, who seems to drift into a series of sexual encounters and near-comic sexual frustrations. Except for the blue movie running through his head at several points (literally blue: it consists of black-and-white, blue-tinted views of the naked Alice making love with a uniformed naval officer) and a point-of-view shot in which Alice smiles at him while he mentally 'hears' her voice from an earlier scene, we seldom know exactly what Bill is thinking. Or is most of what we see intended to suggest his dream thoughts? If so, exactly when does his dream begin and end? These questions are unanswerable and perhaps unimportant because, unlike the Schnitzler novella, which consists mostly of the central character's internal monologue, the film gives the story an entirely ambiguous ontological status.

Kubrick decided to cut Bill's extensive voice-over from an early draft of the script; instead he shows the character almost completely from the outside, relying on the *mise en scène* and Cruise's understated reactions to create psychological effects. This technique contributes to the feeling that Bill is being carried along impassively, rather like someone in a dream. In effect, his aimless journey is both a fantasy of sexual revenge and a guilty response to his own sexuality. Nearly everyone he meets comes on to him sexually, but his chief response is attempted dignity in the face of all kinds of fears, including infidelity, homosexuality, HIV-AIDS, incest/paedophilia and punishment from a father-figure such as Ziegler. At the orgy, where we might expect him to display at least a few excited reactions, his face is covered by an ornate but inexpressive mask that barely shows his eyes; he's a nearly ridiculous little man who wanders blankly through a strange sexual fun-house and then (as in a typical anxiety dream) suffers the embarrassment of having to remove his mask in front of the entire crowd.

The orgy was a major concern for Kubrick throughout his preparation for the film. Despite the anything-goes, pornography-on-demand environment of late twentieth-century media, some viewers expected a kinky sexual shock they had never seen. The Warner publicity campaign for *Eyes Wide Shut* and Kubrick's reputation as the director of

A Clockwork Orange obviously contributed to this expectation and may have led to disappointment in certain quarters. In fact, Bill's masked walk through the Somerton mansion was designed to show glimpses of fucking and sucking but, in order to obtain an R rating in the US, Kubrick placed computer-generated figures in the *mise en scène* for the North American market, blocking out the more explicit sexual details (his first use of CGI, which would figure more importantly in his plans for *A. I. Artificial Intelligence*). His concession to censorship, however, doesn't have a significant effect. Even without the computerised fig leaves, the orgy is coldly detached, involving none of the techniques – pulsing music, close-ups of genitalia, lingering views of lithe and sweaty bodies, moans and cries of satisfaction – that are the *sine qua non* of movie pornography. In a series of travelling shots from Bill's point of view, we see all sorts of sexual positions and a variety of heterosexual and homosexual activities, but the action is viewed from a relatively discreet distance and has a ritualistic quality that makes both participants and voyeurs seem bored. The entire panorama is intended as an allusion to fashion photographer Helmut Newton's fetishistic, semi-pornographic images in *Vogue* and other magazines during the 1980s. Newton's mostly black-and-white photographs featured half-naked, glamorous models standing or lying beside other, fully clothed models in extravagantly luxurious or formal settings, in poses suggestive of sadomasochism, zoophilia and other kinds of forbidden sexuality; one

of their most distinctive traits, a sign either of Newton's decadence or of his subtly satiric attitude towards the fashion world, was the jaded, blasé or drugged look of the models, who vaguely resembled the stone-faced socialites in *Last Year at Marienbad*.

Kubrick pays as much attention to the eclectic design and decor of Somerton as to the orgy itself, viewing the sexual activity in the context of ornate, rather Moorish architectural designs, marbled and carpeted floors and a richly furnished library. Everything has the feeling of a confused dream about ancient and modern cultures: the interiors look like a cross between Xanadu and the Playboy mansion; the invited guests resemble Catholic monks dressed as Venetian revellers; and the music, written and conducted by the British avant-garde composer Jocelyn Pook, sounds like a religious ritual filtered through postmodern performance art. One of Pook's compositions, 'Backward Priest', was created by recording the voice of a Romanian priest, running it backward and adding a repetitive, percussive musical chord that supposedly comes from Nick Nightingale's piano; another, 'Migrations', sounds vaguely Arabic or North African in origin. To this *mélange* Kubrick adds a kitschy dance tune, 'Strangers in the Night'. He also intended to incorporate chanted verses from the *Bhagavad-Gita*, but removed them when Hindu fundamentalists threatened to protest against the film.[22] In *The Da Vinci Code*, author Dan Brown absurdly opines that Kubrick was trying to send hidden messages about a grail society but got the details wrong. Actually, the point of all the wildly clashing cultural references isn't to create puzzles or secret symbols, but to lend an aura of all-purpose demonic ritual to a slightly weird erotic pageant. Like some types of dream, the orgy is both sinister and silly. Filled with details that would presumably make Jung and Freud jump for joy, it often looks like what Ziegler later claims it to be – an event staged to frighten Bill.

Kubrick's alienating treatment of the Somerton orgy points up the fact that *Eyes Wide Shut* is as much about money as about sex. As Tim Kreider has observed, the first words in the film are 'Honey, have you seen my wallet?' and the last scene is a shopping trip to FAO Schwartz; in between, we meet several prostitutes – one of whom is a girl working her way through college who owns a textbook entitled *Introducing Sociology* – and we're constantly reminded that Bill Harford is a prosperous doctor who serves extremely wealthy patients.[23] The importance of money is somewhat less evident in *Traumnovella*, which has no character like Zeigler, and this may be one reason why Jonathan Rosenbaum feels that Kubrick is more of a 'moralist' than Schnitzler (p. 265). In various ways the film suggests that Bill's guilt and shame when he returns home isn't simply the result of his potential unfaithfulness. In fact, for whatever fearful or accidental reasons, Bill hasn't committed adultery; his greater failing has to do with a tacit acceptance or complicity in Victor Ziegler's behaviour. At the big Christmas party, he jokingly tells Alice that they've been invited because of his willingness to make 'house calls'. Not long afterward Ziegler summons him upstairs to the fancy bathroom to help with a prostitute who, while having sex with Ziegler, has nearly died from a drug overdose. When Bill revives the woman, Ziegler tells him, 'You saved my ass', making it clear that the fate of the woman isn't the real concern. Bill replies

ambiguously, 'I'm glad I was here.' Ziegler pointedly asks Bill to keep quiet about the incident. 'Of course,' Bill says, in a man-to-man tone.

The lengthy conversation in Ziegler's library/billiard room near the end of the film
brings these moral issues to roost – although, as Rosenbaum has pointed out, Ziegler seems
like such a nice fellow that audiences might not fully grasp the situation. Kubrick originally intended to cast Harvey Keitel in the role, probably because Keitel often plays gangster
or low-life characters and is roughly the same size and body configuration as Cruise. Sydney
Pollack is a completely different type; tall and burly-chested, he's best known as an actor for
playing a small role in *Tootsie* (1982), a film he directed. He gives the impression of an intelligent, kindly and rather earthy father-figure, and his performance creates a disjunction
between the character's outward charm and actual corruption.

In this regard and others, the scene between Pollack and Cruise makes a nice contrast
with the one between Kirk Douglas and Adolphe Menjou near the end of *Paths of Glory*. In
both cases a monstrous but almost likeable representative of prestige and power has a private conversation with a younger man who is concerned about injustice, and in both cases
the characters are surrounded by leather-bound books and emblems of 'culture'. In *Eyes
Wide Shut*, however, the scene is less dynamically blocked and the star can't give vent to
moral outrage. Here as elsewhere in the film, Bill Harford is a relatively passive figure.
Immediately after viewing the body in the morgue, he's called to Ziegler's mansion, where,
escorted to the library by a tall, strong-looking male 'secretary', he arrives in a state of
exhaustion and guilt. Ziegler pours him a glass of twenty-five-year-old Scotch, pleads unsuccessfully with him to accept a full case of the whisky as a gift and toys uneasily with an
ivory ball on the red surface of the billiard table (the only instance in the lengthy scene
when an actor is given the opportunity to convey emotion by manipulating a prop). The
Steadicam follows Ziegler as he paces around the table and struggles for words. 'I . . . I was
just, erh . . . . Listen, Bill, the reason I asked you to come over, I, I . . . I need to talk to you
about something.' At first, the older man is deferential, suggesting that Bill 'might have
the wrong idea about one or two things' but, as the conversation develops, he makes veiled
threats. Explaining that he was one of the people at the orgy, he denounces 'Nick what-
ever-the-fuck his name was' and reveals that Bill has been followed all day.

Bill says little and hardly moves; in close-ups, he reacts to Ziegler's long speech with
puzzlement, surprise and muted anger, finally putting his hands on the edge of the billiard
table and slumping over in embarrassment. 'Victor, what can I say?' he asks. 'I had
absolutely no idea you were involved in any way.' Ziegler crosses to the drinks table, pours
more Scotch, says that if Bill knew the names of the people at the orgy he wouldn't 'sleep
well', and walks to the other side of the room to sit in a chair. In an extreme deep-focus shot
Bill turns his back on Ziegler, folds his arms and walks a couple of paces into the foreground. 'There was a woman there,' he says, 'who tried to warn me.' Zeigler gets up and
walks forward, describing the woman as a 'hooker' and claiming that everything at
the party was a 'charade'. Bill slumps into a chair, briefly holds his forehead in his hand,

clutches both hands together almost prayerfully and then asks Ziegler if the hooker is the dead woman described in today's newspaper. When Ziegler says yes, Bill shows his only flash of anger: standing, he turns and asks, 'Do you mind telling me what kind of fucking charade ends up with somebody turning up dead?' Ziegler's genial mask almost drops away: 'Let's cut the bullshit, alright? You've been way out of your depth for the last twenty-four hours . . . . She got her brains fucked out, *period* . . . . She OD'd. There was nothing suspicious. Her door was locked from the inside. The police are happy. End of story.' Then he becomes paternal, telling Bill that it was only 'a matter of time' before this particular woman died from drugs. 'Remember, you told her so yourself? Remember the one with the great tits who OD'd in my bathroom?'

Kubrick photographs the last shot of this sequence expressionistically. As Bill hangs his head and Ziegler steps up behind him to put reassuring hands on his shoulders, an unmotivated blue light falls mysteriously across the left side of both men's faces. 'Life goes on,' Ziegler says. 'It always does until it doesn't. But you know that, don't you?' Cut to Bill and Alice's bedroom, which is bathed in the same blue light, ostensibly from the moon. Alice lies sleeping, with Bill's mask from the orgy resting on the pillow next to her. (In the Schnitzler novella the husband's failure to return the mask is inadvertent, rather like a Freudian slip; in the film, the presence of the mask is unexplained.) When Bill sees the

mask he puts his hand to his heart, and on the soundtrack we hear the piercing piano notes of Ligeti's '*Musica Ricercata* II'. Bill breaks into tears, curls up in a foetal position on the bed next to Alice and promises to tell her 'everything'.

Cut to a close-up of Alice on the next morning; her eyes red from tears, she smokes a cigarette while Bill looks remorseful. She remembers the shopping trip they've promised their daughter and we cut to the toy store, which again has no equivalent in Schnitzler. Bill, Alice and Helena walk in a circle, the Steadicam retreating in front of them as numerous extras walk past like figures in a play or a dream. Bill has a hangdog look and asks Alice what they should do. As in the Schnitzler novella, she tells him to be grateful that their marriage has survived its 'adventures', whether they were 'real or only a dream'. Bill remarks that 'no dream is ever just a dream', and wants to be awake 'forever'. Alice rejects this idea and responds in existential terms: she loves Bill now and thinks that as soon as possible they should 'fuck'.

This last word, which we've heard at several other junctures in Kubrick's last film, is significantly given to a woman. A grotesque term for what is sometimes an act of love, 'fuck' has a sucking, lower-body sound and derives from an Anglo-Saxon word that connotes violence or repeated blows, as when Ziegler says 'she got her brains fucked out'. Kidman delivers it in a soft, wryly amused voice that conveys both tenderness and a tough awareness of how much the unsteady edifice of everyday, companionate marriage is built on primal urges. One could argue that, by ending the film in this way, Kubrick shows himself to be a sexual conservative, since he confirms the importance of monogamous married relations and the heterosexual, nuclear family. One could also argue by the same logic that *Eyes Wide Shut* has a 'happy' ending, which would mean that it differs from any Kubrick movie, with the possible exception of *Killer's Kiss*. Without doubt the film honours Kubrick's third marriage, which was long and apparently happy. But his implicit view of sexuality is by no means simple or complacent. The Spanish critic Celestino Deleyto offers what seems to me an accurate summation of the film's sexual themes:

> it explores in complex and convincing ways the links between love and sex, between affective relationships and sexual fantasy, between sex as a male construct signifying anxiety, guilt and death and sex as a crucial ingredient in a healthy relationship, between sex as commodity and sex as emotion.[24]

As Rosenbaum has argued, *Eyes Wide Shut* also shows the tenuous, conflicted and always complicated links between dreams and responsibilities. Whatever optimism there might be in the last scene is extremely hard won, and the film has the courage to leave its characters relatively unchanged: Bill remains the successful, compromised doctor and Alice the beautiful, jobless wife, and their lives still involve guilt and resentment. Tomorrow and the next day they will have similar adventures, which they may or may not survive.

Notes

1. Michael Herr, 'Foreword', in Stanley Kubrick, Michael Herr and Gustav Hasford, *Full Metal Jacket: The Screenplay* (New York: Alfred A. Knopf, 1987), p. vi.

2. Thomas Doherty, 'Full Metal Genre: Stanley Kubrick's Vietnam Combat Movie', in Mario Falsetto (ed.), *Perspectives on Stanley Kubrick* (New York: G. K. Hall, 1996), p. 315. All further references are to this edition, and page numbers are indicated in the text.

3. Brad Stevens, '"Is That You, John Wayne? Is This Me?" Problems of Identity in Stanley Kubrick's *Full Metal Jacket*', *Senses of Cinema* <www.sensesofcinema.com/contents/02/21/full_metal.html>:2.

4. Bill Krohn, '*Full Metal Jacket*', *The Kubrick Site* <www.visual-memory.co.uk/amk/doc/0104.html>: 2. All further references are to this posting, and page numbers are indicated in the text. A longer version of Krohn's essay can be found in Jonathan Crary and Sanford Kwinter (eds), *Incorporations* (New York: Urzone, 1992), pp. 428–35.

5. Stanley Kubrick and Michael Herr, *Full Metal Jacket: A Screenplay* (undated), p. 8. All further references are to this script, and page numbers are indicated in the text. I'm grateful to Jonathan Rosenbaum and Bill Krohn for providing me with the manuscript. Matthew Modine's diary of his work on the film, plus reviews and news reports from the time when the film was released, provide strong evidence that this is the final shooting script. It shouldn't be confused with the published screenplay listed in Note 1, which is based on the released picture. See Krohn, '*Full Metal Jacket*', and Aly Sujo, 'Was *Full Metal Jacket* Even Bleaker before Trims?', *Chicago Sun-Times Weekend* (11 September 1987), p. 28.

6. Matthew Modine, *Full Metal Jacket Diary* (New York: Rugged Land, 2005), n.p. All further references are to this edition, which is without page numbers.

7. Gustav Hasford, *The Short-Timers* (New York: Bantam Books, 1983), pp. 175–80.

8. Gene D. Phillips and Rodney Hill (eds), *The Encyclopedia of Stanley Kubrick* (New York: Checkmark Books, 2002), p. 160.

9. Paula Willoquet-Maricondi, 'Full-Metal Jacketing, or Masculinity in the Making', *Cinema Journal* vol. 33 no. 2 (1994), p. 19.

10. For a roughly similar analysis of the gender politics of Kubrick's film, see Willoquet-Maricondi, 'Full-Metal Jacketing'.

11. Quoted by Mark Bowden, 'The Things They Carried: One Man's Memoir of the 1991 Persian Gulf War', *The New York Times Book Review* (2 March 2003), p. 8.

12. See Kubrick's 1987 interview with Gene Siskel, in Gene D. Phillips (ed.), *Stanley Kubrick Interviews* (Jackson: University Press of Mississippi, 2001), p. 186.

13. Ermey is quoted from an interview with the New York *Daily News* in Phillips and Hill, *The Encyclopedia of Stanley Kubrick*, p. 103.

14. Stanley Kubrick and Frederic Raphael, *Eyes Wide Shut, a Screenplay*, and Arthur Schnitzler, 'Dream Story', trans. J. M. Q. Davies (New York: Warner Books, 1999), p. 176. Subsequent quotations are from this edition, and page numbers are indicated in the text.

15. Jonathan Rosenbaum, *Essential Cinema: On the Necessity of Film Canons* (Baltimore, MD: Johns Hopkins University Press, 2004), p. 270.

16. Frederic Raphael, *Eyes Wide Open: A Memoir of Stanley Kubrick* (New York: Ballantine, 1999), p. 160. Subsequent quotations are from this edition, and page numbers are indicated in the text.

17. Frederic Raphael further discusses the film (indicating his contempt for Cruise and Kidman, whom he describes as 'coldly calculating') in 'The Pumpkinification of Stanley K.', in Geoffrey Cocks, James Diedrick and Glenn Perusek, *Depth of Field: Stanley Kubrick* (Madison: University of Wisconsin Press, 1961), pp. 62–73.

18. Carl Schorske, *Fin-de-Siècle Vienna: Politics and Culture* (New York: Vintage, 1981), p. 223.

19. For additional discussion of this topic, see Peter Lowenberg, 'Freud, Schnitzler, and *Eyes Wide Shut*', in Cocks *et al.*, *Depth of Field*, pp. 255–79.

20. Michel Chion, *Eyes Wide Shut*, trans. Trista Selous (London: BFI, 2002), pp. 70–6. All further references are to this edition, and page numbers are indicated in the text.

21. Christian Appelt, 'The Craft of Seeing', in Reichmann and Flagge (eds), *Stanley Kubrick*, p. 261.

22. N. C. Menon, 'Kubrick's *Eyes Wide Shut* slights Hinduism, feel US Indians', *The Hindustan Times* (26 July 1999), <www.media-watch.org/articles/0799/220.html>

23. Tim Kreider, 'Introducing Sociology: A Review of *Eyes Wide Shut*', in Cocks *et al.*, *Depth of Field*, pp. 280–97.

24. Celestino Deleyto, '1999, A Closet Odyssey: Sexual Discourses in *Eyes Wide Shut*', <www.atlantisjournal.org/HTML%20Files/Tables%20of%20contents/28.1%20(2006).htm>

Part Six

EPILOGUE

I. Afterthoughts

In the absence of a grand synthesis or a key to Kubrick's work, which I believe would be impossible, it may be useful to offer some remarks on the themes that have emerged from this study. From the beginning I've emphasised that Kubrick's position as an author is paradoxical and almost unique. For most of his career he seemed both inside and outside the American film industry. In some ways he might be compared to Martin Scorsese or Woody Allen, who made their home in New York rather than Hollywood; but Kubrick, after shooting three early pictures in California, moved much further than Scorsese and Allen from the centres of US entertainment and managed to keep a greater control as producer. Even though his career was enabled by historical conditions – the breakdown of the classic studio system, the advent of 'art' cinema, the rise in foreign productions of American movies and so forth – his position in history is unusual. He can't be placed among the classic auteurs, or among the New York television directors who entered movies in the 1950s and 1960s or among the directors of the 'New Hollywood'. Part of the aura surrounding his name and much of the argument I've made for his late-modernist attributes derives from his special status and apparently aloof individuality, coupled with the sense that nothing in his films (with the exception of *Spartacus*) happened unless he allowed it to happen.

Unlike many directors, Kubrick never suffered the experience of having his projects re-cut, re-shot, or abandoned by the organisations that financed and distributed them. *Dr. Strangelove*, *2001* and *The Shining* were slightly revised after their premieres, but Kubrick did the revisions. He left no 'director's cuts' or alternative versions to signify a conflict between the artist and the money men. By the end of his career, the US movie industry was moving into the digital era and being absorbed into home entertainment, but Kubrick continued to make personal films in his own style, eschewing the tight framing and skittish editing typical of movies in the age of Avid technology. Although his films were sometimes strikingly different from one another and derived from a variety of literary sources, his career as a whole was unified by his stylistic, emotional and intellectual concerns, and in qualitative terms the level of his achievement was remarkably consistent – more like a writer or painter than a movie director.

Almost from the beginning, Kubrick was a total film-maker who combined the sensibility of a literary intellectual with the technical expertise of a photographer/editor and the instincts of a showman. The strength of his work came from his ability to link together these and other apparently irreconcilable oppositions. He had a sensitive understanding that movies are a medium of light and sound, but at the same time, his films were characterised by novelistic or theatrical word-play. He disavowed the old Hollywood codes of lighting to such a degree that even *2001* and *Barry Lyndon* owe something to his early experience as a street photographer; and yet his visual 'realism' was counterbalanced by his interest in myth, fairy tales and the Freudian unconscious. A dialectic or tension between the rational and irrational can be seen everywhere in his work, so that he usually leaves the impression of a fastidious, highly controlled or 'cool' technician dealing with absurd, violent or sexually 'hot' material. As one instance, consider the characteristic 'tunnel' shots that I and other critics have noticed in his films, some of which are vividly spectacular (Davy's nightmare in *Killer's Kiss*; Colonel Dax's walk down the trench in *Paths of Glory*; the B-52 hurtling between mountains in *Dr. Strangelove*; Bowman's journey through the star gate in *2001*; Danny Torrance's exploration of the hotel hallways in *The Shining*); and others fairly simple or ordinary (a car moving down a foggy road at the beginning of *Lolita*; a nurse rolling dinner down a hospital corridor in *A Clockwork Orange*; Lord Bullingdon advancing uneasily along the entrance to a men's drinking and gambling room in *Barry Lyndon*; Sergeant Hartman reviewing a line of recruits in *Full Metal Jacket*; Bill and Alice Harford hurriedly walking along their apartment hallway as they prepare to leave for a party in *Eyes Wide Shut*). Most of these shots involve a camera with a wide-angle lens moving forward or backward along a corridor of some kind; but Kubrick seems less interested in the specific technique than in the quality of the image itself, which can be achieved by various means. He creates the sensation of a series of lines sharply converging towards a distant horizon and of a steady, smooth, fairly rapid movement towards or away from a vanishing point, which is sometimes obscured by fog, smoke or a turning hallway. The image is orderly in its composition, pleasurably dynamic in its streamlined movement and almost phallic in its energy; but at the same time, either overtly or very subtly, it generates a feeling of anxiety, as if we were moving forward or backward through a demonic space that might burst open into something threatening or unknown.

This orderly presentation of a strange, unnerving energy is typical of Kubrick's work, but in intellectual terms his career involves not so much a coherent world view as a trajectory, an interaction of his social, technological and aesthetic interests with historical forces. At the deepest level, one key to his art can be found in the emotional qualities of his films, which I've argued are strongly marked with grotesque effects. He makes toilet jokes; he uses actors who have eccentric faces and performing styles; he puts masks on the players or encourages them to behave like caricatures; and he repeatedly blurs the distinction between the animate and inanimate by showing us mannequins, dolls, figures in wheel-chairs or computers that seem alive. Running beneath all these things is an anxiety about the body – its secretions, its orifices, its inevitable decay and death – mingled with a deri-sive sense of humour, so that the audience is caught somewhere between shock and laughter. Beginning with *Lolita*, the films also tend to swerve unpredictably between different modes or tonal qualities, creating a grotesque clash between acting styles or between realism and black comedy. Kubrick is essentially a satirist whose subject is human folly or barbarism; in the interest of satire, he's drawn to a family of 'estranging' effects – the grotesquely mis-shapen, the uncanny, the fantastic, the Kafkaesque – and he repeatedly conjoins methodical orderliness and horrific absurdity.

Kubrick's treatment of male sexuality, one of his leading subjects, is nearly always inflected with darkly psychoanalytic themes, but like Freud he was capable of hard-won respect for marriage. His attitude towards science and machines is equally complex, and it interacts in interesting ways with the social and sexual implications of his films. One of the cinema's foremost technicians and engineers, Kubrick was well grounded in physics and mathematics and obviously attracted to a kind of speculative, scientific futurism. In *2001*, he suggests that humanity may be evolving towards pure machine intelligence, leav-ing behind its grotesque organic shell and finding a kind of immortality; but in *A Clockwork Orange* he offers a nightmare view of a 'mechanical', reified society in which sexuality becomes a reflex and art a commodified stimulus. As his career progresses, his romantic identification with the criminal as a kind of artist or elite outsider (as evidenced in *The Killing*, *Lolita* and *A Clockwork Orange*) is increasingly shadowed by his social pessimism, and partly for this reason it's difficult to say exactly what political position his films occupy. His career began with a photograph of a news vendor mourning the death of F. D. R., a hero to his family and to most New Yorkers in the 1940s, but the image was despairing, marking the end of an era and the beginning of what would become a Cold War. Kubrick's subse-quent films, made in the period of the Cuban missile crisis, the Vietnam War and the increasingly reactionary drift in US politics, convey liberal, libertarian, anarchic and, in some respects, conservative attitudes; the conservative impulses, however, might be said to dominate in the sense that there is very little room in his work for utopian idealism. The exception to the rule might be in certain of his uses of myth or fairy tale, as in *2001* or in the boy's victory over a menacing adult in *The Shining*, but I would hesitate to call either film optimistic.

All these issues seem to me to coalesce in one of Kubrick's most ambitious projects, *A. I. Artificial Intelligence*, which was brought to the screen by Steven Spielberg a couple of years after Kubrick's death. In lieu of any further summary and as a way of achieving some sort of closure, I now want to offer a fairly wide-ranging meditation on that film, in the process moving beyond the subject of Kubrick as auteur. My discussion takes a different form than previous chapters on individual pictures, but it engages with some of the same topics. Like the book as a whole, it begins by emphasising the theme of death – the death of both an individual and a period in film history – as well as the problem of emotional affect.

II. Love and Death in *A. I. Artificial Intelligence*

At the end of the Steven Spielberg/Stanley Kubrick production of *A. I. Artificial Intelligence* (2001), a blond, innocent-looking boy, played by the remarkable child actor Haley Joel Osment, goes to bed with his beautiful, dark-haired mother, played by the equally remarkable Frances O'Connor. The two are alone in what looks like a California-modern house located somewhere beyond the city. Significantly absent are the boy's father and brother, who, much earlier in the film, caused the boy to be sent away from home. The day is fading, suffusing the room with earthen colours. 'I really ought to be tucking *you* in,' the mother says as her son covers her with a bedspread. 'How strange, I can hardly keep my eyes open … Such a beautiful day!' In close-up, she gazes adoringly at the boy. 'I love you, David,' she says. 'I *do* love you. I have *always* loved you.' A reverse-angle shows the boy smiling through tears and embracing her. On the soundtrack, a voice-of-god narrator tells us that this 'was the everlasting moment [David] had been waiting for, and the moment had passed, for Monica was sleeping'. Dissolve to an overhead shot of the boy crawling into bed, where he lies on his back next to his mother, who is posed almost like a stone figure atop a catafalque. The boy blissfully closes his eyes, the room grows dark, a John Williams piano score reminiscent of Schubert rises on the soundtrack and the camera begins craning back and away. The narrator speaks again, as if reading the last lines from a child's bedtime story: 'So David went to sleep. And for the first time in his life, he went to that place where dreams are born.' The camera continues craning back, moving out of the bedroom window, and we see that the sleeping couple is being watched over by a robotic teddy bear at the foot of the bed, who moves his furry arms and head in benediction. Outside, blue night has fallen and, as the camera cranes up and away, the lights in the house go out one by one.

Several intelligent critics and not a few friends whose opinions I value have said that they dislike this scene and the movie as a whole, finding in it a sentimentality they associate with Spielberg and a pseudo-profundity they associate with Kubrick.[1] Even when they express admiration for one or both directors, they complain that the teddy bear is no E. T. and the bedtime-story narration no substitute for the cinematic razzle-dazzle of *2001*. I've heard reports of audiences laughing at the end of *A. I.*, and I once encountered a couple on an elevator who had just returned from the film and were grumbling about the time they had wasted. As for me, I've watched it five times, and on each occasion I've been moved to copious tears. I should perhaps note that as I grow older I seem to shed tears more easily in the movies, even when I know my emotional buttons are being pushed; then, too, the last scene in *A. I.* probably has a personal resonance for me, because my mother

died when I was about the age that the boy appears to be in the story. At any rate, David's cry of 'Mommy! Where are you?' at a point near the end, when he returns home after a millennium of longing, is voiced in a tone of such desperate excitement and anxiety that it wrenches my heart. In the concluding shot-reverse shot, when he hears his mother's declaration of love and embraces her, I weep – and I feel in tune with the film, because tears are one of its most important motifs. To those who are unmoved, I can only say, in the words of William Butler Yeats, who is quoted twice in *A. I.*, 'the world's more full of weeping than you can understand'.

But would laughter or at least a wry smile be totally inappropriate? Despite all the fairy-tale sweetness, David is experiencing a kind of Freudian wet dream. The film is fully aware of this implication; it tells a straightforward Oedipal story containing several overt references to Freud – as in an earlier scene when David surprises his mother in the bathroom, where she is sitting on a toilet reading a book entitled *Freud and Women* (a volume Frances O'Connor chose for the shot). Throughout, the Disneyish atmosphere is inflected by an art-cinema irony. As in Kubrick's *The Shining*, we get Freud with revisionist vengeance: Father isn't simply an imaginary danger but a real one – a deadly threat who needs to be expunged so that the son can fulfil his romance with Mother. The closing moments of the film also seem to confirm Freud's ideas about Thanatos, neatly linking the fairy tale's drive towards closure with the human death drive, or with what Freud called the 'conservative' instincts, through which we strive to return to 'an old state of things, an initial state from which the living entity has departed and to which it is striving to return'.[2] To make things more complicated, another irony runs deeper, threatening to undercut even Freud. As everyone who is familiar with *A. I.* knows, the story takes place in the far distant future, thus producing the sense of 'cognitive estrangement' that Darko Suvin and other theorists have equated with literary science fiction.[3] David isn't a 'real' boy but a 'mecha' – a computerised replicant, operating with relative autonomy, who is programmed by a scientist and an army of corporate technicians to feel love for his organic 'mother' and to want, like some futuristic Pinocchio, to become truly human. Hard-wired to experience Oedipal desire, he can weep and feel joy or fear, but he can't pee and can't eat spinach or any other kind of food. He has lived on the earth for thousands of years and will never grow older. He can dream, but in one sense he dreams of electric sheep. As for the mother he loves with single-minded obsession, she herself in the final scene is a kind of simulacrum or reconstruction with a limited memory, brought to life for a single day and awakened like Sleeping Beauty by virtue of a preserved lock of her hair, which was frozen for centuries at the bottom of the sea. Even the house is a simulacrum, fashioned by other robots on the basis of David's memory bank.

Perhaps the ultimate irony is that, while the scene concludes a film that poses the question of what it means to be human, while it effectively dramatises childhood trauma and loss, and while it stirs me profoundly, it also makes its own status as artifice quite evident. What am I crying about, except a fantasy staged by robots for the benefit of an artificial boy who was invented by a corporation; and what am I watching, except a movie manufactured by a horde of Hollywood technicians from another corporation? The credits at the end of *A. I.* list scores of technical specialists, headed by robot designer Stan Winston, effects supervisors Michael Lantieri, Dennis Muren and Scott Farrar, and digital experts from Industrial Light and Magic and Pacific Data Images. Because of these contributors, I sometimes find it difficult to trust the evidence I see on the screen. For example, the teddy bear gently moving his arms and head in the closing scene is not just a robotic 'super-toy', as the story would have it, but also a 'special effect' – a doll animated partly by robotics and partly by computer-generated imagery (CGI). It was never fully there in front of the camera, occupying what is sometimes called the 'pro-cinematic' space, even though it forms part of the *mise en scène* in such realistic fashion that it's almost indistinguishable from the real players.

A. I. was released in a year when Stephen Hawking told his fellow scientists that they should begin developing advanced forms of genetic engineering to compensate for 'Moore's Law', or the theory that computers will soon surpass human intelligence. That same year, children could purchase an electronic toy resembling a live insect; Sony Corporation announced SDR-4X, a humanoid robot with an extensive vocabulary who is designed to live with people in their homes; and a war in Afghanistan was fought with the assistance of robotic aircraft called 'drones'. Meanwhile, Hollywood created a new category for the Academy Awards to honour feature-length animated films that use CGI, and digital animators around the world spoke repeatedly of their desire to achieve the 'holy grail' of computer-generated 'synthespians' who seamlessly interact with live players on the screen. No doubt *A. I.* is symptomatic of all these events, but it has a special relationship to computerised imagery, which is the most spectacular of a series of digital technologies that have changed the manufacture and look of contemporary movies. A non-photographic or semi-photographic special effect, CGI brings into question the status of visual evidence, apparently lending credence to Jean Baudrillard's theory of the simulacrum, and reinforcing fears, such as the ones expressed in a recent book by Paul Virillo, that under postmodernity the individual's relation to reality is collapsing.[4] One of the most intelligent writers on the subject, Sean Cubitt, doubts that CGI actually functions in this way, and I would agree;[5] nevertheless, as Cubitt notes, the digital has been charged in some quarters with being guilty of 'the murder of reality and of the human' (*Cubitt*, p. 125). How logical, then, that *A. I.* should make extensive use of CGI. The film is about the robotic post-human, and it uses a technique that's occasionally described as 'post-cinematic'. Am I weeping for the death of David's mother, for the death of humans, for the death of photography, or for the death of movies?

A. I. and CGI

To answer the question above, which by no means exhausts my interest in *A. I.*, it may help to briefly consider another emotionally powerful and equally maternal scene from an older and ostensibly quite different Hollywood film. Three-quarters of the way through the Samuel Goldwyn/William Wyler production of *The Best Years of Our Lives* (1946), a World War II veteran named Homer prepares for bed, and in the process exposes his war wounds to the camera. Homer is a former enlisted man who has lost both of his hands and who skilfully manipulates a pair of mechanical hooks attached to his wrists. By day he's self-sufficient, lighting his own cigarettes, eating with a knife and fork and playing chopsticks on the piano. In the evening before going to bed, however, he needs his loving but inarticulate father to help him remove the hooks, and he feels helpless and unmanned. At one point, he invites his former high-school sweetheart, who still loves him, to visit his bedroom and see his condition. For me personally, this is one of the most poignant moments in the history of Hollywood, in part because of my knowledge that the sailor is played by Harold Russell, an amateur actor who had lost his hands in a training accident during the war. This fact was well known to the film's original audience. *Best Years* was a highly publicised feature, second only to *Gone with the Wind* (1939) in its initial box-office profits, and it won seven Academy Awards, two of which went to Russell. But the emotional efficacy of the scene also derives from the dignity and discretion with which it is staged by Wyler and photographed by Gregg Toland. The camera stands completely still, at a respectful middle distance, viewing the two actors on the same plane, without the elaborate deep-focus perspective that was the hallmark of Toland's style. When Russell removes his hooks and puts on his pyjama top, Wyler doesn't try to analyse the action with shot-reverse shots or close-ups. Non-diegetic music can be heard throughout, but there is no dramatic lighting and no tricks of costume or special effects. In other words, although the film is obviously fictional, it wants the camera to bear witness to history. Nearly everything conspires to show us that the sailor has no hands.

I've often shown this scene in the classroom in conjunction with André Bazin's famous essay on the ontology of the photographic image, in which Bazin argues that photography has an 'objective' quality (today's film theorists tend to say 'indexical'), since 'between the originating subject and its reproduction there intervenes only the instrumentality of a nonliving agent'. For the first time in history, Bazin tells us, 'an image of the world is formed automatically, without the creative intervention of man [sic]'. The paradox of the situation, at least insofar as Bazin is concerned, is that the purely mechanical becomes the servant of the organic. Photography, he says, has the power to affect us 'like a phenomenon in nature, like a flower or a snowflake whose vegetable or earthly origins are an inseparable part of their beauty'.[6]

Bazin was a great admirer of *The Best Years of Our Lives*, which he praised in another essay for its self-effacing 'neutrality and transparency of style'.[7] From our current perspective it's possible to see both his arguments and Wyler's film as symptoms of an international movement towards humanist realism in the decade after the war – a phenomenon determined by the political and social temper of the times, and made possible by new forms of recording technology. But in a still larger context, as R. L. Rutsky has shown, theories about photography have long involved a distinction between the organic and the mechanical that has contradictory implications, sometimes reinforcing humanism and sometimes threatening it. Behind the invention of cinema, Rutsky notes, there is both a 'Mummy myth' of the kind postulated by Bazin, who sometimes speaks of photography as if it were a means of embalming time and forestalling death, and a 'Frankenstein myth' of the kind suggested by Lev Kuleshov, whose experiments with montage involved a sort of cutting and reassembling of the human body.[8] Thus, Susan Sontag can argue that photography is 'treacherous' because photographic images 'do not seem to be statements about the world so much as pieces of it'.[9] Even when bodily anxiety or a fear of violence against nature isn't present in theoretical writings, the photographic machine is often placed in contested relation to the human sensorium – in Dziga Vertov's manifestoes, for example, where we repeatedly encounter contrasts between the camera and the human eye: 'I am kino-eye, I am a mechanical eye. I, a machine, show you the world as only I can see it.' Along similar lines, early photographers such as Eadweard Muybridge and E. J. Marey, who were motivated less by the aesthetic desire for representation than by a technological/scientific urge, always treated photography as an extension and improvement of the eye, or as what Rutsky calls 'a kind of prosthesis' (p. 31).

The scene from *Best Years* is about prosthesis, and it uses sophisticated camera technology in an apparently artless way, giving us empirical evidence of a wounded human body.

Whenever I show it to contemporary students, however, they seem sceptical of the idea that photography has an indexical relation to the world, and they tend to doubt that the actor who plays the sailor in the film really has no hands. One reason for their scepticism, I suspect, is that they've never heard of Russell, and they've all seen Robert Zemeckis's *Forrest Gump* (1994), which contains several scenes involving a paraplegic Vietnam veteran acted by Gary Sinise, whose legs have been imperceptibly 'erased' by means of CGI. The effect in *Gump* is at least technically similar to an earlier Zemeckis film, *Death Becomes Her* (1992), in which digital imaging is used for comic and spectacular ends, enabling Meryl Streep's head to go spinning around on her neck and Goldie Hawn to carry on conversations after a gaping hole has been blown through her stomach. The major difference is that the trick with the wounded veteran in *Gump*, like the majority of trick shots in narrative movies since the beginning of cinema, is intended to be invisible. To find an example of an invisible trick prior to the digital age, we need only consider another moment in *The Best Years of Our Lives*. Just prior to the scene in which Homer invites his sweetheart up to his room, he looks at some old high-school photographs of himself, showing him passing a football and dribbling a basketball. If you study the photos, you'll notice that they've been doctored by the film-makers, who have pasted Harold Russell's head onto the bodies of young athletes.

Best Years relies upon our willingness to ignore such details in the interest of social realism. By contrast, the computer-enhanced scenes in a movie like *Death Becomes Her* feel more like a cartoon or a *trompe l'oeil*; and, as Sean Cubitt remarks, 'despite its name, *trompe l'oeil* wants not to trick, but to be discovered in the act of trickery' (p. 127). We can, in fact, make distinctions among degrees or kinds of disbelief that special effects elicit. Some want to be accepted as 'invisible' even though they look artificial to the knowing eye (matte printing, glass shots and process screens in classic Hollywood); some deliberately call attention to themselves as 'movie magic' (dream sequences, expressionist distortions of the visible world and cataclysms in action-adventure movies); and some are unnoticed or completely undetectable (the arched eyebrow that was 'painted' by computer onto the face of Jodie Foster for a close-up in Zemeckis's *Contact* [1997]).

Given the ubiquity and historical importance of special effects, my own students are inclined to accept Christian Metz's notion that all cinema is essentially a trick, beginning with the phenomenon of persistence of vision upon which the medium is founded.[10] They also tend to agree with Tom Gunning and André Gaudreault that cinematic spectatorship was originally founded on a kind of incredulity or sceptical wonder; hence, there was no radical difference between the way early viewers regarded the Lumières' train arriving at a station and the way they regarded Melies's magic act, since both experiences involved a sense of astonishment in the face of what was known to be a mechanical illusion.[11] In my own view, the situation is more complicated. The old theoretical distinction between movies as document and movies as magic makes sense as a description of two film-making practices, and the documentary practice isn't threatened by digital technology. In fact, digital cameras have opened up vast new possibilities for film-makers who work in the tradition of neo-realism or documentary, and who want to explore the camera's ability to function more or less autonomously, recording accidents or contingency in everyday life. It should nevertheless be noted that, even when we're treated as incredulous spectators who are aware that some kind of visual trick has been projected onto the screen, CGI seems to undermine documentary authority in the entertainment film. It brings movies closer to the spirit of comic books and animation, it makes some tricks less easily detectable and it threatens a certain discourse about realism and humanism in the cinema. Perhaps it's no accident that CGI has often been used to show morphing androids and missing body parts, as if the world were coming apart before our eyes, or as if the mechanical were supplanting and not simply serving the organic.

A. I. is filled with such moments – for example, in the scene in which David's face melts after he eats spinach, or in the scenes of the 'Flesh Fair', in which CGI is used to show robots with their humanoid surfaces ripped away and their arms and legs torn asunder. (Spielberg hired actual amputees to perform in several shots at the Fair, but he also used a full range of technical tricks; at one point we see a robot played by an African-American amputee picking up a white mechanical hand from a junk pile of spare parts and inserting it onto the stump of his wrist.) One of the most spectacular of these effects occurs at the very beginning of the film, and is clearly designed to showcase CGI's ability to split actors apart and blur the distinctions between human and mechanical. Professor Hobby (William Hurt) calls a meeting of his corporation in order to demonstrate the strengths and limitations of their new 'artificial being' – an attractive and compliant robot 'secretary' named 'Sheila'. At the end of the demonstration, Hobby orders Sheila to 'open', whereupon her face slides apart, revealing an inner network of electronic wiring. As viewers of the film, we recognise that Sheila is played by a flesh-and-blood actor, and that CGI has been used to morph her face into a machine image; the illusion, however, is almost perfect, and is neatly capped when the mechanical face re-closes like a jewel box. Hobby remarks that this new model is only a toy, and goes on to explain his vision of creating 'a mecha of a qualitatively different order'. As he speaks, we see Sheila take out a compact and adjust her make-up. Dissolve to a scene that takes place twenty months later, in which Monica, the flesh-and-blood mother played by Frances O'Connor, takes out a compact and adjusts her own make-up.

In one sense the trick shot of Sheila's face isn't unusual, because movies have always enjoyed splitting actors apart. The first special effect is usually said to have been the Edison Company's *The Execution of Mary Queen of Scots* (1895), which employed a 'substitution shot' to show an actor being beheaded. (The camera was stopped, the actor playing Mary was replaced by a dummy and the camera was restarted to show the executioner chopping off the dummy's head.) Digital effects clearly have their own phenomenology and their favoured images, especially in scenes involving impossible 'camera movements,' morphing shapes and crowds of figures running across landscapes; they can also show us purely electronic, non-verisimilar images that are unlike anything we've seen before. In Hollywood, however, they tend to be used for exactly the same purposes as older technology like matte shots, optical printers and rear or front projection – that is, to achieve magical transformations or to combine verisimilar images in order to produce a kind of invisible collage. In this sense, *A. I.* is typical of Hollywood. Even so, because *A. I.* is explicitly about the distinction between the 'real' and the 'artificial', and because it depicts a future in which humans are replaced by robots, it seems a particularly appropriate use of CGI. Indeed, the film as a whole can be understood as an allegory of cinema, involving a somewhat contradictory attitude towards the future of the medium.

Notice, moreover, that even though *A. I.* envisions the death of the human, it invites us to understand its creation in humanist terms, as a kind of dialogue between two auteurs about the relationship between the organic, the mechanical and the spiritual. In the history of Hollywood there have been several instances when two celebrated directors of different temperaments worked on the same picture – Murnau and Flaherty on *Tabu* (1931), Hawks and Wyler on *Come and Get It* (1936), Mamoulian and Preminger on *Laura* (1944) – but none is more interesting or well publicised than *A. I.*: on the one hand we have Kubrick, a symbol of mid-century cool, a devotee of black humour, a technophile influenced by street photography and Wellesian expressionism and an intellectual whose movie career was partly built on challenges to censorship; on the other hand we have Spielberg, a populist and postmodernist who alternates retro-styled adventure movies with liberal projects about Important Themes. Spielberg may have written and directed *A. I.*, but Kubrick conceived the idea and worked on it intermittently for over almost two decades before his death. Kubrick is therefore figured as the ghost in the machine and Spielberg as his eulogist. Some commentary on the two seems inevitable as a way of accounting for *A. I.*'s particular way of achieving closure and its unusual commentary on gods, humans and robots. It may also help to answer another of my questions: why am I crying in a movie for which Stanley Kubrick is at least partly responsible?

Puppet Masters

A. I. originated shortly after the release of Kubrick's *2001*, a film that suggests that machines might someday achieve an *improvement* over humankind, and a film that has continuing relevance in a period when computer intelligence and biological engineering have brought us to the point where the definition of the human is no longer clear. Kubrick's outer-space epic had been inspired by a short story and *A. I.* began in much the same fashion, with Brian Aldiss's 'Super-Toys Last All Summer Long', which appeared in *Harper's Bazaar* in 1969. The Aldiss story depicts a future when two-thirds of the earth's population is starving, when birth-control laws are enacted to protect resources and when engineers and corporate executives live in luxurious but entirely artificial enclaves fitted with electronic windows that emit hyper-realistic scenes of sunlit gardens. Monica Swinton, the childless wife of the managing director of Synthank Corporation, has been provided with one of the company's most advanced products – a 'synthetic life form' named David, who looks and behaves like a real boy, and whose best friend is an electronic teddy bear. Unfortunately, Monica can't develop a truly maternal attitude towards David. Her husband nevertheless announces a programme to market more such products, which he predicts will surpass the company's recent success with a line of miniature dinosaurs. Meanwhile, David uses crayons to compose a series of unfinished messages to Monica ('Dear Mummy, I love you and Daddy and the sun is shining –' 'Dear Mummy, I'm your little boy and not Teddy and I love you but Teddy –'.) At the end of the story, Monica discovers that she has won the parenthood lottery from the Ministry of Population and will be allowed to become pregnant. David, who will probably be abandoned, has a conversation with his teddy bear: 'I suppose Mummy and Daddy are real, aren't they?' 'You ask such silly questions,' the bear replies. 'Nobody knows what *real* really means.'

In the early 1990s, Kubrick collaborated with Aldiss in an attempt to turn this story into a film, and at various points he commissioned other writers, including Arthur Clarke, Ian Watson and Bob Shaw. He was never fully satisfied with the results, but three of his objectives remained constant. First, he wanted the story to be told from the point of view of robots, for whom it would elicit sympathy; as Aldiss remarked, 'Stanley embraces android technology and thinks it might eventually take over – and be an improvement over the human race.'[12] Second, he wanted to structure the story along the lines of Carlo Collodi's nineteenth-century fairy tale, *Pinocchio* (1883), which he would subject to what Roman Jacobson terms a 'metaphoric transformation'. Instead of a hand-carved Italian street urchin with an unusual nose, we would be given an industrially manufactured product resembling an innocent and rather suburban American boy; the boy's adventures, however, would be loosely based on those of Collodi's puppet. (Many of the characters and incidents in the completed film retain this quality: Professor Hobby, the Blue Fairy, Gigolo Joe, the Flesh Fair, the visit to Rouge City, the swarm of fish that convey David underwater, etc.) Finally, he wanted to unify Collodi's picaresque tale by treating the boy's adventures in Freudian terms, as an Oedipal quest.

Because he loved high-tech, and because he anticipated a lengthy production schedule, Kubrick actually tried to have a special-effects crew build a robot to play the role of David.[13] This proved unworkable, but a new idea occurred to him when he saw Spielberg's *Jurassic Park* (1993), in which ground-breaking CGI effects are used to create dinosaurs that move freely through a Bazinian *mise en scène*, looking rather like the ones made by the fictional Synthank in Aldiss's story. During the same period, computer animators were producing 'synthespians' or 'vactors' to play extras and stunt roles in live-action movies, and videogame developers were experimenting with characters that possessed Artificial Intelligence. The time was ripe for 'virtual humans', and Spielberg's film suggested how they might be created. As it happened, Kubrick and Spielberg had already developed a friendship and were in regular communication. Thus, when Kubrick grew more frustrated and uncertain about *A. I.*, he suggested that he might serve as producer and Spielberg as writer/director of the film. (When the film was eventually released, Kubrick was, in fact, listed as producer. Spielberg wrote the screenplay from a ninety-page treatment prepared for Kubrick by Ian Watson; he also consulted some 600 drawings Kubrick had commissioned from Chris Baker, and he hired Baker to work on the Hollywood production.)

Critics tend to describe Kubrick as 'cold' and Spielberg as 'warm', but, as I've already tried to explain in regard to Kubrick, that claim seems oversimplified. It's better to say that Kubrick was a fastidious stylist who favoured slow, measured, sometimes over-the-top performances and crystal-clear imagery, whereas Spielberg is a flashy rhetorician, more inclined to sentiment, who works with dazzling speed and who produces fast-paced narratives with a somewhat garish and smoky look. (The garish atmosphere is exacerbated by his photographer on *A. I.*, Janusz Kaminski, who loves to show beams of light penetrating through studio fog.) In any case, the two figures converge in their love of movie magic, and Spielberg was good 'casting' for this film because he brought to *A. I.* a vast knowledge of digital technology, a gift for telling stories about suburban families, and a certain affinity with the Disney aspects of the story; indeed 'When You Wish upon a Star', the theme from Disney's *Pinocchio* (1940), had figured importantly in *Close Encounters of the Third Kind* (1977).

There is, in fact, a sort of lineal relationship between Collodi, Disney and Spielberg. Although the romantic movement taught us to think of children's stories as simple, unaffected and genuine, Collodi's fascinating, often dark narrative about a puppet who wants to become a boy belongs to a period when the Brothers Grimm, Hans Christian Andersen and Rudyard Kipling were bringing the European fairy and folk tale to the apex of literary respectability. As folklore historian Jack Zipes points out, this was also the time when modern nation-states were 'cultivating particular types of literature as commensurate expressions of national cultures'.[14] The nineteenth-century tales were derived from a much earlier oral tradition of *Zaubermärchen*, but they were addressed to the bourgeoisie and were part of a struggle for ideological hegemony. For similar reasons, the fairy tale figured importantly in early cinema, particularly in Méliès's *féeries* and in Porter's *Jack and the Beanstalk*. It remained for Disney in the late 1930s and early 1940s to appropriate the genre and turn it into a truly middle-class American form, or into what Zipes describes as a Horatio-Alger myth about patriarchy, perseverance, cleanliness, hard work and the rise to success. Disney's films were made by a Taylorised industry, but they celebrated the individual imagination and appeared to spring from Disney's own brow. The lovely princesses, handsome princes and cutely anthropomorphised animals were treated as Walt's puppets, even when they were drawn by a host of animators and supervised by gifted directors like Ben Sharpsteen, who was in charge of the adaptation of *Pinocchio*. But to expose Disney's ideological aims and modes of production, as several writers have done, is not to break his spell, for the classic Disney films are superbly crafted narratives, and like their sources they have a genius for tapping into elemental anxieties. The grinning witch addressing the camera in *Snow White* (1937), the death of the mother in *Bambi* (1942), the abandonment of the child in *Dumbo* (1940), the transformation of Lampwick in *Pinocchio* – these events are burned into the screen memories of generations of children, and they can never be expunged by happy endings.

For his own part, Spielberg has repeatedly drawn upon the Disney films, evoking nostalgia for middle-class Americana and encouraging audiences to regress into childhood; it's as if the pop culture of the 1930s, 1940s and 1950s offers him a repository of 'authentic' materials, roughly analogous to what gothic architecture offered the English romantics during the industrial revolution. A talented director of stories about monstrous predators, he is also sharply attuned to the anxieties of childhood, which he treats in affecting and ultimately optimistic fashion. Thus, Spielberg's version of *A. I.* eschews the dark sexuality Kubrick had intended to convey through the Joe Gigolo character, and it frequently alludes in affectionate ways to classic Hollywood, reminding us not only of Sharpsteen's *Pinocchio* and *Dumbo*, but also of *The Wizard of Oz* (1939) and the Astaire/Kelly musicals. Everywhere it shows its indebtedness to comic books and animated films and, in line with contemporary practice for the Disney Company, it uses celebrity actors (Robin Williams, Ben Kingsley, Meryl Streep and Chris Rock) as voices for the CGI figures.

One is tempted to speculate about whether Spielberg could have experienced an anxiety of influence during the making of *A. I.*, or whether he and Kubrick, who were undoubtedly friends, were at any point engaged in a psychic contest with one another. I doubt this was the case and, even if it was, Spielberg seems to me to win the contest. Nevertheless, the last scene of *A. I.* isn't typical of Spielberg. Its particular mixture of sadness and intellectual irony feels less harmonious than dialectical, rather like a deconstruction of Spielberg's sentiment that somehow leaves all his emotional gestures in force. He, Kubrick, Aldiss and Ian Watson might be its authors, but none of them is its puppet master. To further account for the scene, we need to broaden our perspective, for *A. I.* is a film about the curious affinity between Artificial Intelligence and psychoanalysis, and it involves a good deal of metaphysical speculation about such big concepts as the self and God. The central themes of the film can be traced back to a long tradition of western philosophical idealism – to Plato, for example, who believed that human beings are puppets formed by a *demiurge*; to Renaissance neo-Platonists like Marsilio Ficino, who argued that the visible world is a kind of machine that mediates between earth and heaven; and to romantic authors like Heinrich von Kleist, who proposed that theatrical marionettes have spirit or soul. This quasi-religious tradition, which provided a basis for most of western high art prior to the age of Enlightenment, is intriguingly discussed in Victoria Nelson's *The Secret Life of Puppets*, a book that was published in the same year as *A. I.*'s first screenings. Nelson points out that there has been a resurgence of Platonism in our own day, but this time in pop-culture genres like science fiction or fantasy, where it often takes a sublimated or displaced form, allowing 'the benign supernatural' to emerge from the shadows of modernism's fascination with 'the demonic grotesque'.[15] As I hope to show, *A. I.* contributes to exactly this phenomenon, and could be described as one of its most emotionally forceful manifestations.

The Robot's Soul

Several viewers of *A. I.* have told me that they think the film should have ended earlier, at the point when David and Teddy travel far beneath the waters of global warming that engulf Manhattan, ultimately arriving at the remains of Coney Island. The old amusement park contains a kitschy theme park based on the characters and events in *Pinocchio*, and in its midst is a statue of the Blue Fairy. As soon as David arrives, however, a giant Ferris wheel pitches forward and crashes atop his amphibious helicopter, pinning it undersea. Mesmerised by the statue in front of him, David ignores his situation and begins to pray: 'Blue Fairy, please, please make me into a real boy!' As he incessantly repeats his prayer, the camera cranes backward, the image fades and the narrator tells us that David went on praying until the seas froze over.

This is certainly a more spectacular ending than the one we have, and more of a downer. For those of us who believe that David isn't really real, it sums up the film's 'Frankenstein' theme, showing how Professor Hobby's arrogance leads to the destruction of civilisation and the death of a pathetically artificial creature. It also seems to echo the closing of the first 'act' in *A. I.*'s narrative, when we see David abandoned at the bottom of his family swimming pool. The film might well have stopped at Coney Island, and for a moment it seems to; but then it starts up again, jumping 2,000 years into the future, where its third and final act brings other issues into focus. David has been engaged in an odyssey, albeit one in which he has never been distracted from a single, urgent goal; it seems appropriate, therefore, that he should be given a *nostos* in which, however briefly or ironically, he rejoins the woman he loves, banishes her suitors and reclaims his kingdom. The scene in which he and Monica sleep together is suffused with the gauzy, golden light of nostalgia, and is both triumphant and deeply sad. In some respects it may run counter to Stanley Kubrick's original intent, because one of its apparent aims is to suggest nostalgia not simply for childhood, but also for human imagination in a world of purely mechanical intelligence. It never quite achieves that aim, however, and as a result it has fascinating implications about Hollywood, about the machine as a bearer of life, and about the simulacrum as a mediator between matter and spirit.

The first of these implications is easy to explain, for what is David if not an emblem of Hollywood? He's an image of white male innocence and resourcefulness who touches my heart even when I know he's artificial; he's frozen in time and will never grow older; he's an illusion created by an actor, a director and a team of technical magicians; he's programmed to enact the Oedipal scenario; and, above all, he's a commodity – in this case a star personality or brand name, cleverly packaged by a corporation that plans to construct many more just like him. As Professor Hobby tells his staff at the beginning of the film, 'Ours will be a perfect child caught in a freeze frame . . . . Our little mecha will not only open up a compelling market, it will fill a great human need.' And as the baffled mother says to her husband when he brings David home as a sort of toy or gift who can function as a substitute child, 'He's so real, but he's not. But outside he just *looks* so real!'

Despite the fact that he isn't 'acted' by robotics or CGI, David is also an emblem of advanced technology and of an anxiety over the human body that Scott Bukatman finds at the heart of most science fiction (such an anxiety is clearly present in Kubrick's *2001*). The body, Bukatman writes, 'has long been the repressed content of science fiction, as the genre obsessively substitutes the rational for the corporeal, and the technological for the organic'.[16] In one sense, Spielberg reverses the process. He chooses not to animate David and thereby completely displace the organic because the illusion of David's human presence needs to be complete if he is to convince either the audience or the live-action characters in the film. Unlike Kubrick, who consistently found ways to alienate the audience, Spielberg wants us to identify strongly with his leading characters, and he knows that computer animation has yet to reach the stage where it can create truly believable human figures in major speaking roles. The most elaborate attempt to do so is *Final Fantasy* (2001), a feature-length sci-fi adventure modelled on videogames, which was released in the United States at almost the same moment as *A. I.*, and which, for all its use of CGI, looks waxen and stilted, seldom rising even to the level of *trompe l'oeil*. More recently, Robert Zemeckis has put Tom Hanks and several other actors into motion-capture suits for the computer-animated *Polar Express* (2004), in which the figures on the screen look almost dead. Even so, contemporary animators continue to speak of photo-realism as an attainable goal, and they sound as if they were trying to produce exactly the same psychological effect that young David has on his mother. According to John Lasseter, the director of the Pixar/Walt Disney company's computer-animated *Toy Story* (1995), 'I'm interested in creating a film with characters that people obviously know don't exist. But then they look at it and say, "It seems so real. I know it doesn't – but wait . . . . No, they can't be alive, no. Are they?"'[17]

The effect Lasseter describes is essentially that of good movie magic since the beginning of the medium, and also the effect of the commodity fetish, whose promise of 'real' gratification is always teasingly deferred. Where *A. I.* is concerned, however, both emotional identification with the leading character and engagement with movie magic are somewhat estranged, because David is explicitly shown as a machine and a commodity. The situation is similar to what we find in at least one version of the many scripts of *Blade Runner*, except that here the plot is reversed: the leading character is known to be artificial at the beginning and we're asked to accept him as human in the course of the story.[18] Haley Joel Osment's performance is especially interesting in this regard because *A. I.* requires him to start with a slightly digitalised or pantomimic style of acting, very similar to what the Russian futurists called 'bio-mechanics', and then to shift, at the moment when David's mother imprints his circuits with Oedipal desire, into an analogue, Stanislavskian style that reveals his 'inner' life. (Even in the final stage of his development, he never blinks his eyes.)

The important question posed by the last scene, in which the emotions expressed by Osment are particularly subtle and moving, is whether the film regards David's acquisition of so-called humanity as progress, regression or neither. This question isn't easily resolved. *A. I.* often uses the keywords of romantic idealism ('God', 'love', 'spirit', 'dreams' and 'genius'), but it submits these words to a certain amount of irony or scientific scepticism. At the beginning of the film Professor Hobby, who is both a Dr Frankenstein and a surrogate movie director, boasts that he is about to achieve a great leap forward by creating a 'mecha with a mind . . . who will love its parents'. He wants to produce many copies of this mecha for the marketplace, but he describes them in the rhetoric of pure romanticism: 'Love will be the key by which they acquire a kind of subconscious never before achieved, an inner world of metaphor, of intuition, of self motivation, of dreams.' Hobby descends from a long line of scientist-as-*demiurge* characters who have populated western culture since the Renaissance (famous examples in the modern period include the puppet masters in E. T. A. Hoffmann's supernatural tales, the fictional Thomas Edison in Villiers de l'Isle-Adam's *L'Eve future* and Rotwang in Fritz Lang's *Metropolis*) and, like most of his ancestors, he is treated unsympathetically. Despite his godlike role ('Didn't God create Adam to love him?'), he fails to see what we eventually learn – that robots, who until now have served purely instrumental needs as secretaries, cooks, nannies, entertainers and sex workers, *already* have an ability to love and to act in self-motivated ways.

When Teddy (who insists he's '*not* a toy') is forced by David's 'real-life' brother (who wears a mechanical brace on his legs) to make a choice between David and the brother, he suffers a psychological double bind that almost destroys his circuits; and when Gigolo Joe encounters David at the Flesh Fair, he deliberately chooses to befriend the boy and assist him. With the qualified exception of Monica, who suffers a crisis when she must abandon David, none of the humans in the film is as loving and sympathetic as the robots, and none is more inherently capable of feeling emotion. David may be different from other robots, but what makes him unusual isn't so much his ability to love as his ability to fill a prescribed role in the nuclear family. Unlike his fellow machines, he isn't created as a proletarian or a skilled worker in the service industries. Combining Agape and Eros, he both loves and is *in* love with Monica, and therefore aspires to *become* a particular kind of human. At this level he resembles the robot played by Robin Williams in a much less interesting film, *Bicentennial Man* (1999), who is possessed with a suicidal desire to become human, even to the point of experiencing mortality. We might say that his tragedy is that he wants to be something less than he is.

Like many humans, David has a fascination with magic and the supernatural, as when he encounters a kitschy statue of the Virgin Mary in Rouge City and wonders if she is the Blue Fairy. His friend Gigolo Joe explains that the statue is only a symbol of the humans' rather contemptible desire to know who made them. (One could also say that the statue, rather like a robot, is a simulacrum mediating between the divine and the earthly.) This issue never troubles David, who is concerned only with finding his mother and reclaiming her love. 'Mommy doesn't hate me, because I'm special and unique,' he says to Gigolo Joe. But when David travels to Manhattan and confronts his maker, he encounters a nightmarish form of mechanical reproduction in the service of serial commodities. Copies of himself are suspended on hooks along the walls of Hobby's corporation. 'I thought I was one of a kind,' David says to Hobby. 'My son was one of a kind,' Hobby replies. 'You are the *first* of a kind.' Hobby is already packaging scores of boys who resemble his dead son, and he plans to market them under the brand-name of 'David'. His workshop also contains packages for a female product named 'Darlene'. We can only guess what her story might be like (the film is far too Freudian to know for sure), but David's seems to end in a murderous assault on his mechanical twin, a revolt against the patriarch, an attempted suicide and a futile prayer to the Blue Fairy. Only after he's discovered under the ice by a future generation of robots does he have a chance to become real. 'These robots were originals,' one of the futuristic mechas says to the others when they remove David from the ice. 'They knew living people!' In a final twist, humanism and 'spirit' survive. Like a precious archeological find or a rare zoo animal, the robot boy is given special care by robots of the future, who bring his organic mother to life for a single day and fulfil his greatest wish.

The final section of the film was undoubtedly a problem for Spielberg, because it posits a situation beyond human understanding. Kubrick faced similar difficulties in the last segment of *2001*, which he wisely chose to keep ambiguous and non-verbal; but *A. I.* is further complicated by the fact that we need to see events from the radically different perspectives of a futuristic intelligence and a human child. Unfortunately, Spielberg chose to represent the technically advanced androids with a rather conventional design that looks a bit like a CGI version of the 'Grey', a pop-culture figure who has influenced the look of space aliens in almost every sci-fi movie after *Close Encounters of the Third Kind*. It doesn't help that the chief robot speaks to David in the voice of Ben Kingsley, who sounds as if he were narrating *Masterpiece Theater*. But these faintly risible touches could have been intended as such, because the conversation between David and the robot of the future has been mediated or managed for the benefit of a human boy's comprehension. (A window behind the two when they talk seems almost like an HDTV screen showing an imaginary natural world.) Because David is so thoroughly programmed as a suburban boy, it makes sense that signs of gender, nationality and even Hollywood movies should be used in an attempt to communicate with him.

At the end, David becomes a paradoxical representative of humanity, which the film defines in Freudian terms. This move is typical of both Spielberg and Kubrick; of the two, however, Kubrick was the more deliberate and forthright in the way he deployed psychoanalytical themes. As we've seen, when he was working with Diane Johnson on the screenplay of *The Shining*, he became interested in Bruno Bettelheim's *The Uses of Enchantment*, which is filled with ahistorical, somewhat vulgarly psychoanalytical interpretations of literary fairy tales. Bettelheim was also an influence on the development of *A. I.*, and one wonders if either Kubrick or Spielberg read the following passage from another of Bettelheim's books, *Freud and Man's Soul* (1984), which insists that Freud's use of the term 'psyche' has something in common with the spiritual idea of 'soul' and ought to be translated as such:

> Freud's atheism is well known – he went out of his way to assert it. There is nothing
> supernatural about his idea of the soul, and it has nothing to do with immortality; if
> anything endures after us, it is other people's memories of us – and what we create . . . . It is
> intangible, but it nevertheless exercises a powerful influence on our lives. It is what makes
> us human; it is what is so essentially human about us that no other term could equally
> convey what Freud had in mind.[19]

Bettelheim is symptomatic of the way psychoanalysis (like art) became the last refuge
of spirituality in an increasingly secularised and scientific age. But if memory is what
makes us spiritual and human, how is it that machines can also be given memory, and
why have computer engineers turned memory into the basis of what Sherry Turkle describes
as the 'emergent' field of Artificial Intelligence? In a 1998 paper on 'Artificial Intelligence
and Psychoanalysis', Turkle observes that the two intellectual domains in question would
appear to be worlds apart:

> Psychoanalysis looks for what is most human: the body, sexuality, what follows from
> being born of woman and raised in a family. Artificial intelligence looks deliberately for
> what is least specifically human: the foundation of its theoretical vision is the thesis that
> the essence of mental life is a set of principles that could be shared by people and
> machines.[20]

And yet, as Turkle goes on to demonstrate, the culture of psychoanalysis and the culture of
computers also have a great deal in common: both make use of a 'biological aesthetic', both
involve a fragmented or de-centred conception of the self, both theorise that repression
and the unconscious are central to the workings of the mind and both dissolve the line
between subjective and objective reflection. Turkle concludes that psychoanalysis and
emergent A. I. can provide each other with 'sustaining myths', in the process overthrowing
certain paradigms. The mind of the computer unsettles behaviourist psychology in much
the same way as it unsettles complacent notions of the ego. 'Artificial intelligence,' Turkle
remarks, 'is to be feared as are Freud and Derrida, not as are Skinner and Carnap' (p. 245).

In the concluding scenes of *A. I.*, the pure machine entities of the future seem to have
evolved beyond the biological differences that constitute Freud's theory, and they inhabit
a world so rational that it bears no signs of sex, capitalism, and nationality. Even so, they have
memory, and an intense historical interest in David, which they express as a kind of nostalgia for humanist idealism. 'You are so important to us,' their representative says, 'you are
unique . . . . You are the enduring memory of the human race, the most lasting proof of
their genius.' After downloading David's memory cells and viewing his life like a video-
tape running at fast speed, this same robot confesses, 'I often felt a sort of envy of human
beings; of that thing they called spirit.' When the robots decide to grant David's wish by
reuniting him briefly with his mother, they view the action from the vantage point of a

table-top TV screen, as if they were archivists looking down at an old movie that offers a key to the human psyche.

None of this irony detracts from the emotions represented in the last scene. David has brought his mother back from the dead in order to have a single moment when the two can express their love for one another and when David can reconcile himself with her death. During his adventures he has seen things she can barely understand and for the first time he possesses a knowledge superior to hers. Spielberg focuses our attention on the faces of the two actors, particularly on Haley Joel Osment. As the camera shows in empirical fashion, here is a real-life boy who has only just acquired his mature teeth, but whose weary smile reveals that death is the mother of beauty. What makes the scene distinctive, however, is that every emotion evoked by Osment and O'Connor is bracketed or qualified by the unusual fictional situation. The mother, the child and the house are too perfect, like idealised figures from Hollywood. Something uncanny inflects everything – a feeling of 'un-homeliness', as if we could sense ghostly futuristic robots designed by CGI somewhere off in the distance, looking down upon David and his mother, who are themselves artificial. The effect isn't so shocking as David's uncanny laughter during a family dinner at an earlier point in the film, but it asserts its presence like a chilling afterthought or an overlay to an otherwise touching reunion.

Freud's essay on the uncanny is based at least in part on his analysis of the animated dolls in E. T. A. Hoffmann's stories, and on 'the impression made by wax-work figures, ingeniously constructed dolls and automata'. One of its conclusions, implicitly evident in Kubrick's *The Shining* and *Eyes Wide Shut*, is that uncanny feelings are related to the primal fear of castration and death.[21] R. L. Rutsky notes that this fear can also be understood through Lacan's rewriting of Freud, as a threat to the 'phallus' or to the idea of Cartesian self-hood; thus, when technology appears animated or strangely 'undead', we tend to lose our faith in the 'authority of a unitary, living soul or spirit over the fragmentation and contingency of the object-world' (p. 39). Freud and Lacan seem to hover in the background of the last scene in *A. I.*, alongside those CGI robots – especially when the childlike automaton embraces his maternal 'bride' and goes to 'that place where dreams are born'. But they don't rule the story, which can also be viewed as another in the long history of tales about the way statues, dolls and robots fascinate us because they seem to embody spirit. Vast oppositions – grief and irony, sentiment and intellect, nostalgia and strangeness, humanism and anti-humanism, rationalism and idealism – are joined in the concluding scene. David is a child who overcomes the trauma of a dead parent, but at the same time a machine whose deepest 'human' tragedy is that he's created in our image, a projection of us. We witness a fundamental experience of love and death, and at the same time an Oedipal fantasy staged by machines for the benefit of a mechanically reproduced commodity from a dead American culture.

After my first viewing of this scene, I recalled a 1976 short story about robots by Peter Wollen, entitled 'Friendship's Death', which Wollen later turned into a movie. The story concerns a space alien named Friendship, who looks like a human being but is in fact a

robot equipped with 'artificial intelligence and a very sophisticated system of plastic sur-
gery and prosthesis'. Friendship is sent by his programmers as an envoy to earth, where
he hopes to have a conversation with Noam Chomsky at MIT. Unfortunately, an error in nav-
igation causes him to land in Jordan during the 1970 war between the Jordanians and
Palestinians. At the same moment all his communications with his home are cut off, thus
giving him complete autonomy. In a conversation with a British journalist who is the only
person to learn his true identity, Friendship says that during his short visit he has begun to
see how human society is strongly marked by class division and class struggle. Lines of
power have been drawn between the bourgeoisie and the proletariat, between industrial
nations and the Third World, between men and women, and between humans and animals. The most basic division of all is that between the human and the non-human, although
the definition of human seems to change over time and certain humanitarian principles have
been extended to the whole of the organic world. The one thing that always seems to be
walled off from the human, Friendship observes, is the machine, which is regarded as
instrumental and not sentient. This seems unreasonable to Friendship, for have not many
of Earth's philosophers likened human beings to machines? (The most important example, as Wollen knows, is Descartes.) Suddenly the reporter who narrates the story feels
uneasy, because he begins to see the drift of the conversation: '[Friendship] could not possibly look at machines in the same way. He was one himself. Moreover, he had intelligence,
privacy and autonomy; he felt, although he was not a human, he was clearly entitled to
the same consideration.' When the reporter last sees Friendship, the robot is on his way
to join the Palestinian militia and to die in struggle.[22]

Like Wollen, but in less political terms, Spielberg and Kubrick indicate that solidarity,
love and even sex are grounded less in biology than in intelligence. More importantly, they
reveal that the human/not-human distinction lies at the very bedrock of ideology. The last
scene of *A. I.*, therefore, moves beyond irony to a place where rationality is troubled, where
empathy and intelligence reinforce one another and where the 'oceanic' feeling Freud once
ascribed to religious experience comes flooding back into force. It allows us to understand
David's tragic condition on a level that both transcends and contains oppositions, so that
we can share his grief and victory in a 'humane' fashion but in a much larger context than
humanism normally allows. I weep for David as a boy *and* as a machine, even as I watch
him living out a fantasy of modernity. In a hyper-modern America where, in the wake of
September 11, 2001, there was much discussion of family and home, much sober reflection
on the excesses of modern entertainment and much nostalgia for an older, supposedly more
'human' national life, such a scene is rare indeed, and affecting in more ways than one.

Notes

1. Critical reaction to the film was mixed. One of the most lengthy and discerning reviews was
    Jonathan Rosenbaum, 'The Best of Both Worlds', *Chicago Reader* (13 July 2001), pp. 32–6, reprinted
    in Rosenbaum, *Essential Cinema: On the Necessity of Film Canons*, pp. 271–9. See also Geoffrey

O'Brien, 'Very Special Effects', *The New York Review of Books* (9 August 2001), and Andrew Sarris, 'A. I.=(2001+E. T.)2', *The New York Observer* (25 June 2001), p. 1.

2. Sigmund Freud, 'Beyond the Pleasure Principle', in *The Standard Edition of the Complete Psychological Works of Sigmund Freud*, trans. James Strachey (London: Hogarth Press, 1929), vol. 17, p. 38. For a fascinating discussion of the relation between narrative closure and the death drive in Hitchcock's *Psycho*, see Laura Mulvey, 'Death Drives', in Richard Allen and Sam Ishii-Gonzales (eds), *Hitchcock Past and Future* (New York: Routledge, 2004), pp. 231–42.

3. Darko Suvin, *Metamorphoses of Science Fiction* (New Haven, CT: Yale University Press, 1979). See also Carl Freedman, *Critical Theory and Science Fiction* (Hanover, CT: Wesleyan University Press, 1999).

4. Paul Virillo, *The Vision Machine*, trans. Julie Rose (London: BFI, 1994).

5. Sean Cubitt, 'Introduction: *Le reel, c'est l'impossible*: The Sublime Time of Special Effects' in Sean Cubitt and John Caughie (eds), *Screen: Special Issue on FX, CGI, and the Question of Spectacle* vol. 40 no. 2 (Summer 1999), pp. 123–30. Page numbers hereafter noted in the text. See also Sean Cubitt, 'Phalke, Méliès, and Special Effects Today', *Wide Angle* vol. 21 no. 1 (January 1999), pp. 115–48.

6. André Bazin, *What Is Cinema?*, trans. Hugh Gray (Berkeley: University of California Press, 1967), p. 13.

7. André Bazin, 'William Wyler, or the Jansenist of Directing', trans. Alain Piette and Bert Cardullo, in Bazin, *Bazin at Work*, ed. Bert Cardullo (New York: Routledge, 1997), p. 12.

8. R. L. Rutsky, *High Techne: Art and Technology from the Machine Aesthetic to the Posthuman* (Minneapolis: University of Minnesota Press, 1999), p. 34. Page numbers hereafter noted in the text.

9. Susan Sontag, *On Photography* (New York: Farrar, Straus and Giroux, 1978), p. 4.

10. Christian Metz, 'Trucage and the Film', *Critical Inquiry* (Summer 1977), pp. 657–75.

11. Tom Gunning, 'An Aesthetic of Astonishment: Early Films and the (In)Credulous Spectator', in Leo Braudy and Marshall Cohen (eds), *Film Theory and Criticism*, 5th edn (New York: Oxford University Press, 1999), pp. 818–32; André Gaudreault, 'Theatricality, Narrativity and "Trickality": Reevaluating the Cinema of Georges Méliès', *Journal of Popular Film and Television* vol. 15 no. 3 (Autumn), pp. 110–19.

12. Aldiss is quoted in the introduction to 'Super-Toys Last All Summer Long', which is reprinted in an extremely useful website devoted to Stanley Kubrick: ‹www.visual-memory.co.uk/ amk/doc/0068.html›

13. One of Kubrick's ideas was to have experimental director Chris Cunningham create the scenes involving the robot. Tests of these scenes were apparently made, but were judged unsatisfactory. (For an example of Cunningham's sexy and uncanny work with robotic figures, see his video of Bjork's 'All Is Full of Love'.)

14. Jack Zipes, 'Breaking the Disney Spell', in Elizabeth Bell, Linda Haas and Laura Sells (eds), *From Mouse to Mermaid: The Politics of Film, Gender, and Culture* (Bloomington: Indiana University Press, 1995), p. 25. For a good discussion of the historical and literary context of Collodi's story, see Nicolas J. Perella, 'An Essay on *Pinocchio*', in Carlo Collodi, *The Adventures of Pinocchio, Story of a Puppet*, trans. Nicolas J. Perella (Berkeley: University of California Press, 1986), pp. 1–70.

15. Victoria Nelson, *The Secret Life of Puppets* (Cambridge, MA: Harvard University Press, 2001), p. xi. Nelson's fascinating book is strikingly relevant to *A. I.*, though she was not able to write about the film. Her thesis, which is elaborated through a rich and diverse exploration of western art and philosophy, is that the 'larger mainstream culture' of the twenty-first century 'subscribes to a non-rational, supernatural, quasi-religious view of the universe', and that our consumption of art forms of the fantastic is 'one way that we as nonbelievers allow ourselves, unconsciously, to believe' (p. vii).

16. Scott Bukatman, *Terminal Identity: The Virtual Subject in Post-Modern Science Fiction* (Durham, NC: Duke University Press, 1993), p. 19.

17. Lasseter is quoted in a website created by the PBS programme *NOVA*, which devoted one of its programmes to the history of special effects in Hollywood: <www.pbs.org/cgi-bin/wgbh>

18. For a discussion of the scripts of *Blade Runner* and the ambiguous effect of the film's ending, see William M. Kolb, 'Script to Screen: *Blade Runner* in Perspective', in Judith B. Kerman (ed.), *Retrofitting Blade Runner* (Bowling Green: Popular Press, 1991), pp. 132–53.

19. Bruno Bettelheim, *Freud and Man's Soul* (New York: Vintage Books, 1984), p. 77.

20. Sherry Turkle, 'Artificial Intelligence and Psychoanalysis: A New Alliance', *Daedalus* vol. 117 no. 1 (Winter 1998), p. 241. See also Sherry Turkle, *The Second Self: Computers and the Human Spirit* (New York: Simon & Schuster, 1984).

21. Sigmund Freud, 'The 'Uncanny',' in *The Standard Edition of the Complete Psychological Works of Sigmund Freud*, vol. 17, p. 226.

22. 'Friendship's Death', in Peter Wollen, *Readings and Writings: Semiotic Counter-Strategies* (London: Verso, 1982), pp. 140–52.

Filmography

(The information below is derived from the films and also from scholarly sources, among them Gene D. Phillips and Rodney Hill (eds), *The Encyclopedia of Stanley Kubrick* (2002); Hans-Peter Reichmann and Ingeborg Flagge (eds), *Stanley Kubrick* (2004); and Alison Castle (ed.), *The Stanley Kubrick Archives* (2005). Credits for *Spartacus* and *A. I. Artificial Intelligence* are abbreviated.)

DAY OF THE FIGHT (US, 1950–1)

Director: Stanley Kubrick
Screenplay: Robert Rein and Stanley Kubrick
Photography: Stanley Kubrick and Alexander Singer
Assistant Director: Alexander Singer
Editor: Julian Bergman and Stanley Kubrick
Sound: Stanley Kubrick
Music/Music Direction: Gerald Fried
Cast: Douglas Edwards (narrator), Walter Cartier, Vincent Cartier, Nate Fleischer, Bobby James, Stanley Kubrick, Alexander Singer, Judy Singer
Production Company: Stanley Kubrick Productions, distributed by RKO *Screenliner*
Producers: Stanley Kubrick and (uncredited) Jay Bonafield
Running Time: 16 min.
Gauge: 35mm, b/w, mono
First Screening: Paramount Theater, New York, 26 April 1951

FLYING PADRE (US, 1950–1)

Director: Stanley Kubrick
Screenplay: Stanley Kubrick
Photography: Stanley Kubrick
Music: Nathaniel Shilkret
Sound: Harold R. Vivian
Editor: Isaac Kleinerman
Cast: Bob Hite (narrator), Rev. Fred Stadtmueller
Production Company: Stanley Kubrick Films for RKO
Producer: Burton Benjamin
Running Time: 9 min.
Gauge: 35mm, b/w, mono
First Screening: 1951

THE SEAFARERS (US, 1953)

Director: Stanley Kubrick
Screenplay: Will Chasen
Photography: Stanley Kubrick
Editor: Stanley Kubrick
Sound: Stanley Kubrick
Cast: Don Hollenbeck (narrator), members of the Seafarers Union
Producer: Lester Coope
Running Time: 30 min.
Gauge: 35mm, colour, mono
First Screening: New York, 15 October 1953

FEAR AND DESIRE (US, 1951–3)

Working Titles: *Shape of Fear, The Trap*
Director: Stanley Kubrick
Screenplay: Howard O. Sackler and Stanley
    Kubrick, based on the script 'The Trap' by
    Howard O. Sackler
Photography: Stanley Kubrick
Assistant Director: Steve Hahn
Dialogue Director: Toba Kubrick
Art Director: Herbert Lebowitz
Make-up: Chet Fabian
Title Design: Barney Ettengoff
Editor: Stanley Kubrick
Music/Music Direction: Gerald Fried
Cast: David Allen (narrator), Frank Silvera
    (Mac), Kenneth Harp (Lt Corby/enemy
    general), Virginia Leith (girl), Paul
    Mazursky (Pvt. Sidney), Steve Coit
    (Pvt. Fletcher/aide-de-camp)
Producers: Stanley Kubrick, Martin Perveler
Production Manager: Robert Dierks
Production Company: Stanley Kubrick
    Productions, distributed by Joseph Burstyn
Locations: San Gabriel Mountains, Bakersfield,
    Azuga, CA
Running Time: 68 min.
Gauge: 35mm (1:1.33), b/w, mono
First Screening: Guild Theater, New York,
    1 April 1953

KILLER'S KISS (US, 1955)

Working Titles: *Kiss Me, Kill Me, The Nymph and
    the Maniac, Along Came a Spider*
Director: Stanley Kubrick
Screenplay: Howard O. Sackler and Stanley
    Kubrick (uncredited), story by Stanley
    Kubrick
Photography: Stanley Kubrick (camera

operators, Jesse Paley and Max Glen)
Assistant Director: Ernest Nukanen
Sound: Stanley Kubrick (Titra Studios
    recording engineers, Walter Ruckersberg
    and Clifford Van Pragg)
Editor: Stanley Kubrick
Music: Gerald Fried (Love theme from the song
    'Once', by Norman Gimbel and Arden Clar)
Choreography: David Vaughn
Cast: Frank Silvera (Vincent Rapallo), Jamie
    Smith (Davy Gordon), Irene Kane (Gloria
    Price), Jerry Jarret (Manager), Ruth Sobotka
    (Iris Price, dancer), Mike Dana/Felice
    Orlandi/Ralph Roberts/Phil Stevenson
    (gangsters), Julius Skippy Adelman (owner
    of mannequin factory)
Production Company: Minotaur Productions,
    distributed by United Artists
Producers: Morris Bousel and Stanley Kubrick
Locations: New York City – Pleasureland Dance
    Hall (49th St), Theatre de Lys (Greenwich
    Village), 121 Christopher St, various
    Manhattan locales
Running Time: 67 min.
Gauge: 35mm (1:1.33), b/w, mono
First Screening: Loew's Metropolitan, New
    York, 28 September 1955

THE KILLING (US, 1955–6)

Working Titles: *Day of Violence, Clean Break, Bed
    of Fear*
Director: Stanley Kubrick
Screenplay: Stanley Kubrick, Jim Thompson
    (dialogue), from the novel *Clean Break* by
    Lionel White
Photography: Lucien Ballard
Camera Operator: Dick Tower
Assistant Director: Milton Carter
Second Unit Director: Alexander Singer

Sound: Earl Snyder

Editor: Betty Steinberg

Art Director: Ruth Sobotka

Set Decoration: Harry Reif

Wardrobe: Jack Masters and Rudy Harrington

Make-up: Robert Littlefield

Special Effects: Dave Kohler

Music: Gerald Fried

Music Editor: Gilbert Marchant

Production Assistant: Marguerite Olson

Director's Assistant: Joyce Hartman

Photographic Effects: Jack Rabin, Louis Dewitt

Cast: Sterling Hayden (Johnny Clay), Colleen
    Gray (Fay), Vince Edwards (Val Cannon), Jay
    C. Flippen (Marvin Ungar), Ted de Corsia
    (Randy Kennan), Marie Windsor (Sherry
    Peatty), Elisha Cook Jr (George Peatty), Joe
    Sawyer (Mike O'Reilly), James Edwards
    (parking attendant), Timothy Carey (Nikki
    Arane), Kola Kwariani (Maurice
    Oboukhoff), Jay Adler (Leo), Tito Vuolo
    (Joe), Dorothy Adams (Ruthie O'Reilly),
    Joseph Turkel (Tiny), William Benedict
    (airline clerk), James Griffith (Mr Grimes),
    Charles R. Cane/Robert Williams
    (plainclothes police at airport), Saul Gorss
    (track guard), Hal J. Moore (track
    announcer), Richard Reeves/Frank Richards
    (track employees), Art Gilmore (narrator),
    Herbert Ellis, Cecil Elliott, Steve Mitchell,
    Mary Carroll

Production Company: Harris–Kubrick
    Productions, distributed by United Artists

Producer: James B. Harris

Associate Producer: Alexander Singer

Production Manager: Clarence Eurist

Locations: Golden Gate Racetrack and Bay
    Meadows Race Track, San Francisco;
    various locales in Los Angeles; United
    Artists Studio, Los Angeles

Running Time: 84 min.

Gauge: 35 mm (1:1.33), b/w, mono (RCA Sound
    System)

First Screening: Mayfair, New York, 20 May
    1956

PATHS OF GLORY (US, 1957)

Director: Stanley Kubrick

Screenplay: Stanley Kubrick, Calder
    Willingham, Jim Thompson, from the
    novel *Paths of Glory* by Humphrey Cobb

Photography: George Krause

Camera Operator: Hannes Staudinger

Editor: Eva Kroll

Sound: Martin Muller

Art Direction: Ludwig Reiber

Costumes: Ilse Dubois

Make-up: Arthur Schramm

Military Advisor: Baron von Waldenfels

Music: Gerald Fried (also *Kunstlerleben* by
    Johann Strauss, *Marseillaise* and *Das Lied
    vom treuen Husaren*)

Cast: Kirk Douglas (Col. Dax), Ralph Meeker
    (Cpl Paris), Adolphe Menjou (Gen.
    Broulard), George Macready (Gen. Mireau),
    Wayne Morris (Lt Roget), Richard Anderson
    (Maj. Saint-Aubin), Joseph Turkel (Pvt.
    Arnaud), Timothy Carey (Pvt. Ferol), Peter
    Capell (Judge, also narrator of opening
    sequence), Susanne Christian (German
    captive), Bert Freed (Sgt Boulanger), Emile
    Meyer (priest), John Stein (Capt. Rousseau),
    Jen Dibbs (Pvt. Lejeune), Jerry Hauser
    (café proprietor), Harold Benedict (Capt.
    Nichols), Frederic Bell (shell-shock victim),
    Paul Bos (Maj. Gouderc), Leon Briggs
    (Capt. Sancy), Wally Friedrichs (Col.
    De Guerville), Halder Hanson (doctor),
    Rolf Kralovitz (K. P.), Ira Moore (Capt.

Renouart), Marshall Rainer (Pvt. Duval),
James B. Harris (Pvt. in the attack)
Production Companies: Harris–Kubrick
Productions/Bryna Productions, distributed
by United Artists
Producer: James B. Harris
Production Managers: Georg von Block and
John Pommer
Locations: Schleissheim Palace, Bernried, Lake
Starnberg and Puchheim (Bavaria), Bavaria
Studios, Munich
Running Time: 87 min.
Gauge: 35mm (1:1.66, with option for 1:1.85),
b/w, mono
First Screening: Fine Arts Theater, Beverly Hills,
20 December 1957

SPARTACUS (US, 1959–60)

Director: Stanley Kubrick
Screenplay: Dalton Trumbo, from the novel
Spartacus by Howard Fast
Cast: Kirk Douglas (Spartacus),
Laurence Olivier (Crassus), Jean Simmons
(Varinia), Charles Laughton (Gracchus),
Peter Ustinov (Batiatus), Tony Curtis
(Antonius)
Production Company: Bryna Productions for
Universal Pictures
Producers: Edward Lewis and Kirk Douglas
Running Time: 196 min. (original version)

LOLITA (UK/US, 1960–2)

Director: Stanley Kubrick
Screenplay: Vladimir Nabokov (James B. Harris
and Stanley Kubrick uncredited), from the
novel *Lolita* by Valdimir Nabokov
Photography: Oswald Morris (Robert Gaffney,
second unit)

Camera Operator: Dennis Coop
Editor: Anthony Harvey
Sound: Len Shilton (recording), H. L. Bird
(mixing)
Art Directors: Bill Andrews and Syd Cain
Set Dressers: Peter James and Andrew Low
Costumes: Gene Coffin (for Shelley Winters)
Wardrobe: Elsa Fennel
Make-up: George Partelton
Title Design: Chambers & Partners
Music: Nelson Riddle (Lolita's theme by Bob
Harris, 'Put Your Dreams Away' by George
David Weiss [uncredited])
Cast: James Mason (Humbert Humbert),
Shelley Winters (Charlotte Haze), Sue Lyon
(Dolores 'Lolita' Haze), Peter Sellers (Claire
Quilty), Diana Decker (Jean Farlow), Jerry
Stovin (John Farlow), Suzanne Gibbs (Mona
Farlow), Gary Cockrell (Richard T. 'Dick'
Schiller), Marianne Stone (Vivian
Darkbloom), Cec Linder (doctor), Lois
Maxwell (nurse), William Greene (George
Swine), C. Denier Warren (Potts), Isobel
Lucas (Louise), Maxine Holden (hotel
receptionist), James Dyrenforth (Beale),
Roberta Shore (Lorna), Eris Lane (Roy),
Shirley Douglas (Mrs Starch), Roland Brand
(Bill), Colin Maitland (Charlie), Irvine
Allen (hospital attendant), Marion Mathie
(Miss Lebone), Craig Sams (Rex), John
Harrison (Tom)
Production Companies: Seven Arts
Productions, Allied Artists, Anya,
Transworld, distributed by Metro Goldwyn
Mayer
Producer: James B. Harris
Production Supervisor: Raymond Anzarut
Production Manager: Robert Sterne
Locations: Albany, NY; Gettysburg, NY; Hague,
NY; Ticonderoga, NY; Middleboro, VT;

Portland, ME; Dover, NH; Pittsfield, NH;
Mills Cabins Motel, Rt. 1, Saco, ME; Boston,
MA; Shrewsbury, MA; Sharon, MA; Westerly,
RI; Route 128, US; Elstree Studios, London
Running Time: 152 min.
Gauge: 35mm (1:1.66), b/w, mono (RCA Sound
System)
First Screening: Loew's State Theater and
Murray Hill Theater, New York, 12 June
1962

DR. STRANGELOVE, OR HOW I LEARNED TO STOP WORRYING AND LOVE THE BOMB (UK/US, 1963–4)

Director: Stanley Kubrick
Screenplay: Stanley Kubrick, Peter George,
Terry Southern, from the novel *Red Alert* by
Peter Bryant (Peter George)
Assistant Director: Eric Rattray
Photography: Gilbert Taylor
Editor: Anthony Harvey
Sound: John Cox (recording), H. L. Bird
(mixing)
Production Design: Ken Adam
Art Director: Peter Murton
Wardrobe: Brigit Sellers
Make-up: Stuart Freeborn
Special Effects: Wally Veevers
Technical Advisor: Capt. John Crewsdon
Title Design: Pablo Ferro (Ferro, Mohammed &
Schwartz)
Music: Laurie Johnson ('We'll Meet Again' by
Lew Ross Parker, Hughie Charles; 'Try a
Little Tenderness' by Harry Woods, Jimmy
Campbell, Reg Connelly; 'When Johnny
Comes Marching Home' by Patrick S.
Gilmore; 'Greensleeves')
Cast: Peter Sellers (Group Capt. Lionel
Mandrake/President Merkin Muffley/Dr

Strangelove), George C. Scott (Gen. Buck
Turgidson), Sterling Hayden (Gen. Jack D.
Ripper), Keenan Wynn (Col. 'Bat' Guano),
Slim Pickens (Maj. T. J. 'King' Kong), Peter
Bull (Ambassador de Sadesky), James Earl
Jones (Lt Lothar Zugg), Tracy Reed (Miss
Scott), Jack Creely (Mr Staines), Frank Berry
(Lt H. R. Dietrich), Glenn Beck (Lt W. D.
Kivel), Roy Stephens (Frank), Shane
Rimmer (Capt. G. A. 'Ace' Owens), Paul
Tamarin (Lt B. Goldberg), Gordon Tanner
(Gen. Faceman), Laurence Herder/John
McCarthy/Hal Galili (soldiers at Burpleson
Air Base)
Production Company: Hawk Films Ltd,
distributed by Columbia Pictures
Producer: Stanley Kubrick
Executive Producers: Victor Lyndon and Leon
Minoff
Locations: London Airport, IBM facilities,
Shepperton Studios, London
Running Time: 95 min.
Gauge: 35mm (1: 1.66), b/w, mono
(Westrex)
First Screening: Columbia Theatre, London,
29 January 1964

2001: A SPACE ODYSSEY (UK/US, 1968)

Director: Stanley Kubrick
Screenplay: Stanley Kubrick and Arthur C.
Clarke, based on the short story 'The
Sentinel' by Arthur C. Clarke
Photography: Geoffrey Unsworth
Additional Photography: John Alcott
Second Unit Photography: Robert Gaffney
Camera Operator: Kelvin Pike
Editor: Ray Lovejoy
Sound: A. W. Watkins (recording), Ed Winston
Ryder (editing), H. L. Bird (mixing)

Production Designers: Antony Masters, Harry
    Lange and Ernest Archer
Art Director: John Hoesli
Costumes: Hardy Amies
Make-up: Colin Arthur and Stuart Freeborn
Special Effects: Stanley Kubrick, Wally Veevers,
    Douglas Trumbull, Con Pederson, Tom
    Howard, Colin J. Cantwell, Bryan Loftus,
    Frederick Martin, Bruce Logan, David
    Osborne, John Jack Malick
Technical Advisor: Frederick Ordway III
Music: Aram Khachaturyan, Ballettsuite
    Gayaneh; György Ligeti, *Atmospheres,
    Requiem, Lux Aeterna*; Johann Strauss, *An der
    schönen blauen Donau*; Richard Strauss, *Also
    sprach Zarathustra*, op. 30
Cast: Keir Dullea (David Bowman), Gary
    Lockwood (Frank Poole), William
    Sylvester (Dr Heywood R. Floyd),
    Daniel Richter (Moonwatcher), Leonard
    Rossiter (Dr Andreas Smyslov), Margaret
    Tyzack (Elena), Robert Beatty (Ralph
    Halvorsen), Sean Sullivan (Robert
    Michaels), Douglas Rain (HAL 9000),
    Frank Miller (voice of Mission Control),
    Vivian Kubrick ('Squirt' Floyd), Bill Weston
    (astronaut), Edward Bishop (Aries 1B Capt.),
    Glenn Beck (astronaut), Robert Beatty (Dr
    Halvorsen), Sean Sullivan (Dr Michaels),
    David Allen Gifford (Poole's father), Ann
    Gillis (Poole's mother), Edwina
    Carroll/Penny Brahms/Heather Downham
    (flight attendants), John Ashley/Jimmy
    Bell/David Charkham/Simon
    Davis/Jonathan Daw/Peter Delmar/Terry
    Dugan/David Fleetwood/Danny
    Grover/Brian Hawley/David Hines/Tony
    Jackson/Mike Lovell/Scott MacKee/
    Laurence Marchant/Darryl Paes/Joe
    Rafelo/Andy Wallace/Bob Wilyman (apes),

Martin Amor (interviewer), Kenneth
    Kendall (BBC-12 announcer), Krystina Marr
    (Russian scientist)
Production Company: Stanley Kubrick
    Productions/Polaris Films, distributed by
    Metro Goldwyn Mayer
Producers: Stanley Kubrick and Victor Lyndon
Locations: Page, AZ; Monument Valley, UT;
    Outer Hebrides; Isle of Harris, Scotland;
    Elstree EMI Studios, EMI-MGM Studios;
    Borehamwood Studios, Herts; Shepperton
    Studios, Middlesex
Running time: 141 min. (cut from 160 min.
    after premiere)
Gauge: 70mm (1:2.20), Super Panavision, colour
    (Technicolour prints, Metrocolour), 4-Track
    Stereo (35mm)/6-Track (70mm print)/DTS
    70mm (re-screening)
First Screening: Uptown Theater, Washington,
    DC, 6 April 1968

A CLOCKWORK ORANGE (UK/US, 1971)

Director: Stanley Kubrick
Screenplay: Stanley Kubrick, from the novel
    A Clockwork Orange by Anthony Burgess
Photography: John Alcott
Camera Operators: Ernie Day and Mike Molloy
Editor: Bill Butler
Sound: John Jordan (recording), Brian Blamey
    (editing), Bill Rowe and Eddie Haben
    (mixing)
Assistant Directors: Derek Cracknell and Dusty
    Symonds
Assistant Editors: Gary Shepard, Peter Burgess,
    and David Beesley
Art Direction: Russell Hagg, Peter Shields
    (Paintings and sculptures: Herman
    Makkink, Liz Moore, Cornelius Makkink,
    Christiane Kubrick)

Production Design: John Barry

Costumes: Milena Canonero

Wardrobe: Ron Beck

Make-up: George Partleton, Fred Williamson, Barbara Daily, Leonard of London and Olga Angelinetta

Music: Pieces from Henry Purcell, *Music for the Funeral of Queen Mary*; James Yorkston, *Molly Malone*; Gioacchino Rossini, overtures to *The Thieving Magpie* and *William Tell*; Walter Carlos, *Beethoviana*, *Timesteps*; Ludwig van Beethoven, *Symphony Nr. 9 d-minor op. 125*, 2nd and 4th movements; Edward Elgar, *Pomp and Circumstance, op. 39*, marches 1 and 4; Nicolai Rimskii-Korsakov, *Scheherazade*; Terry Tucker, *Overture to the Sun*; Terry Tucker, 'I Want to Marry a Lighthouse Keeper'; Arthur Freed and Nacio Brown, 'Singin' in the Rain'

Arrangements and Electronic Adaptation: Walter Carlos

Casting: Jimmy Liggat

Cast: Malcolm McDowell (Alexander DeLarge), Patrick Magee (Mr Alexander), Michael Bates (Barnes), Warren Clarke (Dim), John Clive (stage actor), Adrianne Couri (Mrs Alexander), Carl Duering (Dr Brodsky), Paul Farrell (tramp), Clive Francis (Joe), Michael Gover (prison governer), Miriam Karlin (Mrs Weathers, the cat lady), James Marcus (Georgie), Aubrey Morris (Deltoid), Godfrey Quigley (prison chaplain), Sheila Raynor (Alex's mother), Madge Ryan (Dr Branom), John Savident (Dolin), Anthony Sharp (Minister of the Interior), Philip Stone (Alex's father), Pauline Taylor (psychiatrist), Margaret Tyzack (Rubenstein), Steven Berkoff (policeman), Michael Tarn (Pete), David Prowse (Julian), Jan Adair/Vivienne Chandler (handmaidens), John J. Carley (man from CID), Richard Connaught (Billy Boy), Carol Drinkwater (sister Feeley), Cheryl Grunwald (raped girl), Gillian Hills (Sonietta), Barbara Scott (Marty), Virginia Weatherhill (actress), Neil Wilson (prison civil servant), Katya Wyeth (girl in Ascot fantasy)

Production Companies: Polaris Productions, Hawk Films Ltd, Shepperton, for Warner Bros.

Producer: Stanley Kubrick

Executive Producers: Si Litvinoff and Max L. Rabb

Associate Producer: Bernard Williams

Assistant to the Producer: Jan Harlan

Locations: Aylesbury, Buckinghamshire; Brunel University, Uxbridge, Middlesex; Edgewarebury Hotel, Barnet Lane, Elstree, Hertfordshire; Festival Embankment, London; Wandsworth, London; Joydens Wood, Bexleyheath, Kent; Shenley Lodge, Shenley, Hertfordshire; Southmere Lake, Binsey Walk, Yarnton Way, Thamesmead South Estate, London; Princess Alexandra Hospital, Harlow, Essex; Woolwich Barracks; South Norwood Technical College; Pinewood Studios, London; EMI-MGM Studios, Borehamwood, Hertfordshire

Running time: 137 min.

Gauge: 35mm (1:1.66), colour (Technicolour), mono, Dolby Digital (reissue)

First Screening: Cinema I, New York, 19 December 1971

Barry Lyndon (UK/US, 1975)

Director: Stanley Kubrick
Screenplay: Stanley Kubrick, from the novel
    The Memoirs of Barry Lyndon by William
    Makepeace Thackeray
Photography: John Alcott
Second Unit Photography: Paddy Carey
Editor: Tony Lawson
Sound: Robin Gregory (recording), Rodney
    Howard (editing) and Bill Rowe (mixing)
Production Design: Ken Adam
Art Direction: Roy Walker and Jan Schlubach
Set Decoration: Vernon Dixon
Costumes: Ulla Britt Soderlund and Milena
    Canonero
Hair Design: Leonard
Music: Leonard Rosenman, adapted pieces by
    George Friedrich Handel (*Sarabande*),
    Friedrich II (*Hohenfriedberger March*),
    Wolfgang Amadeus Mozart (march from
    Idomeno), Franz Schubert (*Deutscher Tanz
    Nr. 1, C-dur* and *Trio for Piano in Es-dur*, op.
    100), Giovanni Paisiello (*Cavatina* from *Il
    barbiere di Siviglia*), Antonio Vivaldi
    (*Concerto for Violoncello in e-minor*), Johann
    Sebastian Bach (*Adagio* from *Concerto for
    two Harpsichords and Orchestra in c-minor*),
    Jean-Marie Leclair (*Le rondeau de Paris*),
    Sean O'Riada (*Women of Ireland* and *Tin
    Whistle*); folksongs arranged by The
    Chieftans and Leonard Rosenman ('Piper's
    Maggot Jig', 'British Grenadiers',
    'Lilliburlero', 'Ad lib Drum')
Choreography: Geraldine Stephenson
Cast: Ryan O'Neal (Redmond Barry, later Barry
    Lyndon), Marisa Berenson (Lady Lyndon),
    Patrick Magee (Chevalier de Balibari),
    Hardy Kruger (Capt. Potsdorf); Steven
    Berkoff (Lord Ludd), Gay Hamilton (Nora
Brady), Marie Kean (Mrs Barry), Diana
    Korner (German woman), Murray Melvin
    (Rev. Samuel Runt), Frank Middlemass (Sir
    Charles Lyndon), Andre Morell (Lord
    Wendover), Arthur O'Sullivan (Capt.
    Feeney), Godfrey Quigley (Capt. Grogan),
    Leonard Rossiter (Capt. Quinn), Phillip
    Stone (Graham), Leon Vitali (Lord
    Bullingdon), Dominic Savage (young
    Bullingdon), Roger Booth (King George III),
    Anthony Sharp (Lord Harlan)
Production Companies: Peregrine Films/Hawk
    Films Ltd, for Warner Bros.
Producer: Stanley Kubrick
Associate Producer: Bernard Williams
Executive Producer: Jan Harlan
Production Managers: Terence Clegg, Douglas
    Twiddy and Rudolph Hertzog
Locations: *Germany*: Hohenzollern Castle,
    Hechingen; Ludwigsburg Palace; New
    Palace, Potsdam-Sanssouci. *England*:
    Castle Howard, Coneysthorpe, North
    Yorkshire; Stourhead garden, Warminster,
    Wiltshire; Wilton House, Salisbury,
    Wiltshire; Glastonbury Rural Life
    Museum; Glastonbury Abbey; Bath
    surroundings, Somerset; Longleat House,
    Warminster, Wiltshire; Petworth House,
    Petworth, West Sussex; Huntingdonshire;
    Blenheim Palace, Oxfordshire. *Ireland*:
    County Kerkenny: Comaragh Mountains,
    Rathgormack, County Waterford; Carric-
    on-Suir, Tipperary; Dublin Powerscourt
    Castle; Kells Priory, Kells; Cahir Castle.
    EMI-MGM Studios, Borehamwood,
    Hertfordshire
Running Time: 187 min.
Gauge: 35mm (1:166), colour (Eastmancolour),
    mono. Special lenses by Carl Zeiss, Mitchell
    BNC engineering by Ed DiGiulio

First Screening: Warner West End and ABC-
Cinemas Bayswater, London, 11 December
1975

THE SHINING (UK/US, 1980)

Director: Stanley Kubrick
Screenplay: Stanley Kubrick and Diane
Johnson, based on the novel *The Shining* by
Stephen King
Photography: John Alcott
Steadicam: Garrett Brown
Aerial Photography: Greg McGillivray
Editor: Ray Lovejoy
Sound: Richard Daniel and Ivan Sharrock
(recording), Dino DiCampo and Jack T.
Knight (editing), Wyn Ryder and Bill Rowe
(mixing)
Production Design: Roy Walker
Art Direction: Les Tomkins
Set Dresser: Tessa Davis
Costumes: Milena Canonero
Make-up: Tom Smith and Barbara Daly
Hair: Leonard
Music: Wendy Carlos and Rachel Elkind, music
pieces by Bela Bartok (*Music for strings,
percussion, and celesta*), György Ligeti
(*Lontano*), Krzysztof Penderecki (*Urenja, The
Awakening of Jacob, Polymorphia, De Natura
Sonoris Nr. 1 and 2*)
Cast: Jack Nicholson (Jack Torrance), Danny
Lloyd (Danny Torrance), Shelley Duvall
(Wendy Torrance), Scatman Carothers
(Dick Halloran), Barry Nelson (Stuart
Ullman), Philip Stone (Delbert Grady), Joe
Turkel (Lloyd), Anne Jackson (doctor), Tony
Burton (Larry Durkin), Lia Beldam (young
woman in bath), Billie Gibson (old woman
in bath), Barry Dennen (Bill Watson), David
Baxt (Ranger Manning), Lisa and Louise

Burns (Grady sisters), Robin Pappas (nurse),
Alison Coleridge (secretary), Kate Phelps
(receptionist), Norman Gay (injured guest),
Vivian Kubrick (smoking guest)
Production Companies: Peregrine Films/Hawk
Films Ltd, for Warner Bros. in association
with the Producers Circle Company
Producer: Stanley Kubrick
Executive Producer: Jan Harlan
Production Manager: Douglas Twiddy
Assistant to the Director: Leon Vitali
Locations: Timberline Lodge Hotel, Mount
Hood, OR; Yosemite National Park Valley;
Bretton Woods, NH; Glacier National Park;
EMI-Elstree Studios, London
Running Time: 146 min. (US), 119 min.
(Europe)
Gauge: 35mm (1:1.66), colour, mono
First Screening: Criterion Sutton and Lowe's
Orpheum, New York, 23 May 1980

FULL METAL JACKET (UK/US, 1987)

Director: Stanley Kubrick
Screenplay: Stanley Kubrick, Michael Herr and
Gustav Hasford, based on the novel *The
Short-Timers* by Gustav Hasford
Photography: Douglas Milsome
Aerial Photography: Ken Arlidge
Steadicam Photography: Jean-Marc Bringuier
Editor: Martin Hunter
Sound: Nigel Galt (recording), Joe Illing
(editing), Edward Tise (mixing)
Production Design: Anton Furst
Art Direction: Rod Stratfold, Les Tomkins and
Keith Pain
Set Designer: Stephen Simmonds
Costumes: Keith Denny
Special Effects: Alan Barnard, Jeff Clifford and
Peter Dawson

Assistant Directors: Terry Needham and
   Christopher Thompson
Music: Abigail Mead (Vivian Kubrick).
   Recorded songs by Tom T. Hall ('Hello
   Vietnam'); Lee Hazelwood ('These Boots
   Were Made for Walking'); Domingo
   Samudio ('Wooly Bully'); J. Barry, E.
   Greenwich, P. Spector ('The Chapel of
   Love'); Chris Kenner ('I Like It Like That');
   A. Franzler, C. White, T. Wilson, J. Harris
   ('Surfin' Bird'); Jimmy Dood ('Mickey
   Mouse March'); Mick Jagger, Keith Richards
   ('Paint It Black'); Jacques Offenbach, Hector
   Cremieux, Etienne Trefeu (*The Marine
   Hymn*)
Cast: Matthew Modine (Pvt. 'Joker' Davis),
   Vincent D'Onofrio (Pvt. Leonard 'Gomer
   Pyle' Lawrence), R. Lee Ermey (Gunnery Sgt
   Hartman), Adam Baldwin ('Animal
   Mother'), Arliss Howard ('Cowboy'), Dorian
   Harewood ('Eightball'), Kevyn Major
   Howard ('Rafterman'), Ed O'Ross (Lt
   'Touchdown' Tinoshky), Kerion Jecchinnis
   ('Crazy Earl'), John Terry (Lt Lockhart),
   Bruce Boa (Poge Col.), Kirk Taylor (Pvt.
   Payback), Jon Stafford (Doc Jay), Tim
   Colceri (door gunner), Ian Tyler (Lt Cleves),
   Sal Lopez (T. H. E. Rock), Papillon Soo Soo
   (Da Nang prostitute), Ngoc Le (sniper),
   Peter Edmond (Pvt. 'Snowball' Brown),
   Leanne Hong (prostitute with motorbike),
   Tan Hung Francione (pimp), Marcus
   D'Amico ('Hand Job'), Costas Dino
   Chimona (Chili), Gil Kopel (Stork), Keith
   Hodiak (Daddy D. A.), Peter Merrill
   (TV journalist), Herbert Norville
   (Daytona Dave), Nguyen Hue Phong
   (camera thief)
Production Company: Warner Bros.
Producer: Stanley Kubrick

Co-Producer: Phillip Hobbs
Executive Producer: Jan Harlan
Associate Producer: Michael Herr
Production Manager: Phil Kohler
Locations: Bassingbourn Barracks, Royston,
   Cambridge, Cambridgeshire; Beckton
   Gasworks, East London; Dorset; Epping
   Forest, Essex; Norfolk Broads; Pinewood
   Studios, London
Running Time: 116 mins.
First Screening: National Manhattan Twin,
   Eighth St Playhouse and others, New York,
   26 June 1987

EYES WIDE SHUT (UK/US, 1999)

Working Titles: *EWS, Rhapsody*
Director: Stanley Kubrick
Screenplay: Stanley Kubrick and Frederic
   Raphael, from the novella *Traumnovella
   (Rhapsody – A Dream Novel)* by Arthur
   Schnitzler
Photography: Larry Smith, Patrick Turley and
   Malik Sayeed
Second Unit Photography: Arthur Jaffa
Editor: Nigel Galt
Sound: Tony Bell, Paul Conway and Eddy Tise
Production Designers: Les Tomkins and Roy
   Walker
Art Direction: John Fenner and Kevin Phibbs
Set Decoration: Lisa Leone and Terry Wells Sr
Paintings: Christiane Kubrick and Katharina
   Kubrick Hobbs
Costumes: Marit Allen and Cerutti
Special Effects: Garth Inns and Charles
   Staffell
Music: Jocelyn Pook (*Naval Officer, Masked Ball,
   Migrations*) and Jocelyn Pook and Harvey
   Brough (*The Dream, Backwards Priests*).
   Music pieces by Dimitri Shostakovich

(*Waltz Nr. 2* from *Jazz Suite*), György Ligeti (*Musica Ricercata II: Mesto, rigido e ceremoniale*), Franz Liszt (*Nuages gris*), Wayne Shanklin ('*Chanson d'Amour*'), Jimmy McHugh and Dorothy Fields ('I'm in the Mood for Love'), Gus Kahn and Isham Jones ('It Had to Be You'), Georges Garvarentz and Charles Aznavour ('Old Fashioned Way'), Victor Young and Edward Heyman ('When I Fall in Love'), Harry Warren and Al Dubin ('I Only Have Eyes for You'), Chris Isaak ('Baby Did a Bad, Bad Thing'), Duke Ellington and Paul Francis Webster ('I Got It Bad'), Ted Shapiro, Jimmy Campbell and Reg Connelly ('If I Had You'), Oscar Levant and Edward Heyman ('Blame It on My Youth'), Bert Kaempfert, Charles Singleton and Eddie Snyder ('Strangers in the Night'), Benjamin Page and Christopher Kiler ('I Want a Boy for Christmas'), Rudolph Sieczynski (*Wein, du Stadt meiner Traume*)

Cast: Tom Cruise (Dr William Harford), Nicole Kidman (Alice Harford), Madison Eginton (Helena Harford), Jackie Sawris (Roz), Sydney Pollack (Victor Ziegler), Leslie Lowe (Illona), Peter Benson (bandleader), Todd Field (Nick Nightingale), Michael Doven (Ziegler's 'secretary'), Sky Dumont (Sandor Szavost), Louise Taylor (Gale), Stewart Thorndike (Nuala), Randall Paul (Harris), Julienne Davis (Mandy), Lisa Leone (Lisa), Kevin Connealy (Lou Nathanson), Marie Richardson (Marion), Thomas Gibson (Carl), Mariana Hewett (Rosa), Gary Goba (officer), Vinessa Shaw (Domino), Florian Windorfer (head waiter at Café Sonata), Rade Serbedzija (Milich), Leelee Sobieski (Milich's daughter), Sam Douglas (cab driver), Angus McInnes (gateman), Abigail Good (mysterious woman), Brian W. Cook (butler), Leon Vitali (red cloak), Carmela Marner (waitress), Alan Cumming (desk clerk), Fay Masterson (Sally), Phil Davies (pursuer), Cindy Dolenc (girl at Sharky's), Clark Hayes (hospital receptionist), Treva Etienne (morgue orderly), Christiane Kubrick (woman behind Harford at Café Sonata), Alex Hobbs (boy in examination room), Katharina Kubrick Hobbs (mother of boy in examination room)

Production Companies: Warner Bros., Hobby Films and Pole Star

Producer: Stanley Kubrick

Executive Producer: Jan Harlan

Production Manager: Margaret Adams

Production Coordinator: Kate Garbett

Locations: *England*: Chelsea & Westminster Hospital, Chelsea; Hamleys, Hatton Garden, Islington; Madame Jo Jo's, Soho; Worship Street; Research Centre, Bracknell, Berkshire; Elveden Hall, Highclere Castle, Newbury, Berkshire; Mentmore Towers, Buckinghamshire; Pinewood Studios, London. *New York*: Central Park West.

Running Time: 159 min.

Gauge: 35mm (1:1.85), colour (DeLuxe), DTS/Dolby Digital/SDDS

First Screening: Mann's Village Theater, Westwood, Los Angeles, 13 July 1999

A. I. ARTIFICIAL INTELLIGENCE (US, 2001)

Director: Steven Spielberg

Screenplay: Steven Spielberg, based on the short story 'Super-Toys Last All Summer Long' by Brian Aldiss and the film project developed by Stanley Kubrick

Cast: Haley Joel Osment (David Swinton), Jude Law (Gigolo Joe), Frances O'Connor

(Monica Swinton), Sam Robards (Henry
Swinton), William Hurt (Professor Allen
Hobby)
Production Companies: Warner Bros.,
DreamWorks SKG, Amblin Entertainment
and Stanley Kubrick Productions
Producer: Steven Spielberg
Running Time: 143 min.

Select Bibliography

Note: As this book went to press, University of the Arts London announced that in late 2007 it would become the home of Stanley Kubrick's extensive archive of material related to his films

Appel Jr, Alfred (ed.), *The Annotated* Lolita (New York: Vintage Books, 1991).

Auerbach, Erich, *Scenes from the Drama of European Literature* (New York: Meridian Books, 1959).

Bakhtin, Mikhail, *Rabelais and His World*, trans. Helene Iswolsky (Bloomington: Indiana University Press, 1968).

Baxter, John, *Stanley Kubrick: A Biography* (New York: Carroll & Graf, 1997).

Bazin, André, *What Is Cinema?*, trans. Hugh Gray (Berkeley: University of California Press, 1967).

_____, *Bazin at Work*, ed. Bert Cardullo (New York: Routledge, 1997).

Bettelheim, Bruno, *Freud and Man's Soul* (New York: Vintage Books, 1984).

Bizony, Piers, *2001: Filming the Future* (London: Aurum Press, 2000).

Bordwell, David, 'The Art Cinema as a Mode of Film Practice', in Leo Braudy and Marshall Cohen (eds), *Film Theory and Criticism*, 5th edn (New York: Oxford University Press, 1999), pp. 716–24.

_____ *Figures Traced in Light: On Cinematic Staging* (Berkeley: University of California Press, 2005).

Breton, André (ed.), *Anthology of Black Humor*, trans. Mark Polizzotti (San Francisco, CA: City Lights Books, 1997).

Bukatman, Scott, *Terminal Identity: The Virtual Subject in Post-Modern Science Fiction* (Durham, NC: Duke University Press, 1993).

Burgess, Anthony, *A Clockwork Orange* (London: Penguin Books, 1972).

Burrow, Colin, 'Not Quite Nasty', *The London Review of Books* vol. 28 no. 3 (9 February 2006), p. 20.

Castle, Alison (ed.), *The Stanley Kubrick Archives* (Cologne: Taschen, 2005).

Cherchi Usai, Paolo, 'Checkmating the General: Stanley Kubrick's *Fear and Desire*', *Image* vol. 38 nos 1–2, p. 27.

Chion, Michel, *Kubrick's Cinema Odyssey*, trans. Claudia Gorbman (London: BFI, 2001).

_____, *Eyes Wide Shut*, trans. Trista Selous (London: BFI, 2002).

_____, *Stanley Kubrick, l'humain ni plus ni moins* (Paris: Cahier du cinéma, 2005).

Ciment, Michel, *Kubrick: The Definitive Edition* (New York: Faber and Faber, 2001).

Cocks, Geoffrey, *The Wolf at the Door: Stanley Kubrick, History, and the Holocaust* (New York: Peter Lang, 2004).

Cohn, Joel G., 'Ferro-Gross: Titles, Trailers, and Spots, with Feeling', *T-Print*, vol. 26 no. 6 (November–December 1972), p. 49.

Cook, David A., 'American Horror: *The Shining*', *Literature/Film Quarterly* vol. 12 no. 1 (1984), pp. 2–5.

_____, *Lost Illusions: American Cinema in the Shadow of Watergate and Vietnam, 1970–1979* (Berkeley: University of California Press, 2000).

Corliss, Richard, *Lolita* (London: BFI, 1994).

Crone, Rainer (ed.), *Stanley Kubrick, Drama and Shadows: Photographs, 1945–50* (London: Phaidon, 2005).

Cubitt, Sean, 'Phalke, Melies, and Special Effects Today', *Wide Angle* vol. 21 no. 1 (January 1999), pp. 115–48.

_____ and John Caughie (eds), *Screen: Special Issue on FX, CGI, and the Question of Spectacle* vol. 40 no. 2 (Summer 1999).

Deleuze, Gilles, *Cinema 2: The Time-Image*, trans. Hugh Tomlinson and Robert Galeta (Minneapolis: University of Minnesota Press, 1989).

Deleyto, Celestino, '1999, A Closet Odyssey: Sexual Discourses in *Eyes Wide Shut*', ‹www.atlantisjournal.org/HTML%20Files/Tables%20of%20contents/28.1%20(2006).htm›

Devries, Daniel, *The Films of Stanley Kubrick* (Grand Rapids, MI: Erdman Publishing Co., 1973).

Dimendberg, Edward, *Film Noir and the Spaces of Modernity* (Cambridge, MA: Harvard University Press, 2004).

D'Lugo, Marvin, '*Barry Lyndon*: Kubrick on the Rules of the Game', *Explorations in National Cinemas, The 1977 Film Studies Annual: Part One* (Pleasantville, NY: Redgrave Publishing Company), pp. 37–45.

Douglas, Kirk, *The Ragman's Son* (New York: Pocket Books, 1989).

Duncan, Paul, *Stanley Kubrick: The Complete Films* (Cologne: Taschen, 2003).

Durgnat, Raymond, 'Paint It Black: The Family Tree of Film Noir', *Film Comment* 6 (November 1974), p. 6.

Ebert, Roger, *The Great Movies* (New York: Broadway Books, 2002).

Eliot, T. S., *Selected Prose*, ed. John Hayward (Harmondsworth: Peregrine, 1963).

Falsetto, Mario (ed.), *Perspectives on Stanley Kubrick* (New York: G. K. Hall, 1996).

_____ (ed.), *Stanley Kubrick: A Narrative and Stylistic Analysis*, 2nd edn (Westport, CT: Praeger, 2001).

Freedman, Carl, 'Kubrick's *2001* and the Possibility of a Science-Fiction Cinema', *Science Fiction Studies* vol. 23 (1996), pp. 300–17.

_____, *Critical Theory and Science Fiction* (Hanover, CT: Wesleyan University Press, 1999).

Friedman, Lester D., *Citizen Spielberg* (Champaign: University of Illinois Press, 2006).

Freud, Sigmund, *The Standard Edition of the Complete Psychological Works of Sigmund Freud*, trans. James Strachey (London: Hogarth Press, 1929).

Frewin, Anthony, 'Colour Him Kubrick!', *Stopsmiling* no. 23, 2005, pp. 60–3, 91–3.

Garcia Mainar, Luis M., *Narrative and Stylistic Patters in the Films of Stanley Kubrick* (Rochester, NY: Camden House, 1999).

Gaudreault, André, 'Theatricality, Narrativity, and "Trickality": Reevaluating the Cinema of George Melies', *Journal of Popular Film and Television* vol. 15 no. 3 (Autumn), pp. 110–19.

Ghamari-Tabrizi, Sharon, *The Worlds of Herman Kahn* (Cambridge, MA: Harvard University Press, 2005).

Godard, Jean-Luc, *Godard on Godard*, ed. and trans. Tom Milne (New York: Viking Press, 1972).

Gorbman, Claudia, 'Ears Wide Open: Kubrick's Use of Music', in Phil Powrie and Robynn Stilwell (eds), *Changing Tunes: The Use of Pre-Existing Music in Film* (Aldershot: Ashgate, 2006), pp. 3–18.

Gunning, Tom, 'An Aesthetic of Astonishment: Early Film and the (In)credulous Spectator', in Leo Braudy and Marshall Cohen (eds), *Film Theory and Criticism*, 5th edn (New York: Oxford University Press, 1999), pp. 818–32.

Haskell, Molly, *From Reverence to Rape: The Treatment of Women in the Movies* (Harmondsworth: Penguin, 1974).

Herr, Michael, *Kubrick* (New York: Grove Press, 2000).

Hoile, Christopher, 'The Uncanny and the Fairy Tale in Kubrick's *The Shining*', *Literature/Film Quarterly* vol. 12 no. 1 (1984), pp. 6–12.

Horkheimer, Max and Theodor Adorno, *The Dialectic of Enlightenment: Philosophical Fragments*, ed. Gunzelin Schmid Noerr, trans. Edmund Jephcott (Stanford, CA: Stanford University Press, 2000).

Howard, James, *Stanley Kubrick Companion* (London: B. T. Batsford Ltd, 1999).

Jackson, Kevin, 'Real Horrorshow: A Short Lexicon of Nasdat', *Sight and Sound* (September 1999), p. 27.

Jackson, Rosemary, *Fantasy: The Literature of Subversion* (London: Methuen, 1981).

Jameson, Fredric, *Signatures of the Visible* (New York: Routledge, 1990).

Jenkins, Greg, *Stanley Kubrick and the Art of Adaptation: Three Novels, Three Films* (Jefferson, NC: McFarland Publishing, 1997).

Kagan, Norman, *The Cinema of Stanley Kubrick* (New York: Continuum, 1997).

Kerman, Judith B. (ed.), *Retrofitting* Blade Runner (Bowling Green, OH: Popular Press, 1991).

Keyser, Wolfgang, *The Grotesque in Art and Literature*, trans. Ulrich Weisstein (Bloomington: Indiana University Press, 1963).

Kissinger, Henry, *The Necessity for Choice: Prospects of American Foreign Policy* (New York: Harper & Brothers, 1961).

Kolker, Robert, *A Cinema of Loneliness* (New York: Oxford University Press, 2000).

_____ (ed.), *Stanley Kubrick's* 2001: A Space Odyssey (New York: Oxford University Press, 2006).

Kosloff, Sarah, *Invisible Storytellers: Voice-Over Narration in American Film* (Berkeley: University of California Press, 1998).

Krohn, Bill, '*Full Metal Jacket*', in Jonathan Crary and Sanford Kwinter (eds), *Incorporations* (New York: Urzone, 1992), pp. 428–35.

Kubrick, Stanley, *Stanley Kubrick's* A Clockwork Orange (New York: Ballantine Books, 1972).

_____, Michael Herr and Gustav Hasford, *Full Metal Jacket: The Screenplay* (New York: Alfred A. Knopf, 1987).

_____ and Frederic Raphael, *Eyes Wide Shut, a Screenplay* and Arthur Schnitzler, 'Dream Story', trans. J. M. O. Davies (New York: Warner Books, 1999).

The Kubrick Site ‹www.visual-memory.co.uk›

Kurzweil, Ray, *The Age of Spiritual Machines: When Computers Exceed Human* (London: Penguin, 2000).

LoBrutto, Vincent, *Stanley Kubrick: A Biography* (New York: Da Capo Press, 1999).

Maland, Charles, 'Dr Strangelove (1964), Nightmare Comedy and the Ideology of Liberal Consensus', in Peter C. Rollins (ed.), Hollywood as Historian: American Films in a Cultural Context (Lexington: University of Kentucky Press, 1983), pp. 209–10.

McDougal, Stuart Y. (ed.), Stanley Kubrick's A Clockwork Orange (New York: Cambridge University Press, 2003).

Menand, Louis, 'Fat Man: Herman Kahn and the Nuclear Age', The New Yorker (27 June 2005), pp. 95–7.

Metz, Christian, 'Trucage and the Film', Critical Inquiry (Summer 1977), pp. 657–75.

Modine, Matthew, Full Metal Jacket Diary (New York: Rugged Land, 2005).

Müller-Tamm and Katharina Sykora (eds), Puppen, Körper, Automaten: Phantasmen der Moderne (Dusseldorf, Kunstsammlung Nordrhein-Westfalen: Oktagon, 2004).

Mulvey, Laura, 'Death Drives', in Richard Allen and Sam Ishii-Gonzales (eds) Hitchcock Past and Future (New York: Routledge, 2004), pp. 231–42.

Nabokov, Vladimir, Lolita (New York: Second Vintage International Edition, 1997).

Naremore, James, Acting in the Cinema (Berkeley: University of California Press, 1988).

————, 'Hitchcock and Humor', in Richard Allen and Sam Ishii-Gonzales (eds), Hitchcock Past and Future (London: Routledge, 2004), pp. 22–6.

Nelson, Thomas Allen, Kubrick: Inside a Film Artist's Maze (Bloomington: Indiana University Press, 2000).

Nelson, Victoria, The Secret Life of Puppets (Cambridge, MA: Harvard University Press, 2001).

Paul, William, Laughing/Screaming: Modern Hollywood Horror and Comedy (New York: Columbia University Press, 1994).

Peucker, Brigitte, 'Kubrick and Kafka: The Corporeal Uncanny', Modernism/ Modernity 8, 4 (2001), pp. 663–74.

Phillips, Gene D., Stanley Kubrick: A Film Odyssey (New York: Popular Library, 1975).

———— (ed.), Stanley Kubrick Interviews (Jackson: University Press of Mississippi, 2001).

———— and Rodney Hill (eds), The Encyclopedia of Stanley Kubrick (New York: Checkmark Books, 2002).

Pipolo, Tony, "The Modernist and the Misanthrope: The Cinema of Stanley Kubrick", Cineaste, vol. 27 no.2, 2002, pp. 4–15.

Polito, Robert, Savage Art: A Biography of Jim Thompson (New York: Vintage Books, 1996).

Raphael, Frederic, Eyes Wide Open: A Memoir of Stanley Kubrick (New York: Ballantine, 1999).

Reichmann, Hans-Peter and Ingeborg Flagge (eds), Stanley Kubrick, Kinematograph no. 20 (Frankfurt am Main: Deutsches Filmmuseum, 2004).

Richter, Dan, Moonwatcher's Memoir: A Diary of 2001: A Space Odyssey (New York: Carroll & Graf, 2002).

Rodowick, D. N., The Crisis of Political Modernism: Criticism and Ideology in Contemporary Film Theory (Champaign: University of Illinois Press, 1988).

Rosenbaum, Jonathan, 'The Pluck of Barry Lyndon', Film Comment (March–April 1977), pp. 26–8.

————, Essential Cinema: On the Necessity of Film Canons (Baltimore, MD: Johns Hopkins University Press, 2004).

Ruskin, John, *The Genius of John Ruskin*, ed. John D. Rosenberg (New York: George Brazillier, 1963).

Rutsky, R. L., *High Techne: Art and Technology from the Machine Aesthetic to the Posthuman* (Minneapolis: University of Minnesota Press, 1999).

Ryan, Michael and Douglas Kellner, *Camera Politica: The Politics and Ideology of Contemporary Hollywood Film* (Bloomington: Indiana University Press, 1990).

Sarris, Andrew, *The American Cinema: Directors and Directions, 1929–1968* (New York: E. P. Dutton & Co., 1968).

_____, 'Science Fiction: *The Forbin Project*', in *The Primal Screen: Essays on Film and Related Topics* (New York: Simon & Schuster, 1973).

Schorske, Carl, *Fin-de-Siècle Vienna: Politics and Culture* (New York: Vintage, 1981).

Schwam, Stephanie (ed.), *The Making of* 2001: *A Space Odyssey* (New York: Modern Library, 2000).

Sikov, Ed, *Mr. Strangelove: A Biography of Peter Sellers* (New York: Hyperion, 2002).

Sklar, Robert, 'Stanley Kubrick and the American Film Industry', *Current Research in Film Audience, Economics, and Law* vol. 4, 1988, pp. 112–18.

Sontag, Susan, *On Photography* (New York: Farrar, Straus and Giroux, 1978).

Southern, Terry, 'Terry Southern's Interview with Stanley Kubrick', <www.terrysouthern.com/archive/SKint.htm>

Sperb, Jason, *The Kubrick Façade: Faces and Voices in the Films of Stanley Kubrick* (Lanham, MD: Scarecrow Press, 2006).

Stam, Robert, *Literature through Film: Realism, Magic, and the Art of Adaptation* (London: Blackwell, 2005).

Stephenson, William, 'The Perception of "History" in Kubrick's *Barry Lyndon*', *Literature/Film Quarterly* vol. 9 no. 4 (1981), pp. 251–60.

Stevens, Brad, '"Is That You, John Wayne? Is This Me?" Problems of Identity in Stanley Kubrick's *Full Metal Jacket*', *Senses of Cinema* <www.sensesofcinema.com/contents/02/21/full_metal.html>

Stork, David G. (ed.), *Hal's Legacy: 2001's Computer as Dream and Reality* (Cambridge, MA: MIT Press, 1997).

Suvin, Darko, *Metamorphoses of Science Fiction* (New Haven, CT: Yale University Press, 1979).

Theweleit, Klaus, *Male Fantasies: Volume I: Women, Floods, Bodies, History*, trans. Stephen Conway (Minneapolis: University of Minnesota Press, 1987).

Thompson, Philip, *The Grotesque* (London: Methuen, 1972).

Thomson, David, *A Biographical Dictionary of Film*, 3rd edn (New York: Alfred A. Knopf, 1994).

Todorov, Tzvetan, *The Fantastic: A Structural Approach to a Literary Genre*, trans. Richard Howard (Ithaca, NY: Cornell University Press, 1973).

_____, *The Poetics of Prose*, trans. Richard Howard (Ithaca: Cornell University Press, 1977).

Turkle, Sherry, *The Second Self: Computers and the Human Spirit* (New York: Simon & Schuster, 1984).

_____, 'Artificial Intelligence and Psychoanalysis: A New Alliance', *Dedalus* vol. 117 no. 1 (Winter 1998).

Virillo, Paul, *The Vision Machine*, trans. Julie Rose (London: BFI, 1994).

Vizzard, Jack, *See No Evil* (New York: Simon &
    Schuster, 1970).

Walker, Alexander, Sybil Taylor and Ulrich
    Rachti, *Stanley Kubrick, Director* (New York:
    W. W. Norton & Company, 1999).

Waller, Gregory A. (ed.), *Moviegoing in America*
    (Malden, MA: Blackwell, 2002).

Wilinsky, Barbara, *Sure Seaters: The Emergence of
    Art House Cinema* (Minneapolis: University
    of Minnesota Press, 2001).

Willoquet-Maricondi, Paula, 'Full-Metal
    Jacketing, or Masculinity in the Making',
    Cinema Journal vol. 33 no. 2 (1994), pp. 17–23.

Winston, Mathew, '*Humour noir* and Black Humor', in
    Harry Levin (ed.), *Veins of Humor* (Cambridge, MA:
    Harvard University Press, 1972), pp. 269–84.

Wollen, Peter, *Readings and Writings: Semiotic
    Counter-Strategies* (London: Verso, 1982).

Wood, Robin, *Hollywood from Vietnam to Reagan*
    (New York: Columbia University Press,
    1986).

Zipes, Jack, 'Breaking the Disney Spell', in
    Elizabeth Bell, Linda Haas and Laura
    Sells (eds), *From Mouse to Mermaid: The
    Politics of Film, Gender, and Culture*
    (Bloomington: Indiana University Press,
    1995), pp. 20–8.

Index

Page numbers in **bold** indicate detailed analysis; those in *italic* refer to illustrations. *n* = endnote.